Cuba's Digital Revolution

Reframing Media, Technology, and Culture in Latin/o America

CUBA'S DIGITAL REVOLUTION

Citizen Innovation and State Policy

EDITED BY
Ted A. Henken and Sara Garcia Santamaria

University of Florida Press
Gainesville

Publication of this paperback edition made possible by a Sustaining the Humanities through the American Rescue Plan grant from the National Endowment for the Humanities.

Copyright 2021 by Ted A. Henken and Sara Garcia Santamaria
All rights reserved
Chapter 1 "The Past, Present, and Future of the Cuban Internet" by Larry Press is licensed under CC BY 4.0.
Published in the United States of America

First cloth printing, 2021
First paperback printing, 2022

27 26 25 24 23 22   6 5 4 3 2 1

Library of Congress Cataloging-in-Publication Data
Names: Henken, Ted, editor. | Garcia Santamaria, Sara, 1984– editor.
Title: Cuba's digital revolution : citizen innovation and state policy /
    edited by Ted A. Henken and Sara Garcia Santamaria.
Description: Gainesville : University of Florida Press, [2021] | Series:
    Reframing media, technology, and culture in Latin/o America | Includes
    bibliographical references and index.
Identifiers: LCCN 2020045517 (print) | LCCN 2020045518 (ebook) | ISBN
    9781683402022 (hardback) | ISBN 9781683402374 (pdf) | ISBN 9781683403517 (pbk.)
Subjects: LCSH: Information technology—Cuba. | Technological
    innovations—Social aspects—Cuba. | Information society—Cuba. |
    Digital communications—Cuba. | Written communication—Technological
    innovations—Cuba.
Classification: LCC HC79.T4 C83 2021 (print) | LCC HC79.T4 (ebook) | DDC
    303.48/3097291—dc23
LC record available at https://lccn.loc.gov/2020045517
LC ebook record available at https://lccn.loc.gov/2020045518

University of Florida Press
2046 NE Waldo Road
Suite 2100
Gainesville, FL 32609
http://upress.ufl.edu

Contents

List of Figures vii
List of Tables ix

Introduction: *In Medias Res*; Who Will Control Cuba's Digital
Revolution? 1
Ted A. Henken

PART I. HISTORY, MEDIA, AND TECHNOLOGY

1. The Past, Present, and Future of the Cuban Internet 29
Larry Press

2. Historical Itineraries and Cyclic Trajectories: Alternative Media,
Communication Technologies, and Social Change in Cuba 51
Edel Lima Sarmiento

PART II. POLITICS

3. Information and Communication Technology, State Power, and
Civil Society: Cuban Internet Development in the Context of the
Normalization of Relations with the United States 73
Olga Khrustaleva

4. Ghost in the Machine: The Incompatibility of Cuba's State Media
Monopoly with the Existence of Independent Digital Media and the
Democratization of Communication 95
Alexei Padilla Herrera and Eloy Viera Cañive

5. The Press Model in Cuba: Between Ideological Hegemony and the
Reinvention of Civic Journalism 116
Carlos Manuel Rodríguez Arechavaleta

6. Digital Critique in Cuba 136
Marie Laure Geoffray

Part III. Journalism

7. From *Generación Y* to *14ymedio*: Beyond the Blog on Cuba's Digital Frontier   157
   Ted A. Henken

8. Independent Journalism in Cuba: Between Fantasy and the Ontological Rupture   180
   Sara Garcia Santamaria

9. Perceptions of and Strategies for Autonomy among Journalists Working for Cuban State Media   200
   Anne Natvig

10. Independent Media on the Margins: Two Cases of Journalistic Professionalization in Cuba's Digital Media Ecosystem   219
    Abel Somohano Fernández and Mireya Márquez-Ramírez

Part IV. Business and Economy

11. Online Marketing of Touristic Cuba: Branding a "Tech-Free" Destination   241
    Rebecca Ogden

12. "A Una Cuba Alternativa"? Digital Millennials, Social Influencing, and *Cuentapropismo* in Havana   262
    Jennifer Cearns

Part V. Culture and Society

13. Without Initiation Ceremonies: Cuban Literary and Cultural E-zines, 2000–2010   285
    Walfrido Dorta

14. Images of Ourselves: Cuban Mediascapes and the Postsocialist "Woman of Fashion"   306
    Paloma Duong

List of Contributors   327
Index   333

Figures

0.1. "Propiedad privada" (private property), political cartoon, Omar Santana, *El Nuevo Herald*, Miami, 2018   3

0.2. *El paquete*—The Internet without Internet   5

0.3. "Real Life vs. Twitter," Twitter feed, Camilo Condis, March 11, 2019   9

0.4. "The Spaniard, the Taíno, and Technological Sovereignty" (cartoon, Lázaro Saavedra)   14

0.5. "The Anti-Internet Authoritarian and Imposed Consensus" (cartoon, Lázaro Saavedra)   16

1.1. Generations of Internet regulation policy   36

3.1. Free Wi-Fi at Kcho's Studio   79

3.2. "With Internet I can . . ."   86

7.1. "Censoring the Heretical, from Rome to Havana" (cartoon, Lázaro Saavedra)   162

7.2. The minidisk   164

7.3. *Ventana 14*'s YouTube page   171

7.4. Screenshot of *14ymedio*'s membership page   172

7.5. "Reimagining José Martí's *Patria* as a Blog" (cartoon, Lázaro Saavedra)   174

8.1. "Sensitizing Concepts in Discourse Theory: Expanding the Field of Discursivity"   184

11.1. Stills from the "Auténtica Cuba" promotional video   249

11.2. Still from The Wind Collective's "Mi Cuba querida" video   251

11.3. Still from The Wind Collective's "Mi Cuba querida" video   253

11.4. Still from The Wind Collective's "Mi Cuba querida" video   254

12.1. WhatsApp thread seeking "alternative" lesbian cultural events   272

13.1. Cover image of *Cacharro(s)*—Issue 2, September–October 2003   292

13.2. Cover image of *The Revolution Evening Post*—Episode 5, 2006   298

14.1. "Yindra" fashion advertisement   311

Tables

1.1. Cuban IDI and sub-index rankings   34
2.1. Periods of emergence of alternative media in Cuban history, 1868 to present   66

INTRODUCTION

In Medias Res
Who Will Control Cuba's Digital Revolution?

TED A. HENKEN

Fidel was the first to realize the value that the Internet would have in truly *democratizing communication*. He said it seemed to have been created for revolutionaries, given its capacity of spreading messages at an insignificant cost and with infinite reach.

President Miguel Díaz-Canel, February 8, 2019 (emphasis added)[1]

[The flash drive] is much more than a technological device. This tiny object that fits in your pocket, *that's freedom*. For many Cubans it's the difference between being informed and ignorant, between silence and the word, between censorship and journalism.

Yoani Sánchez, April 16, 2016 (emphasis added)[2]

The state socialist model officially instituted in Cuba in 1961, two years after the revolutionary triumph of 1959, gave the Communist Party (*Partido Comunista de Cuba*, PCC) a monopoly over both party politics and the mass media. By the time the PCC was formally founded in 1965, all preexisting media outlets had either been nationalized or shuttered. Subsequently, the Cuban government used its media hegemony to socialize citizens in its vision of a "revolutionary" society. This effort transformed all channels of broadcast media into state propaganda starting with *Granma*, Cuba's national daily newspaper whose masthead unequivocally proclaims it the "Official Organ of the Central Committee of the PCC." However, since the collapse of the Soviet Union in 1991 and the subsequent global proliferation of new information and communication technologies (ICTs) in the subsequent thirty years, the Cuban government's media hegemony has progressively eroded and Cuban citizens—working independently of if not always in opposition to the government—have increasingly become active participants in the worldwide digital revolution, remaking the Cuban media landscape in the process.

This second, informational, communicational, and technological revolution—a phenomenon we label Cuba's *digital* revolution—has erupted within (*in medias res*) the Cuban Revolution, leading to a dynamic and unpredictable struggle over the meaning, impact, scope, and direction of both. Indeed, the dueling epigraphs cited above declare in no uncertain terms that the global digital revolution has democratized communication and expanded freedom in Cuba in recent years. Of course, Cuban President Miguel Díaz-Canel and the pioneering independent digital journalist Yoani Sánchez would agree on little else about the direction of this change or the uses to which these new media technologies should be put. Who will control Cuba's digital revolution? Who will benefit from it? To what ends will it be applied? Who will be left behind? Will digital technology "remake" or perhaps "remix" the Cuban Revolution, as the government aims to do with its "computerization" of society policy? Or are the many diverse digital developments currently unfolding in Cuba which we chronicle here contributing to something more akin to an "unmaking" or "upending" of the Revolution? Thus, this volume seeks to answer these and other related questions by convening a diverse group of global scholars[3] and highlighting their original, cutting-edge scholarship that critically analyzes the many and sometimes contradictory ways Cubans are using new media technologies to transform Cuban society from within.[4] While the book's authors approach this phenomenon from a rich variety of disciplinary perspectives, our main common contention is that technology is radically reconfiguring the evolution of the cultural, economic, and political project that is the Cuban Revolution in myriad unprecedented ways.

* * *

The Cuban Internet has been characterized by government censorship, private self-censorship, high costs, slow speeds, and limited access. However, since 2013 the island has seen transformations in both top-down, government-enabled, paid public Web access and the ever-creative, bottom-up *inventos* or workarounds that Cubans themselves have designed to independently produce, distribute, and access digital content. These developments began with the spread of a diverse and often contentious Cuban "blogosphere" starting around 2005 and were followed by the subsequent growth of various collective projects of "citizen journalism" since 2008 (Henken 2011; Henken and Van de Voort 2015). These pioneering experiments in "indymedia" *a la cubana* have culminated since 2014 in the appearance of an increasingly rich variety of independent digital journalism projects, all of which have consciously moved "beyond the blog" to embrace the challenge

Introduction: *In Medias Res*; Who Will Control Cuba's Digital Revolution? · 3

Figure 0.1. "*Propiedad privada*" (Private property), Political Cartoon, Omar Santana, *El Nuevo Herald*, Miami, 2018. Translation: "[President] Miguel [Díaz-Canel] says that Cuban journalists are not for sale, they will continue being property of the Communist Party." Used with permission of the cartoonist Omar Santana.

of informing the Cuban public in a more systematic, coordinated, and professional way, targeting the demand for credible and objective reportage unmet by the propagandistic state press (Díaz 2018; Henken 2017). This development has forced journalists working in the official media to reexamine both their reporting style and focus and their heretofore unwavering duty to follow the censorial eye of the Party (figure 0.1).

While many chapters of this book critically analyze different aspects of Cuba's emergent digital independent journalism, others examine how the state press itself—after initially being caught off-guard by these digital gadflies—has been forced to respond by establishing an increasingly nimble Web and social media presence of its own. This has been embedded within a larger state effort at the progressive "*informatización*" (computerization) of Cuban society, an initiative which various chapters of this book also analyze. Indeed, after years of insinuating that Twitter was a CIA front, the Cuban government finally embraced it in late 2018 with the new fifty-eight-year-old President Miguel Díaz-Canel himself joining the microblogging revolution on the patriotic date of October 10 and later urging all his ministers to follow suit and begin to engage Cuba's new "netizens" directly by the end of the year (*The Economist* 2019; Pentón 2019).[5]

This digital turn in Cuba has been facilitated by the opening of Cuba's first public-access cybercafes in June 2013, the possibility of accessing e-mail via cell phone for the first time in 2014, and the establishment of thirty-five public Wi-Fi hot spots across the island in the summer of 2015. The continued expansion of the government's Wi-Fi hot spot plan, which reached two hundred locations in September 2016, and the launch by ETECSA[6] of a pilot program known as *Nauta Hogar,* allowing home Internet access for the first time to two thousand customers in Old Havana in late 2016, along with the establishment of 3G Internet access via cell phone to paying customers for the first time in December 2018, have continued to fuel the growth and social impact of Cuba's digital revolution.[7]

Simultaneously with the government's top-down rollout of greater digital access, tech-savvy, entrepreneurial Cuban millennials have launched a wide array of digital start-ups, most of which exist in a legal limbo of anxious toleration. These include a variety of homegrown (and initially offline) apps that aim to connect Cuban customers to the growing crop of new private businesses on the island (ConoceCuba, AlaMesa, Isladentro, etc.) and various Craigslist-like classified sites—merchandise clearinghouses where Cubans can buy and sell everything from late model smartphones to their own homes (Revolico, Cubisima, etc.). There's even Cubazón, a Cuba-based Amazon clone that allows clients (mostly in the Cuban diaspora) to purchase goods and services from Cuba's emergent private sector for delivery to their friends and family on the island, as well as an Uber-style app called ¡Sube! ("Get In!"), Knales (a Web data retrieval app that uses SMS messaging), and Kwelta (a cultural calendar cum publicity service) (Vela 2019; Sosa Barceló 2017; Press 2017). The island has also seen the spread of multiple independent local area networks or intranets, popularly known as "street nets" (or SNETs, which the government alternately attempted to outlaw or absorb during 2019) (Padgett 2019; Rodríguez Fernández 2019), and Cuba's own infamous "sneaker net," universally referred to as *el paquete* ("the packet"), an island-wide, underground digital data distribution network that rides on the backs of a million flash drives and successfully competes against the often-stale programming on Cuba's handful of official television channels (figure 0.2). Various chapters of the book also investigate trends in this emergent digital entrepreneurial demimonde.[8]

* * *

Figure 0.2. The Internet without Internet. Photo of a Panasonic flat screen television with a built-in media player below and front-loading USB port with a 64-gigabyte flash drive containing the latest video content from *el paquete*. Photo taken by the author, Havana, 2016.

Of course, the spread of Internet access in Cuba has implications that reach far beyond business, entrepreneurship, and economics. The unprecedented increase in access to alternative forms of information from abroad combined with the growing ability of Cuban citizens to communicate horizontally among themselves, producing and sharing their own diverse reportage, experiences, and points of view independently of the government has enormous if as of yet unclear implications for Cuban political life, civil society, and in a variety of public spheres. Indeed, the confluence of the economic development that the digital revolution enables (Machado 2017) together with the fundamental challenge that it presents to closed societies and authoritarian governments has been called "the dictator's dilemma." Defined by Larry Press in the mid-1990s as "the desire to have the benefits of the Internet without the threat of political instability," he imagined dictators asking themselves "how do you give people access to information for health care, education, and commerce while keeping them from [critical alternative] political information?" (Press 2011).

In fact, since December 2018, when Cubans finally gained access to the "anywhere-anytime" convenience of 3G mobile Internet for the first time, the island has seen a nonstop flurry of digital technology–enabled sociopolitical mobilizations, all facilitated by citizens' newfound access to a wide array of social media platforms from Telegram to Twitter, YouTube to Facebook, and WhatsApp to Qbolá. While still very far from anything approaching a "Cuban Spring," this series of hashtagged public denunciations of government policies indicates that the spread of Web access that the government has justified as part of its urgent *informatización* of Cuban society is also a Pandora's box of political headaches. It has unleashed pent-up netizen demands and eroded two of the key pillars of government information control on the island: fear of the consequences of speaking out of turn[9] and isolation from others who harbor similar complaints (Tufekci 2017; Parker 2014). The three most inventive and impactful of these cyber-denunciations to appear during 2019 are the digital campaign that urged Cubans to either vote against (#YoVotoNo) or abstain from voting on (#YoNoVoto) Cuba's new Constitution on February 24, an online demand that ETECSA lower its costly Internet prices (#BajenLosPreciosDeInternet) (Faiola 2019; Zaldívar 2019), and an expression of digital solidarity with the netizen founders of Cuba's various local area networks or SNETs after it became clear in August that new legislation would effectively outlaw their online communities (#YoSoySNET).[10]

These phenomena are vivid recent examples of Cuba's expanding "networked public sphere" (Tufekci 2017), as they have been independently organized, convened mostly through social media, leaderless and horizontal, and later spread, popularized, and reported on via social media. They have also further eroded the government's traditional control over the day-to-day narrative about how life is lived in Cuba that makes it into the international press coverage of the island. Indeed, thirty-one-year-old gay rights and cyber-activist Norges Rodríguez told the *Washington Post* that "when [government authorities] started detaining people [during the unauthorized May LGBT march], they were looking for a leader. But since it was organized through social media, there was no specific leader" (Faiola 2019). Faiola estimated that as many as 2.2 million Cubans are now accessing 3G mobile Internet service, calling the change a "great leap forward [. . .] that's giving rise to a new class of netizens, who are organizing behind causes and social movements in a manner not seen since the Cuban Revolution" itself. Likewise, Abraham Jiménez Enoa, the independent journalist and cofounder of the narrative journalism site *El Estornudo*, wrote in a 2019 *New York Times* op-ed that:

> The Internet has reconfigured society by allowing citizens to express themselves freely on its platforms and feel empowered. An alternative to the official voice imposed for years has emerged. Dissent is moving beyond the online world and materializing in real life.

Still, we should not assume that a handful of Twitter hashtags linked tenuously to brief marches and protests by a relative handful of "connected" and politicized Cuban citizens (however unprecedented they may be) amounts to a social movement capable of posing an existential threat to a regime that remains entrenched in power with no well-known or widely credible political alternatives. Indeed, even Larry Press, who asked the pregnant question above about the either-or "dilemma" that the Internet inevitably poses for dictators, has since developed a more nuanced view of how the digital revolution impacts state hegemony in closed regimes like Cuba. "In the 1990s," he writes, "I would have agreed with [Raúl] Castro[11] that the Internet was destined to bring democracy. Today [2011] I have a more nuanced view—the Internet is used by dictators and terrorists as well as democrats" (Press 2011). Indeed, in May 2013, when he was still Cuba's first vice president, Miguel Díaz-Canel turned more than a few heads when he declared as part of a speech he gave at the closing ceremony of an education conference:

> Today, with the development of information technologies; today, with the development of social networks; today, with the development of computers and the Internet, to prohibit something is nearly an impossible chimera. It makes no sense. Today, news from all sources, from good ones and from bad ones, those that are manipulated, and those that are true, and those that are half-truths, all circulate on the Web and reach people and those people are aware of them. The worst response then, what is it? Silence. (Henken 2013)

While at the time, these words were interpreted by most foreign analysts as a signal of Díaz-Canel's supposed openness to dialogue, diversity of opinion, and a freer media environment if and when he became Cuba's president, it turns out that his main point was not one of openness but of revolutionary engagement—a digital "battle of ideas" of sorts. For him, the Revolution would be mistaken to ignore or disengage from the digital revolution then sweeping the world, ceding ground to Cuba's enemies. Instead, Cuban patriots and revolutionaries must turn on Twitter, tune in to Google, open up their own blogs, and join that revolution as stalwart defenders of Cuban sovereignty and socialism. This explains how he could argue in a much later February 8, 2019, speech at the closing ceremony of an International Pedagogy Conference (quoted above as the opening epigraph) that Fidel Castro himself celebrated the Internet as a "truly democratizing" tool of communication "created for revolutionaries" (*Juventud Rebelde* 2019).

Might the idea that Web 2.0 equals Democracy 2.0 just as easily work in the opposite direction, where it actually facilitates Authoritarianism 2.0 (Calvo Peña 2008)? Indeed, there is an ongoing, spirited debate among those who have studied the complex impact of expanding information and communication technologies on the depth, direction, and civic nature of its political impact (Best and Wade 2005; Kelly and Etling 2008; Etling et al. 2009; Hernández Busto 2010; Tufekci 2017). In other words, just as netizens can use the Web as a democratic public plaza of citizen participation where they can "speak truth to power" and hold authorities to account, so too can governments structure and manipulate the Web in order to strengthen their power, control, and surveillance over citizens. Indeed, Díaz-Canel's point cited above about Fidel Castro's early "realization" that the Internet seemed to have been created especially for revolutionaries, given its democratization of communication, low cost, and infinite reach reminds us of the fact that the "digital revolution" has no predetermined political color and that one person's "revolutionary" may be another's repressor or reactionary.

That is, Cuban government "revolutionaries" may legitimately see the Internet as a powerful tool with which they can challenge the dominant capitalist media narrative about the Revolution (thus the Cuban state media's constant use of terms like "cyberwar" and "la guerra mediática" in its portrayal of foreign coverage of the Revolution), while the island's many, diverse digital activists and independent journalists like Jiménez Enoa, cited above, can also speak convincingly about the Web's empowering facilitation of citizen free expression and dissent in a country with a monolithic, mono-color, and monopolistic Party-controlled official media. Finally, the contrasting cases of China (where Internet access is as ubiquitous as it is inexpensive, but also where the government has firm control over it, having reinvented it in its own authoritarian image) and Cuba (where access remains limited and prohibitively expensive, and where critical sites are routinely censored with impunity) indicate that more and greater connectivity do not automatically lead to "*Revolución 2.0*" (Repnikova and Fang 2018; Garcia Santamaria 2019).

One upside to the slow adoption of digital technology in Cuba is that some of the sober lessons about the risks and downsides of increased reliance on the Internet and the growth of the use of social media have already been absorbed by some of the island's digital mavens. For example, Camilo

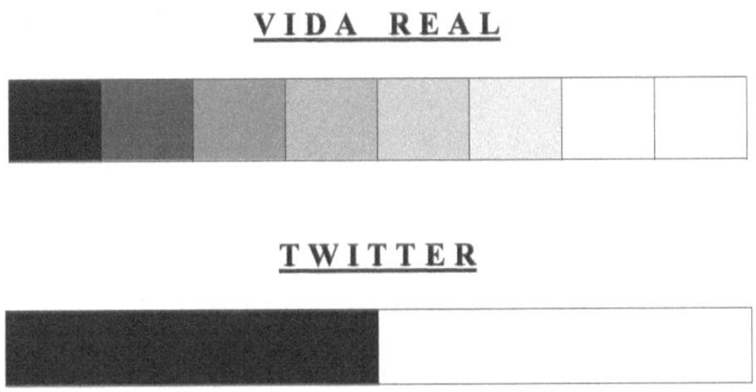

VIDA REAL

[color gradient bar from dark to light across seven cells]

TWITTER

[bar mostly empty with dark segment on the left]

Figure 0.3. Re-creation of "Real Life vs. Twitter," March 11, 2019, Twitter feed, Camilo Condis. Original tweet by Camilo Condis, re-created by the author. Used with permission.

Condis, a Cuban entrepreneur who has emerged as a pioneering Cuban podcaster (*Havana Times* 2019) and consistently sharp-tongued Twitter critic of many Cuban government ministers, has celebrated Twitter as a way to hold government officials accountable as public servants (Faiola 2019; Ávila 2019; Pentón 2019). However, he has also seen his share of polarizing propaganda, innuendo, fake news, fake profiles, personal attacks, and trolling on the site and is under no illusions that it is the silver bullet for civil society. "This confluence of people entering the social networks," notes Condis, "with the leaders within reach of their keyboards and being able to tell them what they think, has changed the dynamics of Cuban society" (Ávila 2019). At the same time, among Condis' most popular tweets to date is a simple but powerful graphic (which I have re-created as figure 0.3 above) that captures the risks of increased social media use on the island (Morán 2019; Zaldívar 2019).[12]

Expanded access to the Internet does not move societies in a single direction partly because different constituencies within any country view the potential of the Web in different ways. Is the Web a place to download development and democracy,[13] find the latest Hollywood blockbuster, fight imperialism, resist "Westoxification," plant the virus of destabilization, or defend national sovereignty? For many governments, especially those like Cuba's that struggle against underdevelopment and the "digital divide" that continues to separate wealthy from poor countries in terms of Internet cost and connectivity, new ICTs have the potential to be harnessed as a veritable "economic miracle" allowing a country to "leapfrog" into the modern era. At the same time, citizen journalists and blogger-activists often understand the Web (and especially the potentialities offered in many Web 2.0 applications and the new generation of smartphones) as a kind of revolutionary "Roman

Senate" where they can open up a closed system carrying out a "netroots" reform movement some have called "blogostroika."

* * *

In the Cuban case, five overarching and as yet unresolved debates about how the global digital revolution interacts with the public sphere drive our interest and inform the questions we seek to answer. Simply stated, they are

- "Liberation technology" and "digital democracy" vs. "slacktivism" and the cult of the amateur
- The "networked public sphere" vs. "networked authoritarianism"
- "Free" global social media platforms vs. "antisocial" mediums that show human disconnection, exploit personal privacy, erode public trust, and undermine democracy
- The potential of Cuba developing open-source software vs. the centralized control of Cuban political and economic life
- *Autonomofobia*: the Cuban government's deeply rooted fear of autonomous civil society

Liberation Technology

"Freedom of the press," A.J. Liebling once sardonically quipped, "is guaranteed only to those who own one" (1960). Thus, the much-ballyhooed promise embedded in phrases like "liberation technology" and "digital democracy" is that the emergence and mass adoption of new information and communication technologies such as personal computers and Web-ready smartphones (what Liebling might call "owning a [digital] press" if he were still around today) would inevitably "free" or democratize the production and distribution of information, irreversibly eroding the concentrated power of traditional state and corporate broadcast media. When first applied to the arrival of home computers in communist China, these hopeful ideas were memorably summarized as "the CP [Communist Party] will never survive the PC [personal computer]." A decade later, President Bill Clinton made the famous, but now clearly bombastic quip that China's crackdown on the Internet was "like trying to nail Jell-O to the wall" (Zhong 2018). In other words, the debatable supposition has been that digital technologies have the potential to help "level the playing field" between authoritarian governments (or even dominant and monopolistic corporations) and marginalized citizens—whether they be Russian voters, Chinese dissidents, or Cuban bloggers. Greater access to the Internet and social media can help these citizens begin to conquer their fear, overcome their isolation, and create more public space to exercise the rights denied them offline (Parker 2014).[14]

Social media's disruptive potential in Cuba arises from the same "leveling" process that it exhibits in other, less authoritarian contexts. It blurs the traditional distinction between the public and the private, the real and the virtual, the professional and the amateur, formal one-to-many broadcasting and informal one-to-one communication, as well as collapsing the local, national, and international spheres. It can also undermine the authority and hegemony of dominant telecom institutions (i.e., the "master switch" wielded by the "mainstream media," which is the party-controlled state media in the case of Cuba) by placing inexpensive broadcast technology in the hands of "the people formerly known as the audience" (Wu 2010; Rosen 2012). Furthermore, it allows for greater independent and horizontal ("peer-to-peer") communication, the sharing of information, and the convening of publics (Mandiberg 2012). Moreover, crowdsourcing, "peer production," and creative nonproprietary collaboration through harnessing the collective "cognitive surplus" of time and energy are all abilities with a disruptive potential to undermine the power of authoritarian regimes and traditional media elites alike (Shirky 2010).

However, simplistic understandings of how digital tools are adopted in different countries often conveniently overlook the fact that many of these technologies facilitate only "weak ties" to so-called slacktivists, while affording nothing truly game-changing to activist outsiders seeking change that requires durable "strong tie" organizations, strategy, and leadership (Gladwell 2010). Moreover, these new technologies can also be used by existing power brokers to expand the hegemony they enjoyed in the traditional media sphere into the emerging digital one (Morozov 2011). For example, political websites in the U.S. exhibit a pronounced winner-take-all pattern whereby only a handful of well-known and well-linked sites receive the lion's share of Web traffic. In our celebration of "user generated content" (UGC) and social media, a key distinction needs to be made between the ability to speak—which the Internet has indeed "democratized" in powerful ways—and being heard, which is far more elusive. As for the contention that the blogging phenomenon amplifies the voice of ordinary citizens, there is likewise a big difference between who posts and who gets read. Finally, while many have celebrated blogs as a step toward greater democratization of the mainstream media, there is a potential downside to the pluralism and "amateurization" of the media that blogs and other forms of social media facilitate, especially if hard-won norms of professional accuracy and objectivity are sacrificed in the process (Keen 2007; Hindman 2009).

Networked Authoritarianism

The recent study, *Twitter and Tear Gas* (Tufekci 2017), explores both the power and fragility of what the author calls the "networked public sphere." Indeed, Zeynep Tufekci reminds us that authoritarian governments across the globe have followed a clear learning curve in the years since the Arab Spring of 2011. In short, they have graduated from the "1.0" world of old-school surveillance, information blocking, fear mongering, and open physical repression to incorporate more subtly effective techniques that have alternately been called "propaganda 2.0" and "networked authoritarianism" (Kalathil and Boas 2003; MacKinnon 2012). These include "demonizing online mediums, mobilizing armies of supporters or paid employees who muddy the online waters with misinformation, information glut, doubt, confusion, harassment, and distraction, making it hard for ordinary people to navigate the networked public sphere, and sort facts from fiction, truth from hoaxes" (Tufekci 2017, xxviii).

Antiestablishment, digitally enabled social movements face the challenge of persuading people to act. However, Tufekci argues that this task is much harder in an environment of "too much information" where all that repressive governments or unaccountable non-state actors have to do is simply "create enough confusion to paralyze people into inaction" (Tufekci 2017, xxix). That is, these governments use the chaotic, open, and "free" nature of the Internet against itself. With a flood of unverified information and potentially "fake" news, authoritarian governments can shift from traditional forms of censorship that sought to block specific anti-regime information or websites (as the Cuban government has done systematically for the past decade) to a new strategy that focuses instead "on making available information unusable" (Tufekci 2017, xxix).[15]

Web 2.0: If it's Free, You're the Product

As the Internet slowly reinvented itself at the turn of the century following the burst of the dot-com bubble, a set of now ubiquitous and seemingly omnipotent new Web companies emerged, including Google, YouTube, Facebook, and Twitter. Though somewhat different in their particular offerings, all were founded on the dual "Web 2.0" understanding that the "special sauce" of the new digital era was not traditional content or even fancy software but the harvesting of users' personal data and the universal attraction of "sharing" and "the social" (Mandiberg 2012; O'Reilly 2012; Wu 2016). While these companies pulled more and more users in with the seductive promise of efficiency, convenience, and universal and nonstop connectedness (all at the unbelievably low price of "free"), their business models were also predicated on the invasion of privacy, the potential spread of unverified "fake" news, and the harvesting and resale of personal information for private profit. They have also tended toward acting as functional monopolies thanks to the logic of "network effects" in the social media world, to a failure to subject them to proper government oversight and regulation as utilities or public services, and to a long-held and generalized irrational exuberance that the emergence of such "cool" companies was an unmitigated good—that they could "do no evil" (Vaidhyanathan 2012, 2018; McNamee 2019).

Ironically, it took another informational leviathan and fierce digital competitor to these Web giants to most forcefully challenge and expose the inherent risks of this new normal. Speaking in mid-2015 at the annual fundraising dinner of a little-known D.C. nonprofit, the Electronic Privacy Information Center (EPIC), Apple's CEO Tim Cook—who succeeded the legendary Steve Jobs in 2011—threw down the gauntlet by reminding his listeners that "some of the most prominent and successful companies [in Silicon Valley] have built their businesses by lulling their customers into complacency about their personal information." However, he was heartened to also note a growing awareness of and potential revolt against their usurious "terms of service" among the world's netizens who were increasingly realizing that "when an online service is free, you're not the customer. You're the product" (Wu 2016, 335). While Cuba's relatively late embrace of mass Internet access and use of social media platforms has largely (if inadvertently) shielded its citizens from these risks, this is no longer the case. Indeed, Marie Laure Geoffray addresses this emerging dilemma in Cuba, which she incisively calls, "the digitalization of critique and the critique of digitalization," in chapter 6.

F/OSS *A LA CUBANA*?

As described briefly by Olga Khrustaleva in her chapter on Cuba's evolving information and communication technology (ICT) policies, Cuba's University of Computer Science (UCI), founded in 2002, was originally conceived with the intention of preparing home-grown programmers who could develop software that was both "technologically sovereign" and commercially uncontaminated or "free." While she argues that UCI has instead been transformed into an incubator more dedicated to cyber-surveillance than free software, the idea of Cuba pioneering a national version of the venerable tradition of free and open-source software (F/OSS) is based in part on its own communitarian political and economic traditions (i.e., socialism), its

Figure 0.4. The Spaniard, the Taíno, and Technological Sovereignty. Translation: *The Spaniard*: "Well yes... Anything... Whatever you want to know... But yes, you tell me and I'll search for it." *The Taíno*: "Ask him to search for that thing about Hatuey to see if it's true." Credit/Source: Lázaro Saavedra, from the series "GALERÍA I-MEIL" (2008–2009), used with permission.

stalwart defiance of Western capitalism and foreign (colonial or imperial) control, and its being effectively cut off from importing (and thus being dominated by) American proprietary computer applications such as those developed by Microsoft (figure 0.4).[16]

Moreover, given the chronic scarcities that have become a way of life on the island over at least the last thirty years, Cuba has also become a breeding ground for innovative, self-taught do-it-yourselfers who excel at developing ingenious work-arounds for everything from decrepit 1950s-era American cars to computer programs. Thus, the idea that the island could become an incubator for nonproprietary software developed by informal collaborative networks of programmers is not so far-fetched. In fact, in 2009 most Cuban government institutions switched from Microsoft Windows to the Linux-based, UCI-developed "Nova" operating system due to the high costs of accessing or purchasing Microsoft's marquee OS application combined with its inability to officially use the company's proprietary software due to the embargo (Lai 2009). Though Microsoft's popular Windows operating system and Office applications—often in pirated versions—are widely used in Cuba, the intent of introducing "Nova" at that time was to wean Cuban users and especially government institutions off of what the government has characterized as "insecure, capitalist-produced corporate software" (Israel 2009).

Like other Linux-based operating systems, Cuba's "Nova" OS is free both in the sense that it is distributed free of charge and in the sense that its source code is open and thus can be adapted by those users with the technical ability to write and alter code. It is also more attractive to the Cuban government than traditional proprietary software because it is less vulnerable to malware and does not have the embedded "black holes" that can be exploited by U.S. security agencies because companies like Microsoft have provided them with access codes, at least according to Héctor Rodríguez, the dean of UCI's School of Free Software (Israel 2009; Lai 2009). Besides, Rodríguez emphasized that free software better matches Cuba's worldview. "The free software movement is closer to the ideology of the Cuban people, above all for the independence and sovereignty," he told *Reuters* (Israel 2009). Ironically, Cuba began the switch to developing "Nova" after the American Free Software guru Richard Stallman visited the island and persuaded government officials to move off Windows (Lai 2009).

Still, it is one thing to promote "technological sovereignty" and F/OSS as a national strategy to counter powerful geopolitical adversaries like the U.S. or dominant software companies like Microsoft, and quite another to promote grassroots programming or cyber-linked communities of "civil society" that exist independently from the government and resist being controlled or co-opted by it. The unceremonious outlawing of Cuba's thriving and heretofore tolerated SNET gaming communities in August 2019 is a bitter lesson showing that Cuba's freedom-loving indie programmers, cyber-pioneers, and digital communities have at least as much to fear from the monolithic and all-controlling approach of the Cuban government as the regime itself claims to fear either the alleged U.S. cyberwar or Microsoft's OS monopoly (BBC 2019; Padgett 2019).

AUTONOMOFOBIA

Finally, how do the common criteria of autonomy of civil society organizations apply to a country that has produced a veritable "sea" of participatory revolutionary organizations—Cuba's so-called mass organizations—committed to building (and now "updating") socialism? Cuban political scientist Armando Chaguaceda (2015) has made a pair of useful analytical observations in this context. First, while facilitating (even mandating) the creation of these participatory organizations, the revolutionary government has simultaneously exhibited a deep suspicion of all autonomous groups—what

Figure 0.5. The Anti-Internet Authoritarian and Imposed Consensus. Translation: "THE INTERNET IS SHIT! Let's see . . . Raise your hand if you want Internet." Credit/Source: Lázaro Saavedra, from the series "GALERÍA I-MEIL" (2008–2009), used with permission.

Chaguaceda calls its *autonomofobia*—leading to the systematic persecution of organizations not explicitly "revolutionary" and not directly controlled or effectively co-opted by the state (figure 0.5). Second, Chaguaceda indicates that while this sea of participation may indeed be "a mile wide," in practice it is often only "an inch deep," given the inability of such organizations to make demands on state institutions or hold their leaders accountable.[17]

In light of the above arguments, in this volume we use Haroldo Dilla and Phillip Oxhorn's definition of civil society as a baseline with which to analyze Cuba's emergent digital reality: "The social fabric formed by a multiplicity of self-constituted, territorially based units which peacefully coexist and collectively *resist subordination* to the state, at the same time that they *demand inclusion* into national political structures" (Dilla and Oxhorn 2002, 11, emphasis in the original). By this definition, institutions of civil society need not be absolutely independent from the state, nor have an oppositional agenda. However, they must exercise significant *autonomy* from the state, have an organic, sui generis *base*, appeal to or derive from elements within the *national territory*, seek to *impact* national issues, and accept *nonviolent coexistence* with other civil and political organizations.

Introduction: *In Medias Res*; Who Will Control Cuba's Digital Revolution? · 17

The emergent character of Internet and social media use in Cuba, combined perhaps with at least an initial hubris and ignorance on the part of the government about its disruptive power, has allowed some of its denizens to begin to share spontaneous critical commentary in what is still an uncharted, ambiguous space (via e-mails, blog posts, Twitter messages, websites, or on Facebook and even in their own YouTube videos), granting them a modicum of safety relative to traditional "public," "alternative," or "dissident" street activities. In other words, while "the street" may still belong to the late Fidel Castro and the Revolution ("*la calle es de Fidel*" being a typical slogan aimed at claiming all public spaces as "revolutionary"), it is much less clear to whom Cuban cyberspace belongs, if anyone. Moreover, Cuba's cyber-pioneers and digital activists have not been content to remain "in the cloud," forever isolated from one another. Instead, they have sought to turn their visibility—long understood as a dangerous liability on the island—into an asset (Geoffray 2013, 14–16), harnessing their transnational digital presence (as "the whole world watches") to serve as a protective shield when they dare to occupy the public sphere.

Given the "worldwide" nature of the Web, traditional understandings of civil society need to be updated when applied to the inherently de-territorialized space of the Internet—what Geoffray calls an "emerging transnational Cuban contentious space" (2013, 20–29). In fact, while nearly all of Cuba's cyber-pioneers are indeed territorially based, they simultaneously inhabit a complex transnational space, often relying on hosting, servers, administrators, webmasters, translators, and even some financing from outside of Cuba, not to mention drawing the bulk of their readers, commentators, and critics from abroad as well. And while early Internet debates in Cuba, such as the so-called *polemica intelectual* or e-mail war of January 2007,[18] were largely restricted to elite writers and artists and took place in cyberspace—making them all but invisible to the larger Cuban public given the extremely low rate of Internet access on the island, especially at that time—the years since then have seen increasingly bold and confident attempts on the part of Cuba's tech-savvy entrepreneurs and cyber-activists to claim a public space for their projects and debates.

Plan of the Book

This volume is divided into five interrelated sections, each of which focuses on a particular aspect of Cuba's digital revolution: I. History, Media, and Technology—chapters 1–2, II. Politics—chapters 3–6, III. Journalism—chapters

7–10, IV. Business and Economy—chapters 11–12, and V. Culture and Society—chapters 13–14.

The first chapter by Larry Press examines the evolution of the Internet and telecommunications policy in Cuba from the early 1990s to the present with an emphasis on the particular dilemmas that the island faces in an increasingly digital age where it has fallen further and further behind the world despite its stated policy of the "computerization" of society. This is followed by a chapter by Edel Lima Sarmiento that retraces the role "alternative" and "oppositional" media have played in Cuban history starting in the late nineteenth century as Cuban rebels sought independence from Spain and continuing through the Republican era when the clandestine press played a key role in undermining the power and legitimacy of a series of brutal, undemocratic Cuban rulers. Lima then applies lessons from these past eras as a way to understand the emergence of various shades of independent media on the island during the most recent twenty-five years.

While all the chapters in the volume deal at least indirectly with the intersection of new media technologies and politics, the four chapters that make up the second section focus explicitly on the political implications of the digital revolution for the Cuban revolution. This includes a chapter by Olga Khrustaleva that examines the emergent tensions between state power and civil society in the digital era in the context of an historic thaw in Cuban-U.S. relations. Chapter 4, coauthored by Alexei Padilla Herrera and Eloy Viera Cañive, examines how the emerging digital public sphere represented by various, diverse independent online media outlets has directly challenged the Cuban Communist Party's Leninist conception of the role of the media in a revolutionary society.

In chapter 5, Carlos Manuel Rodríguez Arechavaleta addresses the tense relationship between the Cuban media and the socialist state (the press and the Party), given the off-again/on-again threat of regime change from the United States. The chapter specifically addresses Cuba's new independent online journalism, the emergence of which is associated with the de-professionalization of the ideologically oriented socialist press model, the recent expansion of Internet access on the island, and the state's ongoing information control and surveillance strategies. Rounding out the politics section is chapter 6, by Marie Laure Geoffray, which provides a theoretical reflection on the various competing uses of digital media in Cuba to better understand how, under authoritarian rule, *critical* uses of digital technology are intertwined with more *routine* uses and how "critique," rather than being defined *a priori* and exclusively understood vis-à-vis its political or nonpolitical intentionality, is in fact shaped by the complex and often contradictory context in which it takes place.

The four chapters that make up the third section focus directly on the current struggle for readership and legitimacy on the island between the "official" state press and the insurgent independent digital press. Chapter 7, written by Ted A. Henken, is an analysis of the key transformations in the fifteen-year media career (2004–2019) of the famed blogger and independent journalist Yoani Sánchez as she has moved from celebrating the unique role "citizen journalists" like her can play in opening up a monopolistic media environment to launching her own daily digital newspaper, *14ymedio*, in May 2014. Chapter 8 by Sara Garcia Santamaria is an innovative study of how young Cuban journalists manage daily pressures and harassment at the state-run media. Specifically, her analysis focuses on the role of collective fantasy for escaping oppression, delaying a final rupture with the system. However, Garcia argues that fantasizing a better system has also been essential for envisaging the contours of the independent media sphere even before it existed. Similarly, chapter 9 by Anne Natvig is based on interviews conducted with state-sector journalists and focuses on how they establish and defend their professional autonomy within the strict frame of what the Cuban Communist Party defines as appropriate public information. Finally, chapter 10, coauthored by Abel Somohano Fernández and Mireya Márquez-Ramírez, is a case study that critically compares how two increasingly prominent, independent digital media projects, *El Estornudo* and *Periodismo de Barrio*, are opening—and even helping to democratize—the Cuban media landscape, but in significantly different ways.

The fourth section of the book looks at the multiple ways that Cubans have sought to monetize their increasing Internet connectivity. Specifically, chapter 11 by Rebecca Ogden chronicles the online marketing effort to promote tourist travel to Cuba as a refreshingly (and ironically) "offline" destination. The chapter argues that both Cuba's tourism ministry and private foreign agencies use digital video to highlight the island's offline authenticity and a return to sensual pleasures as Cuba's principal comparative advantage. Chapter 12 by Jennifer Cearns describes how an emerging generation of Cuban "millennials" are becoming digital entrepreneurs, launching businesses that rely on their newfound access to social media and Internet in Havana. Cearns' chapter also provides useful and original examinations of the well-known but under analyzed "*paquete*" and "SNET" phenomena.

The book's final section highlights the many, often unexpected ways that Cuban culture, society, identity, and even citizenship have been transformed by the increasing availability of digital technology, including the transformation of literary publication and digital music and video production. Specifically, in chapter 13 Walfrido Dorta profiles a group of young Cuban writers and artists who published a series of independent literary "e-zines" in the early 2000s, unwittingly serving as a precursor to the explosion of the Cuban blogosphere between 2007 and 2014 and the independent digital media sphere that followed. In chapter 14 Paloma Duong analyzes the various, competing "postsocialist mediascapes" produced on the island by Cubans themselves as opposed to the ones created by official state media or by an exoticizing foreign gaze. Duong unpacks a variety of images produced by what she labels the postsocialist Cuban "woman of fashion," interrogating not just the images themselves but also the social and media contexts in which they are produced and consumed.

Acknowledgments

Given the fact that many chapters of this volume are based on original ethnographic research and in-depth interviews with Cuba's "digital millennials" (journalists, bloggers, YouTubers, cyber-activists, programmers, computer scientists, tech professionals, government officials, tour operators, entrepreneurs, DJs, artists, musicians, *paqueteros*, and "SNET-izens"), we want to acknowledge their cooperation, openness, and trust in this project and thank them for their participation. While most have preferred to remain anonymous, this book would have been impossible without their input and many diverse voices and experiences. We hope we have reflected their eloquence, talent, and passion accurately in these pages.

We would also like to specifically thank Cuban artists Omar Santana and Lázaro Saavedra for allowing us to use their powerful art in these pages, as well as Cuban graphic designer Rolando Pulido for his fantastic cover image. Additionally, Cuban entrepreneur, Twitter maven, and podcaster Camilo Condis, journalist and blogger Yoani Sánchez, and writer Orlando Luis Pardo Lazo, all granted us permission to reprint images here they had previously launched into Cuba's dynamic and expanding digital mediascape. We also recognize the valuable feedback and sage advice we received at various stages of this project from fellow scholars Ellery Biddle, Bert Hoffmann, and Cristina Venegas.

Finally, we want to give a big thumbs up ("like") to the entire University of Florida Press team, starting with the intrepid and always encouraging acquisitions editor Stephanye Hunter. From the initial proposal, to the draft manuscript, to the reader feedback and revisions, to the final launch and publication of the book itself, Stephanye has been a joy to work with. We are also proud to add our title on Cuba to UFP's Reframing Media, Technology, and Culture in Latin/o America Series, edited by Héctor Fernández L'Hoeste and Juan Carlos Rodríguez. We thank both Juan Carlos and Héctor, as well as two anonymous reviewers, for their insightful feedback and suggestions on the manuscript. Likewise, we thank Lucinda Treadwell for her proofreading expertise and Rafael Munia for his indexing work.

Notes

1. The quote is from a speech given by Díaz-Canel at the closing ceremony of the International Congress of Pedagogy (*Juventud Rebelde* 2019). The original Spanish reads: "*Fidel fue el primero en percatarse del valor que tendría Internet para democratizar realmente la comunicación. Él decía que parecía creada para los revolucionarios, por la capacidad de difundir mensajes a un costo insignificante y con alcance infinito.*"

2. The quote is from a talk Sánchez gave at the seventeenth annual International Symposium of Online Journalism (ISOJ) (Higuera 2016).

3. The sixteen contributors of this collection's fourteen chapters include six Cubans (or Cuban-Americans) who live life "on the hyphen" between Brazil, Mexico, the United States, and Cuba itself, two North Americans, two Brits, two Mexicans, one Norwegian, one Spaniard, one Russian, and one native of France.

4. We are indebted to the pioneering spadework analyzing Cuba's digital turn done by Kalathil and Boas (2003), Bert Hoffmann (2004), Cristina Venegas (2010), Emily Parker (2014), and Oller Alonso and Oliveira Pérez (2016).

5. Indeed, the first epigraph above is taken from a Presidential tweet.

6. ETECSA stands for Empresa de telecomunicaciones de Cuba, S.A., the Cuban government's telecom monopoly.

7. Larry Press provides more detailed information and analysis of Cuba's current Internet connectivity in chapter 1.

8. While all authors in this volume discuss Cuba as a whole (sometimes including parts of its vast and diverse diaspora) in their analysis, there is a Havana-centric focus in much of the ethnographic fieldwork on which the chapters are based.

9. It's not that fear has been overcome. Indeed, it seems to still dominate Cuba's various public spheres. However, defiant transgressions of this fear have become more common.

10. This was followed in 2020 by the even more dramatic explosion onto the international scene of the "artist-activists" behind *Movimiento San Isidro* (#MSI) after a digital recording of the government raid of their headquarters was shared widely via the internet. Despite government efforts to block access to key social media platforms at the time, the real breakthrough of the MSI was its effective breakdown of the government-erected wall of fear and isolation that had previously separated these marginalized "artivists" from Cuba's state-sanctioned artistic mainstream. Indeed, after learning of the previous day's violent crackdown via their cellphones, on November 27 (#27N) upward of 500 mostly young artists and intellectuals from a broad array of disciplines and political ideologies staged an unprecedented, music-fueled, day-long "clap-in" (giving birth to the moniker,

"*La revolución de los aplausos*") outside Havana's Ministry of Culture in solidarity with the MSI briefly forcing officials to the table. The *sine que non* of this breakthrough was its members' savvy use of digital technology to communicate their demands, convene their protests, call government officials to account, and challenge the state media's official narrative of events in real time.

11. In October 1997, Raúl Castro declared: "Glasnost, which undermined the USSR and other socialist countries, consisted in handing over the mass media, one by one, to the enemies of socialism" (Press 2011).

12. Condis' original tweet and graphic can be found here: https://twitter.com/camilocondis/status/1105313141297242113.

13. In September 2016, I posed the question of whether "democracy can be downloaded" via the Internet to former USAID contractor Alan Gross, who spent five years in Cuban prison for bringing BGAN technology into Cuba to enable independent access to the Internet. His unequivocal response: "Democracy can't be downloaded. It can only be uploaded," indicated that, in his view, democratic values and institutions cannot be delivered via technology from abroad but must be cultivated locally.

14. A vivid illustration of this ethos of "technological determinism" combined with the hope that information technology would be placed at the disposition of "the many" was on display in Apple's now classic 1984 Super Bowl commercial. The thirty-second spot launched Apple's "Mac," featured an attractive female athlete wearing a Walkman hurling a hammer into the oppressive digital face of "Big Brother," and ended with the line: "On January 24th, Apple Computer will introduce Macintosh. And you'll see why 1984 won't be like '1984.'" See YouTube, https://www.youtube.com/watch?v=RyhwY07CxkM.

15. For recent comparative international reports on this phenomenon see Bradshaw and Howard (2019) and Shahbaz and Funk (2019).

16. Typically, F/OSS source code is licensed free of charge, encouraging modifications and improvements. The caricature by the Cuban artist Lázaro Saavedra (figure 0.4) satirizes the great difficulty Cubans on the island have gaining access to the Internet thanks to its control by powerful foreign entities. As glossed by Milena Recio in her pioneering study, "La hora de los desconectados," figure 0.4 shows "the Spanish conquistador in a superior position given his Internet access, while the Cuban 'Indians,' timid and at a disadvantage, try to decide among themselves whether they should confirm their own history [by having their adversary] look it up on the Web. [. . .] Hatuey was a Taíno leader who fought against the colonizers and was burned at the stake. The powerful control the channels of communication and are the only ones able to search" (2014, 47).

17. In figure 0.5, Saavedra inverts his satire about the lack of Internet access in Cuba, now aiming his critique inward at the demagogic control exercised by the Cuban government. "The authoritarian subject," writes Recio, "imposes a blanket condemnation of the Internet and attempts to have it pass as consensus. But the 'public' cannot dissent as it does not possess the expressive recourse (arms)" (2014, 47).

18. The "e-mail war" was a spontaneous *polémica intelectual* ("intellectual polemic") that erupted among Cuban artists and intellectuals in January and February 2007 in response to the recognition on national television of a number of censors notorious for their repressive policies of the 1970s. Henken briefly describes it in chapter 7 of this volume.

References

Ávila, Moises. 2019. "Cubans use new found social media heft to challenge leaders." AFP, March 19, 2019.
BBC. 2019. *The Documentary: Cuba's Digital Revolution*. October 12, 2019.
Best, Michael and Keegan W. Wade. 2005. "The Internet and Democracy: Global Catalyst or Democratic Dud?" Berkman Center for Internet and Democracy, Harvard University, September 30, 2005.
Bradshaw, Samantha and Philip N. Howard. 2019. "The Global Disinformation Order: 2019 Global Inventory of Organised Social Media Manipulation." Working Paper 2019.2. Oxford, UK: Project on Computational Propaganda.
Calvo Peña, Beatriz. 2008. "La creación de blogs desde Cuba: el nacimiento de una 'diáspora digital.'" Paper presented at the IV International Conference on Creation and Exile, "Con Cuba en la distancia." Fundación Bancaja, Valencia, Spain, November 17–21, 2008.
Chaguaceda, Armando. 2015. "The Promise Besieged: Participation and Autonomy in Cuba." In *A Contemporary Cuba Reader: The Revolution under Raúl Castro*, edited by Philip Brenner, Marguerite Rose Jiménez, John M. Kirk, and William M. LeoGrande, 111–115. Lanham, MD: Rowman and Littlefield Publishers.
Díaz, Elaine. 2018. "Medios emergentes en Cuba: desafíos, amenazas y oportunidades." *SembraMedia*, January 11, 2018.
Dilla, Haroldo and Philip Oxhorn. 2002. "The Virtues and Misfortunes of Civil Society in Cuba." *Latin American Perspectives* 29, no. 4 (July 2002): 11–30.
The Economist. 2019. "Cuba's leaders adopt social media, not democracy." February 21, 2019.
Etling, Bruce, John Kelly, Rob Faris, and John Palfrey. 2009. "Mapping the Arabic Blogosphere: Politics, Culture and Dissent." Berkman Center for Internet and Democracy, Harvard University, June 17, 2009.
Faiola, Anthony. 2019. "Cubans are using social media to air their grievances—and the government is responding, sometimes," *Washington Post*, July 7, 2019.
Garcia Santamaria, Sara. 2019. "Periodismo alternativo cubano: Un acercamiento a la violencia indirecta en perspectiva comparada." *Persona & Sociedad* 33 (2): 113–136.
Geoffray, Marie Laure. 2013. "Internet, Public Space, and Contention in Cuba: Bridging Asymmetries of Access to Public Space through Transnational Dynamics of Contention." Working Paper No. 42, desiguALdades.net, Research Network on Interdependent Inequities in Latin America.
Gladwell, Malcolm. 2010. "Small Change: Why the Revolution Will Not Be Tweeted." *New Yorker*, October 4, 2010.
Havana Times. 2019. "El Enjambre 'se revuelve' con tres tristes tramas." October 30, 2019.
Henken, Ted A. 2011. "Una cartografía de la blogósfera cubana: Entre 'oficialistas' y 'mercenarios.'" *Nueva Sociedad* No. 235, (September-October): 90–109.
Henken, Ted A. 2013. "Quotable (+video): Díaz-Canel on 'the impossible chimera' of information control." *El Yuma* blog, May 6, 2013.
Henken, Ted A. 2017. "Cuba's Digital Millennials: Independent Digital Media and Civil Society on the Island of the Disconnected." *Social Research* 84 (2): 429–456.

Henken, Ted A. and Sjamme van de Voort. 2015. "From Cyberspace to Public Space?: The Emergent Blogosphere and Cuban Civil Society." In *A Contemporary Cuba Reader: The Revolution Under Raúl Castro*, edited by Philip Brenner, Marguerite Rose Jiménez, John M. Kirk, and William M. LeoGrande, 99–110. Lanham, MD: Rowman & Littlefield.

Hernández Busto, Ernesto. 2010. "Los límites de la ciberdisidencia: una polémica." *Penultimos Días*, April 3, 2010.

Higuera, Silvia. 2016. "ISOJ 2016: Yoani Sánchez explica cómo la tecnología ha hecho más libres a los cubanos." *Periodismo en Las Américas* blog, April 16, 2016.

Hindman, Matthew. 2009. *The Myth of Digital Democracy*. Princeton, NJ: Princeton University Press.

Hoffmann, Bert. 2004. *The Politics of the Internet in Third World Development: Challenges in Contrasting Regimes with Case Studies of Costa Rica and Cuba*. New York: Routledge.

Israel, Esteban. 2009. "Cuba launches own Linux variant to counter U.S." Reuters, February 11, 2009.

Jiménez Enoa, Abraham. 2019. "Young People Are Fleeing Cuba. But I'm Staying." *New York Times*, July 3, 2019.

Juventud Rebelde. 2019. "En Pedagogía, como en la Revolución Cubana, no hay ruptura, hay continuidad." February 9, 2019.

Kalathil, Shanthi and Taylor C. Boas. 2003. *Open Neworks, Closed Regimes: The Impact of the Internet on Authoritarian Rule*. Washington, D.C.: Carnegie Endowment for International Peace.

Keen, Andrew. 2007. *The Cult of the Amateur: How Today's Internet is Killing Our Culture and Assaulting Our Economy*. New York: Doubleday.

Kelly, John and Bruce Etling. 2008. "Mapping Iran's Online Public: Politics and Culture in the Persian Blogosphere." Berkman Center for Internet and Democracy, Harvard University, April 6, 2008.

Lai, Eric. 2009. "Software libre! Cuba develops own free Linux called 'Nova.'" *Computer World*, February 12, 2009.

Liebling, A.J. 1960. "The Wayward Press: Do You Belong in Journalism?" *New Yorker*, May 14, 1960: 105.

Machado, Mabel. 2017. "Mi paladar no está en el Paquete. Comunicación en emprendimientos cubanos," in *Información, comunicación y cambio de mentalidad. Nuevas agendas para un nuevo desarrollo*, edited by Rayza Portal Moreno, Raúl Garcés, and Willy Pedroso Aguiar. Havana: Editorial de Ciencias Sociales.

MacKinnon, Rebecca. 2005. "Blogging, Journalism, and Credibility: Battleground and Common Ground." Berkman Center for Internet and Democracy, Harvard University, February 1, 2005.

MacKinnon, Rebecca. 2012. *The Consent of the Networked: The Worldwide Struggle for Internet Freedom*. New York: Basic Books.

Mandiberg, Michael, ed. 2012. *The Social Media Reader*. New York: New York University Press.

McNamee, Roger. 2019. *Zucked: Waking Up to the Facebook Catastrophe*. New York: Penguin.

Morán, Raphael. 2019. "Internet en Cuba: una nueva herramienta de expression." RFI, April 25, 2019.

Morozov, Evgeny. 2011. *The Net Delusion: The Dark Side of Internet Freedom.* New York: Public Affairs.

Oller Alonso, Martín and Dasniel Olivera Pérez, eds. 2016. *Ideology and Professional Culture of Journalists in Cuba: Confidences, Dialogues and Senses of a Profession.* Riga, Latvia: Editorial Académica Española.

O'Reilly, Tim. 2012. "What Is Web 2.0? Design Patterns and Business Models for the Next Generation of Software." In *The Social Media Reader,* edited by Michael Mandiberg, 32–52. New York: New York University Press.

Padgett, Tim. 2019. "Snarled SNET: Seizure of Cuba's Underground Network May Signal Cyber-Crackdown." *WLRN,* August 26, 2019.

Parker, Emily. 2014. *Now I Know Who My Comrades Are: Voices from the Internet Underground.* New York: Sarah Crichton Books.

Pentón, Mario J. 2019. "Cuban officials invite dialogue on Twitter—but only with citizens who don't criticize." *Miami Herald,* March 8, 2019.

Press, Larry. 2011. "The Dictator's Dilemma." *The Internet in Cuba* blog, February 15, 2011.

Press, Larry. 2017. "TechCrunch panel—three Cuban software companies." *The Internet in Cuba* blog, May 30, 2017.

Recio, Milena. 2014. "La hora de los desconectados. Evaluación del diseño de la política de 'acceso social' a Internet en Cuba en un contexto de cambios." *Crítica y Emancipación,* Year VI, No. 11, 291–377.

Repnikova, Maria and Kecheng Fang. 2018. "Authoritarian Participatory Persuasion 2.0: Netizens as Thought Work Collaborators in China." *Journal of Contemporary China* 27 (113): 763–779.

Rodríguez Fernández, Fidel Alejandro. 2019. "Conexiones comunes: Sobre los usos de las redes autónomas de videojuegos en La Habana y el caso SNET." *Revista Científica de Información y Comunicación,* No. 16: 391–414.

Rosen, Jay. 2012. "The People Formerly Known as The Audience." In *The Social Media Reader,* edited by Michael Mandiberg, 13–16. New York: New York University Press.

Shahbaz, Adrian and Allie Funk. 2019. "Freedom on the Net 2019: The Crisis of Social Media." Freedom House. Washington, D.C., 29. https://freedomhouse.org/sites/default/files/2019-11/11042019_Report_FH_FOTN_2019_final_Public_Download.pdf

Shirky, Clay. 2010. *Cognitive Surplus: How Technology Makes Consumers into Collaborators.* New York: Penguin.

Sosa Barceló, Sayli. 2017. "AlaMesa: Todo cubierto y servido en un click." *Invasor,* June 10, 2017.

Tufekci, Zeynep. 2017. *Twitter and Tear Gas: The Power and Fragility of Networked Protest.* New Haven, CT: Yale University Press.

Vaidhyanathan, Siva. 2012. *The Googlization of Everything (and Why We Should Worry).* Berkeley: University of California Press.

Vaidhyanathan, Siva. 2018. *Antisocial Media: How Facebook Disconnects Us and Undermines Democracy.* New York: Oxford University Press.

Vela, Haztel. 2019. "Young Cubans develop app to help with island's transportation woes." WPLG Local10.com, January 25, 2019.

Venegas, Cristina. 2010. *Digital Dilemmas: The State, the Individual, and Digital Media in Cuba*. New Brunswick: Rutgers University Press.

Wu, Tim. 2010. *The Master Switch: The Rise and Fall of Information Empires*. New York: Knopf.

Wu, Tim. 2016. *The Attention Merchants: The Epic Struggle to Get Inside Our Heads*. New York: Knopf.

Zaldívar, Liz Érika. 2019. "Camilo Condis, el emprendedor cubano que usa Twitter." *ADN-Cuba*, June 24, 2019.

Zhong, Raymond. 2018. "How China Walled Off the Internet." *New York Times*, November 18, 2018.

I
HISTORY, MEDIA, AND TECHNOLOGY

1

The Past, Present, and Future of the Cuban Internet

LARRY PRESS

The first two sections of this introductory chapter[1]—summarizing the history of the Cuban Internet and its current state—aim to establish a baseline upon which subsequent chapters of the volume will build. The third section on the future of the Cuban Internet does not attempt to predict that future but describes emerging technology and suggests policy changes the Cuban government could make to take advantage of it. Before the advent of the Internet, Cuba was arguably the leading international computer-networking nation in the Caribbean. Members of Cuba's research and education community used pre-Internet networks for e-mail, document retrieval, and threaded discussions of a variety of technical and social topics. However, when Cuba finally connected to the Internet in 1996, seventeen other nations in Latin America and the Caribbean were already online. The U.S. embargo, the economic downturn after the dissolution of the Soviet Union (i.e., the special period), and political fear of free information (the so-called dictator's dilemma) had delayed Cuba's connection.

Cuba adopted a limited-access Internet policy in 1996, and today the Cuban Internet is arguably the worst in Latin America and the Caribbean—minimal, slow, and unfree—in spite of Cuba being among the leaders in the region in terms of human development, a contradiction I address in some detail below. The economy has stabilized, restrictions on the importation of networking equipment have been lifted, and the Internet has been shown to be a tool for political control as well as free expression. However, bureaucracy and vested interests have developed within ETECSA (*Empresa de Telecomunicaciones de Cuba, S.A.*), Cuba's government-monopoly Internet service provider.

Cuban technology languished along with its policy. They relied on slow, expensive geostationary orbit satellites for international connectivity until

2013, when they installed an undersea cable via Venezuela and began opening public-access *telepuntos* or "navigation rooms." Since that time, they have added nearly seven hundred public Wi-Fi hot spots, digital home connectivity to over seventy thousand customers, and most recently launched 3G mobile access in December 2018, which was serving 1.8 million (35 percent) of Cuba's 5.3 million mobile phone users by the end of January 2019. This was followed by 4G trials in the first half of 2019. These series of government-initiated stopgap measures are available in limited locations and use obsolete technology to deliver inferior performance at prices that are high relative to other nations and to Cuban incomes.

The government tolerates the offline circulation of a wide array of digital material downloaded from the Internet and transferred from person to person via USB drives. Known popularly as *el paquete semanal* (the weekly packet), this phenomenon is widespread and monetized, but its tolerance is based on its compiler's strict self-censorship of political, religious, and pornographic content (Henken 2021). This innovative grassroots digital workaround has attracted wide media attention abroad (Kessler 2015; Fenton 2016; Parish 2018) since it reveals Cuba's where-there's-a-will-there's-a-way, maker, DIY culture borne of scarcity and fueled by the population's scrappy resolve.

If Cuba aspires to a truly modern Internet, they should consider what they are doing today as providing an interim stopgap and plan to leapfrog to next-generation technology and policy by 2025. Such a policy should be designed to meet economic and social goals, not to maintain its telecom monopoly, stifling bureaucracy, and lucrative revenue stream. I derive my suggestions from considerations of both global and local trends in policy and technology and Cuba's own human resources, values, and culture. Cuba has fallen behind the world, but they are taking stopgap measures today and could deploy next-generation technology in the future. Given political fear, vested interests, and the Cuban government's often-impenetrable bureaucracy, next-generation policy will be a tougher problem. I will speculate on that future policy and technology in the final section of the chapter, but first, let's review the past and the present.

The Past

Before the Internet, companies like IBM and DEC (Digital Equipment Corporation) used proprietary protocols to network their computers and the U.S. government-built defense networks of identical computers (Press 1996d). Later, X.25 and UUCP, open standards that allowed dissimilar computers to communicate, were developed. In the 1980s, Cubans began using X.25 and UUCP networks for limited international communication. They used Russian X.25 networks for access to scientific articles and e-mail, but UUCP was more important. UUCP networking was central to communication within the nascent international networking community and Cubans used it for e-mail, file transfer, and Usenet News, a large, eclectic collection of global threaded discussions on technology, science, politics, culture, and many other topics (Mesher et al. 1992; Press and Snyder 1992). Usenet News Groups were user discussion forums, not sites dedicated to publishing news for the general public.

Four Cuban organizations had international UUCP links and were serving client organizations (Press 1996a; Press 1996b; Press 1996c):

- CIGB, the Center for Genetic Engineering and Biotechnology, served subnets in eight organizations with 950 active accounts. (Several users might share a single account).
- CENIAI, the Center for Automated Interchange of Information of the Cuban Academy of Sciences, served ten subnets with 732 active accounts.
- TinoRed served the 150 (at the time) Youth Computer Clubs around the nation and thirty-two NGOs with 413 active accounts.
- Infomed served the medical community with five hundred active accounts.

Note that in those days (the late 1980s and early 1990s), computer networking was just beginning and Cuba, with its large, well-educated population and fewer than three thousand accounts, was among the leading Caribbean nations. However, UUCP was an asynchronous protocol—data was transferred several times a day in batches, so interactive applications were not possible and X.25 was inefficient relative to TCP/IP, the protocol used on the Internet; and Cuba did not have a link to the Internet.[2] The U.S. embargo and Cuba's economic depression that followed the dissolution of the Soviet Union delayed their connection to the Internet and, in September 1996, when CENIAI established Cuba's first Internet connection (Press 2011a), seventeen Caribbean nations were already online (Crepin-Leblond 1996). Despite the U.S. embargo, Cuba's Internet link was to the U.S. National Science Foundation network under their International Networking Program for research and education networks in developing nations and provided by Sprint (Press 1996d).[3]

While Cuba was late to the Internet, it had experience with small TCP/IP networks within the nation and CENIAI Director Jesús Martínez, Carlos

Armas of CIGB, and others had been active in regional and international Internet organizations. Cuban networkers shared the values and enthusiasm of the international networking community, believing, correctly, that the Internet would profoundly affect individuals, organizations, and society (Press 2011a; Press 2015b).[4] Today, Cuba's nascent Internet developer and entrepreneur community is reminiscent of that optimistic time (Press 2015h).

Cuban officials also took note of the Internet and established an inter-ministerial commission to determine Cuban Internet policy. The Cuban Communist Party Plenum of March 1996 may have been decisive. The meeting was held less than two weeks after President Clinton signed the Helms-Burton Act codifying the Cuban embargo into U.S. law for the first time and aimed at providing "assistance, through appropriate NGOs, for the support of individuals and organizations to promote nonviolent democratic change in Cuba" (U.S. Congress 1996). At the meeting, Carlos Lage, Executive Secretary of the Council of Ministers, spoke of the economic advantages of the Internet, but Raúl Castro, who was familiar with a well-known study of Cuban NGOs by Gillian Gunn, feared them (Gunn 1995). His view was that "glasnost, which undermined the USSR and other socialist countries, consisted in handing over the mass media, one by one, to the enemies of socialism" (Press 2011b). The Center for the Study of the Americas (CEA), perhaps Cuba's most important, influential, and innovative think tank of this period, was also shuttered in 1996 due to government fears of the growth of independent NGOs and civil society organizations (Pérez-Stable 1998; Giuliano 1998).

The hardliners prevailed, and, while internal TCP/IP networks were allowed, Internet access was strictly limited (Rohter 1996; Valdés and Rivera 1999). It is noteworthy that Fidel Castro allowed the hardline decision but understood the importance of the Internet and supported TinoRed and the Youth Computer Clubs (Press 2013c). However, two years later, TinoRed no longer served NGOs and Cuba had made little progress while other developing nations—notably China (Press et al. 2003)—forged ahead.

In the late 1990s, my colleagues and I developed a framework for assessing the state of the Internet in a developing nation along six dimensions: *pervasiveness, geographic dispersion, sectoral absorption, connectivity infrastructure, organizational infrastructure,* and *sophistication of use* (Press et al. 1998; Wolcott et al. 2001). Using our framework, we conducted a study of the Cuban Internet and in October 1997 ranked Cuba at our lowest level on five of the six dimensions (Press 1997; Press et al. 1998).

In the early 1990s, Cuba had fewer telephone lines as a proportion of population and GDP than any Caribbean nation but Haiti, and was closer to the low-income nations in terms of infrastructure and services than the lower-middle group into which it fell (Press 1996). The dissolution of the Soviet Union and U.S. embargo exacerbated the deficiency, leading them to create ETECSA, a joint venture between the Ministry of Communications (MINCOM) (51 percent) and Grupo Domus of Mexico (49 percent). In April 1995, Domos sold 25 percent of their interest to STET International Netherlands, a wholly owned subsidiary of the Italian State Telecommunication Company. Domos defaulted on their capital commitment and lost their equity, leaving STET with 29.29 percent of ETECSA, the Cuban government 49 percent, and a coalition of banks the remainder. In 2011, Telecom Italia sold its share of ETECSA to a company called Rafin S.A., which the Central Bank of Cuba describes as a non-banking financial institution.[5] The International Telecommunication Union (ITU) describes ETECSA as "one of the last state telecommunication-sector monopolies" but that seems inconsistent with the attribution of ownership to Rafin and banks, raising questions about finance and decision-making authority at ETECSA (Press 2014d).

The Internet impacts commerce, education, entertainment, government, etc. in a nation, but it is shaped in turn by the values, laws, politics, and economy of that same nation. Society shapes infrastructure and infrastructure shapes society. While Internet access was limited, Cuban networking was (Press 1998b)

- Relatively noncommercial—the first four internationally connected networks dealt with science, education, biotechnology, and medicine.
- Geographically dispersed relative to other developing nations—Internet connectivity was only available in the capital city in twenty-nine of the forty-four African nations with Internet connectivity, whereas Infomed had a presence in every Cuban province and TinoRed was present in nearly every municipality.
- Focused intra-nationally, not internationally.

Because of political fear, the poor economy during the special period after the dissolution of the Soviet Union, and the U.S. embargo, global Internet access was limited. As a result, Cuba is far behind most of the rest of the world in Internet today.

The Present

Today, the Cuban Internet is arguably the worst in Latin America and the Caribbean—minimal, slow, and unfree. The ITU publishes an annual

Table 1.1. Cuban IDI and sub-index rankings

	2017	2016
IDI	137	135
Access sub-index	166	169
Use sub-index	151	143
Skill sub-index	62	57

Source: Devised by the author based on ITU 2018a, b and ITU 2017a, b, c.

information society analysis (ITU 2018a, b), which features an ICT Development Index (IDI) for each nation. The IDI is a composite of three sub-indices: *access*, *use*, and *skill*.[6] Table 1 shows Cuba's 2016–2017 rank among 176 nations (ITU 2017a, b, c).[7] Cuba's IDI rank dropped during the year and is the lowest in Latin America and the Caribbean. Cuba's *access* and *use* sub-indices are only slightly better than those of Haiti, which is last in the region. Those stand in contrast to the skill sub-index in which Cuba ranks sixty-second, sixth in the region after Chile, Argentina, Venezuela, Saint Kitts and Nevis, and the Bahamas.

The Cuban Internet is also considered *unfree* by Freedom House, which annually assesses nations' Internet freedom using a three-dimension index: obstacles to access, limits on content, and violation of user rights. Freedom House studies sixty-five nations and Cuba ranked sixty-first, fifty-ninth, and fifty-eighth respectively on these dimensions in 2018. Overall, Cuba ranked sixty-first and only China, Iran, Ethiopia, and Syria ranked lower (Freedom House 2018a). For a detailed discussion of the Cuba findings, see Freedom House's annual "Freedom on the Net" report on Cuba (2018b). This dismal record stands in stark contrast to Cuba's ranking in another annual report, the Human Development Report of the United Nations Development Programme (UNDP 2018a). The report centers on the U.N.'s Human Development Index (HDI). The HDI considers 145 indicators in computing a summary measure of achievements on their three key dimensions of human development: *a long and healthy life*, *access to knowledge*, and *a decent standard of living*. In 2014, the Cuban HDI ranked forty-fourth in the world among 187 nations and was second only to Chile in Latin America and the Caribbean (Press 2014c). In 2017, Cuba ranked seventy-third globally and had fallen to twelfth place in Latin America and the Caribbean (UNDP 2018b). Cuba remained constant as the rest of the world progressed.

The state of the Cuban Internet is far worse than one would expect in a nation with a relatively high UNDP Human Development Index. How might we explain the discrepancy? The historical impediments to the Internet in

1996 have eased. The economy has improved since the 1990s and the availability of Chinese equipment has eroded the impact of the embargo (Press 2015a). President Obama's attempted rapprochement between 2014 and 2016 (Press 2017g) included sending high-level delegations of U.S. telecom officials to Cuba (Press 2015g; Press 2016g; Press 2016d), making an historic state visit to Cuba (Press 2016d), and organizing a meeting with tech entrepreneurs during his visit, but little came of that (Press 2016b).[8]

While the historical impediments have diminished in importance, other factors have affected the discrepancy between the IDI and HDI. Cuba's health and education systems have increased HDI (and the *skill* component of the IDI) while other factors have impeded the development of the Cuban Internet:

- The lack of freedom discussed above.
- Bureaucracy and vested financial interests (Press 2014d; Press 2016i).
- Restrictions on self-employment of computer programmers (Camacho 2017; Press 2017c).
- Emphasis on the national intranet rather than the Global Internet (Press 2018; Press 2018e).
- Cuban reluctance to engage with U.S. IT companies both before and after President Obama's visit (Laughlin 2017; Press 2016b).[9]

Underlying all of this is Cuba's obsolete regulatory and infrastructure-ownership policy (Press 2016a). Based on high-quality data from 193 countries, the ITU's information and communication technology "regulatory tracker" uses fifty indicators organized across four pillars: regulatory authority, regulatory mandate, regulatory regime, and competition framework. Using these criteria, the ITU defined four ICT policy generations (G1-G4) up until 2018, after which there emerged a fifth generation (G5). Cuba is one of the twenty-eight remaining first-generation nations in the world (ITU 2017a; ITU 2017b, see figure 1.1 below):

- G1: Regulated public monopolies—command and control approach.
- G2: Basic reform—partial liberalization and privatization across the layers.
- G3: Enabling investment, innovation and access—dual focus on stimulating competition in service and content delivery, and consumer protection.
- G4: Integrated regulation—led by economic and social policy goals.
- G5: Collaborative regulation—collaboration among regulators aimed at digital policy design that accelerates digital transformation.

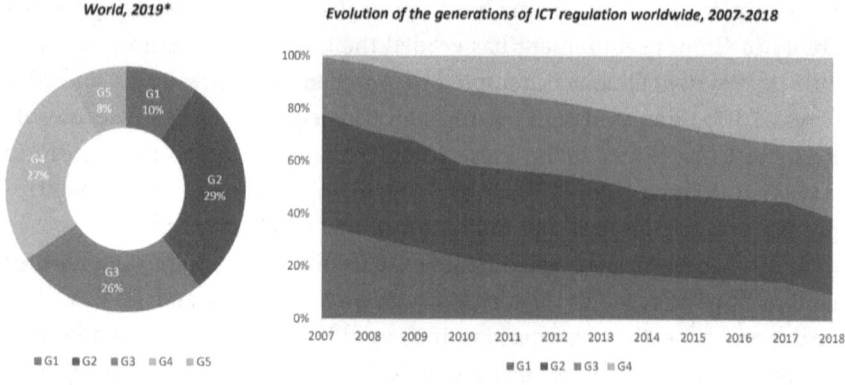

Figure 1.1. Generations of internet regulation policy. International Telecommunications Union (ITU 2017a, b, c; 2020: 19).

In 2017 Cuba ranked 172nd among 190 nations (ITU 2017a). Only Bolivia ranked below Cuba among the thirty-one Latin American and Caribbean nations. Cuba was ranked 157th in 2007—remaining static while others evolved. In 2018, Cuba fell to 179th place among the 193 countries included in the rankings that year (ITU 2019; 2020).

While the current state of the Internet in Cuba is indeed grim, it has improved with the activation of the ALBA-1 undersea cable connecting Cuba to the Internet via Venezuela (Madory 2013). Prior to 2013, international traffic was routed over slow, low-capacity geostationary satellite links. The cable enabled Cuba to begin expanding Internet access and in 2014, they announced that the computerization (*informatización*) of society was a priority (*Granma* 2014). Since that time, ETECSA has introduced four public-access offerings:

- Navigation rooms (*telepuntos*) where Internet access was available for a fee. Today there are 918 computers in 259 navigation rooms, ninety-five of which are in Youth Clubs (ETECSA 2019c).[10]
- Wi-Fi access points, hot spots where people could access the Internet using a laptop, tablet, or smartphone, provided they had previously purchased a *Nauta* card allowing an hour of network access for $1 (down from an original $2). Today there are 956 of these hot spots (ETECSA 2019b).
- Fixed digital access from homes. The service, known as "*Nauta Hogar*," is only available in certain neighborhoods since it requires an equipment upgrade in the local telephone central office and

depends upon the condition of the wiring to a home. There are currently 70,418 connected homes, 95 percent of which connect at 1 Mbps, the lowest download speed available (Guevara 2019).
- Third generation (3G) mobile access became available in December 2018, and during the first month of operation around 859,000 accounts were opened (Guevara 2019; Press 2018j). 4G access is also available in limited areas.
- ETECSA also offers Internet access to enterprises at speeds ranging from 19.2 Kbps to 1 Gbps, point-to-point links, domain registration, data center, and e-mail service to enterprises. Prices for global Internet access are significantly higher than for the national intranet (ETECSA 2019a).

Mobile access is the most important of the public online offerings. During the limited 3G-rollout period of December 4–6, 2018, Internet activity roughly doubled over previous levels and when the initial rollout was complete, they roughly doubled again. During the first month after completion of the rollout, there were nearly two million transactions and the revenue was over thirteen million CUC (Press 2019e). Despite these advances, the Internet service initiatives available through ETECSA described above have things in common:

- They are very expensive relative to world prices and Cuban incomes.
- Access is limited to certain locations.
- Connectivity is slow, cutting user productivity and making some modern applications impossible.
- They use obsolete technology (apart from the Wi-Fi hot spots and limited 4G mobile).

In addition to online access, Internet content is available offline through *el paquete semanal*, a weekly digital distribution of entertainment, software, games, news, etc. on portable hard disks and flash drives (Dye et al. 2018; Press 2015c).[11] *El paquete* is updated weekly, distributed throughout the island by a decentralized, ad hoc two-tier "organization" of largely autonomous people, and may be Cuba's largest private employer. Four "maestro" organizations, called *casas matrices* or "compilation houses," three in Havana and one in Santiago de Cuba, compile weekly terabyte collections that are distributed throughout Cuba by many independent *paqueteros* or "distributors." While it is technically illegal, the Cuban government tolerates *el paquete* because its content is non-political and satisfies public demand for Internet content. The unwritten rule of thumb adhered to by all compilers in order to garner continued government tolerance and avoid police crackdown seems to be "no politics and no porn" (Henken 2017; Henken 2021).

SNET was a community-built and operated network in Havana (Pujol et al. 2017; García Martínez 2017) which offered access to *el paquete* and many Internet-like services—social networks, discussion forums, software libraries, access to video streaming, etc. In 2017, fifty-six thousand users were registered in discussion forums alone. SNET could have been legitimatized by the government and given Internet access (Press 2016e), but it was subsequently taken over by the government (Hernández Busto 2019; Pérez Díaz 2019g; Press 2019b; Press 2019c; Press 2019j).

History and culture shape the Cuban Internet. For example, Roberto, a *paquetero*, knows his customers, gives them technical assistance, tailors their content to suit their tastes, and charges differently depending upon their ability to pay. Another *paquetero*, Carla, says, "I basically sell it to my customers and friends. They already know me, and other *paqueteros* don't come here, since it's already covered by me. There's a market base for everyone in Havana" (Dye et al. 2018). The creators of *Ninjacuba*, an online service for matching technical professionals with projects, say they want to build a sustainable company, not become a "unicorn" startup (Press 2017e). Cuba might bring a degree of social entrepreneurship to the Internet.

The Future

This section focuses on future policy and technology. If Cuba aspires to a truly modern Internet, policymakers should consider today's offerings and policies as interim stopgaps and plan to leapfrog to next-generation technology and fourth-generation policy that is designed to meet economic and social goals, not to maintain political stability and telecommunication monopoly, bureaucracy, and revenue. I will discuss policy changes and technologies that are becoming available.

We have seen that Cuba is stuck at first-generation regulation with infrastructure ownership and decision making centralized in ETECSA and MINCOM. The usual transition from first-generation policy is to invite global companies to bid on the right to install infrastructure in return for a license to provide service for a limited time. For example, Madory has suggested that Cuba follow the example of Myanmar, which in 2013 was a near Internet "greenfield" with a government-monopoly service provider. They called for bids from mobile Internet service providers and over a dozen companies responded. The two winners pledged to provide mobile connectivity in 90 percent of the country and paid $500 million in return for fifteen-year licenses (Madory 2014).

Myanmar's IDI rank rose from 150th among 176 nations in 2013 to 135th in 2017 (ITU 2017), but might they have done better? With a market-driven approach, company profit projections determine investment levels, but Cuba has the opportunity to prioritize economic and social policy goals and those goals might be better served by viewing the Internet as infrastructure, like streets and sidewalks, rather than a market commodity. As African Internet scholar Steve Song states: "The strategic goal of infrastructure is not to derive economic benefit from the asset itself, but to generate economic benefit by maximizing the use of the asset" (Song 2018).

How might this infrastructure approach play out in Cuba? One possibility would be to decentralize infrastructure ownership and operation by creating municipal networks.[12] While that would be politically difficult, this might be a good time to do it since Cuba's new constitution decentralizes executive governance by reducing provincial government and strengthening municipal government (Frank 2019). Municipal networks would connect to a national backbone and, through that, to international links operated by ETECSA. ETECSA would also support the municipal networks by consulting, and by purchasing international bandwidth, telecommunication equipment, infrastructure installation equipment, etc. Locally elected officials would control the municipal networks, and representatives of the municipal networks would shape ETECSA policy.[13]

Cooperatives, where customers jointly own and manage the network, are another form of decentralization (Song 2019). SNET was the world's largest community network not connected to the Internet before it was confiscated. Guifi Net in Spain is a larger community network that is connected to the Internet; ETECSA could have followed the Spanish example (Press 2017a; Press 2017f) and could have also collaborated with *el paquete* by providing them with connectivity and distributing their content,[14] but has not done so. If they are unwilling to revisit the SNET decision, municipal networks might be easier to achieve politically. Cuban schools and other organizations could also make use of local area network-based courseware that is periodically updated from the Internet, for example, educational material from the Khan Academy and MIT (Press 2016h).

ETECSA is currently deploying fifteen-year-old 3G mobile and some 4G technology and charging a price most Cubans cannot afford.[15] Once they develop enough "backhaul" capacity to support it, I would advocate a drastic 3G price cut, better yet make it free—in other words, consider it infrastructure rather than a marketable service. Doing so would generate new, innovative applications. It would also expand the population of experienced, demanding users, ready for future technology. The economic and social benefits of free 3G Internet connectivity would outweigh the costs (Press 2018b).

I would also advise Cuba to become more open to cooperation with U.S. companies and organizations. For example, Google worked hard to establish Cuban relationships, but little has come of their efforts (Press 2014a; Press 2016b; Press 2016f) and there are rumors that Cuba rebuffed a major wireless infrastructure offer from Google. One can imagine Google deploying wholesale fiber in Havana as they have in three African capitals (Press 2016j) or a YouTube production space as they have in several cities (Press 2018j).[16]

Cuba should also be planning to adopt future technology. For a start, they need another undersea cable. I do not know the capacity of the current ALBA-1 undersea cable, but even if it is far from saturated, Cuba needs a second cable. The ALBA-1 landing point is at the east end of the island and a second landing point near Havana would reduce the load on the domestic backbone, lower latency time, and provide backup. Terrestrial capacity conservation would cover the cost of the cable. Ronald Bechtold, chief information officer at the Pentagon, said the U.S. cable at Guantánamo would "be for the entire island in anticipation that one day they'll be able to extend it into mainland Cuba," but that was denied later (Press 2015d). In 1996, Deputy Assistant Secretary of State Daniel Sepúlveda led a U.S. delegation to Havana to discuss telecommunications and the Internet. At the time, he said there were at least a half-dozen U.S.-Cuba undersea cable proposals, but none have been built (Press 2016a).

Satellite technology is changing rapidly. Several years ago, I suggested that ETECSA use geostationary satellites to provide connectivity in rural towns as a stopgap measure (Press 2013a; Press 2017h). While that remains an interim option, future low- and middle-earth orbit (LEO and MEO) satellite constellations may play an important role in the future of the Cuban Internet (Press 2018i; Press 2019h). Cuba uses SES O3b MEO satellites for international connectivity today (Press 2017d), and SES will deploy significantly improved satellites beginning in 2021 (Press 2018j). OneWeb, SpaceX, Telesat, Amazon, and China's Hongyun Project will be deploying constellations of LEO satellites between now and 2025 (Press 2017d; Press 2017g; Press 2017i; Press 2017j; Press 2019g). These satellites will be capable of connecting Cuba's mobile network, municipal networks, organizations like schools or clinics, and rural homes, thereby saving Cuba the expense of investing in their national backbone. To satisfy the FCC, SpaceX, OneWeb, and Telesat have deadlines for covering the U.S. so Cuba, being near the southeastern U.S., could receive early coverage. The Hongyun project will focus first on rural China and, since Havana is around the same latitude as southern China, Hongyun may also offer service in Cuba. Furthermore, China has a strategic motivation for doing so (Press 2019d).

Cuba should also be planning for future terrestrial wireless technology. Much of the world is currently using 4G mobile communication technology, but the transition to 5G wireless has begun. When mature, 5G will enable new applications and be competitive for fixed as well as mobile connectivity. 5G will require many "small cells" because it uses high-frequency radio signals that do not travel as far as 3G or 4G signals and are more easily blocked by obstructions like trees and buildings. For example, there are about 154,000 cell towers in the U.S. today and an industry association estimates that there will be eight hundred thousand small cells by 2026 (CTIA 2018). The U.S. embargo and Cuba's emphasis on education have left them with an innovative do-it-yourself ethic and one can imagine non-professionals or municipal employees rather than ETECSA employees installing "small cells" in their neighborhoods (Press 2018a). Cuba's strategic and commercial ties with China give them an important advantage regarding 5G wireless. Huawei, which dominates the Cuban Internet infrastructure market, is the world leader in 5G development and, if the Cuban government were willing, Havana could possibly have 5G coverage before Miami (Press 2019f).

Looking toward the future, we must also recognize the potential downside to Cuba achieving a ubiquitous Internet. We saw that Freedom House considers the Cuban Internet to be unfree, and Cuba has used the Internet as an international political weapon (Press 2013b; Press 2020) and is using it as a domestic political tool, most recently when government trolls waged a pro-ETECSA Twitter campaign to counter public complaints about high prices (Inventario 2019). The example of Myanmar, mentioned above, also offers a cautionary tale. Privatization of the mobile phone network led to a rapid rise in Internet utilization, but it also contributed to the Facebook-facilitated Rohingya genocide (Mozur 2018). Russia[17] has waged cyberwar against businesses and societies for a decade and Europeans have experience defending against them.[18] Imagine what the Cuban government could do with Russia-style access to Facebook data or the fake news they could create and circulate on YouTube (Press 2019a). Many of our current problems with the Internet are a by-product of the advertising business model of companies like Google and Facebook (Wu 2016). There are alternative ways to finance the Internet—they license television sets in Great Britain; we pay Netflix and others for content in the U.S., and Cubans pay for *el paquete* (though it is heavily subsidized by piracy and contains advertisements). Might Cuba show us a future Internet financed without reliance on advertising and the concomitant risks to privacy, media filter bubbles, and ubiquitous fake news?

Conclusion

We saw that Cuba was among the leading Caribbean nations in pre-Internet international networking. They connected to Soviet networks for access to scientific articles, databases, and e-mail and they communicated with the nascent global networking community—exchanging e-mail, transferring files, and participating in threaded discussions on technology, science, politics, culture, and many other topics. However, financial problems, difficulty in obtaining equipment because of the embargo, and fear of the role free information had played in the dissolution of the Soviet Union, led to a decision to control access to the Internet.

Cuba connected to the Internet in 1996, but by that time they had fallen behind other nations in the region, access was strictly limited, and international traffic was routed over low-capacity geostationary satellites. In 2013, an undersea cable connecting Cuba with Venezuela was installed, increasing international capacity, and four forms of public access followed: navigation rooms, Wi-Fi hot spots, home ADSL, and mobile connectivity are now available in some parts of the country to those who can afford them.[19] These are expensive, slow, and (apart from the Wi-Fi hot spots) use obsolete technology. Cuba remains one of the least connected nations in the world and ETECSA is one of the few remaining government-monopoly Internet service providers.

Looking toward the future, this chapter discusses steps the island's telecommunication policymakers could take if they aspire to a ubiquitous, modern Internet.[20] Policy trends and options, next-generation technology, and Cuba's human resources, values, and culture were all considered in formulating suggestions. Cuba has fallen behind the world, but they are taking stopgap measures today and could deploy next-generation technology when it is ready. Next-generation policy will be a tougher problem.

Notes

1. This work is licensed under a Creative Commons Attribution 4.0 International License (https://creativecommons.org/licenses/by/4.0/).

2. For a summary of nontechnical reasons for the ascendance of TCP/IP, see Haverty 2019.

3. Note that the speed of that first international Internet link was only 64 Kbps and it was soon saturated. Still, limited interactive applications like text chat and text document

retrieval were possible. Text documents were retrieved by requesting them in formatted e-mail messages or by accessing a Gopher server (Press and Armas 1996). Gopher was a protocol for text document retrieval with links to related documents and CENIAI maintained a Gopher server in Uruguay, which had a relatively fast international connection.

4. Based on our experience as early Internet users, we expected it to lead to advances in science, technology, commerce, education, medicine, democracy, global unity, etc. We were naïve in not anticipating negative applications, impact on retail, entertainment and other industries, politics, etc.

5. An unsubstantiated rumor asserts that the Castro brothers owned Rafin (i.e., *Inversiones de Raúl y Fidel*).

6. For details on their methodology, see ITU 2018a.

7. 2017 is the latest year for which the IDI is available. The methodology is being revised.

8. While Trump has made a show of reversing Obama's opening, nothing in his new policy directly affected the Cuban Internet (Press 2017k). However, his antagonistic approach has hardened Cuban rhetoric and solidified China's role as Cuba's IT infrastructure source.

9. Trump's disavowal of President Obama's policy did not directly affect the Cuban Internet (Press 2017a; Press 2017m) and his Cuba Internet Task Force (2019) generated political rhetoric, but nothing more (Press 2018c; Press 2018g).

Google has been active in Cuba with top executive visits and regular staff visits. They reportedly made significant infrastructure proposals, but Cuba has only allowed them to donate Chromebooks for a Wi-Fi hotspot and install servers to speed access to Google content (Press 2016c; Press 2016f). Google has also signed MOUs with a variety of state technological, telecom, cultural, and educational entities but how far those agreements have moved toward actual collaboration is unclear.

While Cuban President Miguel Díaz-Canel has met with U.S. executives (Press 2018d), Cuban policy toward the U.S. does not seem to have changed under his administration (Press 2017l).

10. Navigation room connectivity has been unchanged in recent years, suggesting that this is no longer a priority.

11. Weekly contents of some of Cuba's *paquete* compilation houses or "*casas matrices*" are published online at http://paquetedecuba.com/. Volume 50 of the academic journal *Cuban Studies* (2021) has recently published a four-article dossier on *el paquete*.

12. Publicly owned infrastructure can be efficient. State-owned Antel provides telecommunication services throughout Uruguay, including in the most remote areas (Baca et al. 2018). Antel is the sole provider of wired (ADSL and FTTP) connectivity in the country, yet only Barbados and Saint Kitts and Nevis outrank Uruguay on the IDI (ITU 2017) and there are many examples of effective community networks in other nations. There are numerous successful large and small municipal networks in Latin America (Baca et al. 2018) and throughout the world.

The Internet was designed to be decentralized. It was invented to interconnect heterogeneous networks and it is a collection of interconnected, autonomous networks.

13. These municipal networks would not be homogeneous. For example, a large city like Havana might follow the example of Stockholm, which operates a municipal backbone and provides wholesale access to retail Internet service providers (Press 2014).

14. Much of the content is pirated and ETECSA would not be able to host that.

With their penchant for innovation and stress on education, Cuba has an excess of available technical talent (Press 2015e).

15. Remittances from Cuban expatriates and family members living abroad account for a significant portion of ETECSA revenue.

16. Cubans are well educated and could create entertainment, education, and artistic content for the Spanish-speaking world.

17. Russia is not alone. China has done extensive industrial espionage and Iran and North Korea have also waged cyber-attacks (Carlin and Graff 2018) as have the U.S. and Israel in the case of Stuxnet.

18. Many governments have acted to safeguard privacy and security and fight attacks on infrastructure and lies, fake news, and filter bubbles designed to undermine democracy. Cuba can learn from nations like Estonia (Amaro 2018) with its security and privacy technology and Ukraine for fighting political and social attacks (Cain 2019). They should also consider the European Union General Data Protection Regulation for safeguarding citizens' personal data and give them control over it.

19. ADSL (asynchronous digital subscriber line) is a slow technology that uses copper telephone lines.

20. This is just a starting point. Cuba should consult a variety of international experts on forthcoming technology and alternative infrastructure ownership and regulation models.

References

Amaro, Silvia. 2018. "Estonia is unconcerned about a possible Russian cyberattack, president says." CNBC, August 14, 2018.

Baca, Carlos, Luca Belli, Erick Huerta, and Karla Velasco. 2018. "Community Networks in Latin America: Challenges, Regulations, and Solutions." *Internet Society*, November 13, 2018.

Cain, Geoffrey. 2019. "Ukraine's War on Russian Disinformation Is a Lesson for America." *The New Republic*, March 29, 2019.

Camacho, Armando. 2017. "Cuentapropismo tecnológico en Cuba?" *The Internet in Cuba* blog, May 11, 2017.

Carlin, John P. and Garrett M. Graff. 2018. *Dawn of the Code War: America's Battle Against Russia, China, and the Rising Global Cyber Threat*. New York: Public Affairs.

Crepin-Leblond, Oliver M.J. 1996. "International E-mail accessibility list." *OpenNET*, November 28, 1996.

CTIA (Cellular Telecommunications and Internet Association). 2018. "What is a Small Cell? A Brief Explainer." *CTIA* blog, March 27, 2018.

Cuba Internet Task Force. 2019. "Final Report." Bureau of Western Hemisphere Affairs, U.S. Department of State, June 16 2019. https://www.state.gov/cuba-internet-task-force-final-report/.

Dye, Michaelanne, David Demer, Josiah Mangiameli, Amy S. Bruckman, and Neha Ku-

mar. 2018. "El Paquete Semanal: The Week's Internet in Havana." *Proceedings of ACM CHI 2018* (April).
ETECSA. 2019a. "Conectividad." June 25, 2019. http://www.etecsa.cu/internet_conectividad/conectividad/.
ETECSA. 2019b. "Espacios públicos de conexión inalámbrica (WIFI)." Database, June 25, 2019. http://www.etecsa.cu/internet_conectividad/areas_wifi/.
ETECSA. 2019c. "Salas de navegación." Database, June 25, 2019. http://www.etecsa.cu/internet_conectividad/salas_de_navegacion/.
Fenton, William. 2016. "Black Markets and Secret Thumb Drives: How Cubans Get Online." *PC Magazine*, March 21, 2016.
Frank, Marc. 2019. "Communist Cuba seeks improved governance." Reuters, January 17, 2019.
Freedom House. 2018a. "Freedom on the Net, 2018." Freedom House (October).
Freedom House. 2018b. "Freedom on the Net, Cuba." Freedom House (October).
García Martínez, Antonio. 2017. "Inside Cuba's D.I.Y. Internet Revolution." *Wired*, July 26, 2017.
Giuliano, Maurizio. 1998. *El caso CEA: Intelectuales e inquisidores en Cuba. ¿Perestroika en la isla?* Miami: Ediciones Universal.
Granma. 2014. "La informatización de la sociedad, una prioridad para Cuba." Editorial, December 12, 2014.
Guevara, Yurisander. 2019. "Una nueva etapa en la informatización cubana." *Juventud Rebelde*, January 18, 2019.
Gunn, Gillian. 1995. "Cuba's NGOs: Government Puppets or Seeds of Civil Society?" *Cuba Briefing Paper Series* No. 7, Georgetown University Caribbean Project (February).
Haverty, Jack. 2019. "Internet History—Commercialization." Internet History archive, February 16, 2019. http://mailman.postel.org/pipermail/internet-history/2019-February/004979.html.
Henken, Ted A. 2017. "Cuba's Digital Millennials: Independent Digital Media and Civil Society on the Island of the Disconnected." *Social Research* 84 (2), 429–456.
Henken, Ted A. 2021. "The Opium of the Paquete: State Censorship, Private Self-Censorship, and the Content Distribution Strategies of Cuba's Emergent, Independent Digital Media Startups." *Cuban Studies* 50.
Hernández Busto, Ernesto. 2019. "Cuba y los derechos informáticos." *El País*, August 13, 2019.
Inventario. 2019. Twitter thread. June 20, 2019. https://twitter.com/invntario/status/1141693759698157568.
ITU. 2017a. "ICT Regulatory Tracker: Cuba." https://www.itu.int/net4/itu-d/irt/#/country-card/CUB.
ITU (International Telecommunication Union). 2017b. "ICT Regulatory Tracker—Overview." https://www.itu.int/net4/itu-d/irt/#/about-tracker.
ITU. 2017c. "Measuring the Information Society Report 2017 Volume 1." https://www.itu.int/en/ITU-D/Statistics/Documents/publications/misr2017/MISR2017_Volume1.pdf.
ITU. 2018a. "ICT Development Index, 2017." December 2018. https://www.itu.int/en/ITU-D/Statistics/Pages/publications/mis2017/methodology.aspx.

ITU. 2018b. "ITU Measuring Information Society Report–Cuba page." December 2018. https://www.itu.int/net4/itu-d/irt/#/country-card/CUB.

ITU. 2019. "The ICT Development Index (IDI): Conceptual framework and methodology." https://www.itu.int/en/ITU-D/Statistics/Pages/publications/mis/methodology.aspx.

ITU. 2020. "Global ICT Regulatory Outlook 2020: Pointing the way forward to collaborative regulation." April 16, 2020. http://handle.itu.int/11.1002/pub/81510992-en.

Kessler, Sarah. 2015. "In Cuba, An Underground Network Armed with USB Drives Does the Work of Google and YouTube." *Fast Company*, July 7, 2015.

Laughlin, Kirk. 2017. "Stubborn and Paranoid: Cuba's Determined Effort to Never Emerge as a Nearshore Hub." *Nearshore Americas* blog, August 29, 2017.

Madory, Doug. 2013. "Mystery Cable Activated in Cuba." *Oracle/Dyn* blog, January 20, 2013.

Madory, Doug. 2014. "What's Next for Cuba?" *Oracle/Dyn* blog, December 18, 2014.

Mesher, Gene M., Robert Owen Briggs, Seymour Goodman, Larry Press, and Joel M. Snyder. 1992. "Cuba, Communism, and Computing." *Communications of the ACM* 35 (11), November 1992, 27–29, 112.

Mozur, Paul. 2018. "A Genocide Incited on Facebook, With Posts from Myanmar's Military." *The New York Times*, October 15, 2018.

Parish, Nick. 2018. "Inside *El Paquete*, Cuba's Social Network." *With Internet*, March 8, 2018.

Pérez Díaz, Marita. 2019. "SNet, the Cuban street network, resists disappearing." *OnCuba*, August 12, 2019.

Pérez-Stable, Marifeli. 1998. "El Caso CEA." *Encuentro de la cultura cubana* 10 (Fall): 85–88.

Press, Larry. 1996a. "Cuban Computer Networks and Their Impact." *Cuba in Transition* 6 (Proceedings of the Association for the Study of the Cuban Economy Annual Conference), November: 338–345.

Press, Larry. 1996b. "Cuban Telecommunication Infrastructure and investment." *Cuba in Transition* 6 (Proceedings of the Association for the Study of the Cuban Economy Annual Conference), November: 145–154.

Press, Larry. 1996c. "Cuban Telecommunications, Computer Networking, and U.S. Policy Implications." RAND Corporation, Santa Monica, CA, July: DRU-1330-1-OSD,.

Press, Larry. 1996d. "Seeding networks: the federal role." *Communications of the ACM* 39 (10), October: 11–18.

Press, Larry. 1997. Internet Diffusion Summary, Cuba, October. http://som.csudh.edu/fac/lpress/devnat/nations/cuba/cubadim.htm.

Press, Larry. 1998a. "Cuban Computer Networks and their Determinants." RAND Corporation, Santa Monica, CA, February: DRR-1914-OSD. (Not cleared for open publication.)

Press, Larry. 1998b. "We Shape our Tools and they Shape Us (A Cuban Example)." *OnTheInternet* 4 (2), March/April: 38–39.

Press, Larry. 2011a. "Cuba's first Internet connection." *The Internet in Cuba* blog, February 27, 2011.

Press, Larry. 2011b. "The Dictator's Dilemma." *The Internet in Cuba* blog, February 15, 2011.

Press, Larry. 2013a. "A Cuban approach to achieving Internet connectivity." *The Internet in Cuba* blog, December 26, 2013.

Press, Larry. 2013b. "Eliécer Ávila and Operation Truth—who is on the payroll?" *The Internet in Cuba* blog, November 1, 2013.

Press, Larry. 2013c. "Fidel likes the Internet, but does that matter?" *The Internet in Cuba* blog, August 18, 2013.

Press, Larry. 2014a. "Is the Internet a priority for Cuba? The ball is in their court." *The Internet in Cuba* blog, December 19, 2014.

Press, Larry. 2014b. "The Cuban Internet in context." *The Internet in Cuba* blog, December 13, 2014.

Press, Larry. 2014c. "Stockholm: 19 years of municipal broadband success." *CIS 471* blog, June 26, 2014.

Press, Larry. 2014d. "Who owns ETECSA and who runs the show?" *The Internet in Cuba* blog, December 22, 2014.

Press, Larry. 2015a. "Cuban infrastructure investment—China won the first round." *The Internet in Cuba* blog, September 28, 2015.

Press, Larry. 2015b. "The Cuban Internet—a look back and looking forward." *The Internet in Cuba* blog, August 6, 2015.

Press, Larry. 2015c. "El paquete update—Cuba's largest private employer?" *The Internet in Cuba* blog, September 14, 2015.

Press, Larry. 2015d. "Guantánamo is in the news, but not the undersea cable to Guantánamo." *The Internet in Cuba* blog, February 6, 2015.

Press, Larry. 2015e. "A high-level U.S. delegation is in Havana to discuss telecommunication and the Internet." *The Internet in Cuba* blog, March 25, 2015.

Press, Larry. 2015g. "US-Cuba talks on telecommunication and the Internet." *The Internet in Cuba* blog, April 2, 2015.

Press, Larry. 2015h. "Will the nascent Cuban startup community thrive?" *The Internet in Cuba* blog, May 21, 2015.

Press, Larry. 2016b. "Disappointment after President Obama's trip to Cuba." *The Internet in Cuba* blog, June 28, 2016.

Press, Larry. 2016c. "Google Global Cache coming to Cuba." *The Internet in Cuba* blog, December 9, 2016.

Press, Larry. 2016d. "Internet-related announcements around President Obama's trip to Cuba." *The Internet in Cuba* blog, March 25, 2016.

Press, Larry. 2016e. "Might Cuba's street net, SNET, become legitimate?" *The Internet in Cuba* blog, March 3, 2016.

Press, Larry. 2016f. "Opening of the Google+Kcho tech center—much ado about not much (again)." *The Internet in Cuba* blog, March 30, 2016.

Press, Larry. 2016g. "A second high-level US delegation to Havana to discuss telecommunication and the Internet." *The Internet in Cuba* blog, January 25, 2016.

Press, Larry. 2016h. "Teaching material for Cuba—El Paquete Educativo?" *The Internet in Cuba* blog, March 16, 2016.

Press, Larry. 2016i. "What stopped the Cuban Internet in 1996 and what is stopping it today?" *The Internet in Cuba* blog, April 26, 2016.

Press, Larry. 2016j. "Wishful thinking—Google Fiber in Havana." *The Internet in Cuba* blog, December 2, 2016.

Press, Larry. 2017a. "Could SNET become Cuba's Guifi.net?" *The Internet in Cuba* blog, November 21, 2017.

Press, Larry. 2017b. "Crooked media interviews on Cuba." *The Internet in Cuba* blog, May 25, 2017.

Press, Larry. 2017c. "Cuba's self-employed computer programmers." *The Internet in Cuba* blog, April 15, 2017.

Press, Larry. 2017d. "Cuban satellite connectivity—today and (maybe?) tomorrow." *The Internet in Cuba* blog, December 14, 2017.

Press, Larry. 2017e. "Cuban tech entrepreneurs—new values?" *The Internet in Cuba* blog, June 5, 2017.

Press, Larry. 2017f. "Data on SNET and a few suggestions for ETECSA." *The Internet in Cuba* blog, November 9, 2017.

Press, Larry. 2017g. "OneWeb Satellite Internet Project Status Update." *CircleID*, August 24, 2017.

Press, Larry. 2017h. "Satellite links for interim Internet access in rural Cuba." *Internet in Cuba* blog, May 15.

Press, Larry. 2017i. "SpaceX Satellite Internet Project Status Update." *CircleID*, August 15, 2017.

Press, Larry. 2017j. "Telesat, a Fourth Satellite Internet Competitor." *CircleID*, November 13, 2017.

Press, Larry. 2017k. "Trump's Cuba policy and its impact on the Cuban Internet." *The Internet in Cuba* blog, June 20, 2017.

Press, Larry. 2017l. "Trying to predict Miguel Díaz-Canel's Internet policy." *The Internet in Cuba* blog, May 9, 2017.

Press, Larry. 2017m. "What does Trump's Cuba policy memorandum say about the Internet?" *The Internet in Cuba* blog, July 1, 2017.

Press, Larry. 2018. "Cuba's year-end progress report—emphasis on the national intranet." *The Internet in Cuba* blog, January 9, 2018.

Press, Larry. 2018a. "A 5G, community network strategy for Cuba (and other developing nations)." *The Internet in Cuba* blog, April 2, 2018.

Press, Larry. 2018b. "The case for making 3G mobile Internet access free in Cuba." *The Internet in Cuba* blog, December 11, 2018.

Press, Larry. 2018c. "The Cuba Internet Task Force—a win for Trump, Castro and Putin." *The Internet in Cuba* blog, January 28, 2018.

Press, Larry. 2018d. "Cuban president Miguel Díaz-Canel's meeting with tech company executives." *The Internet in Cuba* blog, October 4, 2018.

Press, Larry. 2018e. "Cuban 'technological sovereignty'—a walled garden strategy?" *The Internet in Cuba* blog, July 2, 2018.

Press, Larry. 2018f. "Cuba rolls out 3G mobile access." *The Internet in Cuba* blog, December 5, 2018.

Press, Larry. 2018h. "How about opening a YouTube video production space in Havana?" *The Internet in Cuba* blog, June 7, 2018.

Press, Larry. 2018i. "Important Developments on Low-Earth Orbit Satellite Internet Service (2017 Review)." *CircleID*, January 2, 2018.

Press, Larry. 2018j. "O3b satellite Internet—today and tomorrow." *CIS 471* blog, March 14, 2018.
Press, Larry. 2018g. "Suggestions for the Cuba Internet Task Force." *The Internet in Cuba* blog, February 11, 2018.
Press, Larry. 2019a. "Cuba censors SMS messages . . . for now." *The Internet in Cuba* blog, January 10, 2019.
Press, Larry. 2019b. "Cuba Claims New Regulations Expand Internet Access to Homes and Businesses, but There's the Downside." *The Internet in Cuba* blog, July 30, 2019.
Press, Larry. 2019c. "Cuba's new WiFi regulations—a step forward, backward or sideways?" *The Internet in Cuba* blog, June 13, 2019.
Press, Larry. 2019d. "Does China's Digital Silk Road to Latin America and the Caribbean run through Cuba?" *The Internet in Cuba* blog, June 3, 2019.
Press, Larry. 2019e. "The first month of Cuban 3G mobile Internet service." *The Internet in Cuba* blog, January 29, 2019.
Press, Larry. 2019f. "Havana can have 5G before Miami." *Internet in Cuba* blog, June 20, 2019.
Press, Larry. 2019g. "Hongyun Project—China's Low-Earth Orbit Broadband Internet Project." *CircleID*, June 4, 2019.
Press, Larry. 2019h. "Low-Earth Orbit (LEO) Satellite Internet Service Developments for 2018." *CircleID*, January 2, 2019.
Press, Larry. 2019i. "Questions Raised by the Takeover of SNET, Havana's Community Network." *The Internet in Cuba* blog, August 21, 2019.
Press, Larry. 2019j. "SNet: Inicio o Final?." *The Internet in Cuba* blog, August 19, 2019.
Press, Larry. 2019k. "Latecomer Amazon Will Be a Formidable Satellite ISP Competitor." *CircleID*, July 19, 2019.
Press, Larry. 2020. "Mass-produced Propaganda—a Cuban Example," *The Internet in Cuba* blog, February 24.
Press, Larry, Grey Burkhart, Grey, William Foster, Seymour Goodman, Peter Wolcott, and Jon Woodard, Jon. 1998. "An Internet Diffusion Framework." *Communications of the ACM* 41, No. 10 (October).
Press, Larry, and Armas Carlos. 1996. "Cuban Network Update," *OnTheInternet* 2 (1), January/February: 46–49.
Press, Larry, William Foster, Peter Wolcott, and William McHenry. 2003. "The Internet in India and China." *The Journal of Information Technologies and International Development* 1 (1), Fall: 41–60.
Press, Larry, and Joel M. Snyder. 1992. "A Look at Cuban Networks." *Matrix News*, 2 (6), Matrix Information and Directory Services, Austin, Texas, June.
Pujol, Eduardo E.P., Will Scott, Eric Wustrow, and J. Alex Halderman. 2017. "Initial Measurements of the Cuban Street Network." *Proceedings of the Internet Measurement Conference, IMC '17* (November): 1–3.
Rohter, Larry. 1996. "Cuban Communists Take Harder Line." *The New York Times*, March 31, 1996.
Salzer, Jerome, David Reed, and David Clark. 1984. "End-to-End Arguments in System Design." *ACM Transactions on Computer Systems* 2 (4): 277–288.

Song, Steve. 2018. "Fibre Feudalism." *Many Possibilities* blog, October 3, 2018.

Song, Steve. 2019. "Rethinking Affordable Access." *Many Possibilities* blog, February 1, 2019.

UNDP (United Nations Development Programme). 2018a. "Human Development Indices and Indicators 2018 statistical update."

UNDP. 2018b. "Human Development Report, Cuba."

U.S. Congress, H.R.927. 1996. "Cuban Liberty and Democratic Solidarity (LIBERTAD) Act of 1996."

Valdés, Nelson P. and Mario A. Rivera. 1999. "The Political Economy of the Internet in Cuba." *Cuba in Transition* 9, 141–154 (Proceedings of the Association for the Study of the Cuban Economy Annual Conference).

Wikipedia. 2019. "Usenet." Queried January 15, 2019.

Wolcott, Peter, Larry Press, William McHenry, Seymour Goodman, and William Foster. 2001. "A Framework for Assessing the Global Diffusion of the Internet." *Journal of the Association for Information Systems* 2 (1), Article 6.

Wu, Tim. 2016. *The Attention Merchants: The Epic Struggle to Get Inside Our Heads*. New York: Knopf.

2

Historical Itineraries and Cyclic Trajectories

Alternative Media, Communication Technologies, and Social Change in Cuba

EDEL LIMA SARMIENTO

The digital revolution has opened up unlimited possibilities not only for expanded connectedness and access to new information, but also for social mobilization and alternative communications. New digital technologies have enabled alternative circuits that help give visibility to the agendas of marginal voices and to challenge the political and economic status quo (Castells 2015). In Cuba, scholars have documented the recent emergence of various alternative media in the digital age, and their possibilities and constraints in a nondemocratic space (Beaulieu 2014; Díaz 2018; Garcia Santamaria 2018; Henken 2011, 2017; Hoffmann 2011; Padilla 2017; Ruiz 2003, 2005). As subsequent chapters in this volume illustrate, the digital revolution is slowly helping democratize political and cultural spaces in Cuba on various fronts, especially journalism.

However, as Downing (2001) asserts, alternative media have a long and complex history that well precedes the so-called digital revolution, starting with different expressions at the margins of the religious and political system that developed after the invention of the printing press (Cadavid 2007). While the alternative media's origin and historical evolution have been left in the background in academic research (Couldry and Curran 2003), this chapter aims to begin to fill that gap by adopting a broader, historical focus. It analyzes various points in Cuban history, when different types of technological affordances have been at the core of social movements and their alternative communication strategies, whether to oppose the Spanish crown or to overthrow different dictatorships.

Starting a century and a half before the digital revolution erupted on the island, rebel political forces were already using alternative media and the technological advances of their time during virtually all the island's most politically tense periods: 1) the Ten Years' War (1868–1878), 2) The Cuban War of Independence (1895–1898), 3) Gerardo Machado's dictatorship (1930–1933), and 4) Fulgencio Batista's dictatorship (1952–1958). This chapter reconstructs the alternative communicational strategies and experiences during these four periods of upheaval. The aim is to establish their similarities with respect to the development of the alternative media of their day, in order to contextualize and better understand the most recent emergence of independent media during what, following Ruiz (2005) and Hoffman (2011), I label "post-totalitarian Castroism" (1989 to date). This is a period I touch on briefly here but that is analyzed in much greater depth and detail in all subsequent chapters of this volume.

Theoretically, this study is based on an inclusive approach to the concept of "alternative media," covering more specific localized terms such as the *independentista* (independence), *separatista* (separatist), or *insurrecta* (insurrectionist) presses of the late nineteenth century (1868–1878 and 1895–1898), the revolutionary or clandestine press during Cuba's Republican period (1930–1933 and 1952–1958), and of course, the alternative or independent media that have emerged with the help of digital technology in recent years (1989 to date). I follow the alternative media typology developed by Jeppesen (2016):[1] the "radical" perspective to characterize the four historical periods selected for this essay (spanning 1868 to 1959) and a combination of the "radical" and "citizen" perspectives for the analysis of the current-day digital media. Radical media convey the alternative visions held by counter-systemic social or revolutionary movements toward hegemonic policies, priorities, or perspectives. Their aim is to subvert the established order and achieve a large-scale change (Downing 2001). In contrast, citizen media function as dialogical spaces for citizen claims and social transformations, without necessarily being politically confrontational (Rodríguez 2001).

The chapter is organized into six sections. The first four briefly examine the role of alternative media in each of the Cuban revolutions up to 1959, including the context of each movement, the most important alternative media and their objectives and links to revolutionary movements. Similarly, I briefly review their contents, internal organization, use of technology, means of distribution, and the repercussions they faced. The fifth section explores the common traits manifested across all the analyzed periods and the current era of alternative digital media. The final section offers a reflection on the significance of the findings as they apply to a deeper understanding of the ways in which today's independent media outlets both fit past patterns and break new, uncharted ground, thanks to the explosion of digital technologies.

Radical Newspapers and the Ten Years' War, 1868–1878

The first wave of radical alternative media in Cuban history appeared during the first war of independence against Spanish colonial rule.[2] This insurrection erupted on October 10, 1868, when wealthy landowners and sugar mill planters rose up in arms. Getting hold of the press was a crucial means for the cause that the initiators of the war understood well. The majority were cultivated men who endorsed civil rights such as the freedom of the press, as established in Article 28 of the Guáimaro Constitution, the governing document exhibiting the ideas of the liberal faction in the insurgency. Nevertheless, due to the limited resources of the insurgents, their journalistic propaganda could only target the "liberated" territories of the island, a region they referred to as *Cuba Libre*.

It would be naive to pretend that such *independentista* publications—lacking large print runs, regular frequency, or chances of reaching the entire island or Spanish-controlled urban centers—could compete in influence against the established legal press, which enjoyed much better technological resources for production and distribution. Comparatively, this legal press did possess all these advantages, but was severely limited by a rigid prepublication censorship that guaranteed the narrative control of the conflict by the Spanish authorities (García 1869). The principal newspapers of those days were *Diario de La Marina*, *La Prensa*, and *La Voz de Cuba*. However, not all the legal press was pro-Spanish, as evidenced by the brief period of press freedom enjoyed in January 1869.

Once the conditions were appropriate, after the seizure of the town of Bayamo by rebel forces, *El Cubano Libre*—the independence movement's official mouthpiece—began publishing between October 1868 and January 1869, when the locals decided to burn their city to the ground before handing it over to Spanish troops. In those days, the aforementioned radical paper was read aloud in the public plaza and among the rebel troops, so that everyone, even the illiterate, could be informed about the progress of the insurrection (Sánchez 1998).

The independence press reached its peak during the 1869–1871 period (Fornet 2014). The printing quality of these periodicals improved thanks to Cuban émigrés in the United States, who acquired a modern printing press baptized as La Libertad ("Freedom") and used a clandestine fleet to smuggle it into the island (Labrada 2018). Eventually, however, this press would prove insufficient for the cause given the concomitant scarcity of newsprint, ink, and other stocks. The first few years of the war were the best of times for the separatist press, but later years would be characterized by rebel exhaustion and lack of resources due to internal divisions among the revolutionary forces. This was combined with a notorious decrease in external aid, a key source of support that, as we shall see, has always been a decisive factor in the development of alternative media in Cuba, regardless of the historical period.

The standout alternative publications of the early years were *El Mambí* (1869–1871), *El Cubano Libre* in its second period, *El Tínima* (1869–1870), and *La Estrella Solitaria* (1869–1870), all of which were published at La Libertad printing hub in Camagüey. By the end of the war, only *El Cubano Libre* still existed, albeit with a very irregular publishing frequency. It was renamed *Boletín de la Guerra* in late 1873, until it changed its name once again to *La República* in 1876. With an alternative discourse vis-à-vis the official one imposed by the legal press, all of these publications echoed the themes and structure of the first *El Cubano Libre* (Romero 2012). Contents commonly consisted of an editorial; a war bulletin containing decrees, edicts, and other documents issued by rebel authorities; speeches and pronouncements of their leaders; chronicles of current affairs; denunciations of Spanish crimes; and a poetic segment where the Spanish troops were mocked and ridiculed (Ponte 1957, 11).

Behind these publications were cultured men of letters or professionals with experience in the craft of journalism. Thus, the editorial boards of these journals stood out for their high cultural level, their simultaneous roles as journalists and combatants, and the inclusion of women in an era when they were largely proscribed from such activities. This element showcases the transgressive character of radical media, which according to Downing (2001) typically break free from some of the rules imposed by convention, if rarely with all of them.

For the distribution of the *independentista* press into liberated territories, insurgents devised a functional network of alternative communication known as the *correo mambí* (or "the Mambí mail"). Correspondence, parcels, mail, newspapers, and other clandestine documents traveled on an underground railroad of sorts "from prefecture to prefecture, without stopping in any of them other than for necessary change of messengers" (Rosal 1874, 26, author's translation). The mail then found its way into cities and villages with the help of *laborantes*[3] who carried the parcels "hidden in padded saddles, pommel holsters, between hay bales, or wrapped in papers at the center of ill-fated coal sacks" (Ponte 1957, 12, author's translation). The intended audience for these publications was the rebels themselves, the specific recipients to whom they were delivered clandestinely in various villages, and the Spanish authorities (Camps 1890). Supporting the work of the rebel press on the island, the Cuban exile community also launched their own publications. They were responsible for disseminating separatist ideas abroad and for garnering support and funds for the Cuban independence movement. Between 1868 and 1878, various Cuban newspapers circulated in the United States, Mexico, and France (Casasús 1953). Most enjoyed a short-lived existence, but some did span the entire campaign.

To summarize this period, *independentista* newspapers published during the Ten Years' War deployed the characteristics of radical communication as defined by Downing (2001). Amid difficult conditions, systematic harassment, and limited resources, they also suffered from an ephemeral publishing life and irregular printing frequency. Their greatest achievement of this stage was to serve as the official mouthpiece for the rebel government-in-arms, therefore developing an informational channel that, albeit precarious, functioned as an insurrectionist alternative to the press system controlled by colonial authorities. In terms of journalism, the failed war of 1868 taught its successors a valuable lesson for the upcoming independence campaign: to accomplish its aim, winning the struggle over information and propaganda was as important as winning the one on the battlefield.

The Press's Push toward Independence, 1895–1898

On February 24, 1895, the final Cuban War of Independence erupted. Unlike the previous uprising, this time the Cuban Revolutionary Party (PRC), led by the famed exiled intellectual José Martí, devised an organized plan with the support of their fellow Cubans both inside the country and abroad. At the beginning of the war, the colonial press was strikingly different from its Ten Years' War predecessor. The partisan publications mirrored the confrontational spirit of the two political parties remaining after the Pact of Zanjón (which ended the armed struggle in 1878). On one side was the so-called *integrista* press with *Diario de la Marina* and *La Unión Constitucional* leading the pack with the aim of defending the "integration" of Cuba into the Spanish union. On the other side were the numerous publications representing the autonomist faction that advocated for a continued colonial status but with political autonomy.

However, alongside these two partisan factions of the legal press, during the inter-war period (1878–1895) there arose a new press openly committed to independence on the island. Before 1895, "there existed fourteen newspapers advocating for the island's independence" (Flores 1895, 505, author's translation). This permissive environment toward different political ideas sprouted as early as 1891, when the Supreme Tribunal of Spain revoked a Havana's High Court sentence against the publisher of *La Libertad* for his article: "Why Are We Separatists?" ruling that it was not a criminal offense to hold independentist ideas as long as one did not incite rebellion (Fornet 2014).

With the start of the conflagration, Spanish authorities imposed prepublication censorship. The alternative legal press, once sympathetic to separatist causes, disappeared, whereas the autonomist press remained muzzled. The independence movement this time organized an alternative press system that would soon spread to all the country's provinces following the war itself, which successfully spread from east to west. Similarly, radical newspapers in this period doubled in format and length with respect to their predecessors from the previous war and were more stable in their publishing frequency (Fornet 2014). Undoubtedly, these were much better conditions to counteract the Spanish-controlled legal press, the circulation of which was forced to contract to the island's large cities as the war unfolded. "Journalism flourishes in *Cuba Libre*, manifesting itself in little pink or green biweekly and monthly newspapers that one finds everywhere in the field," wrote American correspondent Grover Flint (1898, 242).

Half a year after the war began, the first insurrectionist newspaper to appear was, once again, *El Cubano Libre,* reissued from 1868 to highlight the continuity between both wars. In Oriente province, both *Boletín de la Guerra* and *La Independencia* were created. In 1896, *La República* and *La Sanidad* emerged in Las Villas province, later joined by *Las Villas* and *La Nación*. All survived until the end of the war. Unlike the rest of the country, Cuba's western provinces saw *independentista* flyers disappear virtually upon first publication, due to a lack of resources and the intensity of military actions (Torriente 1964).

According to the printing regulations established by the civil government of the Republic in Arms, journals were required to publish the Liberation Army's military reports and ordinances. They also covered revolutionary victories, arrivals of maritime expeditions and letters from Cubans in exile. For example, *El Cubano Libre* typically published an op-ed or feature article on the cover, followed by military statements, laws, speeches, and ordinances, and occasionally a segment devoted to wire reports, a poetry section, a section titled "Manigüeras" composed of mocking, ironic *criollo* humor (Ponte 1957). These publications typically owned their printing presses, either brought in from abroad or seized from the enemy, which could be easily hidden in the most inhospitable mountains. Staff at printing headquarters normally consisted of a director, a manager, and typographers (Fornet 2014). Editorially, the pages benefited from an "army" of journalists within the actual army, as more than fifty high-ranking military men dominated the craft (*Los periodistas en la Revolución* 1938).

From one corner of the island to the other, across Cuba's liberated territories, these newspapers circulated thanks to the aforementioned *Mambí* mail, deemed the best public service organized by the i*ndependentista* forces (Fornet 2014). Across rebel encampments, printouts "pass[ed] from hand to hand, from saddlebag to saddlebag, until they become crumpled, blurred, and soiled, but never too old to be read and discussed over the campfire" (Flint 1898, 244). Different ploys were developed to introduce these publications into Cuba's Spanish-occupied cities. Additionally, maritime courier was used to deliver these publications to foreign destinations, via a clandestine fleet of small ships that kept regular communications with neighboring islands (Fornet 2014).

The separatist press was wholeheartedly supported by the Cuban press in exile, as it never ceased to exist since the end of the previous war, as exemplified by *El Yara* (1878–1899) in Key West, and *El Porvenir* (1890–1898) in New York. The new War of Independence triggered a growth of these publications in cities that hosted significant Cuban exile communities (Llaverías 1932). For example, *Patria*, created in 1892 by José Martí, stood out not only for the quality of its writing, but also for being considered the official organ of the Cuban Revolutionary Party. Together, these papers offered a vision that advocated for the war and devised the features of the new republic to be established after independence.

By the end of the war in 1898, the *independentista* press had turned into a parallel army for the revolution. Whether published in Cuba or in exile, this press circulated across the country and clandestinely penetrated the island's many towns and villages to inform readers about war development. It helped garner solidarity and support for the Cuban cause and functioned as a cohesive element in the emancipatory ideals. The printing press and the *Mambí* mail were the fundamental tools for the constitution and dissemination of these radical media, just as their own resources and funds raised abroad were crucial for their survival.

However, since most publishers held military or political positions, or were part of the intellectual elite, none of the alternative press that emerged during the two wars of independence could pass as "popular" or "grassroots." Still, this was a radical press with ideals that did offer a direct political challenge to the colonial order. Titles like *El Cubano Libre* and *El Porvenir* continued to be published during the years of U.S. occupation (1899–1902), and well beyond the establishment of the Cuban Republic. However, they gradually lost their subversive and transformative character as a result of their publishers' privileged insertion into the "ruling class" of the new society.

Challenging the Machado Dictatorship: 1930–1933

The first decades of the Republican period that followed Cuba's independence were once again agitated by a mass uprising, against the so-called Machadato (Machado dictatorship). It is a key period in the emergence of an alternative radical media. By the end of 1930, a far-reaching sociopolitical movement had surfaced against president Gerardo Machado based on popular discontent over the country's economic crisis, his anti-constitutional reelection, and his increasingly repressive approach to governing. Among Machado's detractors were key segments of the press. Various publications of the day duly reflected the island's drastic situation and demanded his resignation. However, they were promptly silenced through the imposition of illegal prepublication censorship (Lima Sarmiento 2014). Within this environment of pervasive censorship and disinformation, the political forces opposing the regime created alternative media to overcome the siege and clandestinely publicize their own proposals.

However, not all of the clandestine, oppositional media are radically alternative in nature. If we were to subscribe to Downing's (2001) definition, the movement which these media represent, as well as their informational vehicles, must not only aim to replace a government with another one but also aspire to strike at the core of existing socioeconomic structures, whatever the magnitude of the transformation. Hence, according to their objectives and programs, true radical media to emerge during the *Machadato* include the mouthpieces of organizations like the ABC, the University Student Directory (DEU), and Cuba's Communist Party.

The ABC was a cell-structured organization with a right-wing orientation, founded in 1931 by middle-class intellectuals, professors, and students, with the aim of overthrowing Machado through terrorist actions. Clandestinely distributed in November 1932, its political manifesto advocated for Cuba's full political and economic independence, establishing the need to reconstruct the institutions and contribute to the nationalization of the country's economy (Pérez 2013). Propaganda was a central pillar in this battle, hence the ABC counted on support from the most powerful media outlets in the anti-Machado revolution. By the beginning of 1933, the media intensified its work in the face of a weakening regime and growing international pressure on Machado. The ABC's official organ *Denuncia* stabilized its print run, delivering more than thirty thousand issues on a biweekly or monthly basis (Cómo se hacía Denuncia 1934, 13). Its pages featured all the information that the government kept hidden.

Although most texts remained unsigned to avoid reprisals, prestigious journalists like Jorge Mañach and Francisco Ichaso were regular contributors. Issues of the paper were distributed through ABC cells across the country, and even "governmental authorities and Machado himself, had them delivered in official, stamped envelopes from different government Secretariats, since ABC had numerous cell members infiltrated across different state agencies" (Cómo se hacía Denuncia 1934, 13, author's translation). Impressed by the great interest with which ordinary Cubans anticipated each new *Denuncia*'s issue, many observers of the era consider that this *periodiquito* ("little rag") reached a much larger readership than any of its legal, censored counterparts (Lima Sarmiento 2014). *Denuncia* even invited readers to tune in ABC's new radio station. Launched in 1933, it operated clandestinely and never ceased to denounce Machado's tyranny even during his final days, despite the nonstop pursuit of the station's operators by the police.

Besides relying on traditional print media and the novel use of radio inside of Cuba, the ABC also deployed an overseas propaganda strategy against the dictator. Paris-based members of the organization managed to garner the signatures of renowned French journalists in support of their anti-Machado campaign. They managed to publish *El Terror en Cuba*, which showcased the *Machadato*'s crimes. The book prompted a flood of comments in European magazines and newspapers (Carpentier 1933). Thus, the ABC managed to set its agenda in the public sphere through established sources and support networks in order to attract international attention and legitimize the need for political change. Ever since, these kinds of exchange circuits and connections among groups of the Cuban diaspora have remained dynamic and vibrant, just as they had been during the wars of independence and as they are as well in the current day.

Similarly, the DEU also agitated constantly for Machado's overthrow and for the transformation of the country (Soto 1977). The DEU was made up of various factions that handled their own alternative publications. Its official organ, *Alma Mater*, founded in 1922, became clandestine in October 1930 (Contrera 1989). Factors like the criminal prosecution of the magazine, the exile of its director, and differences among its leaders probably led to *Alma Mater*'s being replaced by *Directorio*, a smaller-format publication that was better adapted to clandestine operations. Two issues of *Directorio* reviewed for this study show a striking resemblance to *Denuncia* in both format and content. A split in the DEU gave birth to the *Ala Izquierda Estudiantil* (Student Left Wing), which was more radical and offered a more explicitly anti-imperialist political program than the DEU. Its mouthpiece, *Línea*, denounced the violations committed by the dictatorship and spread the student organization's left-wing program (González 1974). However, relatively few issues were published since its young editors were promptly incarcerated for their revolutionary activities.

As for Cuba's Communist Party, it never knew legal status since its inception in 1925. Between 1931 and 1933, it managed to issue few editions of *El Trabajador* ("The Worker"). The radical press in that period was far from homogeneous, as papers often polemicized among themselves. This intensified antagonism was perhaps more visible in the confrontation between *El Trabajador* and *Denuncia* (Soto 1977). These disparities reflected the variety of political actors who—from many different ideological positions—operated the radical media over this period. Despite their limitations, these publications played important disseminative and supportive roles for both their respective organizations and for broader sectors of society, constituting a cardinal element in the social mobilization behind the collapse of the Machado dictatorship. The existence of media with both a right-wing orientation such as those of the ABC, progressive positioning like that of the DEU, and radical, left-wing views like those of the Student Left Wing and the Communist Party constitute a nod toward Downing's theory (2001) in which "radical" communication stems from subversive objectives (regime change) rather than from a particular political orientation.

In this period, new technologies, such as a radio station, were incorporated as weapons for the battle, managing to reach wider audiences, although the printing press remained important. Other alternative means like pamphlets, rumors, music, and theater, also proved to be useful instruments for protests, combining a diverse array of channels and cultural manifestations for political activism. Following Machado's overthrow in August 1933, most radical newspapers continued operating and eventually contributed to social pressure for democratization that would only crystalize with the passage of the Cuban Constitution of 1940.

Radio Rebelde and the Cuban Revolution, 1952–1958

Decades later, during Fulgencio Batista's military dictatorship, radical alternative media reached an unprecedented level of development thanks to the savvy use of technology. On March 10, 1952, General Batista staged a coup d'état and interrupted the democratic stability the country had enjoyed since

1940. In a context of active civil society, he maneuvered his way into legitimizing himself through bribery and repression, aided by the approval of the White House. Cuba's mass media, by then having achieved notable levels of expansion and development, were not free from those policies. By 1959 there were about fifteen national publications, a dozen provincial newspapers, six national and 146 local radio broadcasters, and five television channels in Havana (García Luis 2013). Most dutifully followed the rules of the game imposed by the dictator because they benefited from subventions or the profits from official advertising deals. Still, the seizure of equipment and even media headquarters, physical aggression against journalists, and prepublication censorship prevailed (Calvo 2014).

Among the many civic and armed movements against Batista to emerge during these years, the 26th of July Movement (M-26-7), led by the young lawyer Fidel Castro, was a clear standout. Its program was outlined in his "History Will Absolve Me" manifesto delivered as a self-defense in court when he was on trial for sedition following the attack on the Moncada Army Barracks in Santiago de Cuba, on July 26, 1953 (thus the name of his subsequent political movement). The document synthesized the country's burdensome situation and laid out the measures to be implemented once the dictatorship was overthrown. The Movement's media strategy can be divided into two stages: the one leading up to the launch of the armed struggle in December 1956 and the one which followed. Prior to the July 1953 attack, the youngsters who would eventually make up the revolutionary movement had released a series of ephemeral, clandestine newspapers. After his release from prison in May 1955, however, Castro employed the opposition newspaper *La Calle* as his preferred channel of denunciation, prompting its immediate closure by the government (Villaescusa 2015).

With the arrival of the yacht *Granma* that delivered the revolutionary leaders onto Cuban coasts on December 2, 1956, and the subsequent insurrection in the Sierra Maestra, M-26-7 implemented an effective media campaign to position the ongoing insurrection on both the national and international agendas. This strategy proved essential in instilling the Cuban and global public with a sympathetic vision of the guerrillas and their cause (Calvo 2014). From his early youth, Castro learned to perform political publicity stunts by employing the press. As a good propagandist, his strategy consisted of creating revolutionary symbols like the beard, the rifle, the bracelet, and the olive-green uniform; of connecting his cause to the revindication of various *independentista* myths including the almost sacred figure of José Martí; the strict, careful choice of words when meeting with reporters, and strategies that would attract international attention, such as the clandestine meeting in the Sierra Maestra with *New York Times* journalist Herbert L. Matthews or the kidnapping of the Argentine Formula One driver Juan Manuel Fangio in Havana (Beaulieu 2014; Calvo 2014; DePalma 2006). Rebels employed the foreign press, the national legal press, and their own clandestine media in their benefit, the latter being the focus of this section.

Shortly after *Granma* disembarked, the biweekly publication *Revolución* appeared as the official mouthpiece of M-26-7, publicizing developments in the insurgency and denouncing regime abuses across the island. The paper achieved a nationwide distribution with a peak print run of twenty thousand issues (Beaulieu 2014). Because a few of their rotary presses fell into the hands of the police, rebels devised a cell structure so that staff at the printing houses did not know the distribution staff. Their only link consisted of a single phone call to arrange for a blind contact to hand over the publication (Vázquez et al. 2008). In 1957, both *Vanguardia Obrera* and *Sierra Maestra* emerged, with different editions in all Cuban provinces, as well as Miami and New York (Soto 1965). Moreover, newspapers appeared with links to different guerrilla fronts. Once again, *El Cubano Libre* was reborn in 1957 in the Sierra Maestra on orders from Ernesto "Che" Guevara.

Still, the most transcendental channel for M-26-7 was Radio Rebelde. The clandestine radio station first went on the air on February 24, 1958, in the Sierra Maestra mountains. Programming carried news on guerrilla operations, towns being seized by the rebels, or the reorganization of M-26-7 abroad. It also broadcast speeches by rebel leaders like Fidel Castro and other patriotic programming. Acquired in Havana, the first transmitter equipment had a limited power of about 120–130 watts (Amores 2010). Upon installation of a second antenna, the signal reached much further with broadcasts regularly taking place in the afternoons and evenings. By the end of the war, however, the station was on the air nearly twenty-four hours a day (Vázquez et al. 2008), with a collective of radio professionals running the station under the direction of experienced journalists of the time (Villaescusa 2015).

By the close of 1958, Radio Rebelde gained even more visibility as broadcasts began to reach not only across the entire country but also to other parts of Latin America (Amores 2010). This was possible due to the support of "La Cadena de la Libertad" (the Chain of Freedom), a network of radio broadcasting stations inside and outside the country that repeated or simulcasted Radio Rebelde programming. Emerging guerrilla fronts also began to control their own broadcasting equipment so that eventually each of the thirty-two guerrilla columns had one. Soon joining this endeavor were broadcasting stations from the liberated territories. Moreover, M-26-7 members in Venezuela arranged for the national broadcasters in that country to record the rebel signal and reproduce it (Amores 2010). Hence, based on its audience reach, Radio Rebelde became the most important medium in the fight against the Batista dictatorship. Indeed, it was able to break the information blockade imposed by government censorship and establish a channel of alternative information with a growing audience on the island, that even while having to listen in secret, was as seduced by the station's broadcasts as were listeners across Latin America.

Other organizations linked to the 26th of July Movement also developed their own radical media apparatuses. These included the Federation of University Students (FEU) and the Popular Socialist Party (PSP, the new name for Cuba's original Communist Party). In 1952, the FEU publication *Alma Mater* reappeared sporadically to express student opposition to Batista's coup. For its part, the Revolutionary Directorate, which was the armed branch of the FEU, released publications like *Al Combate* and *13 de Marzo* starting in 1957. Finally, the PSP produced two publications: *Mella* and *Carta Semanal*, which benefited from a network of agents that enabled newsgathering and national circulation (Vázquez et al. 2008). The latter replaced *Hoy*, the newspaper traditionally published by communists that was closed down by Batista following the Moncada assault.

The effect of radical alternative media in the hands of these revolutionary groups undermined the credibility of the dictatorship's official information as rebels managed to set the agenda with their own version of the conflict both in Cuba and abroad. A wide circulation allowed the clandestine press to reach ordinary Cubans. Also, by the end of the war, Radio Rebelde enjoyed more prestige than any of the dominant, censored media and became the most credible and popular source of information by both the other clandestine press outlets and the international media (Villaescusa 2015). The simulcasting of Radio Rebelde across Cuba and abroad helped amplify its signal, turning it into a transnational medium at the service of a national liberation movement, an experience probably unprecedented at the time.

During this period, the radical media surpassed their Machadato media counterparts in number, type, distribution, reach, and repercussion. Their work should be seen as one of the determining factors in the victory of the revolutionary movement. However, one has to be careful not to romanticize their endurance or legacy, since the rebels' taking of state power led to the integration of Radio Rebelde and the rest of the Cuban press into the docile, propagandistic, and monopolistic media system that exists today, in correspondence with the Soviet-style totalitarian regime established in Cuba following the triumph of the Revolution (Fernández 2016).

One Hundred Fifty Years of Alternative Media

There are five commonalities between the development of the radical media during the four periods described above and the alternative media that have emerged in Cuba during the past thirty years (1989 to date). First, all of them emerged illegally, facing material hardships and defying absolute political powers characterized by repression and deprivation of rights and liberties, whether authoritarian colonialist regimes like the Spanish crown, the Machado and Batista dictatorships, or what Ruiz (2005) or Hoffman (2011) label "post-totalitarian" regimes like Castroism, from 1989 onward.

Unlike past periods, dissident radical media and citizen media do coexist in the present day (Henken 2017). The latter are different from the first in that they exhibit a less confrontational position vis-à-vis the government and a more contained critical discourse. Still, none of them escape the inquisitive eyes or the repressive hands of the Cuban regime, since any news media created outside the authority and control of the state constitutes political defiance (Hoffmann 2011).

Second is the incorporation and use of the different technological advances of the day for either production or distribution of their alternative materials, without replacing the preceding ones. The *independentistas* used the rotary press. The revolutionaries fighting against Machado and Batista employed radio broadcasting in innovative ways without renouncing Gutenberg's invention. Similarly, Cuba's contemporary independent journalists working outside the official media system have turned to the Internet and its many digital platforms, social media, and most recently podcasts to make their voices heard.

However, if journalistic agents that antagonize Castroism have not resorted more frequently to older, established technologies like the printing press or television broadcasting, it is only because these tools are strictly controlled by the government and any attempt to deploy them is swiftly met with repression (Beaulieu 2013; Ruiz 2005). Despite this, some projects managed to survive: magazines like *Vitral* (now disappeared), *Palabra Nueva*, and *Espacio Laical*—all run by the Catholic Church, one of the few actors with a certain degree of independence and state toleration—and the critical video series uploaded to YouTube by the oppositional platform *Estado de SATS* (Fernández 2003; Padilla 2017).

Third, a singular creativity in devising networks of production and distribution for alternative communication has characterized all radical media projects from the early days of opposition to Spanish colonial rule until the present day. The *independentistas* created an effective courier system based on the relay of *Mambí* messengers for internal distribution, and on a sea flotilla for external distribution. The rebels who opposed the Machado and Batista dictatorships organized groups in charge of delivering clandestine press and propaganda, distributed through inventive strategies using their own limited resources or through institutional channels. These days, due to limited Internet access and the blocking of certain websites on the part of the government, alternative information tends to be distributed by underground means through e-mail newsletters, as well as via Cuba's offline exchange networks, especially through the so-called *paquete semanal* (Díaz 2018). Nevertheless, it did not take long for these channels to be "intervened" and controlled by the state as well (Henken 2021). Such obstacles, however, always lead to new initiatives, such as offline, content-downloading apps (Freedom House 2018).

Fourth, there is a tendency for the promoters of alternative media across different periods to be fairly knowledgeable about the formats, styles, and journalistic narratives of their day. *Independentista* newspapers relied on an intellectual elite who were staunch enemies of Spanish domination. The opponents to Machado and Batista also counted on the media directors and trained journalists in their ranks. The first oppositional journalistic associations created in 1989 comprised professional journalists who were expelled from their posts in the official media or intellectuals who eventually became disillusioned with the regime (Beaulieu 2013). During these most recent years, there has been no shortage of initiatives to train or "professionalize" political activists lacking cultural capital or formal, technical education (Ruiz 2003; Beaulieu 2013). Nowadays, many of those who work in Cuba's non-state digital media are young graduates of Cuban universities.

Fifth, in all of the periods, Cubans in exile have always been capable of creating their own alternative media abroad and providing material and financial aid to revolutionary, oppositional, or citizen movements and their means of expression on the island, thus influencing the course of events during times of political turmoil. During both the wars for independence or when facing the Machado and Batista dictatorships, Cubans in exile created their own media to denounce the authorities of their day and gather moral and economic support for their cause. Likewise, today Cuba's "digital diaspora" includes the oppositional news and information sites *CubaNet* (1994), *Cubaencuentro* (2000), *Diario de Cuba* (2009), *CiberCuba* (2014), and *ADN Cuba* (2019), all funded and run from abroad. We should not forget more veteran and controversial media outlets like *Radio Martí* (1985) or *Televisión Martí* (1990), closely linked to Washington's project to undermine Cuba's Communist regime (Ruiz 2005).

Table 2.1. Periods of emergence of alternative media in Cuban history, 1868 to present

Five periods	Name of Era	Type/Example of Most Important Alternative	(Media)
1868–1878	Ten Years' War	Independence press	(e.g., *El Cubano Libre*)
1895–1898	War of 1895	Independence press	(e.g., *El Cubano Libre* and *Patria*)
1930–1933	Machado Dictatorship	Revolutionary media	(e.g., *Denuncia*)
1952–1958	Batista Dictatorship	Revolutionary media	(e.g., *Revolución* and *Radio Rebelde*)
1989-present	Post-totalitarian Castroism	Digital media	(e.g., *14ymedio* and *Diario de Cuba*)

Source: Compiled by the author.

These are the five cohesive traits shared by alternative media of different eras: illegality and repression, use of new technology, creativity in production and distribution, professional expertise, and reliance on the diaspora (see Table 2.1 above). This does not mean that there are also not important differences. Among other aspects, apart from their specific context, alternative communications might differ in their level of radicalization, in their spheres of influence and resources at their disposal, in the target public and reach, and in their various capacities to endure and institutionalize themselves over time.

However, beyond these differences, the aforementioned five qualities have characterized the development and evolution of Cuba's alternative media over the past 150 years. These features have been configured and decisively shaped by common historical contexts of authoritarianism or dictatorship, social or revolutionary movements that aimed to overthrow them or change the political regime through their emancipatory objectives, and the conscious use of existing technologies for such purposes. These factors have led to comparable dimensions in the evolution of alternative media over time, especially in the first four periods of radical media (Downing 2001), when a clear or explicit change of political regime motivated the aims of alternative media. It remains to be seen to what extent contemporary alternative media, both radical and citizen, in the current circumstances, might achieve regime change without accompanying radical political action.

We can conclude that when points of connection arise between social movements throughout history, the same can occur with their informational channels and means of expression. Consequently, this idea of continuity should lead us to understand the history of Cuban alternative media as a comprehensive process spanning more than 150 years, not as one that simply started (or ended) in 1989 with the advent of modern alternative media.

FINAL CONSIDERATIONS

The five traits that tie the different eras together—illegality and repression, use of new technology, innovative means of production and distribution, professional expertise, and the intervention of diasporic communities—are crucial dimensions emerging from this study, that can be further theoretically explored in future research on alternative media with a historical or comparative perspective, both in Cuba and in other postcolonial societies. After establishing these parallels between alternative media through various convulsive periods in Cuban history, it is possible to rethink the assumption that the information era and the advent of digital information technologies are the key drivers that enable and sustain spaces of alternativity. Also, scholarship has paid considerably more attention to the appropriation of technologies for social change as an object of study, marginalizing the very sociopolitical processes that spark the need for change as mere historical background (Gibbs and Hamilton 2001). Hence, we should avoid the trap of circumscribing alternative communications solely to the spread of new digital technologies, social media, or smartphones, since we thus run the risk of overlooking a long, rich, pedagogical past that can shed fresh light on long-standing, complex processes. Even if facilitated by the technologies of their time, alternative communication in Cuba has been a continuous historical, sociopolitical phenomenon, rather than an exceptional, ahistorical phenomenon merely afforded by today's spread of digitalization.

Cuba's alternative communication has been historically connected to the political ideals of their initiators, to their aspirations of change as reflected in their contents, to their clandestine conditions, to their target audiences, and to their alternative processes of production, distribution, and management. The periods analyzed here exhibit long-existing social mobilizations, political activism, and diverse forms of expression and protest—all with varying degrees of success—that helped build the modern Cuban state, either to attain independence from colonial rule at the end of the nineteenth century, or to defy the dictatorial governments of Machado, Batista, and Castroism. The study of alternative media in Cuba must therefore be associated with the long tradition of revolutionary, radical, and transgressive media in permanent struggle against the establishment for the nation's liberty and for the democratization of society.

The contribution of alternative media to the processes of democratization and social change in Cuba in the past, in the present day, and crucially in years to come is contingent upon their ability to construct independent information and create horizontal mechanisms of communication (Ruiz 2005). *El Cubano Libre*, Martí's *Patria*, *Denuncia*, and Radio Rebelde were all successful at such an endeavor. Historically, radical revolutions required alternative communication just as much as they did triumphs on the battlefield. But unlike the past, today the gradual transformations taking place on the island are positioning the digital revolution and its vibrant digital mediasphere on the right path to lead social transformation needed in the country without the need for rifles, bombs, or artillery, but instead through active citizen participation and social mobilization.

Acknowledgments

The author wishes to thank Dr. Mireya Márquez-Ramírez for her translation work, as well as the volume's editors and anonymous reviewers for their helpful suggestions.

Notes

1. Jeppesen's (2016) typology of alternative media includes categories such as "bricolage" (cultural resistance), "citizen" (civic participation), "critical" (questioning and confronting neoliberalism), and "radical" (subverting social order).
2. *El Habanero* (1824–1826)—published by Father Félix Varela in exile in Philadelphia and New York—and *La Voz del Pueblo Cubano* (1852) are recognized as the first radical publications in Cuba's national history.
3. Villagers or city residents that spied for the rebel cause.

References

Amores, Christian. 2010. "El rol desempeñado por la emisora Radio Rebelde en el proceso revolucionario cubano y su transmisión para el resto de América Latina por la Cadena de la Libertad." Undergraduate thesis, Universidad de Pinar del Río, Pinar del Río, Cuba.
Beaulieu, Sarah. 2014. "Política cultural y periodismo en Cuba: trayectorias cruzadas de la prensa oficial y de los medios independientes, 1956–2013." Ph.D. thesis, Universidad de Granada, Granada, Spain.
Cadavid, Amparo. 2007. "OURMedia/NUESTROSMedios. Una red global desde lo local." VI Conferencia de OURMedia/NUESTROSMedios, Sidney, April 9–14.
Calvo, Patricia. 2014. "La Sierra Maestra en las rotativas. El papel de la dimensión pública en la etapa insurreccional cubana, 1953–1958." Ph.D. thesis, Universidad de Santiago de Compostela, Santiago de Compostela, Spain.

Camps y Feliú, Francisco. 1890. *Españoles e insurrectos; recuerdos de la guerra de Cuba*. Havana: A. Álvarez.
Carpentier, Alejo. 1933. "Homenaje a nuestros amigos de París." *Carteles*, No. 37, December 24, 1933: 14, 54, and 62.
Casasús, Juan. 1953. *La emigración cubana y la independencia de la patria*. Havana: Lex.
Castells, Manuel. 2015. *Redes de indignación y esperanza: los movimientos sociales en la era de Internet*. Madrid: Alianza.
"Cómo se hacía Denuncia en su etapa clandestina." 1934. *Denuncia*, June 17, 1934: 13.
Contrera, Nelio. 1989. *Alma Mater, la revista de Mella*. Havana: Ciencias Sociales.
Couldry, Nick and James Curran, eds. 2003. *Contesting Media Power*. Lanham, MD: Rowman and Littlefield.
DePalma, Anthony. 2006. *The Man Who Invented Fidel: Castro, Cuba, and Herbert L. Matthews of The New York Times*. New York: Public Affairs.
Díaz, Elaine. 2018. "Medios emergentes en Cuba: desafíos, amenazas y oportunidades," *Sembramedia*, January 11, 2018.
Downing, John. 2001. *Radical Media: Rebellious Communication and Social Movements*. London: Sage.
Fernández, Damián J. 2003. "La disidencia en Cuba: entre la seducción y la normalización." *Foro Internacional XLIII*, No. 3: 591–607.
Fernández, Waldo. 2016. *La imposición del silencio. Cómo se clausuró la libertad de prensa en Cuba 1959–1960*. Madrid: Hypermedia.
Flint, Grover. 1898. *Marching with Gomez: A war correspondent´s field note-book kept during four months with the Cuban Army*. Boston, New York and London: Lamson, Wolffe.
Flores, Eugenio. 1895. *La guerra de Cuba (Apuntes para su historia)*. Madrid: Hijos de M. G. Hernández.
Fornet, Ambrosio. 2014. *El libro en Cuba. Siglos XVIII y XIX*. Havana: Letras Cubanas.
Freedom House. 2018. "Freedom on the Net, Cuba."
García, Vicente. 1869. *Cuba contra España. Apuntes de un año para la historia de la rebelión de la isla de Cuba*. Madrid: Universal.
García Luis, Julio. 2013. *Revolución, Socialismo, Periodismo. La prensa y los periodistas cubanos ante el siglo XXI*. Havana: Pablo de la Torriente.
Garcia Santamaria, Sara. 2018. "Digital Media and the Promotion of Deliberative Debate in Cuba." A Report by the Internet Policy Observatory at the Annenberg School, University of Pennsylvania, May.
Gibbs, Patricia and James Hamilton. 2001. "Introduction." *Media History* 7 (2): 118–119.
González, Ladislao. 1974. *El Ala Izquierda Estudiantil y su época*. Havana: Ciencias Sociales.
Henken, Ted A. 2011. "Una cartografía de la blogósfera cubana. Entre 'oficialistas' y 'mercenarios.'" *Nueva Sociedad*, No. 235: 90–109.
Henken, Ted A. 2017. "Cuba's Digital Millennials: Independent Digital Media and Civil Society on the Island the Disconnected." *Social Research: An International Quarterly* 84 (2): 429–456.
Henken, Ted A. 2021. "The Opium of the *Paquete*: State Censorship, Private Self-Censorship, and the Content Distribution Strategies of Cuba's Emergent, Independent Digital Media Startups." *Cuban Studies* 50.

Hoffmann, Bert. 2011. "Civil Society 2.0?: How the Internet Changes State-Society Relations in Authoritarian Regimes: The Case of Cuba." *GIGA Working Papers*, No. 156, January.

Jeppesen, Sandra. 2016. "Understanding Alternative Media Power." *Democratic Communiqué*, No. 27: 54–77.

Labrada, Eduardo. 2018. "Tinta y plomo de la prensa mambisa en campaña." *Adelante*, October 30, 2018.

Lima Sarmiento, Edel. 2014. *La prensa cubana y el machadato*. Havana: Ciencias Sociales.

Llaverías, Joaquín. 1932. "Contribuciones a la historia de la prensa en Cuba." In *La prensa en Cuba 1902–1932*, edited by Tomás González, 33–45. Havana: Lapido-Iglesia.

"Los periodistas en la Revolución." 1938. In *El periodismo en Cuba, 1938*, 119. Havana.

Padilla, Alexei. 2017. "Internet e a dinamização da esfera pública em Cuba." *Revista Extraprensa* 10, No. 2: 153–176.

Pérez, Yusleidy. 2013. "Mañach, el ABC y el proceso revolucionario en Cuba." *Perfiles de la Cultura Cubana*, No. 10.

Ponte, Francisco. 1957. *El Cubano Libre; una conferencia universitaria y un estudio adicional*. Havana: Modas Magazine.

Rodríguez, Clemencia. 2001. *Fissures in the Mediascape. An International Study of Citizen's Media*. Cresskill: Hampton Press.

Romero, Cira. 2012. "Prensa mambisa: artillería de la Revolución cubana contra España," *Cubainformación*, September 26, 2012.

Rosal, Antonio del. 1874. *Los mambises. Memorias de un prisionero*. Madrid: Pedro Abienzo.

Ruiz, Fernando J. 2005. "Medios de comunicación alternativa y dictaduras en transición: Cuba en perspectiva comparada." In *Cuba hoy y mañana. Actores e instituciones de una política en transición*, edited by Rafael Rojas, 203–224. México D.F.: Planeta.

Ruiz, Fernando J. 2003. *Otra grieta en la pared. Informe y testimonio de la nueva prensa cubana*. Buenos Aires: Cadal.

Sánchez, Miralys. 1998. *La prensa norteamericana llama a la guerra: 1898*. Havana: Ciencias Sociales.

Soto, Jesús. 1965. *Bibliografía prensa clandestina revolucionaria (1952–1958)*. Havana: Biblioteca Nacional José Martí.

Soto, Lionel. 1977. *La Revolución del 33*, Vol. II. Havana: Ciencias Sociales.

Torriente, Loló de la. 1964. "La prensa en la manigua cubana." *Bohemia*, No. 50, December 11, 1964: 105.

Vázquez, Adelina, Gladys Egües, et al. 2008. *Apuntes de la prensa clandestina y guerrillera (1952–1958)*. Havana: Pablo de la Torriente and Félix Varela.

Villaescusa, Ivette. 2015. *Desafíos en la prensa cubana 1959–1960*. Havana: Editora Historia.

II
POLITICS

3

Information and Communication Technology, State Power, and Civil Society

Cuban Internet Development in the Context of the Normalization of Relations with the United States

OLGA KHRUSTALEVA

In December 2014, when presidents Barack Obama and Raúl Castro announced their intention to reestablish diplomatic relations between their respective countries, the only way for a private citizen to individually connect to the Internet in Cuba was to buy an expensive Nauta access card and visit one of the few parks or hotels recently equipped with a Wi-Fi hot spot. However, over the next five years, Cuba began offering home-based Internet plans, rolled out 3G mobile Internet, and even initiated trials for 4G cell service—all while the spread of cell phones continued apace.[1] The much-ballyhooed reestablishment of diplomatic relations, however, has had very little to do with these domestic developments.

Since that momentous announcement—followed in the summer of 2015 by the opening of embassies in each country's respective capitals (often referred to as "normalization" by the media)—there have been great expectations for "change" on both sides. Change, however, has been understood very differently by the government of each country. For the U.S., the goal was for Cuba to improve its human rights record, institute changes in its authoritarian political system, and provide greater economic opportunities for American companies to do business on the island. In contrast, the Cuban government understood "normalization," first and foremost, as the long-awaited and vehemently demanded beginning of the end of the U.S. embargo.

While small, yet important and historically symbolic, progress was made toward normalization during 2015 and 2016—including the removal of Cuba from the U.S. State Department's "state sponsor of terrorism" list, the resumption of direct commercial flights between the two countries, the lifting of many travel restrictions for Americans, a state visit to Cuba in March 2016 by President Obama,[2] and the end of the so-called wet foot-dry foot migration policy—even before Obama left office on January 17, 2017, the two sides had come to no agreement on many other pending issues, such as the future of the U.S. military base at Guantánamo Bay, the end of the embargo, or the fate of the island's political prisoners, to say nothing of internal changes to the island's one-party political system. Since then, of course, a new administration had taken over in Washington with the goal of canceling the "completely one-sided deal" Obama made in Cuba, in the words of President Donald Trump (2017).

In the midst of these changes, the reestablishment of relations seemed an excellent opportunity for both sides to make progress in an area where there was considerable overlap and mutual interest: technology and telecommunications. American tech and telecom companies were eager to enter a new market and the U.S. government sought to facilitate greater exposure of the Cuban people to "the free flow of information." And for its part, the Cuban government could make further progress upgrading its antiquated telecom infrastructure, speed up Internet technology development, and advance in its stated goal of the *"informatización"* (computerization) of Cuban society (see Padilla Herrera and Viera Cañive, this volume).

However, with historical political tensions, mistrust, and the embargo still in place, bilateral cooperation in the area of technology was much harder to implement in practice than it had at first seemed in theory. Despite initial excitement about possible changes, bilateral relations never actually advanced beyond the formal reestablishment of diplomatic relations to genuine normalization of those relations. Thus, the modest changes that Cuba has seen in terms of greater access to and use of Information and Communication Technologies (ICTs) by everyday Cubans in the five years between 2014 and 2019 owes much more to internal developments on the island, coming from either the ground up (civil society) or the top down (government policy), not as the fruit of the (short-lived) normalization of relations with the United States.

Donald Trump's presidency has demonstrably reversed some of the progress made by the Obama administration in terms of normalizing the notoriously antagonistic relationship between the U.S. and Cuba. The mysterious sonic incidents reported by American diplomats who were stationed at the U.S. Embassy in Havana starting in late 2016 as well as the creation of the Cuba Internet Task Force by the U.S. State Department at the direction of the

White House in early 2018 (ostensibly aimed at expanding Internet access and freedom of expression in Cuba) have further alienated the two countries. And while the creation of the Task Force was much more a political gesture aimed at Florida voters than a real effort to either undermine the Cuban regime or connect and empower the Cuban people, it has been effectively used by the Cuban government to buttress the argument that yet again the Cuban David was under attack by the powerful and hostile American Goliath to the north.

This chapter seeks to gauge the effects of the normalization of diplomatic relations between the U.S. and Cuba on ICT development in Cuba and address the ways in which Cuban Internet development has reflected Cuban power dynamics and conventional geopolitical issues. The research underlying this analysis has focused on a dichotomy underlying analyses of the development of ICT in authoritarian countries: "liberation" vs. "repression" technology (Diamond 2010; Morozov 2011), "forces of light" vs. "forces of darkness" (Deibert and Rohozinski 2010), empowering activists or autocrats (Rød and Weidmann 2015), or the "networked public sphere" vs. "networked authoritarianism" (Tufekci 2017; MacKinnon 2012). However, by treating the Internet as a "carrier of specific purposes," researchers often play down the importance of "competing interests and ideas of different social actors" (Michaelsen 2018). Thus, to fully understand the interconnection between the Internet and political processes, it is necessary to look beyond simplistic dichotomies and focus on how ICT development reflects the underlying power dynamics that predate the development of ICT at both the global and local levels.

In carrying out my research, I chose semi-structured interviews as the main method. During my two research trips to Cuba in November 2016 and April 2017, I interviewed a total of twenty-eight technology experts, computer programmers, journalists, bloggers, tech entrepreneurs, people familiar with Cuban Internet policy and U.S. companies, and individuals with experience in the Cuban telecom sector. Additionally, I interviewed several Cubans who reside in the U.S., both face-to-face and via Skype. I believed that the knowledge and experience of people whose work is closely linked to the development and usage of ICT would give me sufficient information on the subject of ICT in Cuba to evaluate whether and how its development has been connected to the Cuban government's changing bilateral relations with the United States.

This chapter is divided into three sections. In the first one, I address changing U.S.-Cuba relations and their impact on ICT expansion in Cuba. The second section focuses on Cuban "hacks," the multiple online and offline tech *inventos* (inventions) that Cubans have come up with as necessary work-arounds in a politically restrictive and resource-poor telecom environment. The final section explores some of the many emergent Cuban spaces of digital participation and contestation where one can witness both horizontal citizen-to-citizen public convening and communication and the vertical interaction between government representatives and increasingly bold and networked citizens in an expanding Cuban cyberspace.

The Normalization of Distrust: U.S.-Cuban Relations and ICT Development

Hostile relations with the U.S. have had a great influence on Cuban domestic politics and foreign policy for years, in turn impacting the island's tech and telecom policy and development. Indeed, until the 2010s the Internet was viewed more as a threat than an opportunity by the Cuban government. This was the case first because it was initially developed in the U.S. for military defense purposes. Second, it was seen as subversive because of its potential to liberate and diversify the flow of information, undermining the government's media monopoly and leading the populace to question state authority. Third, national security concern was stoked by the fact that U.S. officials had regularly encouraged the expansion of ICT in Cuba as a "Trojan horse."

However, starting in 2009 President Obama relaxed sanctions against Cuba, permitting U.S. telecom companies to establish fiber optic and satellite connections with the island. Then, during his final two years in office, Obama publicly foreswore the past policy of regime change and allowed greater telecom cooperation between the two countries. Still, the Cuban government was never very keen on letting the U.S. play any significant role in ICT development in the country. Looking instead to its powerful geopolitical allies China and Russia, countries that had successfully combined Internet expansion with continued political control (Parker 2014), the Cuban government adopted a defensive strategy that prioritized "digital sovereignty" over high quality or rapid expansion of Internet access.

Of course, Cuba's distrust of the U.S. is not without grounds. For years, developing ways to deploy Internet technology on the island was a part of USAID's "democracy promotion" program, fueling hostility between the two countries. Indeed, in 2014, the Associated Press uncovered documents revealing that USAID financed and operated ZunZuneo, a Cuban version of Twitter that the agency allegedly planned to use to spread anti-Castro messages and stir political unrest. The project was launched in 2009 and was gathering personal data about its users who were unaware that the social network was funded by the U.S. government (Roig-Franzia 2014). Even though its initial popularity was such that it was in danger of running out of funds as it subsidized the connection costs of an increasing number of users on the island, ZunZuneo had no practical subversive impact in Cuba and its importance as a tool of potential subversion was overstated by the Cuban government for propaganda purposes (Mexidor, Menéndez, and Allard 2011). The U.S. has arguably overestimated the potential impact of these "liberation technologies" as well.

Indeed, U.S. efforts promoting ICT development and democratization in Cuba, have been rather contradictory and convoluted. On the one hand, the U.S. has sought to promote free flow of information to combat what it has often referred to as "the Cuban government's internal information blockade." On the other, popular Google, Microsoft, and other messaging apps were unavailable in Cuba for a long time thanks to provisions of the embargo. As *Global Post* reporter Nick Miroff quipped in a 2009 article, "How the U.S. keeps Cuba offline": "Fear not, Web-deprived Cubans. The U.S. government has a new plan to breach the firewall of communist censorship and let free data flow through. First though, it needs to block your access to some really cool software." Indeed, in a confidential e-mail to the CIA and other U.S. government agencies published by Wikileaks, former U.S. Interests Section Chief of Mission in Havana Jonathan Farrar criticized the restrictions as counterproductive.

> The actions by these U.S. companies to stop such services only help the efforts of GOC (Government of Cuba) censors to control the information available to the Cuban people and run directly counter to our own efforts to expand the free flow of information to, from, and within Cuba . . . (Wikileaks 2009)

These inconsistencies have been used by Cuba to justify Internet restrictions and blame its technological backwardness on the embargo. As a result, past policies of both the U.S. and Cuban governments have transformed the Cuban Internet into "a rough and inaccessible space where it is nearly impossible to navigate without being co-opted by the Scylla of state capture or beholden to the Charybdis of foreign support" (Henken and Van de Voort 2015). Still, after the official reestablishment of diplomatic relations and loosening of U.S. sanctions, many private American companies and NGOs started looking into opportunities for investment and business development in Cuba in different areas including technology (Alvarez 2016). What attracted potential investors was an underdeveloped but promising Cuban technology market (sometimes referred to as a "greenfield"), as well as cheap, qualified labor.

In a 2015 report on "Cuba's Readiness for ICT Transformation," the research and consultancy firm Nearshore Americas concluded that Cuban programmers were well educated and used to working for less than $500 a month. According to Nearshore at the time, "in a liberalized environment, Cuba could quickly become a major source of IT outsourcing and research" (Tucker 2015). However, two years later Nearshore's director Kirk Laughlin reluctantly came to the rather pessimistic conclusion that Cuba was "a lost cause and easily the biggest disappointment ever in the short history of Nearshore IT" (2017). According to Laughlin, the main reason for this was the government's fear of subversion, closed-mindedness, and unwillingness to see a partnership with U.S. IT companies as a way to attract capital.

One important U.S. IT company, however, has succeeded in allaying the government's fear of such a partnership, gradually establishing a tech foothold in Cuba over the last five years (2014–2019). That company is Google. Indeed, Google's first forays into Cuba began prior to the official reestablishment of diplomatic relations with a quiet visit to Cuba by Google CEO Eric Schmidt and a small tech and policy team in summer 2014. The short trip included visits to the home office of Yoani Sánchez, famed dissident blogger and founder in May of that same year of the independent digital newspaper *14ymedio* and to the state-run University of Computer Science (UCI).[3]

Then at about the same time the U.S. Embassy opened in Havana (summer 2015), Google made Chrome, Play, and Analytics available in Cuba. A year later, in the spring of 2016—just around the time of President Obama's historic state visit to Havana—the tech giant kicked off a collaboration with Alexis "Kcho" Leiva Machado, a young, successful Afro-Cuban painter and sculptor as well as a staunch Castro government loyalist. At the time, Kcho had already set up Cuba's very first (free) public Wi-Fi hot spot in his art studio in the Romerillo neighborhood in far western Havana.[4] Google expanded on Kcho's offerings by installing its Cardboards and Chromebooks at the site for public use. The significance of the Google Kcho deal was exaggerated by the Western media, as the hot spot had been there before Google came along, and the study room with Chromebooks and an improved Internet connection was in fact only available to the public during very restricted hours and was eventually closed down altogether in 2017 (Rodríguez 2017).

By that time, however, Google had already reached an agreement to install its servers at some ETECSA data centers in Havana as part of its Google Global Cache program (Wamsley 2017). Although Google Cache does not improve Cuba's overall Internet speed, it does make access to Google-owned services such as YouTube significantly faster for island users. Still, contrary to the breathless and bombastic claims of some media reports, Google's

Figure 3.1. A Cuban man uses one of the island's only free Wi-Fi Internet connections as he squats outside of Alexis "Kcho" Leiva Machado's studio in the Romerillo neighborhood of western Havana. Credit: Olga Khrustaleva.

presence in Cuba cannot be considered some kind of Silicon Valley "invasion" of the island (Novak 2016). However, for a tech giant with a mixed track record of doing business in and with authoritarian regimes like China, Google's entry into Cuba and development of a trusting working relationship with various Cuban government agencies and academic, cultural, and technological institutions has been an important strategic step with clear PR benefits for the company—especially as a contrast to the Trump administration's bellicose posture. If Cuba allows more foreign participation in its technology industry in the future, Google will have an advantage because it has already engaged in extensive negotiations with the Cuban authorities and established a small but expanding presence in Cuba as a trusted partner for the government and a welcome provider of Internet services to the Cuban people. Most other companies would have to start from zero.

In its final report released in June 2019, President Trump's Internet Task Force singled out four already well-known obstacles to Internet freedom in Cuba: limited access, high prices, government control, and surveillance. The recommendations of the Task Force included expanding digital safety education and digital literacy and supporting organic network growth, among others (Cuba Internet Task Force 2019). Ironically, the report also highlighted inconsistencies in U.S. telecom policy toward Cuba, stating that many private companies "often feel deterred from entering the [Cuban] market due to uncertainty caused by frequent changes to U.S. regulations concerning Cuba." Indeed, echoing former U.S. Interests Section Chief Jonathan Farrar, cited above, the report went on:

> Other companies have chosen not to offer key products and services, citing reasons ranging from regulatory ambiguity to banks' reluctance to process payments originating in Cuba due to the U.S. embargo. As a result, most Cubans are unable to download popular applications on their mobile devices or benefit from civic tech initiatives, such as Project Shield (Google's effort to protect the human rights community against cyberattacks) because the applications are not offered in Cuba. (Cuba Internet Task Force 2019)

The Task Force also recommended that the U.S. government have better communication with the private sector about the regulations in order to "facilitate exports and services" including Cubans' access to "paid applications and cloud-based technology."

These inconsistencies in U.S. telecom policy together with its clumsy democracy promotion efforts in Cuba have contributed to the government's decision to prioritize a "digital sovereignty" strategy over one that aims to spread access rapidly with the help of U.S. business partners. Even after the reestablishment of diplomatic relations, continued distrust and bilateral hostility made it impossible for the two governments to develop a genuine partnership. The Cuban government took a restrictive approach to Internet development not only to secure its domestic power and thwart opponents inside the country, but also as a response to U.S.-dominated democracy promotion efforts that emphasized the use of technology for "change," a prospect the Cuban government saw simply as subversion. Google might improve the quality of the Cuban Internet, but the company is unlikely to change (or challenge) the government's approach to Internet freedom, control, and surveillance.

Innovation Restricted, *Inventos Cubanos* Multiply

At about the same time Cuba first connected to the Internet in 1996, N. was a student at a small village school in one of Cuba's eastern provinces. In an interview, he made the following point about how he first became enamored of technology:

During those times, computers and technology in general were not something that was known here. But many of us knew that in other places in the world there were computers. In my house, I painted a keyboard on a sheet of paper to study where each letter and each number was so that if one day, I had an opportunity to use a real computer, I would not have fear of working on it. That's how I started.[5]

N. then moved to a city and studied computer science at the university there. He said it was not easy for country people like him to work in big cities, but that's where technology development started. This story is quite typical. Everyone I interviewed first accessed the Internet either when they started college or at a state workplace.[6] While Internet connectivity is limited in Havana and other provincial capitals, in rural areas it is practically nonexistent.

In December 2018, ETECSA started offering paid connections to long awaited 3G mobile Internet service potentially available to 66 percent of the population (Figueredo Reinaldo, Domínguez, and Carmona Tamayo 2018). However, the costs—roughly $8 for 600 MB of data and $34 for 4 GB make the service far out of reach based on an average monthly salary of $30. Still, the 3G rollout is the most important step ETECSA has taken to date to expand Internet access. In the first month (December 6, 2018, to January 7, 2019) ETECSA sold almost $14 million worth of Internet packages (Arego 2019). However, ETECSA reported that it was operating at 160 percent of its technical capacity following the 3G rollout (IPS 2019). Indeed, high prices and low quality led to a series of massive online protests where Cuban netizens reported dropped signals by tweeting #ApagónEtecsa (ETECSA blackout) and demanded lower Internet prices using the hashtag #BajenLosPreciosDeInternet (*14ymedio* 2019a; *El Toque* 2019).

Despite draconian prices, mobile Internet has given Cuban developers new opportunities for local app development and the chance to move beyond what had until then been the "only-in-Cuba" norm for cell phone apps: lightweight offline apps that based their geolocation on pings off of cell towers and had to be updated manually at cell phone repair shops. One of the newest and most innovative ones is called Sube ("Get in"), an Uber-like app that connects taxi drivers with potential fares. The app allows parties to bargain over price prior to agreeing to the deal but payment is made by cash in person since online transactions are not yet available in Cuba. The app developers said that they originally designed and tested Sube using e-mail, but with the launch of 3G they have been able to make a qualitative leap in design that greatly facilitates their work (Ernesto 2019).

In June 2018, Cuba saw the appearance of a messaging app called toDus.

During the first two weeks following the launch it was downloaded two hundred thousand times and quickly became one of the island's most popular apps (Gonźalez 2019). Unlike WhatsApp, IMO, Facebook Messenger, or other international messaging applications, toDus is run on Cuba's national intranet, making the costs much lower and the service inside Cuba much better. However, since it was developed at UCI in collaboration with ETECSA, its widespread adoption raises major data privacy concerns. There is not a word about encryption in toDus's terms and conditions. There is simply a vague pledge not to "share user data with third parties unless the law allows it."

ToDus and other Cuban applications are available via the Android app national distribution site Apklis. Their appearance in recent years reveals the Cuban government's attempt to fulfill the Cuban public's demand for convenient, modern, and affordable digital technology. At the same time, they are further evidence of state promotion of "digital sovereignty." This term has been widely used by the Cuban regime to describe its ICT expansion efforts. Separating the Cuban intranet (over which the government has near total control) from the global Internet (over which it has very limited control) brings additional costs and presents several technical difficulties because of the application design and the two different currencies in which users pay for the services (intranet services can be paid in Cuban national pesos, while Internet access must be paid for in CUCs).[7] However, this seems to be the government's China-inspired strategy to overcome the "dictator's dilemma," enjoying the significant economic and developmental benefits of the digital revolution while minimizing its considerable risks to information control (Press 2011).

By far the most important and uniquely Cuban of these many technological *inventos* is *el paquete semanal* (the weekly package). *El paquete* is nearly a terabyte of the newest films, TV shows, software, games, books, magazines, and other digital content circulated on a weekly basis by a tolerated if technically "unlegal" (Cubans use the word *alegal*) network of compilers and distributors. *El paquete* is a "sneaker net," meaning both that it circulates offline and "on foot" and that it is unregulated. *El paquete* is distributed by an extensive network of people in Havana and Santiago, making its way across the entire island, but its origins are mysterious and likely multiple. With existing Internet speed in Cuba, it would be impossible for a regular Cuban to download even a gigabyte of data in a week, let alone a terabyte. Thus, it is likely that parts of *el paquete* are brought into the island by courier while other parts are downloaded by persons at state institutions with privileged access to high-speed Internet. Over time, the compilation and distribution of *el paquete* has become consolidated into four main *casas matrices* or compilation houses.[8]

More interesting still is the fact that most versions of *el paquete* usually arrive to users with pre-embedded ads for Cuban origin goods and services that differ from province to province. Regional distributors likely get the terabyte of content on Sundays, add local commercials, and deliver it to their clients on Mondays. It also has cached, static versions of classified ads from a popular website called Revolico, a Cuban version of Craigslist and a popular place to sell smartphones, Wi-Fi routers, and even mobile Internet and e-mail access—goods and services either unavailable at state stores, monopolized by ETECSA, or banned outright for import.

Often those who buy *el paquete* from local distributors then resell it piecemeal, so the network of national, regional, and local compilers, distributors, and consumers is very extensive and hard to accurately measure. *El paquete* has been called Cuba's largest private employer (Press 2015) and, as one consumer put it, "an epidemic that cannot be stopped."[9] It has become such a profitable business in some regions that it is distributed not weekly but daily and reaches the most remote parts of Cuba where Internet itself has yet to appear. "Several years ago, we went to climb Pico Turquino,[10] and all the villagers there used *el paquete*. It even reaches that remote jungle," a *paquete* consumer told me in an interview.

What makes *el paquete* "*alegal*" and not strictly illegal is the fact that it is decidedly apolitical and doesn't contain any pornography. Adept in the art of self-censorship to ensure the survival of their business model, most compilers and distributors are determined to keep it this way (Henken 2021). As one *paquete* distributor I interviewed revealed:

> About three months ago one person got detained. Someone made the complaint that [*el paquete*] had pornography and news that spoke against the Cuban government. But in general, *el paquete* [distributors] are very cautious. There is no pornography. Almost no politics. Moreover, after Fidel's death, *el paquete* came with a folder of homage to Fidel.[11]

The rigorous enforcement of the "no politics" rule by *el paquete* has prompted the creation of a competing, clandestine digital compilation known as "*el paketito*" (the little package)—a collection of digital content of the kind that would normally be censored by compilers of *el paquete*. However, to gain access to *el paketito* one has to have direct, personal contact with a member of a rather closed distribution network (Escobar 2017), making its reach and impact quite limited. Yet another alternative to *el paquete*—but not exactly a competitor—is *Mi Mochila* (my backpack), a selection of audiovisual content similar to the traditional *paquete*, but created and distributed by Cuba's network of more than six hundred local Joven Clubs de Computación y Electrónica (JCCEs, Youth Computer Clubs), run by the Union of Communist Youth. The cost of a week's worth of *Mi Mochila*, ten Cuban pesos, is ten times lower than that of the *paquete*. However, the content is much more limited by political criteria so that didactic, government-approved materials predominate (Cibercuba 2018; Henken 2021).

Similar to *el paquete*, homegrown local area networks (LANs) like the so-called street nets or SNETs that virtually blanket Havana have become a popular way to access digital content in Cuba over the past decade. These local wired or sometimes Wi-Fi–enabled networks were set up initially to enable multiplayer gaming, but are also used for all kinds of independent communication and information exchange over the network, which operates "offline" and separately from both the global Internet and national intranet. However, these networks are so rich in content and geographically extensive that observers can be forgiven for assuming that they *are* the Internet (García Martínez 2017; Harris 2015). Indeed, the largest fifty-six-thousand-user-strong network started in 2011 when locals began connecting neighborhood-based LANs for multiuser gaming and file sharing (Pujol, Scott, Wustrow, and Halderman 2017). The SNET's self-imposed rules on permissible content are strict. SNET can ban a user for "violating internal order and security of the country," as well as for damaging the network infrastructure or offering Internet, TV, or other services that are the legal monopoly of ETECSA. The rules also emphasize that SNET is not a space for political debate or religious proselytization (SNET 2016).

In May 2019, the Cuban government announced new regulations allowing private homes and small businesses located close enough to a hot spot to set up their own Wi-Fi networks (*Gaceta Oficial* 2019a, 2019b). However, cables crossing streets and radio transmitter power over one hundred megawatts[12] were explicitly prohibited, which had the effect of outlawing all already existing SNETs (Press 2019). Almost immediately, the hashtag #TodosSomosS-NET (We're all SNET) took Twitter by storm. Dissidents and government sympathizers alike took to the microblogging site to defend the SNET community. The Twitter discussion got so heated that a group of SNET administrators issued a statement calling for everyone to calm down and wait for official information. The administrators—who were then engaged in direct discussions with representatives from Cuba's Ministry of Communications—also expressed the hope that SNET would be legalized even if they had to "adjust or correct certain things" (SNET 2019a).

However, in August 2019 the Ministry of Communication (MINCOM) announced that the regulations would not be changed and no exception would be made for SNET. Moreover, MINCOM proposed that Cuba's Youth Computer Clubs take charge of the SNET nodes and introduce an access fee. (SNET has always been free). Henceforth, the network would mainly offer the preapproved content typical of these Communist Youth-run Clubs, while the games, books, and other materials SNET had become known for would simply vanish. Essentially, this was a government takeover. However, SNET administrators rejected any possible cooperation with Youth Computer Clubs with the following statement:

> SNET disappears and is eliminated permanently and without exceptions. The Youth Computer Clubs will not make any agreement, union, annexation or cooperation with SNET or any node […] It's a farce and a great lack of respect; all the work of more than fifteen years has been thrown away. (SNET 2019b)

The practical elimination of SNET suggests that Cuba's state-directed ICT development and Internet expansion will make no compromises with or exceptions for the island's many bottom-up *inventos*. Still, *el paquete* and SNET have become so successfully embedded in Cuban life because for years they've been virtually the only affordable, functional vehicle allowing horizontal digital sharing and opening a window to the outside world for many Cubans (see Cearns, this volume, for more analysis of SNET). SNET's elimination demonstrates the government's intolerance of any form of alternative community organization—even those that are explicitly apolitical—and raises questions about the fate of *el paquete*. On the one hand, it would take only a single *Granma* article to change the status of *el paquete* from *alegal* to illegal as it distributes content without authorization. On the other hand, it is far more extensive and embedded in people's lives than SNET, as its distribution doesn't require any complex technological equipment. Besides, unlike SNET, *el paquete* is not really a centrally organized communication tool, but rather a diffuse network and mass product. Its elimination may prove both impossible and impolitic.

THE CONTESTED NET: THE CUBAN GOVERNMENT AND CIVIL SOCIETY MEET IN CYBERSPACE

Internet expansion in Cuba has undoubtedly facilitated horizontal communication between different groups of citizens and put the government on the defensive. On the one hand, it monopolizes most ICT development. On the

Figure 3.2. "With Internet I can . . ." Young men outside Alexis "Kcho" Leiva Machado's art studio in western Havana's Romerillo neighborhood talk politics, normalization of diplomatic relations between Cuba and the United States, and Internet expansion. Credit: Olga Khrustaleva.

other, there are multiple processes, arenas, and uses of ICT on which it has little influence. Why then has the government taken the risk of significantly expanding Internet access in recent years (2013–present) thereby threatening its dominance of the communicational field on the island. As I have argued above, this risk is based on the government's calculation that answering rising citizen demand for greater connectivity will also allow it to assert control over the digital revolution on the island, one that the Revolution itself turned its back on in the mid-1990s (see Press, this volume, for this history).

While Internet access is expanding in Cuba, some content remains censored and critical users are routinely surveilled and often detained. The likelihood of reprisal for such criticism is still high because the government closely watches online conversations and monitors selected users' offline activities. For example, ETECSA blocks text messages containing the words "democracy," "dissident," "hunger strike," and "human rights," as well as the names of the most prominent dissidents and independent media outlets from delivery (Sánchez and Escobar 2016). Likewise, in the lead-up to the constitutional referendum that took place on February 26, 2019, ETECSA prevented the delivery of (but applied regular charges to) any text messages advocating abstention (#YoNoVoto) or a "no" vote (#YoVotoNo), while promoting the circulation of messages of support (*14ymedio* 2019b). Indeed, on the day of the vote itself, the critical independent digital media outlet *Tremenda Nota*, recently launched in 2018, found itself blocked for the first time, joining a growing list of the government's digital bêtes noires, including *14ymedio, Cibercuba, Diario de Cuba,* and *Cubanet* (CPJ 2019; OONI 2019). This should come as no surprise since ETECSA remains the most powerful and perplexing actor influencing Internet development in Cuba.

Cuba's University of Computer Science (UCI) is another key Cuban ICT actor. While virtually all Cuban universities are state-run, the UCI stands out as being closely linked to the Cuban government and its "computerization" of society initiative. Founded in 2002, it was originally intended to prepare programmers who could develop Cuba's own "technologically sovereign" and commercially uncontaminated software (Lai 2009). However, because of its close ties with the government's intelligence apparatus, there are credible claims that parts of UCI have been transformed into incubators of a government cyber-surveillance army. Labeled Operación Verdad (Operation Truth), these digital shock troops fight negative online news by trolling critical sites and commending the Cuban government online via fake social media accounts and bots (Jiménez Enoa 2017).

Along these lines, one of my interviewees, the political activist and leader of Somos Más (We are more), Eliécer Ávila[13] shared his experience as a student at UCI during the early 2000s.

> All the students at the university were offered one hundred extra megabytes of Internet per month if we would commit to saying favorable things about [government] policy [online] . . . From then I started reading a lot about different bloggers and it changed my way of thinking. Then I got expelled from a Communist Youth (UJC) project, and almost got expelled from school, but students supported me. [When I graduated] the Cuban government sent me to fulfill my obligatory work service to *el Oriente* where I took care of pigs, made sausage, and worked in agriculture. Everything but using Internet.[14]

Ávila's experience of being banished to work on a farm after graduating with a computer science degree only reinforced his decision to pursue activism after completing his two years of obligatory social service. The one hundred extra megabyte incentive he refers to above is not unique to UCI students. Journalists working for the official media are also provided with privileged Web access to spread positive messages about the Revolution. This practice was revealed to me in an interview with an independent blogger who had previously worked in the state media.

> I started the blog in 2010. At that moment, I still worked at an official newspaper. There was a directive from the Party that all journalists working for the official newspapers had to start a blog or create a Facebook or Twitter account, and fight digitally in favor of "the truths" of the Cuban government via their profiles. [. . .] First, I wrote in a more humorous, indirect way. Then I started to talk more straightforwardly about the reality in Cuba and I was criticized and scolded by my coworkers a lot for what I was writing.[15]

The Cuban government maintains a tight grip on Cuban cyberspace using what Deibert and Rohozinski (2010) refer to as third-generation controls: surveillance, data mining, and counterinformation, defamation, and intimidation of opponents. However, as Internet becomes more accessible to Cuban citizens, various "netizen" spaces and digital "public arenas" have become more visible.

Cuba's new president Miguel Díaz-Canel, who took over from Raúl Castro in 2018, took a different approach to the topic of ICT than his predecessors. More forthcoming and modern, Díaz-Canel did not automatically deem social media a subversive technology and U.S.-based tech companies enemies. Instead, a few months into his presidency, he launched his own Twitter account and encouraged his ministers to do the same. Almost his entire cabinet is now on Twitter, and although social media have largely been used by Cuban officials as just another channel to push the regime's boilerplate agenda, their presence online has led to instances of open, critical exchanges with citizens. Not used to such direct criticism, some ministers have blocked offending users. Others have taken the time to respond, usually defending the Party line. An independent data journalism project called *Inventario* launched in 2018 started a public list of Cuban officials who had blocked critical users (Ibarra 2019).

Conclusion: The Cuban Internet, *entre la espada y la pared*

The expansion of Internet access and the growing online activity of Cuba's "netizens" has led to the emergence of online public spaces where the public and government officials can debate important issues and events.[16] However, it is too early to expect ICTs to transform Cuba's multiple discussion arenas into a shared public space that could effectively or consistently hold state officials accountable to the public. Indeed, the division and mutual suspicion among Cuban civil society activists illustrates the government's continued "overt power" (Gaventa 1980; Lukes 2005). A small group of power-holding Cubans ensure that while they and their loyal inner circle can enjoy certain privileges—in this case access to the Internet and its related digital technologies—regular citizens are deprived of such a possibility; that is, they are excluded from the power network. However, this power network is not always impenetrable. Nevertheless, once someone gets inside, they have to follow a strict set of often unspoken rules in order not to lose their own privileges.

Being expelled from the university or laid off from a job is quite a common consequence of expressing alternative political views. It also serves as a warning that keeps most other "insiders" in line. Three Cubans interviewed for this research personally experienced this kind of "technological and professional excommunication" and about half of all my interviewees admitted to consciously self-censoring for fear of losing the privileges that came with their "insider" status. Traditionally, the more dissident and openly critical of the government a group is, the less access to power and opportunities to be heard it has. And since the government is at the top of this power hierarchy controlling most areas of life—from agriculture to tourism to medicine to telecommunications—it is exceedingly difficult for those active in Cuba's contentious and dissident spheres to shift these dynamics. However, has the advent of ICT, the spread of Internet access, and the use of social media—in short, the "digital revolution"—fundamentally changed this power dynamic?

Scholars of political psychology argue that conformity is a common feature of authoritarian regimes where leaders make sure to foster obedience and suppress individual autonomy through establishing a set of values and norms (Duckitt 1989; Dunn 2014). Before Internet, obedience was mostly achieved through a mix of repression (overt power), isolation of dissidents (covert power), and masterful propaganda (latent power). In countries like China or Cuba, where "behavioral and attitudinal conformity with in-group norms and rules of conduct" (Duckitt 1989, 70) has been taught and enforced for decades, citizens might be less likely to act in pursuit of autonomy out of fear not only of repercussion but also of breaking with the familiar conformist model, even when they have access to ICT.

Quiescence or silent agreement arguably originates from conformity—when citizens do not challenge the authority not primarily out of fear of repression, but because they genuinely accept the established norms and values of the society they live in (Gaventa 1980; Lukes 2005). Conformity diminishes the chances for success of any popular protest movement as it breeds popular indifference to and disinterest in political and social affairs.[17] In Cuba, following years of government discourse praising the Revolution and communism, criticizing the United States, and condemning dissidents as mercenaries, such attitudes become an unthinking and unquestioned norm for many citizens—especially since they lack any alternate sources of information to state propaganda. More diverse sources of information and better access to ICT could arguably change these dynamics.

However, I argue that ICT development in Cuba can hardly be expected to change the current power dynamics dramatically or quickly. Cubans have been disconnected from the world for decades, and to date the main function of ICT is to connect to family and friends abroad, not to engage in politics. When Internet becomes available to the majority of the population, it is likely that its entertainment function will become the second most important one after the mere private communication that currently dominates, as already illustrated by the content and ubiquity of *el paquete*. Moreover, the same conformity which characterizes Cuba's offline spaces can easily extend to the emergent online ones—recall *el paquete*'s producers' voluntary inclusion of a folder of content paying homage to Fidel Castro upon the leader's death and *Vistar* magazine's decision to publish a special edition of their independent digital entertainment magazine to mourn *El Comandante*'s passing.[18] Indeed, while initially caught flat-footed by the digital revolution, the Cuban government has now begun to implement a comprehensive strategy of using the Internet and its related social media tools for surveillance and promoting its agenda online.

Government companies play the dominant role in deploying new technologies and are determined to retain power over ICTs by controlling infrastructure and access and censoring critical online voices. Cuban civil society, while benefiting from the slow but steady development of ICTs and increasing access to the Internet, is still at a distinct disadvantage relative to the government in its popular reach. Moreover, it continues to fight an uphill battle against the norm of popular conformity to the state-sanctioned rules of the game. This explains why in Cuba's case it is still more appropriate to talk about shared spaces, networks, or arenas (Geoffray 2015) rather than a digital public sphere or civil society properly speaking. Finally, with a new, much more reliably aggressive administration in the White House, the Cuban state will find it easier to enforce conformity without having to resort to open coercion, while independent civil society actors will find their spheres of influence once again limited just as they gain greater voice via digital technologies. As the editors of this volume remind us in their introduction with reference to Matthew Hindman's work on the once almost evangelical belief in digital democracy: "there is a big difference between who posts and who gets read" (2009). Likewise, in Cuba's emergent digital ecosystem, there is a big difference between who speaks and who is heard.

Notes

1. In 2008 Raúl Castro legalized the private ownership of cell phones. During the next decade the number of cell phone users went from 330,000 to more than 4.5 million in 2017 or from roughly 3 percent to almost 40 percent of the Cuban population (ONEI 2018).

2. Few could have predicted that a U.S. president would be able to make such a visit with the embargo still in place and the Castros still in power.

3. After his visit to Cuba, Schmidt wrote a blog post on Google+ where he said that "the Internet of Cuba is trapped in the 1990s" and came out against the embargo (Oppmann 2014). The key figure in Google's Cuba deals was Brett Perlmutter, Google's head of Cuba strategy and operations. For several years he has worked quietly building trust with ETECSA officials and increasing Google's presence on the island.

4. To indicate his revolutionary bona fides, Kcho made the password to connect to his hotspot "aquinadieserinde" (here no one is giving up). After the Google deal in 2016 the password was changed to "abajoelbloqueo" (down with the embargo).

5. Author interview with Cuban tech professional, April 2017. All translations from Spanish are my own.

6. Even after the 3G rollout in December 2018 and with Nauta Hogar home Internet plans available, the majority of Cubans still connect to the Internet via their schools and workplaces due to the high cost of mobile and ADSL Internet access.

7. The Cuban convertible peso (CUC) was introduced as the country's second currency in 1994 and was meant for foreigners to pay for luxury goods and services. Cubans' salaries, buses, trains, and prices in local shops and markets have been denominated in the national peso (CUP) for the most part. However, expensive imported durables and electronics such as refrigerators and computers are sold exclusively in CUCs. The conversion rate is 25 CUP = 1 CUC.

8. Recent research indicates that there are three separate, independent *casas matrices* in Havana and one in Santiago, each with its own extensive, island-wide distribution network that includes both regional and local *paqueteros* (distributors). See the extensive dossier on the *paquete* recently edited by Jennifer Cearns and published by *Cuban Studies* 50 (2021).

9. Author interview with a computer scientist and *paquete* consumer, April 2017.

10. Cuba's highest peak located in the Sierra Maestra mountain range in eastern Granma province.

11. Author interview with *paquete* distributor, November 2016.

12. A one-hundred-megawatt power transmitter is strong enough to establish a small private network at a home or guesthouse. However, it does not provide enough power to keep an extensive street network operational.

13. Ávila first became famous in Cuba after a video of his 2008 public confrontation of National Assembly President Ricardo Alarcón went viral. Answering Ávila's question about travel restrictions for Cubans, Alarcón justified them, saying that if everyone was able to board an airplane the sky would get congested (Sánchez 2017). The exchange marked Ávila's life, as he has been under constant scrutiny since. A few days before I

interviewed Ávila, his house was raided by state security who confiscated computers, cell phones, and many of his other belongings. That time he was accused of "reception" of a stolen item, a charge he claimed was completely fabricated.

14. Author interview Ávila, April 2017.

15. Author interview with blogger, April 2017.

16. *Entre la espada y la pared* is literally translated as "between the sword and the wall," the English equivalent would be "between a rock and a hard place."

17. Think of the perfectly named "sheep" in Orwell's *Animal Farm* loudly bleating out "four legs, gooood; two legs, baaad" in unison each time another animal dares to question the status quo or Napoleon's authority.

18. Titled simply "Fidel," this special thirty-third edition appeared in December 2016 and is the only one to date that the government allowed its editors to physically print and distribute: https://vistarmagazine.com/vistar-magazine-n-33/.

References

14ymedio. 2019a. "Cientos de clientes se quejan de Etecsa por fallas en datos móviles." August 26, 2019.

14ymedio. 2019b. "Etecsa cobra pero bloquea los mensajes por el 'No' y la abstención en el referendo." January 7, 2019.

Alvarez, Marcelino J. 2016. "Cuba will fail at tourism, but it can win at creative technology." *Medium*, May 26, 2016.

Arego, Alberto. 2019. "Cuba ingresa más de 12.5 millones de CUC por la venta de paquetes 3G en el primer mes." *Cibercuba*. January 18, 2019.

Cearns, Jennifer, ed. 2021. "Packaging Cuban Media: Communities of Digital Sharing in Cuba and its Diaspora." *Cuban Studies* 50.

Cibercuba. 2018. "Cuba distribuirá por 10 pesos Mi Mochila, el Paquete Semanal oficialista." *Cibercuba*, April 5, 2018.

CPJ (Committee to Protect Journalists). 2019. "Critical news websites blocked during Cuba referendum vote." February 25, 2019.

Cuba Internet Task Force. 2019. "Final Report."

Deibert, Ronald and Rafal Rohozinski. 2010. "Liberation vs. Control in Cyberspace." *Journal of Democracy* 21 (4): 43–57.

Diamond, Larry. 2010. "Liberation Technology." *Journal of Democracy* 21 (3): 69–83.

Duckitt, John. 1989. "Authoritarianism and group identification: A new view of an old construct." *Political Psychology* 10 (1): 63–84.

Dunn, Kris. 2014. "Authoritarianism and Intolerance Under Autocratic and Democratic Regimes." *Journal of Social and Political Psychology* 2 (1): 220–241.

El Toque. 2019. "Etecsa: Bajen Los Precios Del Internet." June 9, 2019.

Ernesto, Miguel. 2019. "Sube, the Cuban Uber Created by Three Entrepreneurs who Dreamed of Map." *Panamerican World*, January 14, 2019.

Escobar, Luz. 2017. "El 'paketito,' un rival clandestino para el 'paquete.'" *14ymedio*, May 5, 2017.

Figueredo Reinaldo, Oscar, L. Eduardo Domínguez, and Edilberto Carmona Tamayo.

2018. "ETECSA: Internet en el móvil a partir del seis de diciembre." *Cubadebate*, December 4, 2018.

Gaceta Oficial. 2019a. Resolución 98, "Reglamento para el empleo de redes de telecomunicaciones inalámbricas de alta velocidad en las bandas de frecuencias de 2.4 Ghz Y 5 Ghz." May 29, 2019.

Gaceta Oficial. 2019b. Resolución 99, "Reglamento para las redes privadas de datos." May 29, 2019.

García Martínez, Antonio. 2017. "Inside Cuba's D.I.Y. Internet Revolution." *Wired*, July 26, 2017.

Gaventa, John. 1980. *Power and Powerlessness: Quiescence and Rebellion in an Appalachian Valley*. Oxford: Clarendon Press.

Geoffray, Marie Laure. 2015. "Transnational Dynamics of Contention in Contemporary Cuba." *Journal of Latin American Studies* 47: 223–249.

González, Orlando. 2019. "Estas fueron las 3 aplicaciones 'made in Cuba' más populares de 2018." *CubaNet*, January 3, 2019.

Harris, Johnny. 2015. "Castro hates the internet, so Cubans created their own." *VOX Magazine*, October 12, 2015.

Henken, Ted A. 2021. "The Opium of the *Paquete*: State Censorship, Private Self-Censorship, and the Content Distribution Strategies of Cuba's Emergent, Independent Digital Media Startups." *Cuban Studies* 50.

Henken, Ted A. and Sjamme van de Voort. 2015. "From Cyberspace to Public Space? The Emergent Blogosphere and Cuban Civil Society." In *A Contemporary Cuba Reader: The Revolution Under Raúl Castro*, edited by Philip Brenner, Marguerite Rose Jiménez, John M. Kirk, and William M. LeoGrande. Lanham, MD: Rowman & Littlefield. 99–110.

Hindman, Matthew. 2009. *The Myth of Digital Democracy*. Princeton, NJ: Princeton University Press.

Ibarra, Glenda B. 2019. "Funcionarios Cubanos En Twitter: Entre Bloqueos Y Torpeza." *El Toque*, March 5, 2019.

IPS (Inter-Press Service). 2019. "Superó la 3G disponibilidad tecnológica de Etecsa." March 6, 2019.

Jiménez Enoa, Abraham. 2017. "How Cuba's Government Fights Negative News." *Havana Times*, August 27, 2017.

Lai, Eric. 2009. "Software libre! Cuba develops own free Linux called 'Nova.'" *Computer World*, February 12, 2009.

Laughlin, Kirk. 2017. "Stubborn and Paranoid: Cuba's Determined Effort to Never Emerge as a Nearshore Hub." *Nearshore Americas* blog, August 29, 2017.

Lukes, Steven. 2005. *Power: A Radical View*. Second edition. New York: Palgrave Macmillan.

MacKinnon, Rebecca. 2012. *The Consent of the Networked: The Worldwide Struggle for Internet Freedom*. New York: Basic Books.

Mexidor, Deisy F., Marina Menéndez, and Jean G. Allard. 2011. "Operación surf." *Granma*, March 8, 2011.

Michaelsen, Marcus. 2018. "Authoritarian Practices in the Digital Age—Transforming

Threats to Power: The International Politics of Authoritarian Internet Control in Iran." *International Journal of Communication* 12: 3856–3876.

Miroff, Nick. 2012. "How the U.S. keeps Cuba offline." *Global Post*, June 27, 2012.

Morozov, Evgeny. 2011. *The Net Delusion*. New York: Public Affairs Press.

Novak, Matt. 2016. "Silicon Valley Has Officially Invaded Cuba." *Gizmodo*, March 22, 2016.

ONEI (Oficina Nacional de Estadística e Información). 2018. "Tecnología de la información y las comunicaciones. Indicadores seleccionados."

Oppmann, Patrick. 2014. "Google executives promote Internet freedoms on Cuba visit." CNN, June 30, 2014.

OONI. 2019. "Cuba blocks independent media amid 2019 constitutional referendum." February 26, 2019.

Parker, Emily. 2014. *Now I Know Who My Comrades Are: Voices from the Internet Underground*. New York: Sarah Crichton Books.

Press, Larry. 2011. "The dictator's dilemma," *The Internet in Cuba* blog, February 15, 2011.

Press, Larry. 2015. "El paquete update—Cuba's largest private employer?" *The Internet in Cuba* blog, September 14, 2015.

Press, Larry. 2019. "Cuba's new WiFi regulations—a step forward, backward or sideways?" *The Internet in Cuba* blog, June 13, 2019.

Pujol, Eduardo P., Will Scott, Eric Wustrow, and J. Alex Halderman. 2017. "Initial Measurements of the Cuban Street Network." *Proceedings of IMC*. https://jhalderm.com/pub/papers/snet-imc17.pdf

Rød, Espen Geelmuyden and Nils B. Weidmann. 2015. "Empowering Activists or Autocrats? The Internet in Authoritarian Regimes." *Journal of Peace Research* 52(3): 338–351.

Rodríguez, Jorge Enrique. 2017. "Kcho Estudio Romerillo, cerrado sin explicaciones y por tiempo indefinido." *Diario de Cuba*, February 10, 2017.

Roig-Franzia, Manuel. 2014. "USAID effort to undermine Cuban government with fake 'Twitter' another anti-Castro failure." *The Washington Post*, April 3, 2014.

Sánchez, Yoani. 2017. "Eliécer Ávila, el 'hombre nuevo' que se volvió opositor." *14ymedio*, April 8, 2017.

Sánchez, Yoani and Reinaldo Escobar. 2016. "Cubacel censura los SMS con las palabras 'democracia' o 'huelga de hambre.'" *14ymedio*, September 3, 2016.

SNET. 2016. "Código de sanciones SNET." http://fontanar1.cubadebate.cu/wp-content/uploads/2016/09/Reglas-Generales-y-Código-de-Sanciones-de-snet.pdf.

SNET. 2019a. "Comunicado Oficial Equipo Administración SNET-Intercambio con MINCOM," June 12, 2019.

SNET. 2019b. "Fin de Snet." Facebook, accessed August 10, 2019.

Trump, Donald. 2017. "Remarks by President Trump on the Policy of the United States Towards Cuba." June 16, 2017.

Tucker, Duncan. 2015. "Cuba Presents a Unique Value Proposition Within the Nearshore IT Market." *Nearshore Americas* blog, July 30, 2015.

Tufekci, Zeynep. 2017. *Twitter and Tear Gas: The Power and Fragility of Networked Protest*. New Haven: Yale University Press.

Wamsley, Laurel. 2017. "Google Spins Up Its First Servers In Cuba." NPR, April 27, 2017.

Wikileaks. 2009. "Reversing the Cut-Off of U.S. Internet Messaging Services in Cuba." https://wikileaks.org/plusd/cables/09HAVANA473_a.html

4

Ghost in the Machine

The Incompatibility of Cuba's State Media Monopoly with the Existence of Independent Digital Media and the Democratization of Communication

ALEXEI PADILLA HERRERA AND ELOY VIERA CAÑIVE

In Cuba, the state exercises a monopoly over the ownership and control of both television and radio, as well as virtually all national and provincial newspapers and magazines, to say nothing about book publishing or academic journals. Despite the vast differences in ideology and the particular exclusion criteria used by private media in capitalist countries vs. those who control the mass media in Cuba (the Cuban Communist Party, abbreviated PCC in Spanish), the result is the same: the marginalization of independent actors, sectors of society, and ideas that challenge the hegemonic interests of national elites.

The nature of the political regime established in Cuba after 1959 does not allow—much less give—legal protection to movements or groups, which (independent of but not necessarily in opposition to the state) fight to democratize the island's media ecosystem, including cyberspace. Aware that Cuban state media do not embrace the diversity and pluralism present in today's society, citizens and/or groups with diverse political goals, ideologies, identities, and positions have recently taken advantage of greater Internet access to create spaces of communication and channels of information that challenge the PCC's monopoly on public discourse.

This chapter attempts to demonstrate that the laws that regulate freedom of speech and the press in Cuba are in fact designed to limit citizens' rights to information and communication. We contrast the notions of freedom according to the Marxist-Leninist conception, and especially the functions that Vladimir I. Lenin attributed to the press in a socialist regime, with fundamental principles of democratic communication. We argue that the dissatisfaction of citizens with the state media monopoly, the consultative processes convened by former president Raúl Castro (2008–2018), and the gradual spread of Internet access have led to the emergence of an increasingly vigorous non-state digital media ecosystem. We also argue that these independent digital media have become consolidated as a viable alternative for information and debate. Finally, we analyze the new Cuban Constitution, approved in a February 2019 plebiscite, arguing that the state's unfolding "Social Communication Policy" together with its "Comprehensive Computerization Policy"[1] only serve to perpetuate the state monopoly over the media and deny legal recognition to Cuba's emergent non-state digital media. However, we also posit that the "ghost" of Cuba's independent digital media will continue to haunt the "machine" of state socialism despite that machine's continued refusal to grant it legal recognition.

The Public Sphere in Socialist Regimes

Historically, socialist regimes have limited the exercise of political and civil rights that would, theoretically, allow for the constitution of public spheres independent from the state, such as freedom of association and assembly. In Cuba, for almost six decades the communist political system, socialist economic model, and Marxist-Leninist ideology have defined the configuration, objectives, and operation of the different spheres that make up the island's public sphere, including the media. Beyond its singularities, the Cuban regime retains aspects present in the former countries of the European socialist bloc and the Soviet Union: A one-party system, a state ideology, no recognition of the legitimacy or relevance of political pluralism, political control and repression of independent civil society groups, and a legal state monopoly on both print and digital media.

Despite this will to power, we can trace an evolution of the Cuban regime into an "early post-totalitarianism" (Linz and Stepan 1996), characterized by the erosion of the regime's structures and people's faith in the ideological postulates that constitute its base. However, many aspects of classical totalitarianism persist, including state control of most economic activities, references to Soviet constitutionalism, the militarized conception of politics and relations between the state and civil society, as well as the physical, institutional, and symbolic violence against dissidents (Chaguaceda and Padilla 2016). Despite the restrictions on political and civil rights, Cuba's public sphere has recently begun to flourish formed by a diversity of independent, sui generis discussion forums (Rittersporn, Rolf, and Behrends 2003; Killingsworth 2012) and some digital media.

This sort of unofficial public sphere in Cuba operates outside state institutions (and often against the law) and is characterized by independent communication channels and the circulation of a far more critical, sometimes oppositional discourse. Active in this area have been the Catholic magazine *Espacio Laical*, its forum *En Diálogo*, the suspended independent think tank *Cuba Posible*, the *Observatorio Crítico* network, the *Estado de Sats* project, and more recently, the independent digital media projects *El Toque*, *Periodismo de Barrio*, *14ymedio*, *Tremenda Nota*, and *El Estornudo*. Here, we must also mention *Diario de Cuba*, *Café Fuerte*, *CubaNet*, and *CiberCuba*, which are digital sites managed from the extensive Cuban diaspora.

Marxism-Leninism, Individual Freedom, and the Democratization of Communication

In his critique of Soviet Marxism, Herbert Marcuse (1975) argues that the socialization of the private sphere sought to replace the freedom of the individual as a private person with the duty of the individual as a member of society. Then society, represented by the Soviet state, defined the value of freedom and its limits and transformed it into an instrument for the achievement of political outcomes. According to the Hungarian scholar László Révész (1977), in Marxist-Leninist theory full freedom is only realized when communism becomes the global hegemonic system. Until then, the intellectual freedom of individuals remains strictly subordinated to the interests of socialist society. In the stage of socialist construction, intellectual freedom is only granted to society as a whole, represented by the party, due to the lack of harmony between individual interests and social interests. Yovchuk (Révész 1977) also recognizes that the "transitory limitation of freedom" is a necessity due to the influences of bourgeois ideology and the constant threats of imperialism. In Cuba, this justification for the limitation of individual freedoms is often referred to as *una plaza sitiada* or "a state of siege."[2]

The single-party political model plays a fundamental role in the Marxist-Leninist conception of freedom. The Communist Party is considered the representative of the "most conscious and progressive element of the people," therefore, the full application of its guidelines is assumed to achieve the emancipation of all individuals. Expressing the will of the people, the interpretation of all legal acts, and all transcendental decisions, corresponds, first of all, to the Party (Révész 1977). This implies an ideological homogenization of citizens—from the real "I" to the communist "we." From the foregoing, we can conclude that Marxist-Leninist principles, in a socialist regime, only recognize freedom as subordinated to the consolidation and advancement of the new regime. Those who intend to fight (or often simply question) this emerging regime are denied their right to freedom.[3] As Fidel Castro declared in his well-known "Words to the Intellectuals" speech in June 1961, "Within the Revolution, everything; against the Revolution, no rights at all."[4]

Lenin theorized a centralized press model oriented by the following fundamentals. The press serves the ruling class (the Party). The state must control the financing of newspapers. Newspapers are part of political organizations and their journalists are political activists. As a result of these postulates, the subordination of the press to the Party bureaucracy created a media system that reflected only the ideas of the Party elite (not the masses, socialist or otherwise) (McNair 1991; see also Natvig in this volume).

Unlike the instrumental and strategic character that Marxism-Leninism attributes to the media, Alfonso Gumucio argues that communication plays a role in the articulation of all human rights and, as a relational process, also includes the exchange of information, "the sharing of knowledge, and recognition of differences." This Bolivian scholar points out that "the right to communication articulates and encompasses all other relative rights, such as access to information, freedom of opinion, freedom of expression, freedom of dissemination" (2013, 1).

Furthermore, Saffon argues that the right to communication encompasses the rights to freedom of the press, expression, and access to information. At the same time, it is distinguished from them because it responds to the needs of the digital era. Among the specific needs that societies must equitably guarantee are both access to information and citizen participation in the processes of information and knowledge production, as a "means to the materialization of essential democratic values." The recognition of communication as an autonomous right implies the assumption of fundamental values such as the "plurality of sources of information and worldviews; the formation of an informed public opinion, and respect for the privacy and dignity of people" as well as "participation in spaces of dialogue, in the construction of consensus and in decision making" (2007, 20–24).

In that sense, the exercise of the right to communication should not depend exclusively on the economic possibilities of people to access and/or produce information, or on their political affiliations or ideological convictions. States must invest resources to guarantee the access of all citizens to information and communication technologies (ICTs) regardless of their economic means or political beliefs. These academic and civil society contributions about the right to communicate and the principles that should guide any initiative for the democratization of communication, demonstrate the incompatibility of Marxist-Leninist notions about freedom, rights, and the role of the media in even a minimalist democratic regime.

Cuba's Constitutionally Controlled Press: A Soviet Import

Leninist postulates about the role of the press in a socialist regime constituted the theoretical basis of the press model adopted in Cuba after the triumph of the Revolution in 1959. Although Fidel Castro initially supported the rights that protected journalists, rejected persecution for ideological reasons, and warned that when the first newspaper was closed, no one else could feel safe (Fernández 2016), the radicalization of the Revolution significantly altered the country's media ecology. To attenuate the hegemony of the private press, in the first months of 1959, the newspapers *Revolución* (run by the July 26th Movement), *Hoy* (run by Cuba's traditional communist party, the Popular Socialist Party), and *Verde Olivo* (the magazine of the Rebel Army), became the main media pillars of the new revolutionary government (García 2013). Subsequently, between 1959 and 1960 the government nationalized all media companies and secured control of all existing electronic and print media (Padilla and Santos 2018). The media became a strategic element for the defense of the regime and, consequently, the presence of dissident voices was limited (Valdés 2009).

In 1965, the media (managed to some extent autonomously by the leadership of the various revolutionary political organizations) were reorganized and unified around the PCC. This resulted in the merger of the previously independent newspapers *Revolución* and *Hoy*, now called *Granma*—the official organ of the Central Committee of the PCC—leaving no doubt about its political affiliation. Two weeks later, *Juventud Rebelde*, the official newspaper of the Union of Young Communists (UJC) was founded. The Department of Revolutionary Orientation of the PCC (now called the Ideological Department) then began to direct propaganda actions and the agenda of the now entirely state/party-run media (García 2013).

Faced with political isolation[5] and pressing economic problems by the late 1960s, exacerbated by the U.S. embargo, Cuba began a process of alignment with the Soviet Union. In 1972, the island joined the Council of Mutual Economic Assistance (CAME), a decision that strengthened political and economic relations between Moscow and Havana. During the so-called institutionalization process that followed the adoption of a Soviet-style communist constitution in 1976, the revolutionary government implemented a system of social, political, and economic organization that echoed the Soviet one (Rojas 2015), adopting Soviet Marxism as an official ideology (Acanda 2002).

The 1976 Constitution (followed most recently by the new one approved in February 2019) legalized decisions taken at the First Congress of the PCC. For example, article 3 declared the subordination of the state and society to the Communist Party.[6] Influenced by the instrumentalism of Marxism-Leninism, the Constitution recognized in its article 53 the freedoms of "speech and the press," but specifically subordinated them to "the ends of the socialist society." That same article established that the "mass media" could only be state or social property and used for the "exclusive service of workers and the interest of society," thus ensuring the material conditions for the exercise of these freedoms while simultaneously outlawing the very existence of private media (Cuba 2010, 64).

Beyond the Constitution, many other legal norms regulate citizens' rights to communication. For example, the Penal Code, adopted in 1987, criminalizes any act that prevents the exercise of constitutionally defined freedom of speech and the press (article 291). Article 103 punishes with up to four years in prison the distribution of an ill-defined "enemy propaganda," understood as the dissemination of false news or "malicious predictions" that cause alarm, discontent, or public disorder. This legal norm also considers "contempt" the threat, slander, insult, or any other act that "outrages or offends" any public authority or official in the exercise of their functions. If the said contemptuous act affects the heads of the executive and legislative branches, the members of the Council of State and Council of Ministers, or the deputies of the National Assembly, the punishment can reach up to three years in prison (article 144). Finally, article 204 condemns anyone who defames or publicly despises the institutions of the Republic, the political, mass, or social organizations of the country, or the heroes and martyrs of the nation (Cuba 1987). Of course, the vagueness of the above statutes is such that they are open to arbitrary application and thus hang like a sword of Damocles over the press, chilling free speech.

The limits to press freedom were reinforced in 1999 when the Cuban parliament passed Law 88 for the Protection of National Independence and the Cuban Economy (known popularly as *la ley mordaza*, or "the gag law"). The legislation criminalizes behaviors that seek to achieve the "objectives of the Helms-Burton Act" (the most recent legal iteration of the U.S. embargo). One of the actions penalized by the norm and especially aimed at the control of free expression and the press is "the collaboration of any citizen with foreign publications or media" (Cuba 1998). This so-called gag law remains in force and was applied in 2003 when Cuban courts condemned seventy-five peaceful opponents, including several independent journalists, to long prison terms. It continues to serve as a major deterrent to the expansion of the activities of various non-state digital media (Henken 2017).

Internet and the Dynamization of Public Space in Cuba

In Cuba, the main antecedents of non-state digital media were the various press agencies and independent journalism organizations created beginning in 1989. These years also saw the emergence of various print publications either sponsored or given protection by the Catholic Church. Despite their ostensibly ecclesiastical character, they also constituted alternative spaces of information, analysis, and discussion about the economic, political, and social problems that affected the country (Crahan 2013). According to Sarah Beaulieu (2013), the birth of Cuban independent journalism took place with the foundation of the Association of Journalists of Cuba (APC) in 1989. This organization grouped together dissident journalists who had been expelled from the official media but who still wished to practice their profession. In 1992, APC became the Cuban Independent Press Agency (APIC). Throughout the 1990s, several other agencies and groups of independent journalists were created. However, it was not until the slow spread of Internet access in Cuba during the second decade of the twenty-first century that a new stage for Cuban non-state media and independent journalism began.

Cuba connected to the Internet in 1996 through an American satellite. The lack of investment in infrastructure and the fear that the United States could use the Internet to empower organizations that opposed the socialist regime led the Cuban government to prioritize access for the official media, universities, and other research institutes, companies, state institutions, international hotels, and embassies, while the general population was left largely disconnected (Recio 2014; Press, this volume). In June 2009, Resolution 99/2009 of the Ministry of Information, Technology, and Communications authorized the Cuban Postal Service (Correos de Cuba) to offer Internet service to the general population, in facilities authorized for that purpose (MIC 2009). In 2015, the Cuban government launched the "National Strategy for the Development of Broadband Connectivity Infrastructure in Cuba." The inaugural document declared the need to take advantage of ICTs as tools for the development of knowledge, the economy, and political and ideological activity. The strategy recognized that at the time Cuba lacked broadband and that only 3.4 percent of households and 25 percent of the population had Internet access (Ministry of Communications 2015).[7] However, in the last three years (2016–2019) Internet connectivity has been systematically increasing.[8]

Despite the legal restrictions and fragmentation of the public sphere in Cuba, the digital environment is consolidating as a space for dispute and attacks, where important debates take place and conflicts and consensus are expressed among various sectors of civil society. Blogs, websites, and social networks like Twitter and Facebook are indicators of the plurality of views and demands present in contemporary Cuban society. Debates between government supporters, opponents, and critics are shaping an often belligerent but increasingly pluralistic public sphere (Henken 2011; Henken and Van de Voort 2015). The spread of Internet access has multiplied both formal and informal channels of news distribution, social networks have proliferated, and a vigorous blogosphere has emerged (roughly between 2005–2014), distributed among numerous sectors (Garcés 2013; Henken, this volume).

The Cuban blogosphere was characterized by the visibility of issues poorly addressed by the official media, an interrogation of national reality, the construction of spaces for dialogue, denunciation, and pressure on issues of public interest (Díaz 2015). In 2010, to compete against the visibility of critical actors and political opponents, journalists, political cadres, and public officials were instructed to create their own blogs and set up profiles on social networks such as Facebook and Twitter to "defend the Revolution" (Rafuls 2015). In 2013, Reflejos was created, a state platform to host Cuban blogs. However, the terms of use for this platform imposed prior censorship by considering "counterrevolutionary" any content that, in their often arbitrary opinion, denigrates "the work of the Revolution," its leaders, the government, the state, the work of official political organizations, security forces, and the official media (Reflejos 2013).

As of 2014, the digital environment entered a new phase, where some digital newspapers and magazines managed from within the island (but independently from state institutions) emerged and began to successfully compete against state media (Marreiro 2014). They are better structured, more deliberate and professional projects than their predecessors in the blogosphere, with more financial and human resources, but have yet to achieve the size or scope of traditional media since they are exclusively digital platforms in a still largely offline country where it is unlawful to print and distribute independent publications (Rafuls 2015). Despite these severe restrictions, the following independent digital media outlets emerged in Cuba after 2014:

OnCuba, Cuba Posible, Periodismo de Barrio, El Toque, El Estornudo, and *14ymedio*. Most of them have been nourished by the collaboration of academics and activists (critics and/or opponents) residing in Cuba and abroad, but many have also benefited from (or even depended upon) the open and unapologetic collaboration of reporters with journalism degrees from Cuban universities.

In authoritarian regimes, communicative interactions in the virtual environment can challenge censorship that attempts to control or repress public opinion (Habermas 2008). However, the initial enthusiasm that foresaw the Internet as a contributor to the democratization of authoritarian regimes has diminished. Although nondemocratic regimes recognize the importance of Internet access for economic development, they maintain limitations to online communication. These regimes—as Cuba's computerization and communication policies show—also have the ability to repress critical and oppositional speech in cyberspace. They can also develop even more effective techniques of surveillance given the growing ubiquity of social media and its related data trail in citizens' everyday lives.

In addition to the use of technological tools for censorship and surveillance, the practice of self-censorship is a key element for maintaining citizens' "discursive discipline" in the virtual environment.[9] The ambiguity of the law in relation to public discourse plays a major role in the induction of self-censorship, by cultivating a sense of collective paranoia that causes citizens to limit the scope of their individual expression. State security bodies, state media, and official blogs not only monitor the development of independent media, but also question its legality and very legitimacy. For example, during 2016 the state press published several articles accusing specific indie media outlets of being mercenaries serving the United States regime change strategy in Cuba (Sánchez Serra 2016)—even after President Barack Obama had publicly forsworn such a policy during his state visit to the island.

The journalist Elaine Díaz, a graduate and former professor of digital media at the University of Havana's School of Communication and founding director of the independent digital newspaper *Periodismo de Barrio*, has said that "most communicators who work for or collaborate with non-state media have suffered threats or been besieged on social networks [by trolls] using fake profiles" (Díaz 2018). In 2016, young, state-employed journalists at the weekly *Vanguardia* (a provincial, party-controlled newspaper) reported having been subject to a "preventive witch hunt," for having collaborated with independent media.[10] This repression has also impacted scholars who have collaborated with non-state media. For example, in 2016 jurist Julio A.

Fernández Estrada, a contributor to *OnCuba*, was fired from the University of Havana after publishing a critical article about Obama's visit to Cuba (Pentón 2016). Due to their publications in non-state media, professors José Raúl Gallego and René Fidel González lost their jobs at the University of Camagüey and the University of Oriente, respectively (Padilla and Santos 2018). As there is no specific legal norm that regulates the exercise of journalism in Cuba, Cuban authorities have applied the Penal Code to criminalize the work of independent journalists. Sol García and Henry Constantín, journalists for the magazine *La Hora de Cuba*, and Ileana García, a collaborator at *CiberCuba*, have been threatened with a criminal prosecution for committing the crime of "usurpation of legal capacity" (Freedom House 2018), which prohibits "carrying out acts pertaining to a profession the exercise of which one is not duly prepared" (Cuba 1987).

The removal of content on platforms managed by state entities is another method used to silence critical voices. For example, in February 2016, the monitoring group at the official blogging platform *Reflejos* announced the closure of the *Proyecto Arcoiris* blog (Rainbow Project, an autonomous collective that fights for the rights of the LGBT community). The reason for the ban was a critical post stating that none of those responsible for the repressive policies against homosexuals carried out during the 1960s—including President Raúl Castro himself—had ever apologized (IPS 2016). Another method used by authorities is blocking specific websites so they cannot be accessed from Cuba. A report published by the Open Network Interference Observatory confirmed that in 2017 at least forty-one sites were blocked in Cuba (Xynou, Filastò, and Basso 2017). Most were critical news and opinion websites such as *14ymedio*, *MartíNoticias*, *Diario de Cuba*, *Cubaencuentro*, and *Café Fuerte* (*MartíNoticias* 2018). Between December 2017 and August 2019, ETECSA blocked access to *CiberCuba*'s multimedia platform and the digital magazines *El Estornudo*, *Tremenda Nota*, and *ADN Cuba*.

The independent and fairly moderate think tank *Cuba Posible* has also suffered frequent repressive actions. In 2018, the directors claimed that the project's website was affected by several cyberattacks. In addition, smear campaigns executed from informal blogs, surveillance, and direct pressures against its directors, Roberto Veiga and Lenier González, were intended to interrupt the publication of new content on their website. Finally, on May 20, 2019, *Cuba Posible*'s directors reluctantly announced the project's dissolution due to the actions of a "set of actors" that used "all the mechanisms and methods of powerful institutions to dismantle our work" (*Cuba Posible* 2019).

The commitment of the PCC to control critical discourses in cyberspace was confirmed by a video leaked in the summer of 2017,[11] where then first vice president Miguel Díaz-Canel (now Cuba's president) commented that he was analyzing a "flood of proposals and projects with subversive content" on a daily basis. He mentioned the existence of magazines, websites, and digital platforms linked to "stereotypes of cultural warfare" that hid their true intentions of confronting the government "behind a critical posture of freedom of expression." Regarding *OnCuba*, owned by Cuban-American businessman Hugo Cancio and afforded foreign press credentials in Cuba, Díaz-Canel said they would close it down because it was "very aggressive with the Revolution." Aware of the controversy that the closure of the *OnCuba* site would generate, Raúl Castro's heir apparent expressed openly: "They may say that we censor, but everyone censors." Such a statement not only shows the nature of Cuba's authoritarian regime, but also reveals the role of the government in monitoring the emergent alternative media and planning repressive actions against independent digital outlets that are considered "enemies of the state."

In addition to the increasing diversification and professionalization of the Cuban independent digital communication ecosystem, the facts presented above illustrate that for the Cuban regime, non-state media refuse to subordinate themselves to the informational and communicational policies of the PCC and therefore must be contained, defamed, and/or repressed. Their very existence is considered fundamentally incompatible with the current system of government and monopolistic control over the mass media. In the final section below, we argue that Cuba's "Social Communication Policy," the new Constitution, and Decree Law 370 "On the Computerization of Cuban Society," all perpetuate a model that recognizes the right of citizens to communication only when the exercise of that right is restricted to within the parameters of the ideological and political goals set by the Communist Party. That is, political subordination trumps editorial independence and professional journalistic standards.

Unfolding State Policies of Social Communication in Cuba

The "Guidelines of Economic and Social Policy of the Party and the Revolution" (hereafter "Guidelines" or *Lineamientos* in Spanish), approved in 2016 during the Seventh Congress of the PCC, are the official playbook for all future economic reforms initiated by former president Raúl Castro. These "Guidelines" are also supra-legal mechanisms which serve as a basis for the drafting of new legal norms in a wide array of Cuban institutional life. Such norms are prepared by the "Permanent Commission for Implementation and Development of the Guidelines," and in most cases, are not published or publicly debated, preventing citizen participation in the conception of the specific norms that affect their interests.

For example, the government's slowly unfolding "Comprehensive Policy for the Computerization of Society" (*La política integral para la informatización de la sociedad*) as well as its "Social Communication Policy" resulted from this process controlled by the "Permanent Commission." The first policy defines information and communication technology (as a strategic sector for economic growth, recognizes that ICTs will impact the development of society, and defines as fundamental principles: 1) the need to understand ICTs as weapons for the defense of the Revolution that guarantee security in cyberspace against threats, risks, and attacks of any nature; 2) the improvement of human capital; and 3) the promotion of citizens' access to ICTs (Puig 2017). For its part, the so-called Social Communication Policy, approved by the Political Bureau of the PCC and described by President Díaz-Canel (2018) in his closing speech at the tenth UPEC Congress in 2018, considers access to information, communication, and knowledge public goods and citizens' rights; it gives greater authority to media managers; defends the values and symbols of the nation, and is guided by respect for diversity (Rodríguez 2018). According to the president, the document also understands communication as a "strategic resource of the state and government," defines the exclusively public nature of the broadcasting and communication industry, and recognizes that the media can be the property only of the state or society—never in private hands, a stipulation explicitly included in the newly amended Cuban Constitution as well (see below).

Although the text of this Social Communication Policy was not available to the public until July 17, 2019, on December 2, 2018, *Periodismo de Barrio* published an editorial titled: "What Does the New Cuban Communication Policy Say?"[12] The editorial was accompanied by a leaked file purported to be a draft of the policy itself, which, according to the editors, was anonymously sent by e-mail to 105 recipients. Considering the published document, the various statements of President Díaz-Canel—in the leaked video of August 2017 and in his speech at the 2018 UPEC congress—other nuances emerge. The document is blind to the growing complexity of the Cuban media ecosystem because it equates the emergence and consolidation of island-based alternative digital media with the existence of "private digital media hosted outside the country that develop an agenda with hypercritical and demobilizing intentionality."[13] It also affirms that the only relationship between these media and the country is based on the "participation of young Cuban professionals in their management." Finally, it understands the existence of this alternative digital media as a mere function of its journalists receiving foreign payments (the implication being that they are simply "mercenaries" working for the "Yankee dollar").

Making use of its remarkable influence on the Cuban state, the PCC labels as "private" a wide variety of emergent media outlets, many of which actually opt for management models closer to cooperativism, public interest entities, or pro bono nonprofits. The vast majority also operate from within Cuba and rely on multiple kinds of international cooperation (not U.S. government funding) to finance their activities. The willful ignorance of the PCC about the domestic nature of these alternative news outlets fulfills a double objective: the use of current ordinances (Law 88 and the Penal Code) to penalize journalists who work with these independent digital outlets when deemed necessary and to legally justify using the label of "mercenaries" for all new alternative media outlets that support their work with foreign funding—whatever the source.

The postulates and principles of both policies (computerization and social communication) were the basis of recently approved legal norms and others that are still in the process of being developed. The first of these norms was the new Constitution itself, which took effect on April 10, 2019. Although it introduced new positive features related to communication such as the right to habeas data,[14] it does not prohibit prior censorship or set limits on state interference in the communication field. Neither does the Constitution promote citizen participation in the design and execution of public policies of social communication or in media management. Indeed, the drafters of the new Constitution did not seem to understand the need to expressly recognize the right of Cuban citizens, in conditions of material equality and without discrimination on political or ideological grounds, to information and knowledge allowing citizens' free speech without leaving them at the mercy of the laws of the market.

Communication rights were addressed exclusively only in the dimensions that had been imposed by partisan policies defended by the Drafting Commission of the legal text. In that sense, communication was understood merely as an exchange of information among people; hence its inviolability was declared in article 50, including that of private correspondence. Rights to freedom of thought, conscience, and expression were also recognized by the Constitution, but the limitation of the ways of maximizing and extending those rights indicates that the protection offered by the Constitution is limited to the private sphere. For example, the right to freedom of the press was essentially delineated within the same framework established by the

1976 Constitution. Press freedom is thus conditioned to "compliance with the law and the purposes of the socialist society" (Cuba 2019, article 55), a stipulation that allows present and future legislation and their subsequent interpreters to establish limits to the exercise of this right.

Interestingly, when defining that only the "fundamental" means of production of the media have to be "state or social property," the drafters of the Constitution implicitly recognize the possible existence of media that operate under other relations of property or forms of management (private, cooperative, nonprofit, etc.). However, this apparent abandonment of the absolute state monopoly over the media is but a chimera since the Constitution itself establishes as a state prerogative the "principles of organization and operation of all media." If these principles became a legal norm they would follow the guidelines established by the previously described Social Communication Policy that states unequivocally: "Radio, television, print media, and other mass media, as well as the technological platforms used by them, are state or socially owned and cannot be the object, in any instance, of private property" (Cuba 2010, article 53). Thus, the possible legalization of non-state, alternative, or independent media in Cuba will not depend on the laws (or even the Constitution), but on the media policy of the PCC that by declaring all alternative media "private" automatically vetoes any possibility of legal recognition.

Finally, on July 4, 2019, Cuba's national register, *La Gaceta Oficial*, published Decree Law 370, "On the Computerization of Society in Cuba," a rule much more concerned with ensuring national security, defending the state's "technological sovereignty," and controlling citizen communications than with protecting the individual's right to communication. Neither does it guarantee the creation of open technological and social spaces for the free exchange of information, debate, and dialogue. On the contrary, this decree law reproduces the objectives already laid out in the Computerization Policy described above and recognizes that the norm seeks to "consolidate the use and development of ICT as an instrument for the defense of the Revolution and strengthen political defense and cybersecurity against threats, attacks, and risks of all kinds" (article 5). Most notably, the decree law also criminalizes the hosting of any "site" by Cuban citizens on a server located in a foreign country. This measure provoked an immediate, broad-based outcry among all sectors of the alternative media (Díaz 2019) and culminated in a confusing clarification of questionable legality (via a tweet no less) from the Ministry of Communications, which assured the public that the new rule did not refer to blogs or media outlets but exclusively to sites that intended to provide services in Cuba.[15]

Likewise, it criminalized "spreading, through public data transmission networks, information contrary to social interest, morality, good customs and the integrity of people." This statute, unlike that related to hosting on foreign website servers, has recently been used to penalize independent communicators and political opponents. For example, the independent journalists Iliana Hernández, Boris González Arenas, and Camila Acosta have been detained under this measure, suffering the confiscation of their computers and telephones and hit with fines of three thousand Cuban pesos or $100 (*14ymedio* 2020; Matienzo 2020).

Behind such vague and undefined concepts lies an intention contrary to the basic principles of modern law. Instead of law acting to limit the absolute powers of the state, these legal mechanisms become instruments for the state to defend itself against the scarce powers of citizens. Moreover, this is happening in a virtual environment where the party-state has so far been unable to control the growing expressions of citizens. The great overlap between the policies designed by the PCC and the legislation formulated by institutions clearly demonstrates the influence of this organization in the development of state functions. More than influence, the existing fusion in Cuba between the state, the government, and the Communist Party is evident. Under these conditions, it is impossible to guarantee the democratic and diverse exercise of the right to communication and the expression of citizenship.

Conclusion

The socioeconomic and political changes that have taken place in Cuba between 2008 and 2019, the gradual expansion of Internet access, and the popular consultations promoted by former president Raúl Castro contributed to the configuration of a more diverse and plural public space. In this context, debates have multiplied and a wide variety of alternative digital media outlets emerged and became consolidated. However, the mere existence of nonstate communication vehicles directly contradicts both the Leninist postulates outlined above and the policies that guide the operation of the state media monopoly, ideologically subordinated to the PCC. This contradiction is reflected in the behavior of the state when implementing various control mechanisms such as selective blocking of websites, content surveillance, and repression against journalists and other collaborators of alternative media.

Although the Social Communication Policy approved by the PCC and the new Constitution give lip service to the recognition of important rights, they simultaneously ignore the fundamental principles required of a democratizing process of communication. The policy recognizes only two forms of ownership: state and socialist. This ignores the growing complexity of the Cuban media ecosystem and denies legal recognition to the diverse array of alternative digital media whose forms of management and operating principles exceed the narrow limits imposed by these forms of ownership. Without legal guarantees or defensible rights, the existence of alternative media operating from Cuba will depend on the arbitrary tolerance and goodwill of the government and the ever-resourceful efforts of its managers. However, the spaces for debate and alternative media mentioned here constitute forms of "communicational citizenship" and establish the right to communicate by unapologetically exercising it. Regardless of each one's particular thematic focus, political orientation, or editorial line, all are examples of civil society's participation in the struggle for the democratization of communication in Cuba. But this struggle takes place under the most precarious of economic and political conditions, always exposed to the surveillance and harassment of political authorities, state security, and their acolytes in the official media.

Notes

1. In Spanish, "La Política de Comunicación Social del Estado y la Política Integral para la Informatización de la Sociedad."

2. The full original quote—often attributed to St. Ignatius of Loyola, the founder of the Society of Jesus (the Jesuits)—is "En una plaza sitiada, la disidencia es traición" or "In a plaza under siege, dissidence is treason." See editorial "Nuevas dinámicas para los disidentes en Cuba," *The New York Times*, December 28, 2014.

3. The previous reflection challenges the thesis that claims that the cause of restriction of certain fundamental civil and political rights is the so-called state of siege, which results from constant confrontation with the United States. The authors cited show that the limitations on freedom of expression, assembly, association, and the press are not a singularity of the Cuban case, but a characteristic of all Soviet-style regimes, and that external factors are important but secondary. That is, the restriction of freedoms was a necessary condition for the normal reproduction and maintenance of the regime, not just a response to external threat.

4. This quote is usually reduced to its first, most famous line: "Within the Revolution, everything; against the Revolution, nothing." However, Castro goes on to clarify that his meaning pertains to the rights of the Revolution vs. the lack of the right for non- and especially counter-revolutionaries to question it:

> Nothing against the Revolution, because the Revolution has its rights also, and the first right of the Revolution is the right to exist, and no one can stand against the right of the Revolution to be and to exist. No one can rightfully claim a right against the Revolution. Since it takes in the interests of the people and signifies the interests of the entire nation. I believe that this is quite clear. What are the rights of revolutionary or non-revolutionary writers and artists? *Within the Revolution, everything;*

against the Revolution, no rights at all. (Emphasis added; see the original Spanish-language speech here: www.cuba.cu/gobierno/discursos/1961/esp/f300661e.html)

5. In January 1962, a resolution of the Organization of American States (OAS) suspended the participation of the Cuban government in the Inter-American System. Canada and Mexico were the only two countries in the Hemisphere that did not break diplomatic relations with the Castro government at the time.

6. In Cuba, as in former European socialist countries, civil society is subordinated to the objectives of the Party. In this regard, Révész points out that the dubious invocation of the interests of the "working people" in socialist constitutions allows a virtually unlimited interpretation of the interests of the people's vanguard, that is, the Party (1977).

7. National Strategy for the Development of Broadband Connectivity Infrastructure in Cuba. Available at: https://oncubanews.com/wmag/wp-content/uploads/2015/06/Estrategia-Nacional-de-la-Banda-Ancha-en-Cuba.pdf.

8. Chapter 1 of this volume, by Larry Press, provides a statistical breakdown of the growth of Internet access during these years.

9. In this context, it is quite ironic that the so-called weekly package (*el paquete semanal*) is often celebrated as a kind of renegade digital black market for successfully undermining the Cuban government's monopoly over the mass media while its compilers and distributors simultaneously practice systematic self-censorship of all content to prevent the circulation of political and pornographic content (Henken 2021).

10. "Carta de protesta del Comité de Base de la UJC del diario *Vanguardia*," 2016.

11. The video was first published by Estado de Sats: "Response to Miguel Díaz-Canel, part 2," YouTube, August 21, 2017. Available at: https://goo.gl/C7rKcm.

12. https://www.periodismodebarrio.org//2018/12/que-dice-la-nueva-politica-de-comunicacion-cubana/.

13. The original Spanish reads: "medios digitales privados alojados fuera del país que desarrollan una agenda de contenidos con intencionalidad hipercrítica y desmovilizadora."

14. According to Wikipedia, "Habeas data is [. . .] designed to protect [. . .] the data, image, privacy, honor, information, self-determination, and freedom of information of a person. Habeas data can be sought by any citizen [. . .] to find out what information is held about his or her person [who] can request the rectification, actualization, or destruction of the personal data held." Last accessed on August 11, 2019 (https://en.wikipedia.org/wiki/Habeas_data).

15. The tweet can be found here: https://twitter.com/MINCOMCuba/status/114723294 1099147265?s=19. Nevertheless, the Constitution gives authority to interpret the laws first to the National Assembly and the Council of State and second to the Supreme Court—not an individual ministry. Moreover, the Constitution establishes a normative hierarchy whereby a decree law can only be modified by a norm of equal or higher order.

References

14ymedio. 2020. "Iliana Hernández, víctima del Decreto 370." February, 10, 2020. Accessed March 12, 2020. https://twitter.com/mendeley_com/status/864947989797896194 and https://www.14ymedio.com/nacional/Iliana-Hernandez-victima-Decreto_0 _2818518128.html.

Acanda, Jorge. 2002. *Sociedad civil y hegemonía*. Havana: Centro de Investigación y Desarrollo de la Cultura Cubana "Juan Marinello."

ADN Cuba. 2020. "Órganos represivos cubanos multan con 3000 pesos a la periodista Camila Acosta." March 28, 2020. Accessed March 12, 2020. https://adncuba.com/noticias-de-cuba/organos-represivos-cubanos-multan-con-3000-pesos-la-periodista-camila-acosta.

Beaulieu, Sarah. 2013. "Política cultural y periodismo en Cuba: Trayectorias cruzadas de la prensa oficial y de los medios independientes (1956–2013)." Ph.D. dissertation. Department of Philosophy and Letters, University of Granada.

"Carta de protesta del Comité de Base de la UJC del diario *Vanguardia*." 2016. Accessed July 15, 2019. https://www.14ymedio.com/nacional/Vanguardia-Comite_de_Base-UJC_CYMFIL20160702_0001.pdf.

Chaguaceda, Armando and Alexei Padilla. 2016. "Frente al Gran Hermano: emergencias y disputas en el universo mediático cubano." *Puente Democrático*, Year 14, No. 60: 3–8. Accessed July 15, 2019. https://www.cadal.org/publicaciones/archivo/?id=9352.

Crahan, Margaret. 2013. "The religious media in Cuba." Paper presented at the VII Encuentro Internacional de Estudios Sociorreligiosos, Havana.

Cuba Posible. 2019. "Comunicación de la directiva de Cuba Posible." May 20, 2019. Accessed July 22, 2019. https://cubaposible.com/comunicacion-la-directiva-cuba-posible.

Cuba. 2019. "Constitución de la República." Accessed March 25, 2020. http://www.granma.cu/file/pdf/gaceta/Nueva%20Constitución%20240%20KB-1.pdf.

Cuba. 1987. Código Penal. Asamblea Nacional del Poder Popular.

Cuba. 1999. "Ley 88 de 1999 de la Protección de la Independencia Nacional y la Economía de Cuba."

Cuba. 2010. *Constitución de la República de Cuba*. Havana: Editora Política.

Díaz, Elaine. 2014. "Derechos sexuales en Cuba: del silencio a la red." Master's thesis. School of Social Communication, University of Havana.

Díaz, Elaine. 2015. "Un sui generis ecosistema de consumo e intercambio de información." *Cuba Posible*, February 4, 2015. Accessed July 15, 2019. https://cubaposible.com/un-sui-generis-ecosistema-de-consumo-e-intercambio-de-informacion-2-aa5-2-4-5-2/.

Díaz, Elaine. 2018. "Medios emergentes en Cuba: desafíos, amenazas y oportunidades." *SembraMedia*, January 11, 2018. Accessed February 15, 2018. https://www.sembramedia.org/medios-emergentes-en-cuba/.

Díaz, Elaine. 2019. "Cuba aprueba ley que multa a ciudadanos por alojar sitios web en servidores extranjeros." *El Toque*, July 5, 2019. Accessed July 10, 2019. https://eltoque.com/cuba-multa-ciudadanos-web-servidores-extranjeros/.

Díaz-Canel, Miguel. 2018. "Discurso de Díaz-Canel en la clausura del X Congreso de la UPEC." *Granma*, July 15, 2018. Accessed August 6, 2019. http://www.granma.cu/cuba/2018-07-15/discurso-de-diaz-canel-en-la-clausura-del-x-congreso-de-la-upec-15-07-2018-11-07-42.

Faiola, Anthony. 2019. "Cubans are using social media to air their grievances—and the government is responding, sometimes." *The Washington Post*, July 7, 2019. Accessed October 17, 2019. https://www.washingtonpost.com/world/the_americas/cubans-are-using-social-media-to-air-their-grievances--and-the-government-is-responding-sometimes/2019/07/07/01b3cba2-912e-11e9-956a-88c291ab5c38_story.html.

Fernandes, Sujatha. 2006. *Cuba Represent! Cuban Arts, State Power, and the Making of New Revolutionary Cultures*. Durham, NC: Duke University Press.

Fernández, Waldo. 2016. *La imposición del silencio. Cómo se clausuró la libertad de prensa en Cuba, 1959–1960*. Madrid: Hypermedia Ediciones.

Freedom House. 2017. "Freedom on the Net, Cuba 2017." Accessed September 20, 2019. https://freedomhouse.org/report/freedom-net/2017/cuba.

Freedom House. 2018. "Freedom on the Net, Cuba 2018." Accessed September 20, 2019. https://freedomhouse.org/report/freedom-net/2018/cuba.

Gallego, José. 2019. "Apagones en Cuba: Gobierno calla, los ciudadanos hablan." *El Toque*, July 16, 2019. Accessed September 20, 2019. https://eltoque.com/apagones-en-cuba-el-gobierno-calla-los-ciudadanos-hablan/.

Garcés, Raúl. 2013. "La prensa cubana, en la encrucijada." *Cubahora*, March 15, 2013. Accessed September 20, 2019. https://www.cubahora.cu/sociedad/la-prensa-cubana-en-la-encrucijada.

García, Julio. 2013. *Revolución, socialismo, periodismo. La prensa y los periodistas cubanos ante el siglo XXI*. Havana: Editorial Pablo de la Torriente.

Geoffray, Marie Laure. 2015. "Transnational Dynamics of Contention in Contemporary Cuba." *Journal of Latin American Studies* 47 (2): 223–249. Accessed September 23, 2019. https://doi.org/10.1017/S0022216X15000048.

Gumucio, Alfonso. 2012. "El derecho a la comunicación: articulador de los derechos humanos." *Razón y palabra*, No. 80. Accessed August 23, 2019. http://www.razonypalabra.org.mx/N/N80/V80/00_Dagron_V80.pdf

Habermas, Jürgen. 2008. "Comunicação política na sociedade mediática: o impacto da teoría normativa na pesquisa empírica." *Líbero*. São Paulo, Year XI, No. 21: 9–22. Accessed March 12, 2016. https://casperlibero.edu.br/wp-content/uploads/2016/10/artigo_habermas.pdf.

Henken, Ted A. 2011. "A Blogger's Polemic: Debating Independent Cuban Blogger Projects in a Polarized Political Context." *Cuba in Transition* 21: 171–185. Accessed September 25, 2019. https://www.ascecuba.org/asce_proceedings/a-bloggers-polemic-debating-independent-cuban-blogger-projects-in-a-polarized-political-context/.

Henken, Ted A. 2017. "Cuba's Digital Millennials: Independent Digital Media and Civil Society on the Island of the Disconnected." *Social Research* 84 (2): 429–456. Accessed September 25, 2019. https://muse.jhu.edu/article/668229/pdf.

Henken, Ted A. 2021. "The Opium of the *Paquete*: State Censorship, Private Self-Censorship, and the Content Distribution Strategies of Cuba's Emergent, Independent Digital Media Startups." *Cuban Studies* 50.

Henken, Ted A. and Sjamme Van de Voort. 2015. "From Cyberspace to Public Space?: The Emergent Blogosphere and Cuban Civil Society." In *A Contemporary Cuba Reader: The Revolution Under Raúl Castro*, edited by Philip Brenner, Marguerite Rose Jiménez, John M. Kirk, and William M. LeoGrande, 99–110. Lanham, MD: Rowman & Littlefield.

IPS 2016. "Proyecto Arcoíris contra la censura en la plataforma Cubava.cu." February 16, 2016. Accessed November 14, 2019. https://www.ipscuba.net/archivo/proyecto-arcoiris-contra-la-censura-en-la-plataforma-cubava-cu/.

Killingsworth, Matt. 2012. *Civil Society in Communist Eastern Europe: Opposition and Dissent in Totalitarian Regimes*. London: EPCR Press.

Linz, Juan J. and Alfred Stepan. 1996. *Problems of Democratic Transition and Consolidation: Southern Europe, South America, and Post-Communist Europe*. Baltimore, MD, and London: The Johns Hopkins University Press.

MacKinnon, Rebecca. 2012. *The Consent of the Networked: The Worldwide Struggle for Internet Freedom*. New York: Basic Books.

Marreiro, Flávia. 2014. "Continuity and Change in the Cuban Media Under Raúl Castro." Reuters Institute for the Study of Journalism, University of Oxford. Accessed April 19, 2019. https://reutersinstitute.politics.ox.ac.uk/sites/default/files/201710/Continuity_and_change_in_the_Cuban_media_under_Raul_Castro.pdf.

Martí Noticias. 2018. "Cuba bloquea *El Estornudo*, periodista insta a no 'naturalizar' la censura." February 27, 2018. Accessed April 19, 2019. https://www.radiotelevisionmarti.com/a/el-estornudo-publica-nota-al-censor-bloqueado-dentro-cuba/163039.html.

Matienzo, María. 2020. "Boris González Arenas: 'Me vinieron a buscar muy decididos a llevarme.'" *Cubanet*, February 7, 2020. Accessed March 14, 2020. https://www.cubanet.org/destacados/boris-gonzalez-arenas-me-vinieron-a-buscar-decididos-a-llevarme/.

Marcuse, Herbert. 1975. *El marxismo soviético*. Madrid: Alianza.

McNair, Brian. 1991. *Glasnost, Perestroika and Soviet Media*. London & New York: Routledge.

MIC. 2009. Resolución No. 99/ 2009. Accessed July 8, 2017. https://www.mincom.gob.cu/sites/default/files/marcoregulatorio/r_99_-09_ecc_proveedor_de_internet_al_publico_.pdf.

Ministry of Communications, 2015. Accessed July 8, 2017. http://www.ventanapolitica.cu/sites/default/files/estrategia-nacional-de-la-banda-ancha-en-cuba.pdf.

Padilla, Alexei. 2016. "A mídia religiosa na esfera pública em Cuba: o papel desempenhado pela revista *Espacio Laical*." Master's thesis, Department of Philosophy and Human Sciences, Minas Gerais Federal University, Brazil.

Padilla, Alexei and David Corcho. 2018. "Entre el Partido y la Ley: normas que rigen el sistema comunicativo en Cuba." In *Derechos humanos: realidades y desafíos en Cuba*, edited by Marlene Azor, 89–127. Madrid: El Barco Ebrio.

Padilla, Alexei and Caio D. Santos. 2018. "A revolução dos millennials: o confronto simbólico entre a mídia alternativa e o monopólio midiático-estatal Cubano." Paper presented at the 28th Meeting of the Groups of Communication Research, 41st Brazilian Congress of Communication Sciences. Accessed September 14, 2019. http://portalintercom.org.br/anais/nacional2018/resumos/R13-0799-1.pdf.

Pentón, Mario. 2016. "'No es porque escribas, es por lo que escribes,' le dicen a profesor despedido en Cuba." *El Nuevo Herald*, October 26, 2016. Accessed October 15, 2019. https://www.elnuevoherald.com/noticias/mundo/america-latina/cuba-es/article110541172.html.

Puig, Yaima. 2017. "Consejo de Ministros aprueba políticas para la informatización de la sociedad y para otros importantes sectores." *Cubadebate*, March 3, 2017. Accessed July 8, 2017. http://www.cubadebate.cu/noticias/2017/03/03/consejo-de-ministros-aprueba-politicas-para-la-informatizacion-de-la-sociedad-y-otros-importantes-sectores/#.X0e_iMhKjIU.

Rafuls, Gretel. 2015. "Participación política en red: La blogosfera y la toma de decisiones de la esfera pública en Cuba: cuatro casos de estudio entre 2010–2015." Master's thesis, School of Communication, Autonomous University of Barcelona.

Recio, Milena. 2014. "La hora de los desconectados." *Crítica y emancipación*, No. 11.

Reflejos. 2013. "Condiciones de uso." Accessed April 5, 2015. https://cubava.cu/condiciones-de-uso/.

Révész, László. 1977. *Ley y arbitrariedad en la prensa soviética*. Pamplona: Ediciones Universidad de Navarra.

Rittersporn, Gabor T., Malte Rolf, and Jan C. Behrends, eds. 2003. *Sphären von Öffentlichkeit in GesellschaftensowjetischenTyps/Public Spheres in Soviet-Type Societies*. Frankfurt am Main: Peter Lang.

Rodríguez, Andrea. 2018. "Cuba loosens grip on media, allows for more independent reporting." *The Christian Science Monitor*, June 21, 2018. Accessed September 12, 2019. https://www.csmonitor.com/World/Americas/2018/0621/Cuba-loosens-grip-on-media-allows-for-more-independent-reporting.

Rojas, Rafael. 2015. *Historia mínima de la revolución cubana*. Mexico City: Fondo de Cultura Económica.

Saffon, María. 2007. "El derecho a la comunicación: un derecho emergente." Centro de Competencia en Comunicación para América Latina. ANDI, Brasília, Brazil. Accessed September 12, 2019. http://www.andi.org.br/documento/el-derecho-la-comunicacion-un-derecho-emergente.

Sánchez Serra, Oscar. 2016. "Matthew: humanismo, transparencia y manipulación." *Granma*, October 13, 2016. Accessed July 23, 2016. http://www.granma.cu/cuba/2016-10-13/matthew-humanismo-transparencia-y-manipulacion-13-10-2016-00-10-02.

The New York Times. 2014. "Shifting Dynamics for Cuba's Dissidents. Editorial, December 28, 2014. Accessed September 23, 2019. https://www.nytimes.com/2014/12/28/opinion/sunday/shifting-dynamics-for-cubas-dissidents.html.

Tufekci, Zeynep. 2017. *Twitter and Tear Gas: The Power and Fragility of Networked Protest*. New Haven, CT: Yale University Press.

Valdés, Juan. 2009. *El espacio y el límite. Estudios sobre el sistema político cubano*. Havana: Instituto Cubano de Investigaciones Culturales "Juan Marinello," Ruth Casa Editorial.

Xynou, Maria, Arturo Filastò, and Simone Basso. 2017. "Measuring Internet Censorship in Cuba's Park Nets." OONI, August 28, 2017. Accessed September 23, 2019. https://ooni.org/documents/cuba-internet-censorship-2017.pdf.

5

The Press Model in Cuba

Between Ideological Hegemony and the Reinvention of Civic Journalism

CARLOS MANUEL RODRÍGUEZ ARECHAVALETA

In recent decades, the connection between journalistic models and political dynamics (regime persistence or change) has captured the attention of scholars in many different fields. However, it is difficult to define a precise causal relationship between media reforms and democratization processes, or even point to specific models of journalism that encourage social or political change (Repnikova 2017a; Zielonka 2015; Gross and Jakubowicz 2013; Hallin and Mancini 2012; Voltmer 2006; Esser and Pfetsch 2004; Price, Rozumilowicz, and Verhulst 2002; Curran and Jin-Park 2000). In developing countries with authoritarian, hybrid, or transitional regimes, journalism may intensify popular discontent and drive the search for long-term potential alternatives, putting pressure on authorities (Randall 1993). However, the collapse of the Soviet press system in Russia gave rise to a new, local press, with a strong commercial and sensational character, often influenced by its alliances with emerging state and business elites (Vartanova 2012). In contrast, investigative journalism in China has become a significant driver for the stability and adaptability of the Communist regime, *not* for its transformation or replacement (Repnikova 2017b). In short, the political impact of the press system on the process of democratization varies greatly from country to country and depends on complex institutional, socio-structural, and micro-level factors (Lugo-Ocando and Garcia Santamaria 2015; Roudakova 2012; Kitzberger 2009).

Given this context, this chapter addresses the dynamics of change of journalism in Cuba today, a process which is closely connected to the recent *actualización* (updating) of the socialist regime. The current status of the relationship between the Cuban media and the socialist state (the press and the party) is worth highlighting given the continued threat of regime change from the United States under the Trump administration and the particular values of the regime's socialist ideology. I am particularly interested in addressing Cuba's new independent online journalism, the emergence of which is associated with the de-professionalization of the ideologically oriented socialist press model (the official state-party media), the recent expansion of Internet access on the island, and the state's ongoing information control and surveillance strategies.

Given the limited economic reforms enacted since 2008 under Raúl Castro, the state continues to strongly control market freedoms and insists on outlawing private, non-state media outlets, a policy which dramatically hinders the development of independent online journalism. However, this is happening in a context of great uncertainty vis-à-vis the future, ideological polarization, and the confrontation between the state and the emerging independent journalistic model. Indeed, the foundations of these new professional digital journalistic practices, their emerging culture, and dynamic roles, show that the state's ideological press model is being reevaluated. Civic journalism is increasingly recognized as a necessary antidote to the stale, propagandistic state-party model, a state of affairs which in turn drives the development of what I call a "transnational containment sphere" that deepens and dynamizes deliberations about Cuba's future.

Journalism in Authoritarian, Hybrid, and Transitional Regimes

The connection between journalism and the persistence-change dynamic in different political regimes has been an issue of intense scholarly focus. The regulatory emphasis of the press models in Western liberal democracies has been challenged by a growing interest in the dynamic relationship among the press, the state, and the audience in developing countries with authoritarian, hybrid, or transitional regimes (Repnikova 2017b; Zielonka 2015; Gross and Jakubowicz 2013; Hallin and Mancini 2012; Voltmer 2006; Esser and Pfetsch 2004; Price, Rozumilowicz, and Verhulst 2002; Curran and Jin-Park 2000). Unlike the "transitology" approach, which assumes a simple, unidirectional political change from the binary perspective of authoritarianism to liberal democracy, the authors cited here insist that it is essential to understand the media in such regimes within their respective historical, national, and geographic contexts. Doing this requires focusing more on the varied processes of change toward an uncertain future rather than on a presumed teleological vision of history that has a predetermined or desired endpoint (Meng and Rantanen 2015; Roudakova 2012).[1]

Comparative research in countries like Russia and China reveals the interdependence of the state and the market, showing that the presumed antagonism between them in the West is overblown. The state has always required a strong media market, but one that is also politically "functional." The market grew within the parameters set by the state, while the state control mechanisms evolved as media commercialization grew (Repnikova 2017b; Roudakova 2012; Vartanova 2012; Tong and Sparks 2009). In post-Soviet Russia after 1992, for example, the reforms of economic liberalization and the elections provoked an institutional change whose results were uncertain and characterized by the penetration of emerging economic and political actors in the competition for political capital. Business entrepreneurs partnered with political actors in order to meet their mutual goal of becoming the ruling elite that then controlled the media. On the other hand, the transition from the socialist economy to the market economy did not enable rapid economic growth or increase the standard of living of society, while the political activism that characterized the 1980s turned into a social apathy that prioritized individual success and hedonism over collective solutions during the 1990s (Vartanova 2012).

Moreover, the privatization of the media in 1992 did not create a more democratic political communication model. Rather, the political sponsorship and manipulation of the press and its characteristic sensationalism only increased. As McNair wisely says, "The result was the creation of a hybrid (hyper)capitalist system" (quoted in Vartanova 2012, 126), with the bureaucratic state as the main economic agent and the resulting integration of the emerging market and the state into a so-called media industrial complex, which heavily influenced the subsequent policies of the media system. In this context, it is possible to understand the constrained role of the media in creating independent political parties in Russia, since the state played a critical role in the political game (Vartanova 2012). Instead of political parallelism (Hallin and Mancini 2007), we observe the phenomenon of what might be called "political-media cronyism" (Kitzberger 2009; Roudakova 2008). On the other hand, journalism was transformed from being a creative or investigative pursuit to a profession focused principally on advertising and public relations. Vartanova (2012) recognizes the paradoxical coexistence of media independence, given the growing decentralization and autonomy of press offices of state agencies and political parties and the scarce speech freedom resulting from growing political centralization. This was combined with a restructuring of the public sphere under the new "national idea" and the pernicious use of journalism as an instrument for political campaigns and self-censorship in press offices.

The Chinese case in particular could serve as a benchmark to help us evaluate the new dynamics of Cuban journalism. Zhao (2012) proposes communism, nationalism, and developmentalism as the cultural and ideological foundations of the Chinese Communist Party (CCP), emphasizing how the restoration of the Confucian principle of the state's liability has enabled it to instill shared values though moral education and its use as a social control vehicle (2012, 152). During the first Maoist revolutionary period (1940–1975), the Chinese press was part of a general system that promoted ideological mobilization and propaganda managed by the state-party. However, since 1978 the CCP reached an ideological agreement around the goals of reform and openness. In the publishing and cultural industries, the state dramatically reduced its role by subsidizing instead of directly running their operations, and offered them the right to private property. However, the ideology of the state-party served to build different versions of Marxism and socialism in order to create "socialism with Chinese characteristics," with the media serving as a moral guide for the people and the mechanism for economic development and social change.

The state monopolized the production and delivery of news and information, as well as the ownership of big print and broadcasting media. However, the total or partial private ownership of peripheral areas in the media and cultural industries, including film production, television entertainment, advertising, and distribution, was part of a complex state policy (Zhao 2012) that ensured that the state would retain control of the media system and its ideological orientation, without monopolizing production and distribution. Institutions within the state-party took charge of commercialization, set the market dynamics inside the existing structures, and created different control mechanisms like media licensing and journalistic certifications, instituting a professional code of ethics for journalists, and imposing a program of mandatory "ideological" entertainment (Zhao 2012).

However, the growing commercialization of the economy granted the media greater administrative and financial autonomy and enabled it to focus on new targets in order to capture consumer interest. At the same time, the structural management of the media by specialized government agencies enabled a more predictable and stable relation between the state and the media, while also attracting significant interest from private capital. Thus, the regulation of the media gained a growing technocratic character ruled by a market logic that indirectly challenged party ideology (Winfield and Peng 2005; Chan and Qui 2002). China's new journalistic practices are starting to change the perception journalists in the country have about the role of the party's ideological legitimacy for some kinds of public services as a

The Cuban Socialist Press Model

The continuity of authoritarian regimes depends on how they enhance the different mechanisms of ideological legitimacy. As Schedler said, "all their acts of power are a *stage performance of power*; they are *domination acts* and *communication acts* at the same time" (2016, 72, emphasis in the original). Thus, the control and manipulation of the public sphere will aim to amplify the perspectives that support the regime and minimize the critical voices, restricting citizens' capacity to imagine and write about an alternative political future (Dukalski 2017). Thus, of utmost importance are the state's legitimacy and the hegemony of its ideological discourse, which are constantly reconstructed and challenged through the media (Roudakova 2012).

Analyzing the official press model in Cuba requires recognizing that it supports the state's ideological legitimization. Its guidelines, which are inherited from classic Leninist style, are the "Thesis and Conclusions of the First Congress of the Communist Party of Cuba" (PCC), which defined "the bodies of the party and the state [. . .] as important instruments of the ideological and political struggle, [. . .] for educating, informing, guiding, and mobilizing" (PCC 1976).[2] The Union of Cuban Journalists (UPEC) was founded in 1963,[3] but the institutionalization of the official press model did not take place until the First PCC Congress in 1975. In concordance with the socialist ideology adopted by the PCC and the Cuban state, this press model became a political project: a close-knit society, a single party, and a press that impeded the U.S.'s subversive strategies and the internal opposition (García Luis 2014, 86).

It is also crucial to recognize that the longstanding U.S.-Cuba conflict revolves around the ideological discourse of the Cuban state. The key components of this discourse are 1) the insoluble link between state socialism, the homeland (*la patria*), and the nation; 2) national unity (and unanimity) in the event of war, threat, or aggression; and 3) socialism as the only political option (Bobes 2007). Between 1976 and 1992, the regime's legitimacy was based on two fundamental ideas: revolutionary nationalism and Marxism-Leninism. However, as a result of the fall of "really existing socialism" in the Soviet Union, Marxism-Leninism ceased being used as state ideology, while revolutionary nationalism was reinforced as the regime's central doctrine (Rojas 2006).

Research based on interviews with journalists who work in state media outlets have shown that the constant threat from the United States and the destabilizing effect of the Soviet policy of glasnost (openness and transparency)—at the end of the eighties—created a siege mentality, impacting the self-regulation of journalists (García Luis 2013). The constant fear that "anything we say is misinterpreted based on this threat" provokes a defensive attitude of discretion and secrecy from Cuban journalists. In addition, the complex relationship between journalists and their sources—usually state and party officials—undermines their professional role, converting them into mere government/party spokespersons. This in turn transforms any information they may report into ideological propaganda given their common reliance on official press releases written by party functionaries, not journalists (Franco Senén 2016). It would seem that the role of the Cuban press is to create a harmonious, functional, and successful national reality when faced with the chaos, injustice, and violence of the outside world. With unparalleled precision one Cuban journalist defines it with these words: "we have frequently substituted reasoned judgment with propaganda" (Garcés Corra 2013).

Investigations of the most relevant variables impacting journalists' performance reveal that a growing precarity, the erosion of working conditions, and de-professionalization are among the biggest threats (Garcia Santamaria 2018b; Franco Senén 2016; Elizalde 2013). According to a 2013 study conducted by the UPEC, 1,143 members joined between 2008 and 2012 but only 395 (34 percent) of them had a journalism degree (quoted in Elizalde 2013, 69). Additionally, it was estimated that just 50 percent of official print media staff had any journalistic training, which was still better than the 40 percent rate for radio (Garcés Corra 2013). This training deficit could be attributed to inefficient press management boards, spontaneity, and the profession's willful decision-making style (Franco Senén 2016).

But excessive external regulation has been the main point of contention for Cuban journalists. In effect, the Cuban socialist press model—institutionalized based on the Soviet experience—was designed as an instrument of ideological legitimation for the state. Thus, the journalistic profession—its practices, culture, and social roles—are imposed by the orientations and degrees of the Ideological Department of the Central Committee of the PCC, a political organization that supersedes the exercise of journalistic editorial control.[4] Political reliability and a commitment to "socialist ideology" condition the exercise of journalism, leading to progressive de-professionalization

(Garcia Santamaria 2018a). It is worth noting that the very leadership of the Cuban state has recognized these limitations by publicly highlighting the dissemination "of boring, improvised, and superficial materials,"[5] and the tense relationship between the PCC's official ideologues and the directors of the media.[6]

On the other hand, beyond the constraints imposed by external regulation, journalists in Cuban state media are also deeply concerned about the effects of self-regulation (Franco Senén 2016; Elizalde 2013; García Luis 2013). Two stances seem to be fundamental here: the state seems to be ruled by the principle that says the director of the media outlet "as a rule, should publish, and as an exception, consult," so they decide "what can be published and what cannot." However, empirical research shows that journalists are aware of the "anesthetic" effects on one's thinking and capacity of analysis of the verticality and mistrust caused by an excessive external regulation, and of a more efficient self-regulation based on "ethical norms, philosophical principles, political options, and professional culture" (García Luis 2013). "Squaring this circle" has proven impossible because despite the constant discursive references of the state leadership to the need for change, Cuban journalism continues to be constrained by the excessively bureaucratic structural conditions of the partisan Soviet press model and the restrictive conditions on the creative autonomy of state-run media agencies (Garcia Santamaria 2018b).

The limitations of the state journalism model described above reflect certain inconsistencies in the mechanisms of ideological legitimation of the Cuban state. These inconsistencies could certainly jeopardize the hegemony of the official discourse and the ideological consensus rearticulated around the socialist project (Elizalde 2013). The control of this state-centric public sphere—conceived of as a space where the ideals of symmetry, order, and consensus are revealed and promoted by the state itself—enables the state to simultaneously silence any independent questioning or citizen deliberation. However, recently under new conditions an interactive and interdependent space is opening up on the island between official journalists and new independent digital media outlets, a novel development which is driving the creation of a Cuban digital public sphere (Geoffray and Chaguaceda 2014). This is the focus of the following section.

Independent Online Journalism

When the transition from authoritarian/totalitarian regimes occurs, it is necessary that the civil society actors with autonomy, associative resources, and the ability to mobilize, develop and justify credible alternative collective projects (from the bottom up). On the other hand, the political actors inside the authoritarian elite (from the top down) should create a space of negotiation over the minimal and mutually beneficial conditions of engagement (Przeworski 1994). Both scenarios imply the establishment of dialogue and communication (Downing 1996), a condition clearly not met in today's Cuba.

Tarrow emphasizes the role of the symbolic-cultural environment for a social movement, and defines the interactive framework as the driver that either accentuates severity and injustice in a social situation or redefines as unjust or immoral what was once considered unfortunate but tolerable (1997, 215). A key activity of any social movement then will be embedding grievances within global frameworks that identify injustice, assign blame, and suggest solutions (Tarrow 1997). On the other hand, Melucci (1999) stresses that the construction and negotiation of a collective identity is a precondition of any cost-benefit calculation, and the perception of injustice as such. For his part, Glenn (2001) analyzes how social movements lodge complaints concerning injustice and identity when also trying to activate support networks, concluding that a sense of injustice should be combined with an identity, which will define the "us versus them" and provide a sense of agency or awareness of the possible changes and of effective individual action. Such framing will have an important persuasive, associative, and mobilizing effect, aligning this with the identities of preexisting networks.

The elements mentioned above allow me to evaluate the democratizing potential of the public sphere, understood as the space where a set of controversial topics for an audience interested in deliberative practices gains visibility and is publicized. "Publicized" in this sense means giving certain topics and certain communicative interaction practices a public meaning, thus the importance of differentiation and autonomy in the diverse currents that make up a democracy. In authoritarian regimes, which are defined by their "structural uncertainty" (Schedler 2016), it becomes very expensive for the state to (re)produce its legitimacy, hence the significance of its constant efforts to control information and monopolize the public sphere (Dukalski 2017). In such a context, information is not a public good but instead a strategic ideological asset used to ensure the hegemony of the state's self-legitimizing discourse, minimizing the visibility of the communicative dynamics that produce alternative autonomous agendas and interactive frameworks that create more "day-to-day" agendas that threaten the state's information monopoly.

Certainly, the Cuban state has long been able to control the public sphere and thus minimize any potential threat to its ideological hegemony.

Nevertheless, as Geoffray (2013) correctly demonstrates, the liberalization of Internet starting in 2008, and the subsequent development of certain virtual activities, enabled the convergence of certain "arenas" of debate that had previously been isolated from one another. She also recognizes that there were three such "micro-arenas" of debate in Cuba by the mid-2000s: dissidents, state-sheltered intellectuals, and independent artists and intellectuals.[7] The first, reduced to a fragmented and limited "micro-space," was then characterized by its local invisibility and illegality. The second was characterized by the limited debate among critical-minded peers of certain problematic aspects of the regime (without challenging its foundations) aimed at a very select audience.[8] The third, despite being the most contentious and most closely linked to daily life in marginal neighborhoods, relied on official resources to support its activities. This factor led the group to negotiate with authorities and moderate its initial demands. A fourth arena is the Cuban diaspora. It is made up of an ensemble of juxtaposed and fragmented spaces shared by members of the cultural sphere in Cuba with politically and culturally active members of the Cuban diaspora abroad.[9]

These micro- or partial arenas are characterized by their small size (limited audiences), their lack of autonomy vis-à-vis the state, and their poor connectivity and interactivity, qualities that weakened their cohesion and interpersonal communication. In spite of building spaces of debate about the public good, they were limited in terms of their content, poor media reach, and limited visibility and performativity, leading to a situation where their reputations depended on contingent interpersonal contact with intermediaries, not reliable information provided by the public media (Geoffray 2013). Since they were not able to grow beyond the micro-dimension and maintain their heterogeneity, the emergence of these different arenas of debate did not represent a threat for the Cuban State and they could easily be controlled. However, after 2018 the growth of Internet access in Cuba has enabled the convergence of some of these different arenas and the creation of what Geoffray calls a "transnational contentious space" (2013), independent of the official political and cultural sphere, which intensifies the interactions and enables the mutual recognition of some of these contentious actors as legitimate opponents (players of the same game) with a common goal: contributing to social and political change in Cuba from below.[10]

This new transnational contentious space is where certain topics always excluded from the formal agendas of the political sphere and the official media are visualized and become partially public (Garcia Santamaria 2018a). Their controversial character unleashes their potential as topics of debate for certain sectors of Cuban society and the diaspora about the future. This transnational contentious space—heretofore kept at the margins of the political field and under bureaucratic control—represents a growing threat for the ideological hegemony of the Cuban state (Hoffmann 2011). A key player in this emergent, dynamic process has been Cuba's independent digital press, which, despite significant technological restrictions, high access costs, and a context of deep political polarization, has developed an alternative approach to Cuban reality in the last decade.

However, the emergent dynamics of this new transnational contentious space have been accompanied by recent geopolitical developments that have exacerbated Cuba's already high level of ideological polarization. Despite the great optimism created by the restoration of U.S.-Cuba diplomatic relations in December 2014 and the interest former president Barack Obama showed in the island's technological development, the aggressive rhetoric of the Trump administration has deepened the perception of the threat of the Cuban government activating its historic suspicion of any independent internal actor who can construct an alternative narrative to counter the hegemonic ideology of the state. For example, at the closing ceremony of the 9th UPEC Congress on July 14, 2013 (when Obama was still U.S. president but before the historic move toward normalization), the then first vice president of the Council of State and Council of Ministers, Miguel Díaz-Canel, said in this regard:

> Our press has the virtue of being an uncomfortable press for imperialism [. . .]. That's why it is hated by our enemies, both the internal and external counterrevolution. [. . .] As a first step [. . .] of political-ideological subversion focused on our country from the U.S. government, the topic of the media and the press are present, and that's why they encourage *counterrevolutionary people* to have press projects, as they call them, projects of the "*independent press.*" (*CubaDebate* 2013, emphasis added)

As we can see, these words consider the emerging Cuban independent digital press the first step of a planned "political-ideological subversion," funded by the U.S. government. As sources of alternative information—beyond the institutional control of the state—these media that "naively believe in the false libertarian discourse of the apologists of the market" (Díaz-Canel 2018) are "mercenaries of the pen and the word" led by the "operation centers of the psychological war of the U.S. special services," whose mission is to "create anxiety, infuse disappointment, doubt, fear, and confusion" (Capote 2016). These alarmist quotes are excerpted from an article published by *Granma* that accuses the U.S. of strategically manipulating social media and "creating spurious thought leaders with fake profiles," and refers to independent journalists as "cyber-mercenaries, masters of gossip, rumors, and lies," whose goal is to "discredit the revolutionary state and undermine the pillars that sustain [. . .] the Revolution" (Capote 2016). We should not forget that the socialist state defines itself as the exclusive representative of the Cuban nation and that unity in the face of any threat is a necessary condition for its existence. Building a different journalism in Cuba means reconsidering the ideological project of the PCC, which would have a negative impact on this unity, turning such journalism into the internal enemy of the state.

Most independent media startups in Cuba face this challenge of defamation as traitors. For example, Henken (2017) attempts to capture the diversity of these "indie" media outlets by creating the following four categories: digital dissidents, digital millennials, critical digital revolutionaries, and the digital diaspora. He considers *14ymedio* to be the most pioneering and representative of the digital dissident media. Its founders (Yoani Sánchez and her husband, Reinaldo Escobar) evoke the classic values of liberal journalism, like objectivity, certainty, transparency, and responsibility as the lodestar of their work. While labeling them "digital dissidents," Henken recognizes that they prefer to think of themselves as citizen journalists in a context where official journalists are mere propagandists. Still, they avoid doing what they consider a "journalism of extremes" (quoted in Henken 2017). *14ymedio* has established content-sharing agreements with international media outlets like *Yahoo! News*, *EFE*, and *The Miami Herald/El Nuevo Herald*, and has received technical training from a series of North American universities and support from private foundations. For this and other reasons, it has been blocked from island access by ETECSA, Cuba's telecom monopoly.[11]

On the other hand, Henken's digital millennials include a wide array of entertainment and culture magazines that enjoy wide underground digital circulation and state toleration given that they are largely apolitical in content (such as *Play-Off*, *Garbos*, and *Vistar*).[12] Henken's interview (2017) with the founder of the independent digital sports magazine *Play-Off*, Pedro Enrique Rodríguez, reflects his disappointment regarding the "inability to criticize" and the "scarce influence" of the state media on the national public. He is also pessimistic about the uncertainty in which he and other indie media pioneers like him carry out their professional work, clouding the future of these independent media startups. He also cites precarious working conditions (he uses his grandparent's basement as an editorial office), the lack of any legal framework for non-state media, the great difficulty procuring funding given the ban on advertising revenue via state and private companies, and the high cost of public Internet access as major obstacles for growth.

Other digital media startups like *Cibercuba* (now blocked by government servers), *Cachivache Media* (now defunct), *El Toque*, and *El Estornudo* (also blocked) address a variety of topics of Cuban society with different styles and goals. Journalist José Jasán Nieves Cárdenas, founder of *El Toque*, has publicly recognized that among the objectives of his project are strengthening Cuban civil society, increasing the diversity and quality of the information available to Cubans, providing legal and financial support for independent digital media, and raising the public profile of important topics, including human rights, sustainable development, gender equality, social inclusion, and government transparency. *El Toque*'s innovative style of editorial management is interesting as it is conceived of as a horizontal cooperative where agendas are built "from the consensus among people who do not think alike," as well as the interest in developing business tools that allow for the financing of their project. Since it was financially supported by The Netherlands during its inception, *El Toque* is seen by the state media as part of the "neo-counter-revolution" at the service of a foreign power aimed at "destroying the Cuban socialist system" (Nieves Cárdenas 2018). Henken also interviewed one of the founders of the independent online magazine *El Estornudo*, who—like Nieves—tries to avoid any association with political propaganda be it of the official or oppositional variety (Henken 2017). However, this has proven virtually impossible since the site was eventually blocked from island access in February 2018 after being readily available to islanders for its first two years of existence.

The independent media outlets included in Henken's critical digital revolutionary category (*Periodismo de Barrio, Havana Times, La Joven Cuba, Observatorio Crítico*, etc.) recognize themselves as revolutionary advocates of socialist democracy while simultaneously rejecting the control of the press by the PCC. In other words, they believe that the independence of the media is a necessary precondition for its credibility. *Periodismo de Barrio*, an online journalism site that addresses climate change and natural disasters and their local impacts in Cuban communities, has challenged how the government authorities have responded to these events. Like other digital media, it has suffered harassment, censorship, and detentions by state forces. Finally, Henken's digital diaspora includes sites featuring news and information about Cuba but whose servers and directors are located abroad (usually in Spain and Miami). Most of these sites have periodically received funding from the National Endowment for Democracy (NED) a grantee of the United States government as well as public funds from various European governments. These include media outlets like *Diario de Cuba* (Spain) and *Cubanet* (Miami) that typically address both cultural and political topics, like human rights, aware as they are of the need for uncensored information to encourage political change and begin the reconstruction of civil society on the island. Two exceptions to this rule that Henken points out are *OnCuba* and *Progreso Semanal*, both of which are progressive news and opinion outlets recognized as foreign press agencies by the Cuban government in Havana. Their funding comes from those in the U.S. private sector interested in investing in media projects on the island (Henken 2017).

As we can see, Cuban independent digital journalism is a different animal than the U.S. puppet imagined by the Cuban state. It is internally heterogeneous, featuring a variety of objectives and styles, which range from revolutionary criticism to open opposition to the Cuban state. In spite of multiple restrictions, some of these media startups have experimented with innovative digital formats and explored new ways of editorial and financial self-management linked to the emerging national sector of private entrepreneurs. Some of them find in *el paquete* and other informal digital networks the vehicle for distributing their content offline. In general, all of them are alienated from the state journalism model, especially by the lack of autonomy and the role of ideological legitimation played by the PCC and the Cuban state together with the apologetic and triumphalist style of the official press, disconnected as it is from the information needs of Cuban civil society. The funding some of them receive from foreign governments, especially the U.S. government, has heightened the official rhetoric that seeks to paint them all as the "internal enemy" supposedly working at the service of the external one, transforming all into a target of public threats and harassment, censorship, and multiple forms of repression by the state authorities.

From De-Professionalization to Journalistic Renewal

From my point of view, the significance of Cuba's emergent independent digital media lies in its potential renewal of the journalistic profession on the island. Its culture and practices, and how its journalists perceive their public role under new circumstances, focus on producing quality information for an audience interested in participating in the decision-making process, rather than being the instrument of partisan ideological legitimation, giving it a legitimacy sorely lacking in the official press. Liberal values like autonomy, balance, and a commitment to addressing contentious topics that encourage public debate and government accountability are examples of these outlets' journalistic culture and practices. Despite their limited national reach, these independent digital startups have altered the rigid dynamics of the information agenda on the island, putting front and center hot topics like social inclusion, marginality and poverty, minority rights, the environment, political corruption, and the voices of those who challenge the government's hegemonic ideological project. This has created a mechanism of pressure against the strict agenda of the official media and even the discourse of the political leadership.

As a consequence of this dynamic new transnational contentious digital space, the Cuban state has only reaffirmed the restrictive nature of its legal norms. For example, Article 55 of the newly implemented 2019 Constitution subordinates press freedom to "the purposes of society," declaring that the means of social communication, "in any of its forms, are social property of all the people," and "cannot be subject to another type of ownership" (*Granma* 2019). The Social Communication Policy of the Cuban state and government, recently published by the official news and information site *Cubadebate*, sets as its main goal "guaranteeing consensus and national unity around the Homeland, the Socialist Revolution, and the Party," justifying this call with reference to Cuba's official cultural policy as declared by Fidel Castro himself in 1961: "Inside the Revolution, everything; against the Revolution, nothing." Today, just as has been the case throughout the entire revolutionary process, the Revolution remains the only legitimate representative of the interests of the "whole nation"; thus, "none can allege justifiably a right against it."[13] This historic subordination of legal norms to the interests of the Revolution means a limited and instrumental vision of the right to freedom of speech of Cuban journalists and the mass media, enabling the state to control the public information with impunity (IESLEC 2018).

In spite of its incipient development, independent digital journalism faces a variety of barriers. The limited, selective, monitored, and highly regulated Internet access for Cuban citizens is its main barrier. The ideal of universal public access is diminished by four key factors: 1) the ambiguity and restrictiveness of legal provisions; 2) limited coverage and high access costs; 3) the blocking and censorship of critical media sites; and 4) digital surveillance strategies (IESLEC 2018). For example, according to the 1996 Decree 209, all ministerial decrees and resolutions that control the use of technology in Cuba are based on the premise that access to global computer networks will be regulated according to "national interests," so that the information available "matches our ethical principles and does not impact the country's interests and security" (ICTworks 2015). Other legal dispositions such as Resolution 179 from 2008 establish a set of obligations for Internet service providers (ISPs), like ensuring that software is not equipped with encryption technology and forbid the use of applications that affect "the integrity or security of the state." Such monitoring obligations are based on extremely ambiguous criteria that can only result in strict censorship (IESLEC 2018).

Conclusion

The growing interest in the tripartite relationship between the press, the state, and the audience in authoritarian, hybrid, or transitional regimes suggests a dynamic tension in the rearticulation of the state's legitimacy under highly uncertain conditions and in a context of political polarization (Lugo-Ocando and Garcia Santamaria 2015). Journalistic practice in Latin America is normally subordinated to other monopolistic social logics like the market and political cronyism (Kitzberger 2009). However, countries as different from one another as China and Russia have successfully challenged the Western vision of the supposedly natural antagonism between the state on the one hand and liberalizing potential of the market on the other. China has successfully turned investigative journalism into a pragmatic player in its partisan project of governance (Repnikova 2017b).

In Cuba, where new and historically significant party regulations subordinate press freedom to the "purposes of the society" and only recognize the "socialist property of all the people" over the mass media, the hegemony of the official partisan press model, based on the Soviet model, seems to have given ground to the island's many, diverse digital upstarts thanks in part to new social and technological conditions. The evidence reveals a progressive impoverishment and de-professionalization of this model, whose journalistic practice is conditioned by political reliability and ideological commitment, hence the strict regulation of official media by the Ideological Department of the PCC.

Structural factors inherited from the Soviet model, like its excessive bureaucracy and the limited creative autonomy of journalistic agency, deter the informative efficiency of the official media and encourage the development of an independent digital press model that promotes the creation of a contentious transnational space, independent of the official political and cultural sphere. Given that it is not under the ideological control of the Party, this new space or digital public sphere encourages debate on controversial topics of public interest, like inefficient government administration, political corruption, marginalization and poverty, prostitution, environmental concerns, and gender equality, topics that the official media have systematically hidden, thus challenging the ideological hegemony of the state.

It is important to recognize that independent digital journalism is intrinsically differentiated in its routines and journalistic culture(s), as well as in the perception of its social role. However, the profound deception and alienation caused by the official press's long-time role as a partisan ideological legitimation apparatus for the regime in power has led to a broad-based embrace of liberal values like autonomy, impartiality, credibility, transparency, and a focus on contentious topics that enable and enrich public debate by all sectors of Cuba's digital indie demimonde. Unlike in China, however, Cuba's independent online journalists face a number of special barriers like the ambiguity and restrictiveness of existing legal norms, the limited coverage and high cost of Internet access, the blocking and censorship of the critical sites, and the many surveillance and harassment strategies employed by government trolls lurking on the Web.

Because Cuba lacks an environment of economic liberalization that could strengthen the market and enable greater autonomy and differentiation of its media system, the island's pioneering independent journalists exercise their profession in a legal limbo, with little or no access to funding, and are constantly stigmatized and defamed as "mercenaries of the pen and the word" by the political leadership and the official media. Given the return of a threatening geopolitical posture from the U.S. under the Trump administration, the main characteristics of Cuba's emergent independent digital press model will be creative improvisation, extreme ideological polarization, and radical confrontation with the state. Still, the new journalistic practices chronicled here seem to have had an irreversible impact on the dynamics of public opinion on the island today and citizen deliberation about Cuba's uncertain future.

Acknowledgments

The author would like to acknowledge the Research Directorate of the Universidad Iberoamericana, Mexico City, for the financial support for the translation of the chapter, and also the young Cuban journalists enrolled in the Postgraduate in Communication at the University for motivating me to analyze the new dynamics of journalism in Cuba today.

Notes

1. According to the authors, the relative stability of Western societies gives the illusion that they represent the destination point of history, a place toward which non-Western countries are necessarily heading (Meng and Rantanen 2015, 4).

2. According to McNair, "the efficacy of the Party and the efficacy of the media are inseparable" (1991, 11–16).

3. Ernesto Vera, who led the UPEC for twenty years, explains that the organization was founded "on the absolute commitment to the policy and ideology of the Revolution, with its members in permanent combat as soldiers of the Party and of Fidel" (quoted in Arencibia 2017, 57).

4. García Luis is emphatically precise in recognizing that "public communication in Cuba is directly functional to the hegemonic ideology and political system" (2013, 87).

5. When presenting the Central Report at the 6th Party Congress, then President Raúl Castro said: "In this area [the Cuban press], it is also necessary to definitively leave behind the habit of triumphalism, stridency, and formality when addressing the national present and [instead] create written materials and TV and radio programs that capture the attention because of their content and style, and foster debate among public opinion, which requires an increase in professionalism and knowledge of our journalists [. . .]. All these factors explain the common dissemination of boring, improvised, and superficial materials" (PCC 2011: 18).

6. At the 9th Congress of UPEC in 2013, Cuba's first Vice President Miguel Diaz-Canel said, "We have entered a vicious cycle" because "the Party expects a specific reaction from the press, and when an incident or event happens that affects that, the Party becomes further involved in managing rather than guiding, it starts playing the role of the media, which in turn feel constrained [. . .] and it is there where the synergy begins to break [. . .]. We are not informed and communication fails" (Díaz-Canel 2013, 5).

7. These included an explicitly "dissident" micro-arena, semipublic debates within state institutions, and a micro-arena of contentious collectives of self-taught artists and marginalized intellectuals.

8. The imprecise and always fluctuating limits of "allowable" criticism in Cuba forced the protagonists in this micro-arena to restrict the political information shared with foreigners and the international media, control access to their meetings and events, and strategically collaborate with the state (Geoffray 2013, 5).

9. Geoffray (2013) specifically refers to the space of convergence and debate created by *Encuentro de la Cultura Cubana*, an influential diasporic magazine published in Madrid between 1996 and 2009.

10. Geoffray recognizes that the transnational dimension of digital technologies represents a threat for authoritarian governments, particularly in small countries where the state (despite its internal controls) does not have the ability to counteract the mainstream influence of international media to reduce the informational and organizational asymmetry between internal and external players (Geoffray 2013).

11. In Henken's contribution to this volume (chapter 7), he provides a chronological analysis of the fifteen-year media evolution that transformed Sánchez's famed blog *Generación Y* into the digital daily newspaper *14ymedio*.

12. The three parallel digital strategies are via website (hard to reach for most Cubans prior to the arrival of 3G in December 2018), paying for the magazine to be included in the weekly package (an underground weekly compendium of digital material), and monthly e-mail digests for subscribers (Henken 2017).

13. See "¿Qué política se plantea el Estado y el Gobierno para la Comunicación Social?" *Cubadebate*, July 17, 2019.

References

Arencibia, Lorenzo Jesús. 2017. "Periodismo cubano: ¿un callejón sin salida?" *Estudios Latinoamericanos*, Nueva Época, No. 39 (January-June): 51–75.
Bobes, Velia C. 2007. *La Nación Inconclusa. (Re)constituciones de la ciudadanía y la identidad nacional en Cuba*. Mexico City: FLACSO.
Capote, Raúl A. 2016. "La nueva prensa." *Granma*, September 22, 2016.
Chan, J. Man and Linchuan Qui. 2002. "China: Media Liberalization Under Authoritarianism." In *Media Reform: Democratizing the Media, Democratizing the State*, edited by Monroe E. Price, Beata Rozumilowicz, and Stefaan G. Verhulst. London: Routledge.
CPJ (Committee to Protect Journalists). 2016. "Conectar a Cuba: Más espacio para crítica, pero restricciones frenan avance de libertad de prensa." September 21, 2016. https://cpj.org/es/2016/09/conectar-a-cuba-mas-espacio-para-critica-pero-rest/.
Cubadebate. 2019. "¿Qué Política se plantean el Estado y el Gobierno para la Comunicación Social?" July 17, 2019.
Curran, James and Myung Jin-Park. 2000. *De-Westernizing Media Studies*. New York: Routledge.
Díaz-Canel, Miguel. 2013a. "Discurso en la clausura del IX Congreso de la UPEC." *Cubadebate*, August 7, 2013.
Díaz-Canel, Miguel. 2013b. "Se necesita mucho de la prensa cubana para construir un socialismo próspero y sostenible." *Enfoque*, Havana, UPEC, August 2013.
Díaz-Canel, Miguel. 2018. "Discurso en la clausura del X Congreso de la UPEC," Agencia Cubana de Noticias (ACN), July 15, 2018.
Downing, John D. 1996. *Internationalizing Media Theory: Transition, Power, Culture*. London: SAGE Publications.
Dukalski, Alexander. 2017. *The Authoritarian Public Sphere: Legitimation and Autocratic Power in North Korea, Burma, and China*. New York: Routledge.
Elizalde, Rosa María. 2013. "*El consenso de lo possible*," Ph.D. thesis, School of Communications, University of Havana.
Esser, Frank and Barbara Pfetsch. 2004. *Comparing Political Communication: Theories, Cases, and Challenges*. Cambridge, MA: Cambridge University Press.
Franco Senén, A. 2016. "Entre la espada y la pared. ¿Cómo se dirige la prensa en Cuba?" Undergraduate thesis, School of Communications, University of Havana.
Garcés Corra, Raúl. 2013. "Siete tesis sobre la prensa cubana." *Cubadebate*, July 14, 2013.
Garcés Corra, Raúl. 2017. "Cómo se dirige la prensa cubana? Un acercamiento a la gestión de medios desde la perspectiva de sus periodistas y directivos." *Alcance: Revista Cubana de Información y Comunicación* 6, No. 12.
García Luis, Julio. 2013. "La regulación de la prensa en Cuba: referentes morales y deontológicos." *Temas*, No. 74: 82–90.
García Luis, Julio. 2014. *Revolución, Socialismo y Periodismo. La prensa y los periodistas cubanos ante el siglo XXI*. Havana: Editorial Pablo de la Torriente.

Garcia Santamaria, Sara. 2018a. "Digital Media and the Promotion of Deliberative Debate in Cuba." Internet Policy Observatory, Annenberg School of Communications, University of Pennsylvania.

Garcia Santamaria, Sara. 2018b. "The Sovietization of Cuban Journalism. The impact of Foreign Economy Dependency on Media Structures in a Post-Soviet Era." *Journal of Latin American Communication Research* 6 (1–2): 135–151.

Geoffray, Marie Laure. 2013. "Internet, Public Space and Contention in Cuba. Bridging Asymmetries of Access to Public Space through Transnational Dynamics of Contention." DesiguALdades.net, Research Network on Interdependent Inequalities in Latin America, Working Paper Series, No. 42.

Geoffray, Marie Laure and Armando Chaguaceda. 2014. "Medios de comunicación y cambios en la política de información en Cuba desde 1959." *Temas de Comunicación*, No. 29 (July–December): 171–196.

Glenn III, John K. 2001. *Framing Democracy. Civil Society and Civic Movements in Eastern Europe*. Stanford: Stanford University Press.

Granma. 2019. "Constitución de de República de Cuba," January. http://www.granma.cu/file/pdf/gaceta/Nueva%20Constituci%C3%B3n%20240%20KB-1.pdf.

Gross, Peter and Karol Jakubowicz. 2013. *Media Transformations in the Post-Communist World: Eastern Europe's Tortured Path to Change*. London: Lexington Books.

Hallin, Daniel and Paolo Mancini. 2007. *Sistemas Mediáticos Comparados*. Barcelona: Hacer Publishers.

Hallin, Daniel and Paolo Mancini. 2012. *Comparing Media Systems beyond the Western World*. Cambridge, MA: Cambridge University Press.

Henken, Ted A. 2017. "Cuba's Digital Millennials: Independent Digital Media and Civil Society on the Island of the Disconnected." *Social Research* 84 (2), Summer.

Hoffmann, Bert. 2011. "Civil Society 2.0? How the Internet Changes State-Society Relations in Authoritarian Regimes: The Case of Cuba." *GIGA*, No. 156.

ICTworks. 2015. "Internet in Cuba: A New Medium for Individual Freedoms?" September 2, 2015. https://www.ictworks.org/internet-in-cuba-a-new-medium-for-individual-freedoms/#.XxeM1ZNKg6g.

IESLEC. 2018. "Informe Especial sobre la Libertad de Expresión en Cuba," Inter-American Commission of Human Rights, The Organization of American States.

Kitzberger, Philip. 2009. "La relación prensa-gobierno y el giro político en América Latina," *Revista PostData*, No. 14: 157–181.

Lugo-Ocando, Jairo and Sara Garcia Santamaria. 2015. "Media, Hegemony, and Polarization in Latin America." In *Media and Politics in New Democracies: Europe in a Comparative Perspective*, edited by Jan Zielonka. New York: Oxford University Press.

McNair, Brian. 1991. *Glasnost, Perestroika, and the Soviet Media*. London: Routledge.

Melucci, Alberto. 1999. *Acción colectiva, vida cotidiana y democracia*. Mexico City: El Colegio de México.

Meng, Bingchun and Terhi Rantanen. 2015. "A Change of Lens: A Call to Compare the Media in China and Russia." *Critical Studies in Media Communication* 32 (1): 1–15.

Nieves Cárdenas, José Jasán. 2018. "Crear un medio digital en Cuba implica ser consciente de los riesgos." *La Babel Digital*, October 23, 2018.

PCC (Partido Comunista de Cuba). 1976. "Tesis y Resoluciones." First Congress of the Cuban Communist Party, Havana.
PCC (Partido Comunista de Cuba). 2010. "Proyecto de Lineamientos de la Política Económica y Social." Sixth Congress of the Cuban Communist Party, Havana.
Price, Monroe E., Beata Rozumilowicz, and Stefaan Verhulst, eds. 2002. *Media Reform: Democratizing the Media, Democratizing the State*. London: Routledge.
Przeworski, Adam. 1994. "Algunos problemas en el estudio de la transición hacia la democracia." In Guillermo O'Donnell and Phillip Schmitter, *Transiciones desde un gobierno autoritario, Perspectivas Comparadas*: 79–104. Barcelona: Paidós.
Randall, Vicky. 1993. "The Media and Democratization in the Third World." *Third World Quarterly* 14 (3): 625–646.
Repnikova, Maria. 2017a. "Media Openings and Political Transitions. Glasnost versus Yulun Jiandu." *Problems of Post-Communism* 64 (3–4): 141–151.
Repnikova, Maria. 2017b. *Media Politics in China: Improvising Power under Authoritarianism*. Cambridge: Cambridge University Press.
Rojas, Rafael. 2006. "Ideología, cultura y memoria. Dilemas simbólicos de la transición." In *Cuba en el siglo XXI. Ensayos sobre la transición*, edited by Marifeli Pérez-Stable. Madrid: Colibrí Publishers.
Roudakova, Natalia. 2008. "Media-Political Clientelism: Lessons from Anthropology." *Media, Culture & Society* 30 (1): 41–59.
Roudakova, Natalia. 2012. "Comparing Processes: Media, 'Transitions,' and Historical Change." In *Comparing Media Systems beyond the Western World*, edited by Daniel Hallin and Paolo Mancini. Cambridge: Cambridge University Press.
Schedler, Andreas. 2016. *La política de la incertidumbre en los regímenes electorales autoritarios*. Mexico City: FCE-CIDE.
Tarrow, Sidney. 1997. *El poder en movimiento. Los movimientos sociales, la acción colectiva y la política*. Madrid: Alianza Editorial.
Tong, Jingrong and Colin Sparks. 2009. "Investigative Journalism in China Today." *Journalism Studies* 10 (3): 337–352.
Vartanova, Elena. 2012. "The Russian Media Model in the Context of Post-Soviet Dynamics." In *Comparing Media Systems beyond the Western World*, edited by Daniel Hallin and Paolo Mancini. Cambridge: Cambridge University Press.
Voltmer, Katrin. 2006. *Mass Media and Political Communication in New Democracies*. New York: Routledge.
Winfield, Betty H. and Zengjun Peng. 2005. "Market or Party Controls: Chinese Media in Transition." *International Journal for Communication Studies* 67 (3): 255–270.
Zhao, Yuezhi. 2012. "Understanding China's Media System in a World Historical Context." In *Comparing Media Systems beyond the Western World*, edited by Daniel Hallin and Paolo Mancini. Cambridge: Cambridge University Press.
Zielonka, Jan. 2015. *Media and Politics in New Democracies: Europe in a Comparative Perspective*. New York: Oxford University Press.

6

Digital Critique in Cuba

MARIE LAURE GEOFFRAY

In Cuba at the end of the second decade of the twenty-first century, many independent journalists criticize the existing social and political order while claiming they are not "doing politics" or "being political" and even that they are not part of a supposedly emergent civil society—independent of the government. They want to be considered professional journalists, *period*—without qualifying adjectives. Similarly, black market operators known as *paqueteros* who distribute digital Internet content on USB sticks and DVDs often characterize their activity as a professional business, a way to support their families (Vela and Torres 2015). Few are those who state that they are politically motivated and/or seek to contribute to regime change on the island. How can we make sense of this at both the empirical and theoretical levels, since most literature on the Internet and politics in authoritarian regimes actually focuses on the way increased editorial and economic independence and the expansion of popular access to digital technology empowers people and transforms the way political power is wielded in the twenty-first century?

Indeed, academic analyses have given special emphasis to the decidedly *political* dynamics of the liberalization of access to digital technology in authoritarian contexts (over and above their economic, cultural, or sociological dynamics). Some have highlighted how contentious uses of digital technology have given visibility to a plurality of political positions and challenged the state information and communication monopoly (Hoffmann 2012), which in turn has had an impact on the ability of activists to better organize, defend civil liberties, and thus expand democratic discourse and practices (Simon et al. 2002; Shirky 2008). Others, however, have underlined the capacity of authoritarian governments to use digital technology to achieve economic development objectives (Kalathil and Boas 2003) while controlling their wider uses in their territory, notably through content filtering tools, censorship of certain sites, permanent monitoring of online forums and chats, and the development of sophisticated tools allowing for the implementation of targeted repression (Deibert 2003; Morozov 2011). But all have focused on the implicit relationship between the Internet and political power.

This laser-like focus on the political implications of Internet access is the major difference between works on the impact of digital technology in authoritarian versus democratic contexts. Indeed, scholars focusing on democratic contexts tend to take into account how digital technology has come to permeate every aspect of life. They have consistently analyzed the rise of online communities, be they linked by expressive logics or identity politics (Mazzarella 2005; Seargeant and Tagg 2014) as well as routine and noncontentious uses of the Internet (Wellmann and Haythornthwaite 2002; Messin 2007; Martin and Dagiral 2016). In contrast, academics focusing on authoritarian regimes have more often maintained a kind of "exceptionalist" perspective, with a primary, even exclusive focus on politics. Only a handful of studies have tried to understand the way digital technology has become enshrined in people's daily practices and transformed identities in authoritarian contexts *without* directly challenging state power (Parodi and Sautedé 1995; Arsène 2011; Lecomte 2013; Bax 2014). However, just as is the case in India, Brazil, France, and the United States, most people in China, Vietnam, Cuba, Saudi Arabia, and Russia use digital technologies primarily to keep in touch with friends and family, shop, stay informed, and seek entertainment.

However, in such contexts maintaining contact with family and friends abroad may include those once deemed "traitors," "worms," or "scum" for "abandoning the Revolution."[1] Likewise, "shopping" can easily mean engaging in prohibited black market activity, "staying informed" might include reading news from sources deemed counterrevolutionary, and the search for supposedly harmless "entertainment" is likely to include quite a few illegal products and processes—making such activities protopolitical at the very least even if they have no political intentionality per se. Although we need to take actors' discourses about and definitions of their actions seriously, we cannot analyze those actions without taking the broader social and political order in which they interact into account. Given these complexities, the objective of this chapter is to provide a theoretical reflection on the Cuban case study of the uses of emergent digital media in order to better understand how, under authoritarian rule, *critical* uses of digital technology are intertwined with more *routine* uses and how "critique," rather than being defined a priori and exclusively understood vis-à-vis its intentionality, is in fact shaped by the complex and often contradictory context in which it takes place.

The Cuban case is especially relevant to this debate because it illustrates the fact that the gradual liberalization of access to digital technology has not necessarily led to the intensification of its politicization, although it has led to what I call the extension of "critique" (i.e., the growth of deeds and speech that transgress the established authoritarian order). Indeed, when access to the Internet in Cuba was highly restricted prior to 2015, when it began to spread more broadly, only determined activists took the risk of expressing their critical views online (mainly through blogs) and facing the consequences (censorship, harassment, threats, defamation, and sometimes unfair trials followed by imprisonment and/or exile). That is perhaps the main reason they became extremely visible and well known *outside* of Cuba (while remaining largely unknown *within* the island at the time). Examples include Yoani Sánchez, Reinaldo Escobar, Miriam Celaya, Claudia Cadelo, Orlando Luis Pardo Lazo, Regina Coyula, and Luis Felipe Rojas (see Geoffray 2015; Vicari 2014; and Henken 2011, 2017, and in this volume). But, as Internet access has slowly expanded since 2015, uses of digital technology have diversified, and breaching controversial social and political issues has not been a priority for most users on the island. At the same time, in the Cuban context, the close monitoring of Internet use makes it and the means of access to it (many of which are informal or illegal) almost intrinsically critical (if not intentionally so).

At the same time, while these new critical voices are often presented outside of Cuba as devoid of power and resources relative to the Cuban state apparatus (a digital David versus a powerful, hegemonic government Goliath), in fact they often rely on U.S. technology, especially the even more hegemonic GAFAM platforms,[2] and sometimes receive financial sponsorship from both individuals and institutions, mainly in the U.S., but also in Europe and Latin America, although some projects and journalists actively avoid any U.S. government funding. Therefore, the David versus Goliath trope requires some nuance and contextualization. That is, we need to appreciate the irony as we seek to carefully understand how David is actually using global hegemonic power vehicles and resources in order to achieve antiauthoritarian goals in the particular media and political context of Cuba. Starting with French sociologist Dominique Boullier's (2018) theoretical take on the way critique is formulated in the digital era in democratic contexts, I propose a reflection on the contradictions and paradoxes that underpin emerging contentious digital dynamics in authoritarian Cuba.

The chapter begins by presenting a theoretical framework that extends Boullier's work on critique in the realm of digital technologies in democratic contexts to include authoritarian ones. Next, the chapter demonstrates how, despite the lack of political intensification of Internet uses, access to digital technology has allowed for the emergence of collective critical practices, which qualify as critique while they are not necessarily intentionally critical. The chapter's third section focuses on the development of a Cuban sphere of what I call "professionalized critique," peopled by protagonists who challenge the official media sphere, while simultaneously claiming a "professional" and nonpartisan approach.

Digitalization of Critique and Critique of Digitalization

When I started studying contentious uses of the Internet in Cuba, I felt that few sociological theories could help me fully grasp one of the very specific and contradictory underpinnings of the emerging contentious dynamics I could observe: the fact that the new contentious voices, *a priori* devoid of power and resources compared to the Cuban state apparatus, are in fact using U.S. technology, and often receive aid from abroad. Indeed, the sociology of (mass) media in authoritarian contexts generally emphasizes the immense power acquired by state media to craft public opinion and at the same time tends to focus specifically on counter discourses and antihegemonic positions. This perspective needs to be refined. That is why I chose to discuss the work of Dominique Boullier (2016), whose theoretical approach is more interactionist and interested in social actors' abilities and capacities to formulate and voice critique in situations of dispute or controversy.

Rather than a focus on the continuous building of hierarchies of norms, judgments, and action regimes (which one can find in Bourdieu's school of thought for instance, as well as in the Frankfurt school), Boullier underlines the way social actors classify, categorize, and judge actions, norms, and behaviors. They strive to expose and analyze the existence of different forms of critique, in order to give visibility to the whole spectrum of critical possibilities. Their objective is not to criticize the way social norms operate and to point out the gap between the way things are and the way they should be, according to a normative egalitarian perspective.[3] It is rather to make the diversity of social critique visible and accessible.

Moreover, as Boullier tackles both the critique of digital technology and the digitalization of critique, his work is relevant to understand the transformation of the uses of digital technologies in Cuba in a broader way than a narrower focus on contention and politics. Indeed, on the island access to digital technology has changed the way people can voice critique. It has also changed people's relationship to critique. And the study of critique is essential to understand recent social and political transformation in Cuba, as the emergence of visible and public critique tells us something about how society becomes more complex and less determined by politics, despite an apparent lack of political change.

Boullier (2018) identifies four types of critique of digital technology. The first two are traditional forms of critique, which now encompass the digital phenomenon. The last two are oriented toward the specific critique of digital technology. In this theorization of the relationship between technology and critique, critique is "equipped" with "machines" (i.e., each critique creates instruments in order to be heard or read).

The first type of critique is called *critique engagée* in French, which can be translated as "activist critique." It strives to denounce the world as it is, and its objective is to defend a specific vision of the world as it should be. In that perspective, digital technology is criticized in the same way other social phenomena are criticized for their reproduction of domination logics. This type of critique is equipped with a specific machine, in other words, with specific instruments, tools, gadgets, or technologies which are created by activists; for instance developing open source, "copyleft" software can be understood as a concrete response to the global commodification of digital tools as proprietary products to be bought and sold on the market for profit and controlled by their "owner," usually a massive tech company like Apple or Microsoft.

The second type of critique strives to render visible or legible the plurality of possible perspectives on reality, in order to open up social actors' perspectives and have them consider a variety of choices, rather than adhere to a single view or a forced choice between two similar options (Google versus Apple, PC versus Mac, or AT&T versus Verizon). The "machines" which correspond to this category are the "new collective formats," in other words, cooperative endeavors such as Wikipedia, peer-to-peer exchanges or collaborative platforms, which aim to decentralize dynamics of information/content sharing and build consensus through the co-building of knowledge.

The third type of critique qualifies as an "activist critique," as in the first type, although its focus is narrower since it focuses on digital technology itself as a new form of domination. It especially criticizes the way global finance has appropriated digital technology with little regulation, turning an open and "free" technological world, which had emerged as a pluralistic one—composed of military actors (Levine 2018), academics, as well as the geek/tech community and various alternative movements (Cardon and Granjon 2010)—into the realm of global oligopolies. It also underlines the fact that the emergence of a new class of computer and data scientists, with few checks and balances, can constitute a worldwide threat to privacy and democracy. The instruments of this third type of critique are the endeavors that seek to propose alternatives to the power of the oligopolistic GAFAM platforms. In the realm of academia, the movement in favor of open access publishing (against the gatekeeper platforms) can be considered an instrument of this critique.

Like the second, Boullier's fourth type of critique is more reflexive and questions the way knowledge is produced in this new digital era as well as how "big data" could be reappropriated (on this specific question see Boullier 2015). It is thus not only concerned with plurality and diversity or with the power of the market on technology, but also with our collective (in)capacity to control the way technology has appropriated our lives. For instance, social life is now synonymous with social networks; mobile phones have become a kind of extra limb; the existence of big data allows for the testing of correlations between all kinds of variables, thus giving the illusion that journalism or social sciences are no longer relevant. A critique of this emerging mode of knowledge production is necessary, but it is still lagging behind rapid technological progress. Thus, this mode of critique explores how to create instruments, which would allow for the participatory collection of data and thus lead to collective reflexivity about the digital traces we leave everywhere online for others to collect and commercialize.

As we can see, theories elaborated in a democratic context are somewhat incongruous to the Cuban case, as what is considered critique in Cuba is relatively different from what is considered critique elsewhere. Indeed, the fear of disconnection, linked to the Cuban government's very slow and cautious roll out of Internet access for the Cuban people, has led the people to consider digital technology as a rare and utterly positive technology. Although some have voiced critique of the risks involved in expanded digital connectedness, it is widely seen as an unmitigated good and has rarely been criticized based on its potential threats to privacy or public trust. Very few island-based endeavors, such as BlackHat—a collective of young Havana-based techies which emerged in the early 2000s—aim to discuss the extension and consequences of the penetration of the Internet in Cuba in order to alert people about both its enabling qualities and its dark sides.[4] It is the objective of this case study to analyze what can be conceived as digital critique in Cuba, to understand how it is voiced, and with which effects. I will then discuss to what extent digital technologies themselves have or have not become an object of scrutiny of the more general capacity for critique in Cuban society.

The Popular Extension of Social Critique

In authoritarian contexts, most experts consider as critique the voices that challenge the dominant elites and the repressive state apparatus, whatever the content of critique and whatever the means and tools they use to convey this critique. Indeed, under repressive rule, analysts have traditionally focused on the mere existence and expression of dissent, rather than on the content or means used to dissent. Thus, when Raúl Castro's liberalization policies that gradually expanded access to the Internet allowed for the emergence of a Cuban blogosphere, access to digital technology was celebrated as a vehicle for greater political freedom and the expansion of independent civil society.[5]

Indeed, the increase in Internet access allowed these emerging digital critical voices to express themselves, connect with like-minded people on the island, and find transnational support and solidarity (Hoffmann 2012; Henken 2011, 2014; Geoffray 2015). In that sense, Cuba's citizen journalism and blogger movement can be understood as a network of activist critique (Boullier's first category), since their aim—during the emerging phase of the movement—was to express their problems of daily life (scarcity, lack of running water, lack of transportation, etc.) and progressively to denounce the Cuban socialist order and raise consciousness both inside and outside of Cuba about the systematic human rights violations committed by the government. These Cubans indeed were focused on describing the gap between what their social reality was like, how it was framed by the authorities, and how it should be according to popular aspirations on the one hand and international norms and values on the other.

However, we need to underline the fact that within the Cuban repressive political context, such a critique did not entail a questioning of the new digital domination exercised by the then emerging Internet behemoths. Activists welcomed Google's engagement with Cuba, and often asked for other U.S. firms such as Twitter, Facebook, and PayPal to become involved so as to circumvent the obstacles built by the Cuban authorities to prevent people from accessing the Internet without their tight control.[6] Indeed, during Google CEO Eric Schmidt's visit to Cuba in summer 2014, he *both* met with government officials and toured Havana's University of Computer Science (UCI) *and* paid a private visit to the home office of Yoani Sánchez, editor of the independent digital newspaper *14ymedio* and renowned government gadfly (Risen 2014).

Similar paradoxical dynamics can be observed with other social actors. In Cuba, since the early 2000s, increased access to digital technology has led to a diversification of Internet uses. People began using it for commercial purposes (for instance via the popular Revolico classified ads platform), for leisure and entertainment, as well as to maintain family ties with Cuban relatives living abroad. At the same time, since the monitoring of Internet use remains strong in Cuba, the lack of an expansion of political activities should not blind us from observing the actual extension of "critique."

Access to the Internet is still quite expensive in Cuba and there are almost no free hot spots, a fact that forces many Cubans to buy connection time on the black market and thus engage in an illegal activity, which can make them subject to harsh repression. It also leads them to rely on Cuba's homegrown "offline Internet," the famous *paquete semanal* (a weekly digital package of content downloaded from the Internet), which primarily circulates on USB thumb drives. Although the circulation of the *paquete* is largely tolerated by authorities, it remains technically illegal, as producing and selling *el paquete* does not correspond to any of the authorized self-employment license categories. Engaging in such activities thus qualifies as a transgression of the dominant social order.

Moreover, producing and circulating *el paquete* can be understood as grassroots agency to build "new collective formats," which are defined by Boullier (2018) as instruments of the second kind of critique, which allow for the display of a plurality of possibilities. Indeed, these kinds of practices generate horizontal forms of organization in a country where the Communist Party has long prohibited any kind of grassroots organizing, even if it only entails repairing the water pump or fixing the sewage system. *El paquete* is the result of a collaboration between thousands of people, who assemble, circulate, and promote it, making a living from this chain of black market media collaboration.[7] Working for *el paquete* thus allows for the development of more plural ways of experiencing life on the island as it creates dynamics of social organization from below and job offers in the private sector, thus subverting both the ideal of universal state employment and the top-down monitoring of the social order in Cuba. Such reclaiming of collective agency, although not often thought of or presented as such, can be considered a kind of indirect social critique.

Indeed, given the constraints, which still weigh heavily on access to and use of digital technology in Cuba, illegal use and access by Cuban citizens—even when they do not entail any political aim or consciousness—can be understood as a way to seize opportunities in order to make space for more social and business-oriented alternatives, with agency from below. Rather than waiting for the Cuban state to expand *cuentapropismo* (self-employment) to the cultural and media industry, some Cubans are reclaiming their right and capacity to participate in that industry, without first asking permission. In that sense, Marshall McLuhan's famous dictum, "the medium is the message," is quite relevant to the use of digital technology in today's Cuba. The practices employed by ordinary Cuban citizens (as opposed to "digital critical voices" for example) are here more important to my argument, inasmuch as these practices constitute transgressions of the Cuban social and economic order imposed on the population by the Cuban authorities. These transgressive practices thus qualify as social critique.

At the same time, producing and distributing *el paquete* cannot be considered an independent alternative to the power of the GAFAM platforms, since it actually uses those same platforms in order to provide more information and entertainment options to their customers. It is relevant to underline the fact that *el paquete* contributes to diversifying people's access to news, leisure, and entertainment, whereas access used to be restricted to official media controlled by the Ideological Department of the Communist Party. At the same time, the creation of *el paquete* has entailed the commodification of a service, which used to be free, as the Cuban public TV and radio system were and are still accessible for the whole population at no cost. Although it is rather inexpensive by Western standards, as it costs between $1.00 and $3.00 (U.S.), depending on the freshness of the product, many Cubans cannot afford to subscribe to *el paquete*, especially if they are civil servants who do not receive remittances from abroad and have not managed to secure a position in the private sector. The same can be said of Netflix's streaming service, which cost $7.99 per month when it was introduced to Cuba in 2015,[8] putting it out of reach for most Cubans. This is to say nothing of the near impossibility of actually making credit card payments or streaming content from the U.S. in Cuba.

The "new collaborative media formats" created by ingenious Cuban techies, independent journalists, and entrepreneurs as a way to circumvent government's restrictions on the Internet create a paradox: they do circulate more information and more entertainment options than offered by the Cuban state sector, but at the same time they transform a formerly "free"[9] public good into a private commodity that only a few can afford. A reverse trend is here at play: whereas socialism tried to subtract certain goods and services from the market (providing them as citizen and human rights to "the people"), such logics tend to recommodify those goods and services. Moreover, whereas most social and citizen movements in the Western world try to make access to online content increasingly universal, such a progressive, "social" model of access to the Internet as a public good is ironically lacking in nominally "socialist" Cuba.

In the Cuban context, we must thus conclude—contrary to what Boullier seems to imply with his theorizing of critique—that the instruments of critique are not necessarily congruent with the type of critique being voiced. The GAFAM platforms do allow for the Cuban social order to be challenged from within, as they represent an alternative to the official information and communication channels. We must here paradoxically observe that the tools of digital capitalism can be used as vehicles for critique and even relative emancipation in the Cuban context, which still strictly monitors access and use of digital technology. This is true even as the Cuban state still defends certain "social-ist media" principles such as providing public audiovisual services free of charge and free from commercial content (and advertising) with its massive subsidizing of and legal monopolization over the official TV and radio channels and the cinema industry. Of course, Western activists also use GAFAM platforms to voice their concerns, organize, and dissent, but most social movements have simultaneously developed a social and political critique of these platforms, highlighting the danger their increasingly monopolistic power over information and interpersonal communication poses both to personal privacy and civil liberties and to the larger democratic process itself (Vaidhyanathan 2011, 2018; McNamee 2019). This awareness and critique has led many of them to try to craft alternative, noncommercial ways to inform and communicate. However, such debates and endeavors are rare in Cuba.

Nevertheless, the Cuban state, which claims to promote an "anti-hegemonic" economic and political model of society, has rejected out of hand the promotion of an alternative technological or nonproprietary "copyleft" model of society. Indeed, ETECSA recently signed a memorandum of understanding with Google which would connect Cuban networks with Google's in the U.S., thanks to a submarine cable (Marsh 2019). The objective is to boost Internet access for the population, which is sluggish, as it is only powered by another submarine cable between Cuba and Venezuela. Despite the existing tradition of alternative technology on the island and that of talented programmers, who know how to program without access to the Internet, the Cuban state has disengaged from such endeavors, as opposed to the decisions made by the Chinese state, for instance. Cuba thus heads every day more toward technological dependency vis-à-vis the United States and U.S.-based firms, as well as vis-à-vis China (which has developed most of the current Internet infrastructure used on the island) and Russia (cybersecurity technology) even while it trumpets its efforts to secure the island's "technological sovereignty" (*Prensa Latina* 2019).

The Professionalization of Digital Critique

The final part of this chapter focuses on the dynamics of professionalization of intentionally critical uses of digital technology in contemporary Cuba. Indeed, since 2014, many new, independent digital media platforms have been created on the island thanks in part to the recent expansion in access to the Internet, largely replacing the online social critique which blogs practiced between roughly 2004 and 2014 (see Henken, this volume). Whereas this trend was already strong in the Cuban diaspora during the first decade of the twenty-first century (thanks to the creation of pioneering blogs like *Penúltimos Días* and digital news sites such as *Café Fuerte*, *Diario de Cuba*, *CubaNet*, and the renovation of *CubaEncuentro*), the phenomenon emerged later on the island itself.

The emerging digital news platforms on the island work in a somewhat different way from the blogs. Blogs were generally very critical. They were often used to express rebellion vis-à-vis the Cuban state and the socialist social and political order (Hoffmann 2012; Vicari 2014). Thus, they dealt with a limited range of issues, which stemmed from their authors' personal experiences and their subjective desire to address subjects, which they deemed important. In contrast, the emerging news platforms that I highlight here have the ambition of offering a professional, informational service of the same kind as any other news service in the world, often justifying their existence with reference to the moribund, propagandistic nature of official Cuban journalism. Although some explicitly state they want to contribute to regime change (*14ymedio*,[10] *Cubanet*), most new independent media platforms (*OnCuba*,[11] *Periodismo de barrio*, *El Estornudo*, *El Toque*, *Cachivache Media*, *Play-Off*, *Postdata*, and *Negolution*) rather position themselves as alternative information options vis-à-vis the official press. Whatever their particular political stance (or lack thereof), however, they all claim to aim to do professional journalism, working according to standard professional norms without responding to higher (or hidden) political or economic interests.[12] Moreover, their decidedly journalistic endeavors have been recognized by international professional media associations.[13]

These emergent independent digital platforms generally define "professionalism" with three criteria: journalism is skilled work, business-oriented, and defined by ethics. First, these independent journalists were often educated in Cuban state schools of communication or journalism and they underline their professional skills and abilities (fact-checking, innovative communication schemes, computer networks, social networks, etc.), which allow them both to produce relevant information and to be able to have it reach the population despite the limitations of Internet in Cuba.[14] Moreover, the independent news platforms have invested in professional graphic design and self-presentation (as opposed to Cuban bloggers who had tended to favor a proudly amateur, subjective, and emotional approach), so as to give a professional image aligned with professional standards in the capitalist world. Some of the journalists even reject the idea that they are part of an emerging civil society in Cuba, instead insisting that they only seek to be considered professionals, the same as journalists elsewhere.[15]

Secondly, the emerging "news entrepreneurs" present their business model as based on sponsoring, crowdfunding, and advertising.[16] This allows them to diversify their income streams and to break free (in most cases) from both the Cuban state's grip and U.S. government interests, as they are less prone to be the target of powerful individuals or industries, who could seek to influence their editorial line. Moreover, one could imagine that, in an open and more prosperous society, they could also obtain revenue from readers' subscriptions. Of course, the use of advertising can create economic dependence, and this kind of asymmetrical relationship is not to be disregarded when assessing the work done by these new media outlets in the future. Dependence on certain sponsors could also lead to editorial pressure, although under authoritarian rule, grants and sponsorship are often less contingent on following a specific political line. This is the central paradox currently facing Cuba's new crop of independent digital media projects: although most do not want to be associated with any kind of political endeavor, the very existence of nonofficial media is considered dissidence by agencies such as the U.S. National Endowment for Democracy (NED) or the U.S. Agency for International Development (USAID) and by most other active or potential sponsors (an approach not dissimilar to that employed by the Cuban government itself).

Third, this new generation of digital journalists embraces a code of ethical conduct. For them, especially in the polarized Cuban media context, journalism must be done in a "serious and rigorous" way,[17] with "no binding ties with parties or ideologies."[18] Journalism is understood as an activity with "responsibility,"[19] not as a struggle to impose one group's perspective on reality. On the contrary, many of the pioneering practitioners of Cuba's new indie digital journalism see its main objective as the promotion of diversity and open space for debate. Although most of these emerging journalists do not directly address or openly criticize Fidel Castro's perspective on the role of the media as "truth creators" in the service of the Revolution (Santi 1991), they still clearly position themselves as critical social actors who create an alternative information option in an emerging and increasingly diverse media market, where they now compete with official journalists, who in turn need to adjust their own journalism practices to deal with these challenges.[20]

The new independent Cuban digital media thus clearly belong to Boullier's second type of critique: they work collaboratively (*14ymedio* is translated by a team of volunteers that calls itself "Translating Cuba," while *El Toque* welcomes readers' contributions), they strive to promote more plural ways of rendering social reality (looking for untold stories and invisible people), and to show how diverse Cuban society really is. They give a voice to the voiceless and try to give visibility to popular perspectives on reality (*Periodismo de Barrio*, *El Toque*), they offer critical perspectives on the Cuban as well as on the international social and political order (*14ymedio*, *El Estornudo*, *Postdata*), while promoting "the excellent, the exquisite, the exemplary" in Cuba (*OnCuba*) and entertainment (*Cachivache Media*, *Play-Off*), rather than always focusing on what went/goes wrong. In a nutshell, these new media rediscover thousands of shades of grey to describe a Cuban reality, which is often only depicted in black and white by the official Cuban press of course, but also by many mainstream international media based outside Cuba.

One might expect that such independent, alternative voices would also look for alternative means to convey their message, and that their critique of the dominant "revolutionary" social and political order would also lead them to criticize or resist the functioning of the dominant globalized economic order—especially as manifest via the GAFAM platforms. However, only *Periodismo de Barrio* (which employs a Creative Commons license) seems to have engaged in a reflection on issues of power linked to the Internet, social media, and their related technological tools that is not limited to the power unleashed by critical uses of these tools to challenge the Cuban government. Thus, most websites fight censorship and repression with capitalist hegemonic tools, apparently without questioning the irony or contradiction latent in their uses of these tools.

Moreover, there seems to be little interest in the debate over the new domination dynamics entailed by digital capitalism, sometimes referred to as "surveillance capitalism" (Zuboff 2019; McNamee 2019).[21] And Cuba's independent digital news projects do not seem concerned with issues linked to the endless collection of big data. For instance, the latest such scandal, which involved the collection of personal information of eighty-seven million Facebook users by the British firm Cambridge Analytica for political purposes, was not reported at all in *El Toque*, *Periodismo de Barrio*, or *El Estornudo*; and *14ymedio* and *Cubanet* only reproduced press agency cables. *OnCuba* was the only platform that devoted some attention to the subject.

I find it especially relevant to underline such an omission here since Cambridge Analytica intended to influence voter opinion in favor of the political position of those who paid the firm to do so. Its purpose was to manipulate political information during an election, while "free and fair elections" is one of the most crucial rules of the game in contemporary liberal democracies—and sorely lacking in Cuba. Such a matter should be of the utmost importance for new media outlets, which, because they are concerned with professional matters and strive to craft a new professional media sector in Cuba, do also, in the process, strive to transform journalism so as to make it one of the pillars of a new and more democratic future order in their country.

This lack of coverage of the scandal can be interpreted in three different ways. First, perhaps these independent journalists are little concerned with electoral issues in the democratic world, as they would rather focus on the effect of authoritarian rule, which directly affects them. One would nonetheless expect such a position to be publicly clarified. A second possible interpretation is that they do not consider the privacy issue a priority, or that they are not sensitive to big data issues as they face other kinds of restrictions on their activity, linked not so much to market disregard for the law but to the repressive power of the state. As the Chinese example clearly shows, big data collection is not specific to private firms. It is also used by repressive states, as well as by supposedly less repressive, democratic states, as an instrument to control people's use of the Internet and to influence their political behavior. A final interpretation of this silence could be that Cubans are unaware of the challenges at stake given their own daily struggle with mere access to the Internet and against state control, surveillance, and censorship.

Whatever the answer may be, we must conclude that Cuba's new digital media have not yet developed the third type of critique theorized by Boullier, which entails a critical reflection on the technological means used to convey critique. And thus neither have they developed the fourth type of critique, which concerns the production of knowledge and big data issues. Although the Postdata project seems to be interested in the issue of privacy, and thus in data gathering and data protection, probably none of the other new platforms can easily perform critical analysis of big data-related issues—although the Inventario project that seeks to be an interface between large, hard to locate digital data sets and Cuba's digital indie startups may be doing this kind of spadework.

Conclusion

When access to the Internet was still highly restricted in Cuba, contentious uses were highly overrepresented and given great visibility abroad. This situation paved the way for a whole field of academic research on the impact of blogs and new media on the heretofore disconnected island, especially as far as their potential for contributing to democratization. Most works focused on Boullier's first category of critique, that is on those activists who denounced the social and political order in Cuba and strove to spread their neglected or censored perspective of reality.

However, this category of critique is not the most widespread in Cuba. Indeed, the gradual liberalization of Internet access has rather enhanced informal economic activities linked to emerging information and communication technologies (see Cearns, this volume) and led to the professionalization of contentious voices of young, state-educated journalists through the appearance of new alternative media platforms (see Somohano Fernández and Márquez-Ramírez, this volume). Both these types of new digital entrepreneurship are relevant to study, as they can be understood as a growth in the more ordinary, not explicitly political uses of the Internet. At the same time, given the specific constraints that limit the use of the Internet in Cuba, these innovative uses of digital technology should be understood as a kind of social critique as theorized by Boullier. Indeed, although these entrepreneurs cannot always be considered activists, their activities contribute to social change in Cuba as they allow for the growing visibility of the social, economic, cultural, and political diversification of the Cuban reality. They also socialize their readers in the existence of a wide variety of alternative, critical "takes" on that reality—ones that must be answered whether directly or indirectly in the official media.

The Cuban situation thus offers a striking paradox: the Goliath state, often portrayed as all-seeing, all-knowing, and all-powerful, is not equipped with either the political or technological tools to curb its growing dependency on the technology of the U.S.-based GAFAM firms. At the same time, the multiple David-like social actors, who generate social critique, actively benefit from the penetration of such global firms on the island. Goliath is becoming obsolete as the chief arbiter of media, while David is empowered as increasingly more credible and trustworthy. Still, David does not seem to be aware of his similar technological dependency on and vulnerability to the other GAFAM Goliath storming the gates. While he is used to fighting or resisting the Cuban state, he will now need to struggle against or navigate among a two-headed Hydra: the Cuban state and the Internet oligopolies, whose constraints on both ordinary uses of digital technology as well as professional media uses are stronger each day (Smyrnaios 2018).

NOTES

1. In the Cuban context, these are some of the worst, most damning insults. They are meant to dehumanize those who left the island after 1959 and are thus considered counter-revolutionaries—placing them not merely outside the Revolution but squarely *against* it.

2. GAFAM stands for Google, Apple, Facebook, Amazon, and Microsoft, but the idea also includes Twitter, Yahoo, Instagram, Snapchat, Airbnb, etc. Essentially, GAFAM is shorthand for the massive U.S.-based firms that dominate the digital market. In English, it is more common to refer GAFAM as the "Internet oligopoly," the "Big Five," or simply "The Five." See Scott Galloway (2017), *The Four,* which focuses on the so-called hidden DNA of Amazon, Apple, Facebook, and Google.

3. For discussions on these two schools of thought and their transformation over the past twenty years, see Luc Boltanski and Laurent Thévenot, "The sociology of critical capacity," *European Journal of Social Theory* 2, No. 3, 1999: 359–377; Thomas Benatouïl, "A Tale of Two Sociologies: The critical and the pragmatic stance in French Sociology," *European Journal of Social Theory* 2, No. 3, 1999: 379–396; Simon Susen, "Towards a Critical Sociology of Dominant Ideologies: An Unexpected Reunion between Pierre Bourdieu and Luc Boltanski," *Cultural Sociology* 10, No. 2, 2016: 195–246; Magnus Paulsen Hansen, "Non Normative Critique. Foucault and pragmatic sociology as tactical re-politicization," *European Journal of Social Theory* 19, No. 1, 2016: 127–145.

4. See the group's Facebook page: https://www.facebook.com/blackhat4all/.

5. Yoani Sánchez, "Cuba. Dame cable!" *HACER Latin American News*, September 1, 2011.

6. "Presidente ejecutivo de Google visita Cuba," *14ymedio*, June 28, 2014.

7. According to Jon Lee Anderson, forty-five thousand Cubans work in the production and distribution of *el paquete,* and private business owners pay so that advertisements for their goods and services are included in its editions. See "Opening for Business," *The New Yorker*, July 20, 2015.

8. Jessica Glenza, "Netflix launches $7.99 service for Cuba despite average wage of $17 a month," *The Guardian*, February 9, 2015.

9. I should make it clear here that there are two definitions of "free" in digital space: free as in "no cost" versus free meaning "open, nonproprietary." I here refer to what used to be "free" (i.e., a public good, available at no cost).

10. See "Quienes Somos?" *14ymedio*, http://www.14ymedio.com/quienes-somos.html). "We are working so that the moment when every Cuban can read us online freely or buy our paper at a newspaper kiosk comes more quickly."

11. *OnCuba* differs from the other platforms. It is a binational platform, legally based both in Cuba and in the U.S. Directly sponsored by U.S. business interests, it includes advertising from domestic private businesses operated in Cuba. While it operates with the same press credentials that foreign media do, most of its employees are Cuban nationals who have studied journalism in Cuban universities. See Jon Lee Anderson, "Opening for Business," *The New Yorker*, July 20, 2015.

12. According to the declaration on its "Quienes Somos?" page, *14ymedio* focuses on doing "journalism" without concessions to the influence of parties, ideologies, and the market. *El Estornudo* presents itself as "an independent journal of narrative journalism made in Cuba, outside of Cuba, and about Cuba." *Postdata* does data journalism exclusively. See Paola Nalvarte, "Data journalism reaches Cuba," Knight Center for Journalism in the Americas, October 14, 2016. *Play-Off* and *Negolution* are topical monthly digital magazines circulated via PDF that cover sports and business, respectively.

13. Jorge Carrasco from *El Estornudo* received the Gabriel García Márquez journalism award (see https://premioggm.org, September 29, 2017) and *Postdata* was a finalist in the DataJournalism awards (https://awards.journalists.org/entries/postdata-club/).

14. Presentation of the technical strategies of the new media by Raidel Pérez Cuello, telecommunications engineer, Panel, "Cuba-EE.UU.: Estrechando vínculos desde Internet y las comunicaciones," Latin American Studies Association conference, New York, May 2016.

15. An example is Elaine Díaz's presentation at the LASA conference in New York City, May 2016. Also see *14ymedio*'s "Quienes Somos" section and *Postdata*'s presentation of its project: https://awards.journalists.org/entries/postdata-club/.

16. Ibid.

17. See "Sobre nosotros," *El Toque,* https://eltoque.com/sobre-nosotros/. See *Postdata*'s presentation of its project as well: https://awards.journalists.org/entries/postdata-club/.

18. See "Quienes somos," *14ymedio*, http://www.14ymedio.com/quienes-somos.html.

19. Ibid.

20. In order to face these challenges, the Cuban authorities have created their own official websites (*Cubadebate*, created in 2003 and recrafted in 2009, and the online encyclopedia *Ecured*—a closed clone of Wikipedia—in 2010). Likewise, they have urged official journalists to create their own blogs so as to give the impression that revolutionary activists are as present and active online to defend the Cuban government as are its critics. More recently, this official pro-regime pushback has appeared on Twitter as well.

21. The only exception is *Postdata*, a new Cuban data journalism platform, which has addressed the lack of privacy in the widespread leaking of ETECSA's user database (Guerra 2016).

References

Arsène, Séverine. 2011. *Internet et politique en Chine*. Paris: Karthala.
Bax, Trent. 2014. *Youth and Internet Addiction in China*. New York: Routledge.
Boullier, Dominique. 2015. "Les sciences sociales face aux traces du big data." *Revue Française de Science Politique* 65, No. 5: 805–828.
Boullier, Dominique. 2016. *Sociologie du numérique*. Paris: Armand Colin.
Boullier, Dominique. 2018. "Post face." In *La critique du numérique*, edited by Roland Canu, Johann Chaulet, Caroline Datchary, and Julien Figeac. Paris: L'Harmattan.
Cardon, Dominique and Fabien Granjon. 2010. *Médiactivistes*. Paris: Presses de Sciences Po.
Deibert, Ronald. 2003. "Black Code: Censorship, Surveillance, and Militarization of Cyberspace." *Millennium: Journal of International Studies* 32, No. 3.

Galloway, Scott. 2017. *The Four: The Hidden DNA of Amazon, Apple, Facebook, and Google*. New York: Portfolio.

Geoffray, Marie Laure. 2015. "Transnational dynamics of contention in contemporary Cuba." *Journal of Latin American Studies* 47, No. 2: 223–249.

Guerra, Ernesto. 2016. "El caso Etecsa. Problema de privacidad." *Postdata*, September 22, 2016.

Henken, Ted. 2011. "Una cartografía de la blogosfera cubana. Entre 'oficialistas' y 'mercenarios.'" *Nueva Sociedad*, No. 235, September-October: 90–109.

Henken, Ted. 2014. "The Internet and emergent blogosphere in Cuba: Downloading democracy, booting up development or planting the virus of dissidence and destabilization." *Cuba in Transition* 24: 122–126.

Henken, Ted A. 2017. "Cuba's Digital Millennials: Independent Digital Media and Civil Society on the Island of the Disconnected." *Social Research* 84, no. 2: 429–456.

Henken, Ted A. 2021. "The Opium of the *Paquete*: State Censorship, Private Self-Censorship, and the Content Distribution Strategies of Cuba's Emergent, Independent Digital Media Startups." *Cuban Studies* 50.

Hoffmann, Bert. 2012. "Civil society in the digital age: How the Internet changes state-society relations in authoritarian regimes. The case of Cuba." In *Civil Society Activism under Authoritarian Rule. A comparative perspective*, edited by Francesco Cavatorta, 219–244. New York: Routledge.

Kalathil, Shanti and Taylor Boas. 2003. *Open Networks, Closed Regimes: The Impact of the Internet on Authoritarian Rule*. Washington D.C.: Carnegie Endowment for International Peace.

Lecomte, Romain. 2013. "Expression politique et activisme en ligne en contexte autoritaire. Une analyse du cas tunisien." *Réseaux* 5, No. 181: 51–86.

Levine, Yasha. 2018. *Surveillance Valley: The Secret Military History of the Internet*. New York: Public Affairs.

Marsh, Sarah. 2019. "Google, Cuba agree to work toward improving island's connectivity." Reuters, March 28, 2019.

Martin, Olivier and Dagiral Eric. 2016. *L'ordinaire d'internet. Le web dans nos pratiques et relations sociales*. Paris: Armand Colin.

Mazzarella, Sharon R. 2005. *Girl Wide Web: Girls, the Internet, and the Negotiation of Identity*. New York, Peter Lang.

McNamee, Roger. 2019. *Zucked: Waking Up to the Facebook Catastrophe*. New York: Penguin.

Messin, Audrey. 2007. "La culture ordinaire de l'écran : l'usage social d'internet par les jeunes adultes." Ph.D. dissertation, Panthéon-Assas University.

Morozov, Evgeny. 2011. *The Net Delusion: The Dark Side of Internet Freedom*. New York: PublicAffairs.

Parodi, Emmanuel and Eric Sautedé. 1995. "Internet en Chine, une modernité qui tolère mal le contrôle." *Perspectives chinoises* 29, No. 29: 37–43.

Prensa Latina. 2019. "Aboga presidente de Cuba por desarrollar soberanía tecnológica." June 13, 2019.

Risen, Tom. 2014. "Google Makes Internet Freedom Visit to Cuba." *US News and World Report*, June 30, 2014.

Santi, Enrico Mario. 1991. "A Cheap Glasnost: Writing and Journalism in Cuba Today." In *Cuba and the United States: Will the Cold War in the Caribbean End?*, edited by J. S. Tulchin and Rafael Hernández R., 41–42. Boulder, Colorado: Lynne Rienner Publishers.

Seargeant, Philip and Caroline Tagg. 2014. *The Language of Social Media: Identity and Community on the Internet*. London: Palgrave Macmillan.

Shirky, Clay. 2008. *Here Comes Everybody*. New York: Penguin Press.

Simon, Leslie David, Javier Corrales, and Donald Wolfensberger. 2002. *Democracy and the Internet: Allies or Adversaries*. Washington, D.C.: Woodrow Wilson Center Press.

Smyrnaios, Nikos. 2018. *Internet Oligopoly: The Corporate Takeover of Our Digital World*. Emerald Publishing: Bingley.

Vaidhyanathan, Siva. 2011. *The Googlization of Everything (And Why We Should Worry)*. Berkeley: University of California Press.

Vaidhyanathan, Siva. 2018. *Antisocial Media: How Facebook Disconnects Us and Undermines Democracy*. Oxford: Oxford University Press.

Vela, Hatzel and Andrea Torres. 2015. "Smugglers of the '*paquetes*' make a living in Havana." Local 10, December 4, 2015.

Vicari, Estefania. 2014. "Blogging politics in Cuba: The framing of political discourse in the Cuban blogosphere." *Media, Culture, and Society* 36, No. 7: 901–915.

Wellmann, Barry and Caroline Haythornthwaite. 2002. *The Internet in Everyday Life*. Malden, MA: Blackwell Publishers.

Zuboff, Shoshana. 2019. *The Age of Surveillance Capitalism: The Fight for a Human Future at the New Frontier of Power*. New York: PublicAffairs.

III
JOURNALISM

7

From *Generación Y* to *14ymedio*

Beyond the Blog on Cuba's Digital Frontier

TED A. HENKEN

In April 2007, a then virtually unknown returned Cuban émigré named Yoani Sánchez, who had come home to Havana in 2004 after a frustrated two-year attempt at starting a new life in Zurich, launched the blog *Generación Y*. It would rapidly become Cuba's most widely read and influential blog over the next seven years—the fleeting but fecund heyday of the so-called *blogósfera cubana* (2007–2014). Sánchez became admired by regime critics and reviled by government supporters in equal measure during that time thanks to her nonstop stream of brief, richly narrated, "day-in-the-life" posts chronicling what for her (and her eponymous "generation") were the countless broken promises and endless daily indignities of life under the always triumphant banner of the Cuban Revolution (Peters 2007).

Instead of revisiting the storied ascent of Sánchez and *Generación Y* already widely chronicled by many journalists (Israel 2007; *Wall Street Journal* 2007; Vicent 2008; Schmidt-Häuer 2008; McKinley 2008), this chapter seeks to highlight some of the lesser-known but perhaps more telling lessons hidden behind Sánchez's breakout success as a blogger that paved the way for her current project *14ymedio*, because they reveal a pattern of "convergence" later followed by other indie media pioneers on the island. One important distinction in this pattern is that while Sánchez moved gradually from independent blogging to independent journalism, many others who were trained in journalism at Cuban universities have moved from official journalism to independent journalism. That is, her path was to *embrace journalism* in an increasingly professional way whereas their path has been to *embrace independence* so that they could develop professionally as journalists, leaving the official media and its strictures behind. Most notable during her "breakout" years between 2007 and 2010 was Sánchez's open embrace and celebration of "citizen journalism" and blogging as the vehicles *par excellence* of speaking truth to power in an authoritarian political context where the mass media is a legal state monopoly.

However, despite her blog's initial popularity (or perhaps precisely *because* of it), by 2014 Sánchez eventually abandoned the blogging format as her primary media platform in exchange for the larger and much more ambitious independent media project known as *14ymedio*. A digital daily newspaper with aims that reach far beyond the personal, anecdotal, and necessarily subjective tone and scope of a blog, *14ymedio* has sought to produce credible information and reportage on a daily basis for a Cuban public hungry for investigative, accountability,[1] and adversarial journalism that is also professionally responsible. Moreover, the *14ymedio* team has sought to accomplish this journalistic goal in a context where "the news" produced by the official press had long since become synonymous with state propaganda and where "most articles in the independent press [had been] more opinions and allegations than verified information" (Henken 2017). That is, as practiced in Cuba both the long-standing tradition of offline independent journalism and its newer variant known as *periodismo ciudadano digital* (digital citizen journalism) have been more of a passion than a profession, carrying with them the costs and benefits than any passion project entails.

While Sánchez and her colleagues at *14ymedio* were among the first to trade in their often singular and passionate blogs for a more coordinated, collective, and professional effort at credible, objective reporting—shifting away from *periodismo ciudadano* (citizen journalism) toward *periodismo y punto* (journalism, period)—they were far from alone in this pioneering digital media enterprise. Indeed, the recent emergence of a diverse array of Cuban indie media pioneers and enterprises has been described by Cuban journalist Bárbara Maseda, the founding director of the data journalism project *Inventario* (2018), as a succession of three waves.[2] First came indie startups (like *14ymedio*) staffed mostly by people *not* trained as journalists who have aimed at resurrecting Cuban journalism. Then came independent outlets (like *El Toque, Periodismo de Barrio*, and *El Estornudo*) that were founded and are staffed by graduates of Cuban journalism schools who have a more formal command of journalism techniques and have helped improve the quality of the resurrected journalism. They have also either steadfastly refused to work in the state media they were trained for, or in some cases, paid for their indie "freelancing" by being unceremoniously dismissed from their state media jobs.

Finally, and much more recently, "now that independent journalism has accomplished all of the above," indicates Maseda, "new outlets [like *Tremenda Nota* and *YucaByte*] can afford to focus on very specific topics and audiences (a.k.a., do 'niche journalism'), and this is improving the depth of the stories and shaping strong beat coverage." Since covering all three of these waves is well beyond the scope of this chapter, here I focus exclusively on the transformations of Sánchez's indie media project in the fifteen years between her return to Havana in 2004 and May 21, 2019—the five-year anniversary of the founding of *14ymedio*—with an emphasis on its innovations over the past five years (2014–2019) that have moved the digital daily well "beyond the blog."

THE GENESIS OF *GENERACIÓN Y*

Founding and Finding *Consenso*, 2004–2007

While Sánchez and *Generación Y* have become quite famous internationally since she won Spain's Ortega y Gasset journalism prize and was named one of *Time* magazine's one hundred most influential people in May 2008, her blog grew out of the digital magazine *Consenso*, a more deeply collaborative media project launched in December 2004, more than two years before *Generación Y*'s appearance. Hosted at the site DesdeCuba.com, *Consenso* was run collaboratively by Marta Cortízas, Eugenio Leal, Yoani Sánchez, Reinaldo Escobar, Miriam Celaya, and Dimas Castellanos.

From its inception, *Consenso desde Cuba* saw itself as a Web portal for the development of citizen journalism, giving visibility to opinions found neither in Cuba's official media nor in any other publication "conditioned by political requirements," as *Consenso* itself put it. This online magazine or "e-zine"[3] also consciously sought to stake out a moderate, progressive tone distinguishing itself from hardliners of all stripes. Indeed, its masthead declared it: "A space of reflection and debate for Cuban progressive thinking." In its inaugural editorial of December 2004, *Consenso* called for a pluralistic, respectful, and serious tone, rejecting the use of insults and personal attacks common to Cuba's political culture. Its motto was, "Let us come together with respect for our differences" ("ponernos de acuerdo, desde la diferencia"), and it called on Cubans of all political persuasions (and in all places) to renounce verbal violence and begin to learn to debate one another with civility.

In an interview with Sánchez in her Havana home in July 2008, she explained the special importance of citizen journalism in the Cuban context, where the state monopolizes the mass media always using the royal "we," presuming to speak in the name of the Cuban people as subjects rather than dialoguing with them as citizens. "Citizen journalism is shaking the very foundations of traditional journalism," Sánchez observed. For her, citizen journalists are people who are not media professionals but who live in the places where "the news" is happening. Thanks to the increasing ubiquity of mobile and social media technologies, these renegade "former members of the audience" (Rosen 2012) do not have to wait for the "pros" to show up but can themselves write, film, record, and photograph the reality that surrounds them, transforming themselves from idle receptors of information into its transmitters. "That," declared Sánchez, "is a hard blow to Cuba's culture of massification."

Consenso published its last issue in December 2007 at which time both its name and format were changed. Now called *Contodos*, the newly christened "webmag" increasingly resembled a blog in format and in fact had already begun hosting a growing number of individual blogs during 2007, including that of Sánchez herself. In June 2009, *Contodos* itself was discontinued as the DesdeCuba project had by that time morphed once again. In the group's final statement, titled "We Continue to Evolve," posted at *Contodos* on June 22, 2009, the editorial board described the ongoing transformation of their media project saying, "We have definitively adopted citizen journalism as our approach, which rests basically on a portal composed of blogs. The traditional concept of a magazine, with a fixed frequency of issues, a top-down editorial line, and different topical sections, fits neither with our goals nor with our limitations." Of course, the irony here is that it is just this kind of "traditional" journalistic approach that Sánchez would later embrace as the format for her digital daily *14ymedio* in 2014.

The Last Straw: *La Polémica Intelectual*

The spark that led Sánchez to begin blogging in April 2007 was the *polémica intelectual* in January-February 2007. Perhaps the most salient fact about this intellectual debate was that it took place almost entirely *online* via a long series of "reply all" e-mails circulated among Cuban artists and intellectuals. Sánchez herself participated in this *guerrita emáilica* (little war of e-mails), but wound up with the bitter aftertaste of another lost opportunity at being largely shut out of the debate. That led directly to the appearance of her blog two months later.

In January 2007, a number of Cuban artists and intellectuals became alarmed when three of the most infamous cultural commissars from the early 1970s, Luis Pavón Tamayo, Jorge "Papito" Serguera, and Armando Quesada, were successively featured in retrospective celebratory interviews on Cuban state television.[4] Since these figures were notorious among Cuba's intelligentsia for having designed and implemented the repressive cultural policies of the 1970s, many saw their public vindication as an insulting attempt to rewrite history, willfully ignoring the deep scar their dogmatic, Stalinist policies had left on Cuban culture. However, since these outraged intellectuals lacked any independent institution or media presence where they could demand an explanation, they turned almost instinctively to the Internet to express their outrage, beginning an unprecedented debate about the repressive cultural policies of the 1970s, the so-called *quinquenio gris*.

For her part, the young and then unknown Sánchez (she was just thirty-one years old at the time) joined the debate by making the characteristically incisive point that the fact that the debate itself was taking place via e-mail had the consequence of preventing the vast majority of Cubans from participating in it either because they didn't belong to the proper institution (which provided members with a coveted "@cubarte.cult.cu" e-mail address) or lacked the funds to pay Cuba's prohibitive Internet prices.

> If the way of the "*emilios*" [e-mails] is the highest step Cuban intellectuals can count on to carry out an open debate, that in itself demonstrates that they are prohibited from using other media outlets. How can [intellectuals] be the critical conscience of a nation if they can barely share their opinions with their fellow citizens?

For Sánchez, a debate which had begun in such a spontaneous, grassroots, and wide-ranging manner left her exasperated, given that the discussion was officially declared over just when it was gaining momentum and beginning to reach beyond a strictly cultural realm. In fact, a turning point of sorts came for her when she unsuccessfully attempted to gain access to the "public" presentation, "The *Quinquenio Gris*: Revisiting the Term," held on January 30, 2007, at Casa de las Americas, one of Cuba's leading cultural institutions. Young and unaffiliated with any cultural institution, she and a group of other nascent intellectuals found themselves excluded, left outside in the cold for five hours as they demanded entry and chanted, "Desiderio, Desiderio, oye mi criterio" (Desiderio, Desiderio, listen to my opinion).[5]

In response, in her final e-mail message to the group on February 15, 2007, Sánchez hinted at her as yet unrealized intention to continue the debate. "The hour is quickly approaching," she wrote, "for us to make our own space for debate and reflection without waiting for them to include us on the list of invited guests." Her intention was to carry this and other necessary debates forward into a (cyber-)space by using a medium (the blog) that Cuba's old guard cultural commissars would have limited ability to control. "MANY

MORE DEBATES STILL AWAIT US," she ended her declaration in all caps, "AND WE WILL NO LONGER CONTINUE WAITING FOR THEM TO INVITE US TO PARTICIPATE" (Sánchez 2007).

From Cyberspace to Public Space: The Evolution of *Generación Y*, 2007–2014

From Fear to Catharsis

Since its launch in April 2007, *Generación Y* has undergone a constant transformation in a dynamic interaction with its many readers, collaborators, and critics. Feeling suffocated by the Orwellian fear of making her internal

Figure 7.1. Censoring the Heretical, from Rome to Havana. Translation: *Monk 1*: "Look! They censored Galileo's blog." *Monk 2*: "Of course! You know the Earth does NOT move." The original graphic included the following text printed below the image: "Since the publication of the complete documentation of the judgement against Galileo in 1870, all responsibility for Galileo's condemnation has traditionally fallen upon the Catholic Church in Rome, hiding the responsibility of the professors of philosophy who persuaded the theologians that the discoveries of Galileo were heretical. Pope John Paul II opened up an investigation in 1979 regarding the Church's condemnation of the astronomer so as to possibly revise it. In October 1992, a papal commission recognized the Vatican's error." The artist, Lázaro Saavedra, indicated to the author that this illustration was penned as a reaction to the government's blocking of Sánchez's blog in 2008. Credit/Source: Lázaro Saavedra, from the series "GALERÍA I-MEIL" (2008), used with permission.

thoughts public, Sánchez initially conceived of her blog as a modest effort at what she called an "individual catharsis" and "an exercise in cowardice," where she could say online what she was then not brave (or stupid) enough to say in public. She aimed to shake off her fear by writing about precisely what paralyzed her most. "My blog is a kind of personal exorcism," explained Sánchez in our 2008 interview, "where I expose my many accumulated demons: inaction, apathy, dissatisfactions, frustrations, and above all questions."

Indeed, one of the defining elements of *Generación Y* is its constant questioning of reality—a public interrogation of the world in which she and her generation have come of age. Proudly partial, Sánchez claimed at the time to "lack the objectivity of an analyst, the tools of a journalist, and the smooth measure of an academic"—a significant admission for someone who would later aspire to be *una periodista y punto*. However, she celebrated this approach at the time as the very essence of citizen journalism. "My texts are impetuous and subjective," she crowed. "I commit the sacrilege of using the first personal singular and my readers have understood that I only speak of that which I have lived." Perhaps the single most unique characteristic of *Generación Y*, however, immediately distinguishing it from the handful of other independent, critical-minded blogs that existed at the time, was its refusal to hide behind a pseudonym. In a context of polarization and paranoia, the fact that this relatively unknown young woman would make such critical declarations while showing her face and giving her real name provoked both admiration and suspicion from her readers, as well as the eventual blocking of her blog from access via Cuban state-controlled servers (figure 7.1).

Reader Feedback, International Recognition, and "La Red Ciudadana"

During a second stage of *Generación Y*'s development, Sánchez began to react directly to reader feedback as she realized that her exercise in personal catharsis had morphed into an international dialogue about Cuba with readers who could identify with the world she described. Also, during this time a series of leading international media outlets began to run profiles of the Internet and blogs in Cuba, all prominently featuring her unique audacity and wit (*Reuters*, *The Wall Street Journal*, *El País*, Germany's *Die Zeit*, and *The New York Times*). Significantly, the blog's increased international profile along with the sympathy of many of its readers led over time to the development of a netroots *red ciudadana* (citizen network) of international commenters, supporters, and collaborators who began to help Sánchez and the growing independent Cuban blogger community by administering their blogs remotely and translating their posts into various languages.

Another strategy that Sánchez and her colleagues first deployed in the

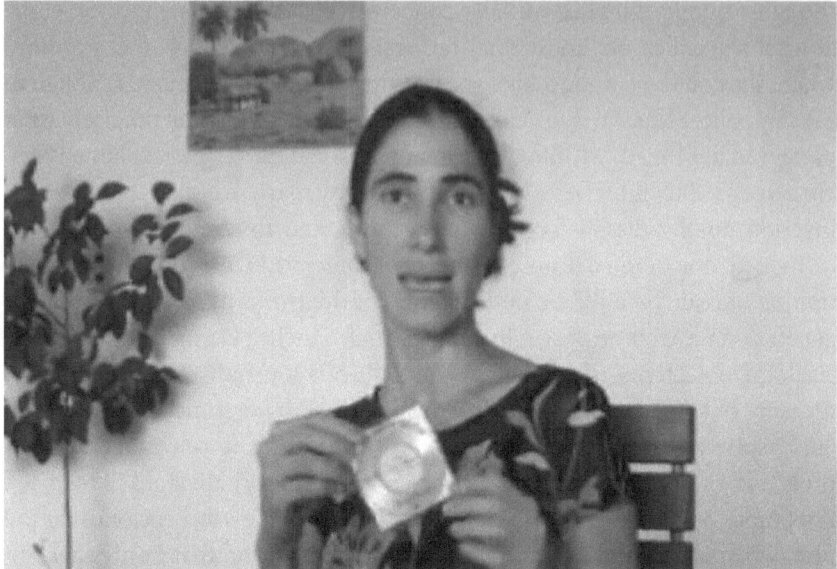

Figure 7.2. The minidisk. Still extracted from a video recording made by the author of Yoani Sánchez in her Havana home, July 2008.

summer of 2008—one that would anticipate the wildly popular digital entertainment distribution network that came to be known as *el paquete*—was copying her entire blog onto a minidisk and distributing it by hand within Cuba, poking a hole in the government's "information blockade" within the island (figure 7.2).[6] Thus, while her *red ciudadana* strategy allowed her to overcome the obstacle of the lack of Internet access to reach her readers *outside* of Cuba, this minidisk strategy was aimed at ensuring her readers *within* the island could gain access to her texts, despite her blog's being censored by the government. As she happily declared in our 2008 interview: "There is nothing more attractive to me than that which has been declared off limits!"

From Cyberspace to Public Space

Sánchez's post, "La red ciudadana," points to the unexpected fact that, "what had begun as an individual impulse is becoming a meeting place for discussion and debate."[7] However, it turned out that this was true in the sense not only that her blog had become a meeting place for her many readers and commenters to come together in cyberspace but also that she and her colleagues began to take the concerns she broached in the cyberspace of her blog into the public space of Havana's streets, government offices, and conference halls for the first time. The first instance of this came in late

August 2008 when Sánchez and a number of her friends led a public protest against the arrest of Gorki Águila, a Cuban punk rocker and lead singer for the group Porno para Ricardo. Their protest seems to have influenced the government's decision to release him after only a few days, a fact Sánchez chronicled in five successive posts, culminating in her August 31 text, "Brief chronicle of a victory."

Emboldened, Sánchez and her fellow bloggers continued to engage in these episodes of guerrilla street theater, now often armed with YouTube-ready handheld cameras or cell phones that could convert local SMS messages into a global Twitter feed, transforming her blog into a medium for broadcasting audacious challenges to state power usually followed by embarrassing episodes of state repression.[8] Perhaps Sánchez's most provocative use of her blog as a platform to broadcast episodes of state repression and restrictions on civic and political freedoms was in October 2009 when a number of Sánchez's colleagues were denied access to an "Último Jueves" debate about the Internet in Cuba held by *Temas* magazine at the Cuban Film Institute's Fresa y Chocolate Café. Anticipating that she too would be denied entry to the supposedly open event, Sánchez slipped in past the guards undetected wearing a tight skirt, silk stockings, and a blond wig (far from her usual "earth mother" style of dress). Her defiant declaration about Internet restrictions in Cuba was captured on film by a friendly videographer and subsequently posted on her blog ("With wig and without Internet" and "Closed doors," October 30, 2009).[9]

Each of the episodes share three key, innovative characteristics that added a daring, "extra-virtual" dimension to Sánchez's blog. First, each episode involved a public action; that is, it involved a Cuban citizen (usually Sánchez accompanied by one or more of her fellow independent bloggers) impertinently speaking "out of turn" in a public space.[10] Second, each episode was an instance of her speaking "truth to power." That is, it inverted the top-down authoritarian power relations typical between Cuban citizens and government officials. As opposed to a commander in chief giving orders for his subjects (or soldiers) to obediently follow, these episodes all involve citizens insisting on being heard as equals and demanding to have their questions and concerns addressed by those officials who supposedly represent their interests. Third, each episode of the taking of public space quickly became part of cyberspace as it was recorded (sometimes surreptitiously) and posted to Sánchez's blog via YouTube—thus transforming it into an international incident where, as the 1960s saying goes, "the whole world is watching."

14YMEDIO: "From a Personal Adventure to a Collective Project," 2014–2019

> We will not do barricade journalism, but journalism in the broadest sense of the word, with neither pedagogical pretensions nor commercial concessions. Informing, sharing opinions, opening spaces for debate, and respecting those who think differently, will help us to harmonize [the values of] freedom of expression with [our] responsibility as citizens.
>
> *14ymedio,* "Who are we?" May 2014

The final transformation to date in the fifteen-year evolution of Sánchez's indie media trajectory from "digital unknown" (*Consenso* and *Contodos*) to "digital dissident," "citizen journalist," and internationally renowned blogger (*Generación Y* and *Voces Cubanas*), to professional journalist and editor (*14ymedio*) began with a long period of strategizing (at home) and travel (abroad) in 2013 and early 2014. In other words, she went from running a *blog* to running a *business*; from being a blogger to becoming a journalist and media director; from relying on a "citizen network" of volunteers—an unpaid webmaster and many translators doing a digital, crowdsourced version of Che Guevara's *trabajo voluntario* based on solidarity (Henken and Porter 2016), to managing a group of employees—reporters, columnists, photographers, editors, webmasters, investors, business partners, lawyers, etc.—based on professional criteria and contractual remuneration.

She also had to figure out how to go from living off the proceeds of awards to developing a sustainable business model based on a reliable stream of revenue. Moreover, all these tasks had to be undertaken at the very moment traditional print journalism was undergoing an unprecedented existential crisis unleashed by the digital revolution, including blogs. Luckily, in this most recent transformation, Sánchez has benefited from the lessons learned during her earlier roles as webmaster of *Consenso*, coeditor of *Contodos*, and coordinator of *Voces Cubanas*, along with the many other collective digital media endeavors of "citizen journalism" she had undertaken between the opening of *Generación Y* in April 2007 and the launch of *14ymedio* in May 2014.

Around the World in a Hundred Days

Given that Sánchez had become Cuba's best internationally known blogger since 2007 (in part because the Cuban government prevented her from leaving twenty times between 2008 and 2013), her successful renewal of her Cuban passport at the end of January 2013 and planned departure for Brazil on February 17 to start a three-and-a-half month, thirteen-country world tour became the most prominent test case of Cuba's new migration law that eliminated the much-hated exit visa. Would the government permit her to travel? Would she be allowed to return? Would she be punished upon return for using her bully pulpit while abroad to blast the regime (García 2013; Cave 2013; Franks 2013; Forero 2013)? Perhaps most importantly, what new project would she launch back home after all the media attention she received abroad faded away (Haven and Orsi 2013)? While the fact that she and many other prominent regime critics were allowed to travel abroad in subsequent months showed that changes were indeed happening in Cuba, it also served as an acknowledgment and vindication of her digital activism since returning to Cuba in 2004. Here was proof that social media–enabled critique (in this case, blogging and tweeting) had effectively broken through the state's long-held media monopoly and impacted an important civil right (Lugo 2013; Kitroeff 2013).

Sánchez certainly took full advantage of the new space ceded by the government during her 100 days abroad, giving literally hundreds of media interviews and public talks everywhere from Prague to Peru and Spain to Switzerland; from the Brazilian parliament to the White House and U.S. Congress; and from New York City to the symbolic capital of the Cuban diaspora, Miami, Florida.[11] However, as she shared in a number of interviews following her March 14 talk at Columbia University's Graduate School of Journalism with journalist Mirta Ojito (Planas 2013; Lugo 2013; Eaton 2013), it was perhaps what she did *away* from the spotlight with a group of new business partners in Spain and Miami that would be the lasting legacy of her historic trip "around the world in a hundred days": establish the logistical, technological, and financial foundations of what would become *14ymedio* a year later.

On a second, month-long trip abroad in October 2013, Sánchez was able to visit Silicon Valley for the first time as well as return to Columbia University, where she was finally able to attend the awards ceremony of the Cabot Prize (four years after having been the first blogger to win the prize's "special mention" in 2009). While in New York City, she also gave a talk titled "Disconnected Dissent" at the Google Ideas Summit. In her remarks, she emphasized what could be accomplished when the boundless creativity of the Cuban people was combined with the almost limitless power and reach of digital technology. Comparing USB drives and offline text messages to the *plátano* (plantain), a Cuban culinary staple, she said that while the latter had been repurposed in Cuban kitchens in times of scarcity to stand in for ground beef, the former had been reinvented by resourceful islanders to provide them "with [the contents of] the Internet without [a connection to the]

Internet." Finally, while she certainly celebrated the fact that digital technology had allowed her and other Cubans like her—working independently of the government—to "open a window" of information and communication among one another and to the outside world, "we will not settle for a window. We want to open the door!" (Sánchez 2013).

From "Informative Object" to "Informative Subject"

If using thumb drives as stand-ins for Internet access and text messages as proxies for Twitter were Sánchez's way of illustrating how Cuban ingenuity was "opening a window" against the island nation's state-enforced media monopoly, the world would soon see what she understood as "opening the door." Just over six months later, on May 21, 2014, Cubans awoke to the appearance of *14ymedio*, an independent newspaper[12] named after both Sánchez's fourteenth-floor home office and the year of its birth. Given that it had been consciously built as a collective endeavor that would move "beyond the blog," utilizing the wide following Sánchez had attracted during the previous seven years at *Generación Y*, the name of the new venture explicitly linked her individual "Y" brand with the idea of a media enterprise that was something more than a personal blog. Meaning literally "Fourteen (*catorce*) and (*y*) a half (*medio*)," the catchy alphanumeric name was steeped in deliberate double entendre, with the "half" meaning both "something more" and "the media" (as in *los medios de comunicación*) (Pham 2014). Since its founding, *14ymedio* has become the island's most prominent and professional independent news-gathering organization. It also has defied the expectations of critics that it would exist simply to denounce the Cuban government or as a vanity project used to steer fame and money in Sánchez's direction (Henken 2017).

Following the launch of the digital start-up in May 2014, Sánchez deliberately chose to cease *being* the story and start *reporting* the stories. While innumerable articles covering the unexpected ascent of Yoani Sánchez the blogger appeared between 2007 and 2014, in the more than five years since she has generally refused giving new interviews about herself with the justification, "we would rather be an informative subject [reporting the news] than an informative object [being the news]."[13] That is, Sánchez began to harvest the notoriety, prize money, credibility, and audience she came to enjoy because of *Generación Y* by the end of her 2013 "world tour," replanting it now as the foundation of *14ymedio*.

As with the many other independent digital media projects to have emerged on the island in the years following *14ymedio*'s launch, Sánchez's brainchild has had to confront a number of challenges during its first five years of existence (2014–2019). The two most important of these have been reaching Cuban readers inside Cuba via an exclusively digital publication in a context of extremely low Internet penetration and high access costs (i.e., why launch an *online* publication to reach a public living on an *offline* island?) and maintaining their journalistic independence while achieving financial sustainability. The latter issue is especially important given the suspicions over sources of financing for independent projects in Cuba together with the financial crisis besetting traditional print journalism globally. Indeed, as quoted above, Sánchez and Escobar openly reject what they call "barricade journalism," refusing "to produce a journalism of extremes." In a 2015 interview conducted after they had been operating nearly a year,[14] they insisted "it is better to arrive late with reliable information than get a scoop that lacks veracity" since their aim is "to inform Cuba's future electors in a transparent and responsible way" by building a journalistic reputation of "objectivity and trustworthiness."

Sánchez and Escobar are acutely aware of their need to remain independent from both "market concessions" and ideological biases. "We are committed to the truth and to independence," they argue, insisting, "We do not align ourselves with any ideology or political interest." At pains to uphold high journalistic standards in a country where official journalism is little more than bald state propaganda and the dissident press suffers from a tradition of placing passion over professionalism, they see their task—as the epigraph that begins this section states—to be one of "informing, sharing opinions, opening spaces for debate, and respecting those who think differently, [with the aim of] harmonizing [the values of] freedom of expression with [our] responsibility as citizens."

Related to the challenges of access, independence, and financial sustainability is the issue of appealing to the diverse interests of the Cuban public while establishing a critical-minded, credible, and professional news source for a population already saturated with political propaganda that passes as news. Indeed, while consistently critical of Cuba's official media, Sánchez has also consistently pointed out her desire to use *14ymedio* as a vehicle to launch a new type of journalism in Cuba, "one based on facts and figures" that creates a "third way" between the passion of the dissident press and the propaganda that defines the official media (Fernández 2015; Higuera 2016).

Finally, there are the ever-present twin issues of the ongoing censorship of *14ymedio*'s content (via the government's blocking of its website for users in Cuba) and the systematic repression, harassment, and occasional detention of its journalists (Weissenstein 2014; Valle 2014; Pham 2014). Indeed, Sánchez and Escobar told me in a 2015 interview that they run the digital daily from their decidedly offline fourteenth-floor office-cum-residence. "We send news out of Cuba using Nauta [e-mail] and later our part-time team members in Spain publish it on our page." While this situation has changed somewhat since the advent of Wi-Fi hot spots, home-based access, and mobile 3G data plans in recent years, the constant barrage of what they plainly referred to as "censorship and repression" has continued unchanged. Not only is the site blocked from national access by the Cuban government, text messages that contain the terms "*14ymedio*" and "Yoani Sánchez" (among many other "objectionable" terms) are not delivered by ETECSA (Sánchez and Escobar 2016). Moreover, their reporters are regularly warned by state security against collaborating with the site and sometimes even brought up on changes of "usurpation of legal capacity" for practicing journalism without proper professional credentials, as was the case in 2017 with the independent journalists Henry Constantín and Sol García Basulto (*14ymedio* 2017b). "At times, they have even been arrested when trying to cover stories or events," Sánchez and Escobar explained. Indeed, this was the case in 2019 for *14ymedio* reporters Luz Escobar and Ricardo Fernández (Escobar 2019; *14ymedio* 2019b).

14ymedio's Financial and Distribution Strategies

The most recent innovation in *14ymedio*'s news format and distribution strategy is called "Ventana 14" (Window 14). First aired via Facebook Live on December 10, 2018—the International Day of Human Rights—Sánchez launched the brief daily morning program in order to summarize each weekday's news (as covered in *14ymedio*) in the form of a ten-minute podcast. It is intended especially for her island-based listeners who are unlikely to be able to read the actual stories or stream or download video files. Also known as "*el cafecito informativo*" (the informative little cup of coffee), the podcast always begins with the sound of Sánchez stirring her morning *café cubano* and taking the first sip of the day together with her audience with the tagline: "I promise you a sip of news: recently brewed, brief, sometimes bitter, but always necessary" (figure 7.3).

Perhaps the most innovative aspect of the podcast—not a format widely used in Cuba—is its multichannel distribution strategy, which is also likely the reason that the majority of its audience listens from within Cuba. The *14ymedio* team makes the show available each morning usually before 9:00 via Sánchez's Facebook page, on YouTube, via Telegram, at the iTunes, iVoox, and Luminary podcast stores, and through WhatsApp. As of late August 2019, *14ymedio* reported that there were more than fifteen thousand subscribers to the show at these various sites (*14ymedio* 2019a).

Figure 7.3. Screenshot of the *"Ventana 14"* YouTube page, September 16, 2019. *14ymedio* YouTube page, used with permission.

In a June 13, 2019, e-mail interview, Sánchez explained that *14ymedio* uses such a wide array of platforms because it understands its main challenge as "seeing to it that our content reaches the largest number of readers within the island, because the residents of Cuba are our principal audience." She further explained that while the *14ymedio* website received a bit more than 587,000 visitors in May 2019 according to Google Analytics (led by the U.S. and Spain), "we reach the Cuban public fundamentally through VPNs [virtual private networks] and anonymous proxies (that hide the user's location) as well as via the *14ymedio* platforms at Telegram and WhatsApp, and via the weekly PDF digest and twice weekly e-mail newsletter." Apart from wanting to counter the common criticism that *14ymedio* has garnered little following on the island, Sánchez has explained why she places such a priority on reaching Cubans on the island:

People always ask me [. . .]: "Who'll be the next president of Cuba?" I say, "I don't know. But what worries me is: Who'll be Cuba's next citizens?" Those citizens need information to make decisions. Because if they don't have information to choose from, they will choose badly. They will choose the person with the most populist discourse; the one who wails like a siren; the one who lies; the one who has the most charismatic stage presence. However, if they have information, they will be able to choose something else. (Higuera 2016)

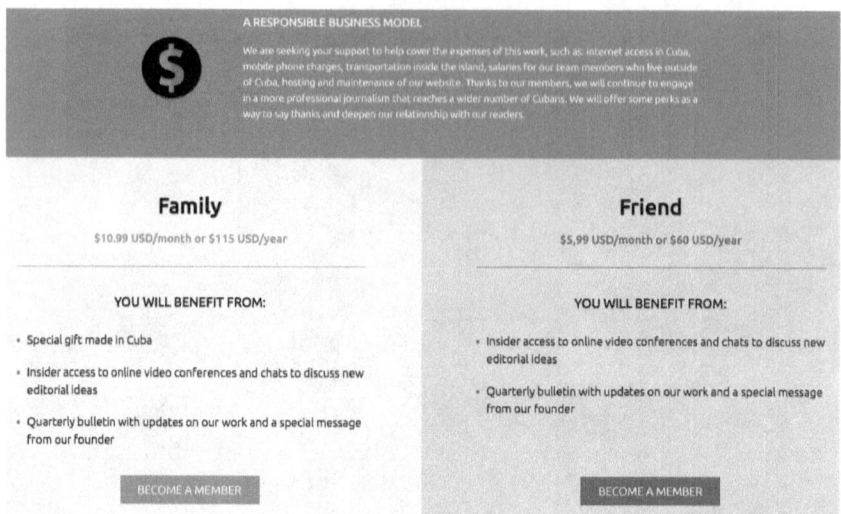

Figure 7.4. Screenshot of *14ymedio*'s membership page. *14ymedio* page, used with permission.

To date, perhaps the most significant shift in *14ymedio*'s trajectory has been its institution of an ambitious membership model in November 2017 (figure 7.4). Its core element has been to invite *14ymedio*'s readers living outside of Cuba—especially the Cuban diaspora—to become part of the renovation of independent journalism back on the island (*14ymedio* 2017a; Moreno 2017). "We are proposing to go beyond a subscription model to instead transform our readers into an active advocate of our work," *14ymedio*'s then head of development and innovation Alejandro González told Jennifer Nelson of the University of Missouri's Reynolds Journalism Institute. The idea, he explained, is to "convince them that by becoming members of *14ymedio*, they are helping independent journalism thrive" (Nelson 2016).

Rejecting funding from political parties, governments, and private interest groups, *14ymedio* aims to be answerable only to its readers and the facts. "We believe that transparency is the foundation of any free society," the finances section of the membership site states, going on to list the operation's expenses and revenue for both 2016 and 2017. Indeed, perhaps following the lead of the independent, left-leaning British newspaper *The Guardian*,[15] every article published at *14ymedio* is followed by a brief message combining a statement of its journalistic mission with a request for financial support so that that mission can be accomplished. "The *14ymedio* team is committed to doing serious journalism that reflects the reality of deep Cuba," it begins. "We invite you to continue supporting us, [. . .] by becoming a member [. . .]. Together we can continue to transform journalism in Cuba."

An August 26, 2019, e-mail to its membership from *14ymedio* titled, "Where are we and where are we going?" highlighted some recent financial and logistical developments. On the one hand, the arrival of 3G to Cuban cell phones enabled the team to report breaking news with greater immediacy. On the other hand, the deterioration of U.S.-Cuban relations had caused "the private institutions that had supported the development of a free press on the island to begin to lose interest," cutting significantly into *14ymedio*'s revenue stream and forcing layoffs. Thus, the daily must now rely even more on its membership program, which in turn has gradually become the media start-up's greatest source of revenue during 2018–2019.

Conclusion

This chronicle of the origin, development, and eventual transformation of *Generación Y* into *14ymedio*, arguably Cuba's most pioneering independent digital media project to have emerged on the island over the last fifteen years, has critically analyzed three key transformative moments (2004, 2007–2009, and 2014) in the evolution of the project in part for what they tell us about this particular media venture but also for how they foreshadowed similar shifts in the trajectory of Cuba's many other emergent indie digital media ventures. Yoani Sánchez and her growing team of collaborators (both in Cuba and abroad) launched the digital magazine *Consenso* at the site Desde-Cuba.com in December 2004. This somewhat traditional media project was shelved in 2007 as the blogging phenomenon gradually took hold in Cuba. Thanks to the broad popularity of *Generación Y*, there followed a shift away from this traditional model of independent journalism toward a conscious embrace of the individual, subjective, interactive, and "social" aspects of the "citizen journalism" movement then sweeping the globe via blogs.

Finally, by 2013 Sánchez and her team had come to realize that while blogs were very effective at giving a "voice" and a public digital platform to those individual stories and opinions systematically silenced in the state-run mass media, they did little to fill the most yawning gap in the Cuban media environment—credible, systematic, and responsible daily reporting that could inform Cuban citizens and serve the public interest by holding those in power accountable. In other words, Cuba did not lack *opinions* (abundantly reflected in its burgeoning blogosphere); it lacked reliable *information* (along with accessible and diverse media platforms in which to find it). As the old Cuban saying goes, "If you have three Cubans, you're bound to get at least six passionately held opinions."

To their credit, like the U.S. politician and public intellectual Daniel

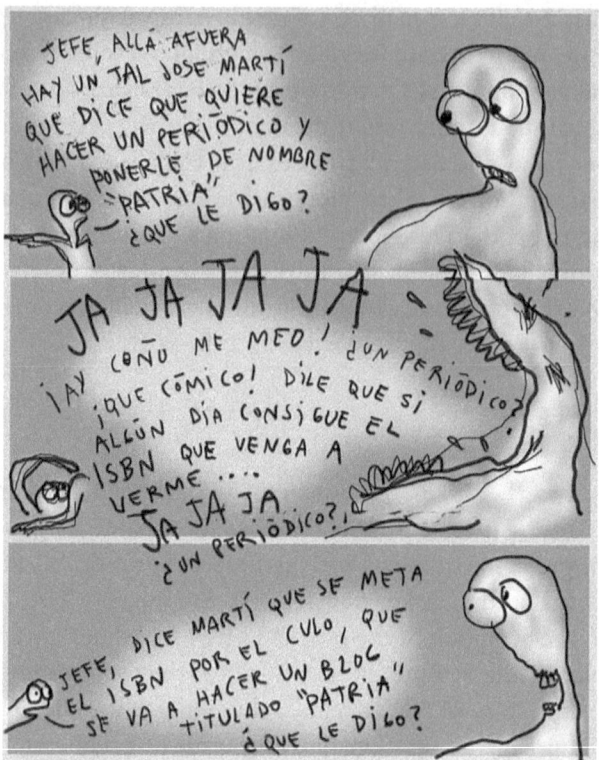

Figure 7.5. Reimagining José Martí's *Patria* as a Blog. Translation: *Minion*: "Boss, Outside, there's a guy named José Martí who says he wants to start a newspaper and name it '*Patria*.' What should I tell him?" *Boss*: "HA HA HA HA. Damn, I'm peeing all over myself! A newspaper? Hilarious! Tell him that if he ever gets an ISBN to come see me... HA HA HA. A newspaper?" *Minion*: "Boss, Martí says that you can shove the ISBN up your ass. He's going to start a blog and name it '*Patria*' instead. What should I tell him?" Credit/Source: Lázaro Saavedra, from the series "GALERÍA I-MEIL" (2009), used with permission.

Patrick Moynihan before them, Sánchez and her team realized that while "everyone is entitled to their own opinions, they are not entitled to their own facts" (Henken 2019). Thus, the final section of this chapter chronicles a third key transformation of Sánchez's indie media odyssey away from the so-called citizen journalism embraced by Cuba's upstart blogosphere between 2007 and 2014 toward a more coordinated, deliberate, and professional approach to news gathering and reporting that is *14ymedio*.

While this transformation mirrors some elements of the rise and fall of the blogging phenomenon in the U.S., the differences in the Cuban case are also instructive. For example, early U.S. bloggers were at pains to distinguish themselves from journalists and distance their ideal of transparency from the traditional journalistic ideal of objectivity. However, in Cuba—where official journalism openly serves the interests of the Party and makes no claim to objectivity—the subjectivity of blogging and the transparency of noncredentialed bloggers who practice "citizen journalism" have served as a vital check on and crack in the dominant system where state propaganda masquerades as "professional journalism." In a context where official journalism is state propaganda, perhaps only citizen journalism (even if or perhaps especially practiced by so-called untrained amateurs) could be expected to do the "classic" work of the journalist: informing the public and reporting the facts with studied balance (figure 7.5).

It is in this sense that the blogging phenomenon in Cuba—while similarly antiestablishment—has led to a far different "antisystemic" outcome than the same phenomenon in the U.S. In Cuba, while many amateur, independent blogs and bloggers have gone the way of the dinosaur, a notable cross section of others—including not only the Cuban journalism "outsider" Sánchez but also the notable former "insider" Elaine Díaz[16]—have used their "fleeting but fecund" blogging experience as a strategic spur, slingshot, or catapult, allowing them to transform the audience, notoriety, and credibility they cultivated as bloggers into the basis for a more serious, sustained, and professional independent digital newspaper or magazine.

That is, blogging did not allow them to "get their foot in the door" of the dominant media system (as was often the case for some U.S. bloggers who later joined mainstream media outlets as columnists). It allowed them to symbolically "kick down the door" of that system, challenging its basic design of obedience to the Party with journalistic independence. An example of this is one of a series of defiant editorials written by Elaine Díaz at *Periodismo de Barrio* where she unequivocally declares: "credibility comes, primordially, from independence. [. . .] Between press and Party there is not, nor can there be, a relationship based on conditions of equality [because] the Party expects submission from the press" (*Periodismo de Barrio* 2016).

NOTES

1. Accountability journalism has been defined by the American Press Institute (API) as "work that encompasses fact-checking, explanatory and investigative reporting, but more generally applies to the journalistic work of holding the powerful accountable" (Elizabeth, Kelley, and Elman 2017).

2. Unless otherwise noted, all direct quotes from Cuban bloggers and independent journalists are from interviews I conducted in recent years. All translations are my own. This quote is from an e-mail interview with Bárbara Maseda on May 29, 2019.

3. See the three examples of other early Cuban e-zines that Walfrido Dorta analyzes in chapter 13 of this volume.

4. Pavón was the military official in charge of the National Council of Culture (CNC), which later became the Ministry of Culture. Serguera was the director of the ICRT (Cuban Institute of Radio and Television). Quesada reigned over Cuban theater (Veltfort 2017, 212).

5. The Cuban intellectual Desiderio Navarro was the unofficial organizer of this and other subsequent meetings and publications related to the *polémica*. See Navarro 2008 and Escobar 2007 for competing analyses of the events.

6. Each minidisk is packaged inside a plastic sleeve and features a photo of Yoani Sánchez, the date the contents were last updated, and the words: "Free distribution and reproduction. *Generación Y*." This image is taken from section 9 of a video recording of an interview the author did with Sánchez in her home in July 2008. The entire fifty-minute video, broken into thirteen Q&A sections, can be accessed here: http://elyuma.blogspot.com/2009/11/arriba-periodismo-ciudadano-abajo.html.

7. The original Spanish reads: "Lo que comenzó como un impulso individual, se está convirtiendo en una plaza de encuentro para la discusión y el debate."

8. Among the more notable uses of this strategy include: a video of Sánchez being denied an exit permit by Cuban immigration authorities, preventing her from traveling to New York to receive the Maria Moors Cabot digital journalism prize from Columbia University ("Lessons of biology," October 14, and "Singing them the forty," October 15, 2008); Sánchez's public challenge to then President Raúl Castro's daughter, Mariela Castro Espín ("Brief encounter with Mariela," December 10, and "Cocky Hen," December 17); the unauthorized presentation of the Cuban writer Orlando Luis Pardo Lazo's book *Boring Home* at the 2009 Havana Book Fair ("*Boring Home*," February 14, and "1971–2009: Gray millennium," February 15, 2009); Sánchez's participation in the Cuban artist Tania Bruguera's performance piece, "A minute of silence," at the 2009 Havana Biennial that spring ("And they gave us the mics . . . ," March 30, and "Performance completed," April 2, 2009); and she and Reinaldo Escobar's filming of a visit to the Internet cafe at Hotel Meliá Cohiba to challenge restrictions against Cuban nationals using hotel Web connections ("In Meliá Cohiba," May 10, 2009).

9. See YouTube, "*Debate sobre Internet en Cuba*," https://www.youtube.com/watch?v=IVHZIVE3dGE.

10. Public space in Cuba is typically thought of as *de Fidel*—that is, government-controlled or "revolutionary" space.

11. She departed Cuba for Brazil on February 17 and returned to Havana from Madrid 103 days later on May 30, 2013. At her request, I organized her March 14–21 itinerary and served as her interpreter in New York and Washington, D.C., with a full schedule of talks at universities and media interviews. I had first met and interviewed Sánchez at her home in Havana in summer 2008, intrigued by her success at deploying rich, succinct, and to me deeply authentic day-in-the-life chronicles into cyberspace, a heretofore uncharted territory for the vast majority of Cubans. I was also attracted by her unique personality, frankness in a country characterized by coded subtleties, and ability to always link her personal stories to Cuba's larger, tragi-heroic, sociopolitical history.

12. This term denotes a media project that is answerable only to its readership and

guided by professional journalistic principles of transparency and objectivity, refusing to accept financial support from any government, political party, or other entity that seeks to use economic support as leverage to exert editorial control over content.

13. The membership page at *14ymedio* makes the following declaration: "*Preferimos ser sujeto informativo que objeto informativo.*"

14. I received responses to my questionnaire from *14ymedio* director Yoani Sánchez and editor in chief Reinaldo Escobar on April 17, 2015. Translations from the Spanish are my own.

15. A similar statement from *The Guardian* reads: "Readers from around the world, like you, make *The Guardian*'s work possible. We need your support to deliver quality, investigative journalism—and to keep it open for everyone. At a time when factual, honest reporting is critical, your support is essential in protecting our editorial independence" (https://www.theguardian.com/us).

16. A former University of Havana professor of digital journalism, Elaine Díaz's popular and trenchant blog *La Polémica Digital* helped her win a yearlong fellowship at Harvard's Nieman Foundation, from which she returned to Cuba in the summer of 2015 to launch the pro bono, public-interest journalism site *Periodismo de Barrio*.

References

14ymedio. 2014. "Who are we?"
14ymedio. 2017a. "14ymedio invita a los lectores a afiliarse." November 14, 2017.
14ymedio. 2017b. "Police Accuse Journalist Henry Constantíin of 'Usurpation of Legal Capacity.'" March 18, 2017.
14ymedio. 2019a. "¿Dónde estamos y hacia dónde vamos?" E-mail message, August 26, 2019.
14ymedio. 2019b. "El reportero Ricardo Fernández está detenido en La Habana, según la Seguridad del Estado." July 14, 2019.
Cave, Damien. 2013. "Yoani Sánchez, Cuban Dissident Blogger, Gets Passport." *The New York Times*, January 31, 2013.
Eaton, Tracey. 2013. "Cuban Dissident Blogger Yoani Sánchez Tours the United States." Florida Center for Investigative Reporting, March 20, 2013.
Elizabeth, Jane, Lori Kelley, and Julie M. Elman. 2017. "Improving accountability reporting: How to make the best of journalism better for audiences." American Press Institute, August 8, 2017.
Escobar, Luz. 2019. "'Regulada' por romper el muro de la mentira oficial." *14ymedio*, May 23, 2019.
Escobar, Reinaldo. 2007. "La polémica intelectual cubana de 2007." *Iberoamericana*, Year VII, No. 28: 157–163.
Fernández, Maité. 2015. "Cómo 14ymedio aspira a convertirse en la principal fuente independiente de noticias de Cuba." *IJNET*, May 27, 2015.
Forero, Juan. 2013. "Yoani Sánchez dissident Cuban blogger behind Generation Y goes on tour." *The Washington Post*, March 11, 2013.
Franks, Jeff. 2013. "Cuban dissident blogger Yoani Sánchez gets passport, will travel." *Reuters*, January 30, 2013.

García, Anne-Marie. 2013. "Cuban dissident blogger starts world tour." *Associated Press*, February 17, 2013.

Haven, Paul and Peter Orsi. 2013. "Cuban blogger returns home to unknown future." *Associated Press*, May 29, 2013.

Henken, Ted A. 2017. "Cuba's Digital Millennials: Independent Digital Media and Civil Society on the Island of the Disconnected." *Social Research* 84, No. 2: 429–456.

Henken, Ted A. 2019. "Book Review: *Voices of Change in Cuba from the Nonstate Sector*." *The Inter-American Dialogue*, April 22, 2019.

Henken, Ted A. and Mary Jo Porter. 2016. "Translating Solidarity." *NACLA Report on the Americas* 48, No. 1 (May): 55–58.

Higuera, Silvia. 2016. "ISOJ 2016: Yoani Sánchez explica cómo la tecnología ha hecho más libres a los cubanos." *Periodismo en Las Américas* blog, April 16, 2016.

Israel, Esteban. 2007. "Cubans go to unusual lengths to post blogs." Reuters, October 9, 2007.

Kitroeff, Natalie. 2013. "Interview with Cuban Blogger Yoani Sánchez." *The Lede* blog, *The New York Times*, March 22, 2013.

Lugo, Gizelle. 2013. "Yoani Sánchez: Dissident Cuban blogger hopeful of digital change." *The Guardian*, March 16, 2013.

McKinley, James C., Jr., 2008. "Cyber-Rebels in Cuba Defy State's Limits." *The New York Times*, March 6, 2008.

Moreno, Chelsea. 2017. "Cuba's *14ymedio* seeks greater independence and engagement with new membership model." Knight Center, *Journalism in the Americas* blog, December 20, 2017.

Navarro, Desiderio. 2008. *La política cultural del período revolucionario: Memoria y reflexión*. Havana: Centro Teórico-Cultural and Colección Criterios.

Nelson, Jennifer. 2016. "New membership model gives Cuban news site financial, editorial independence." Reynolds Journalism Institute, November 17, 2016.

Periodismo de Barrio. 2016. "Las contradicciones del periodismo cubano." July 14, 2016.

Peters, Phil. 2007. "Good Reading." *The Cuban Triangle* blog, August 21, 2007.

Pham, Tiffany. 2014. "How She Did It: Yoani Sánchez Launches Cuban News Outlet *14ymedio*." *Forbes*, November 30, 2014.

Planas, Roque. 2013. "Yoani Sanchez, Cuban Blogger, Plans Independent Newspaper Online." *Huffington Post*, March 15, 2013.

Rosen, Jay. 2012. "The People Formerly Known as The Audience." In *The Social Media Reader*, edited by Michael Mandiberg, 13–16. New York: New York University Press.

Sánchez, Yoani. 2007. "Pavón, Serguera o la política cultural revolucionaria." *Portafolio polémica intelectual*, DesdeCuba.com, January-February 2007.

Sánchez, Yoani. 2013. "Disconnected Dissent." Google Ideas Conference, October 24, 2013. Available on YouTube at https://youtu.be/iMeNMUWEc44.

Sánchez, Yoani and Reinaldo Escobar. 2016. "Cubacel censura los SMS con las palabras 'democracia' o 'huelga de hambre.'" *14ymedio*, September 3, 2016.

Schmidt-Häuer, Christian. 2008. "Insel der blinden Passagiere." *Die Zeit*, January 24, 2008.

Valle, Amir. 2014. "14ymedio, grieta en el muro del monopolio periodístico en Cuba." *Deutsche Welle*, May 21, 2014.

Veltfort, Anna. 2017. *Adiós mi Habana. Las memorias de una gringa y su tiempo en los años revolucionarios de la década de los 60*. Madrid: Editorial Verbum.

Vicent, Mauricio. 2008. "La vida no está en otra parte, está en otra Cuba." *El País*, January 3, 2008.

Wall Street Journal. 2007. "Cuban Revolution: Yoani Sánchez fights tropical totalitarianism, one blog post at a time." December 22, 2007.

Weissenstein, Michael. 2014. "Cuban blogger launching independent newspaper." *Associated Press*, May 20, 2014.

8

Independent Journalism in Cuba
Between Fantasy and the Ontological Rupture

SARA GARCIA SANTAMARIA

In recent years, the consolidation of an independent digital mediasphere in Cuba has allowed the coverage of new social phenomena, giving visibility to a growing plurality of voices. However, some of these new voices, such as independent journalists, still feel uncomfortable framing themselves in political terms. Is not working for an independent media outlet in Cuba a political stance in itself? Things are not so clear-cut, since independent journalists often find themselves caught between a complex identification and rejection of the system, immersed in what Holbraad calls a "visceral allegiance to their Revolution" while at the same time "expressing deep disaffection with it" (2014, 1). Journalists can partially identify with "the Revolution" and agree with its purported values yet still feel immersed in oppressive relationships that dash their professional dreams. Applying this paradox to the study of young Cuban journalists, this chapter examines the ways in which the state-run media manages to grip them and align their practices with the official ontology of a state-people unity.[1] The main argument is that fantasy plays an essential role in enabling young journalists to disconnect from reality and work within a state-media system that they perceive as oppressive.[2]

The concept of fantasy draws on postfoundational discourse analysis, which sees fantasy as a way of concealing the constructed and imperfect nature of discourses, and the instability of our subject position within them.[3] In this paper, fantasy appears as a resource that Cuban journalists use for disconnecting from everyday personal and professional pressures at work, thus enabling them to carry on with their tasks. An immersion in "fantasmatic" logics (logics that articulate fantasy) allows journalists to disconnect from the official media and fantasize about a parallel reality; one that started shaping the contours of the emergent digital media scene well before it existed. The backdrop is that, by providing a scape, fantasies often contribute to the reproduction of the social order, delaying journalists' public contestation and ontological rupture with it (Mouffe 2000).[4]

In this work, I am particularly interested in journalists who are at a crossroads, between identities, and thus still finding their professional selves. Focusing on young journalists becomes interesting because they go through a process of personal, professional, and ideological development that unfolds during their years at university and their first journalistic experiences in the state-run media. Early on in their careers, journalism students are thrown into a system that defends an ontological unity between the state and the people, thus reducing the journalist into a soldier. This conceptualization is based on José Martí, Cuba's hallowed nineteenth-century journalist and national liberation leader, who wrote: "Journalists have so much of a soldier in them!" (¡*Tiene tanto el periodista de soldado!*).[5] In this context, journalists who do not follow their "official" role run the risk of being tagged as *malos cubanos*. Given that the official discourse equates the state with the people, but also with the nation and the Revolution, young journalists who question their officially assigned role can appear as both counterrevolutionary and anti-Cuban; as mercenaries working at the service of "the empire."[6] The interviews suggest that young journalists' resistance to position themselves in political terms is in fact a rejection of the political polarization that pushes them toward the edges of the soldier versus enemy narrative (Henken 2017; Geoffray and Chaguaceda 2015).

This chapter analyzes twenty-one qualitative interviews with journalists trained at Cuban universities and who have worked for the state-run media before switching to the independent sector. The findings indicate that journalists' investment in fantasies allowed them to navigate the apparent paradox of a "visceral" revolutionary investment in the Revolution yet the need for an ontological rupture with it. The interviews reveal that journalists invested in beatific (pleasant) fantasies that helped them conceal their political and emotional self while focusing on a cynical defense of their ultimate freedom and professionalism. While these logics provided comfort, they operated in conjunction with less pleasant ones, with horrific fantasies (one might say nightmares) that created a spiral of fear and collective paranoia that delayed a final rupture with the system.

THE ONTOLOGICAL LOGIC OF THE CUBAN REVOLUTION

Simplistic accounts of an oppressed people who lack all agency can sound familiar, but they contrast with the complexity found by those who have conducted ethnographic research in Cuba (Humphreys 2019; Garcia Santamaria

2018a; Holbraad 2014) and other late socialist states, such as China or Russia (Repnikova 2017; Roudakova 2017).[7] Narratives of "binary socialism" (Yurchak 2003, 6) hide the multiple and often contradicting identities of subjects living under late socialism. In his work on the Soviet Union, Yurchak (2006) acknowledges the analytical failure of "binary" accounts—such as true versus lie, freedom versus captivity, honor versus corruption, or journalism versus propaganda. Binary accounts overlook a crucial paradox: the fact that most people can feel committed to the values and ideals of late socialist countries despite transgressing, reinterpreting, and even rejecting some of the ontological norms and practices inscribed in the official ideology (Yurchak 2006, 8; Holbraad 2014). Therefore, Holbraad (2014, 370) considers that all works that strive for analytical precision need to acknowledge "the visceral character of people's commitment" to the Revolution and its values, even as they decide to break away from them.

In order to understand Cuban journalists' "visceral" and often contradicting positions, simultaneously identifying with and rejecting the revolutionary project, we need to examine the way in which the Revolution has constructed its relationship with "the people." The discursive construction of an all-encompassing Revolution has created the illusion of a complete identification between the people and the state—and their interests. This narrative has reached the realm of journalism and can be observed in the "New Communication Policy for the State and Government," which "guarantees national consensus and unity around the Fatherland, the Socialist Revolution, and the Party" (*Cubadebate* 2019). The policy is explicitly based on Fidel Castro's 1961 speech "Words to the Intellectuals," which considers that "since the Revolution includes the interests of the people, and the Revolution means the interests of the whole nation, nobody can rightly present arguments against it" (*Cubadebate* 2019). Based on this presumed ontological unity, point 2.11 of the New Communication Policy and Article 55 of the 2019 Constitution declare all mass media to be state or social property, including technological platforms. Therefore, independent digital media outlets are by default illegal not only because they are privately owned, but also because they break with the revolutionary consensus.

Since the Revolution presents itself as all-encompassing, it has no outside, and those who have situated themselves beyond the revolutionary project have traditionally been "de-ontologized" and "de-humanized." Either way, they have been denied the opportunity to legitimately confront the project. From this perspective, it follows that independent digital media outlets represent an ontological rupture with the Revolution regardless of their (ontic) content. In fact, breaking away from the unity between the people and the state (and its long chain of synonyms) and the journalistic identities that it generates (the journalist as a soldier) positions independent journalists outside the ontologically totalizing force of the revolutionary project (Garcia Santamaria 2019). Regardless of their political stances, the public contestation of the ontological roots of the system and the practices established around it is, in discourse-theoretical terms, a political act of rupture (Zicman de Barros 2020).

Contesting the Revolutionary Ontology: The Emergence of the Political

This analysis draws on sensitizing concepts from Ernesto Laclau and Chantal Mouffe's (1985) discourse theory, such as identity and agency, which are applied through a logics analysis (Glynos and Howarth 2007; Clarke 2012). Laclau and Mouffe (1985, 112) see discourse as a way of giving sense to social reality by means of performatively structuring and fixing meaning. The attempt to fix meaning through discourse, while fleeting and illusory, is necessary for providing shared frameworks that allow us to make sense of social reality. While meaning can appear as fixed, producing discourses that seem obvious and given, discourses are the result of power relations and certain social actors produce particular articulations that become hegemonic. This means that discursive changes are not automatic nor unlimited. In fact, they depend upon an available reservoir of sedimented articulations and practices that set the range of what is seen as possible (Laclau and Mouffe 1985, 111).

The non-fixity of discourse means that the way in which it articulates meaning, and explains the social world, is always flawed, open to negotiation and rearticulation (Laclau 2005). This is so because there is always meaning that can be articulated differently, as the context changes. In Carpentier's words (2017, 8), the impossibility of fixity "is both enabling and disabling" and, as discourses change, so does the way subjects position themselves within them. The enabling and dis-enabling potential of different discourses is examined here through the lenses of young Cuban journalists and the way in which they identify with the ontological state-people unity of the Revolution.

The impossibility of a discursive closure means that our identification with the truth claims of a discourse, such as the people-state unity or the journalist as a soldier, is always unstable. The fact that subjects position themselves within a given discourse does not mean that their identity is fully or permanently determined by it (Carpentier 2017). In other words, our identity cannot be completely saturated by a single process of identification.

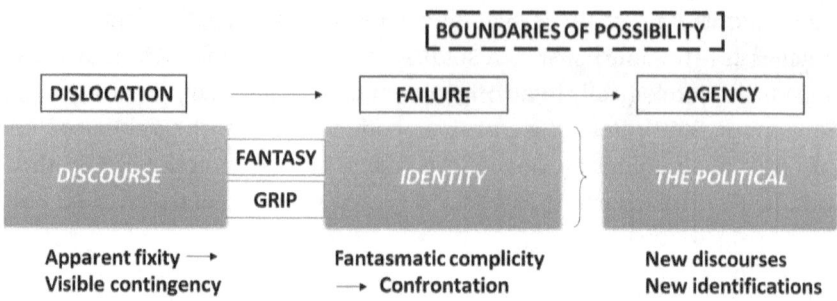

Figure 8.1. "Sensitizing Concepts in Discourse Theory: Expanding the Field of Discursivity." Credit/Source: Adapted by the author from discourse theoretical concepts as they appear defined in the work of Laclau 2005, Glynos and Howarth 2007, and Carpentier 2017.

Instead, it is the product of our (often contradictory) identification with multiple discourses and discursive positions (Buckingham 2008, 6; Barker 2004, 128). Applying these insights to this case study, discourse theory is useful for understanding why Cuban journalists can partially identify with the Revolution yet their identities necessarily overflow the parameters of the official discourse. Journalists can identify as soldiers and, simultaneously, seek independence from their militant duties.

The graphical representation of discourse theory's sensitizing concepts (figure 8.1) shows that, as discourses become dislocated (threatened by competing views), so do subject positions within them and the fantasies that sustain an apparent discourse-identity harmony. What the graph above shows is that dislocation makes available other ways of seeing social reality, enabling subjects to see beyond apparently natural and indisputable (hegemonic) discourses. By enabling the possibility of choosing among different articulations, subjects gain the agency of contesting discourses and practices that once seemed insurmountable (Carpentier 2017; Butler 1997). It is the conjunction of free choice and contestation that is at the roots of political rupture (Gardner 2004; Carpentier 2017; Zicman de Barros 2020).

Individuals are more likely to become political agents in a context in which hegemonic discourses are being dislocated. At this point, it is important to explain that discourse theory makes a conceptual difference between "the political" and "politics." "The political" refers to "the dimension of antagonism that is inherent in human relations," while "politics" is a way of concealing this antagonism, that is, "the ensemble of practices, discourses, and institutions that organize social relations in a way that domesticates hostility" (Mouffe 2000, 101). In order to become political agents, subjects do not need to take a clear political stance; they become political agents because the boundaries of political possibilities have expanded, making room for new subject positions that individuals can choose from. It is by repositioning themselves within a new discursive field that subjects become political agents (Laclau 2005, 107–108).

Dislocation can become apparent when an event or a series of events that cannot be represented and understood within existing discourses takes place. Since there is always an interrelation between discourses and material practices (Carpentier 2017), events can appear in the form of material changes that disrupt stable schemes of meaning. For instance, growing access to the Internet and digital technologies has altered what it means to be a journalist in Cuba (Carpentier 2017; Žižek 2014). Technological changes have facilitated the creation of independent media outlets, bringing about an ontic change that challenges the ideas of the hegemonic discourse. However, it is important to realize that this change also has an ontological nature, a relational nature that alters power relations and facilitates the emergence of new journalistic positions beyond the narrow soldier versus enemy narrative.

A Fantasmatic Logics Approach

The logics analysis of young Cuban journalists who have worked for the state-run media, and broken away from it, is based on twenty-one in-depth interviews with journalists who range between twenty-five and thirty-six years in age. All the interviewees graduated in journalism studies from Cuban universities and therefore had their first journalistic experiences during mandatory internships at state-run companies, mostly official media outlets.[8] Once graduated, most of them continued to work for the state during mandatory social work. The interviews were conducted between March and September 2019 and the interviewees were selected in two phases. First, I conducted a purposive sampling of editors from the main independent media outlets in Cuba. Once I started interviewing them, I followed a snowballing technique by which the interviewees were asked to recommend colleagues with relevant personal experiences who were willing to give an honest account of their experience.

The interviews were manually transcribed and analyzed according to a logics approach. The concept of logics refers to "the rules or grammar" that guide a practice, as well as the contextual elements that (dis)enable this practice to change over time (Glynos and Howarth 2007, 136). In this case study, the practice is the exercise of Cuban journalism and the processes of young journalists' (dis)identification with the hegemonic idea of a state-people unity, which positions the journalist as a soldier (Glynos and Howarth 2007, 136). The goal of this chapter is precisely to examine the ways in which journalists become aware of the logics that shape their professional identity.

Previous literature has identified three main types of logics: social, political, and fantasmatic (Clarke 2012). Social logics describe the way in which social practices work from a synchronic point of view, while political logics examine their historical institution, maintenance, and transformation over time (Glynos and Howarth 2007: 133).[9] However, this chapter is interested in the third type: fantasmatic logics. The goal of fantasmatic logics is to examine why subjects are gripped by certain discourses and practices and become complicit in concealing their incoherence (Glynos and Howarth 2008, 165). From a Lacanian psychoanalytic approach, fantasy is a mechanism that confers safety and harmony, that allows us to go on in our daily lives by telling ourselves we will be fine. It is through fantasies that we escape background pressures, failures, and inconsistencies, freeing our imagination and finding a scapegoat that makes us more resilient in difficult situations. Putting it simply, fantasmatic logics explain the way people "push away reality in fantasy" (Lacan 1999, 107). In the case of Cuban journalism, fantasy can explain to a great degree the late revolutionary paradox of young journalists who work for the state-run media while fantasizing about escaping it.

Fantasies often play a conservative role by stabilizing our identity so we can become functioning members of the social order. By pushing away frustrations, they delay a rupture with the system that originates them. However, when the discourses that grip us become dislocated, the fantasies that mediate our position within them are no longer able to confer us an identity; we experience an identity failure. As new discourses become available, it is in the pursuit of a new identity that we become political agents (Stavrakakis 2005).

Findings and Analysis: Journalistic Fantasies at Work

Analyzing the resilience of young Cuban journalists from a logics approach raises a series of questions. Why are young journalists able to work for the state-run media even when they perceive it as personally and professionally oppressive? What is the role of fantasmatic investment in mediating their identity in a way that becomes compatible with the system? What is the role of fantasy in both enabling and dis-enabling an ontological rupture with "official" journalism?

This section explores a striking paradox: the way in which the state-run media grips young Cuban journalists' practices despite personal and professional malaise. The data reveal that journalists' investment in beatific and horrific fantasies can explain their position within an ontologically totalizing system, and the difficulties escaping it. While journalists' investment in fantasies of well-being have helped them cover up structural coercion and harassment, collective paranoia and a perceived lack of convenient choices have produced a fear that delayed disengagement. Cuban journalists' fantasmatic logics are organized in four main types: political-emotional, cynical, professional, and horrific fantasies.

Rejecting the Political Self

In Cuba, college education is free, but students are required to give something back to society through a period of social work. In practice, this means that all recently graduated journalists need to work for public institutions (mostly the state-run media) for two to three years in order to validate their degrees. The combination of the beatific fantasy of "paying back a debt" to society in exchange for free education, combined with the horrific fantasy of "losing their degree," has served as an efficient way of filling newsrooms with talented young people at virtually no cost while attempting to shape their journalistic practice in a way that supports the system.

Nevertheless, journalists often develop an ambivalent relationship with the regime practices in which they find themselves embedded. The interviews reveal that many young journalists have "viscerally" invested in the Revolution and consider that self-sacrifice and criticism (from within) could lead to positive change. In order to understand self-sacrifice, it is important to remember that in the context of the early 2010s, former president Raúl Castro and other top leaders started calling for greater criticism and an internally led aperture of Cuban journalism. In this sense, official demands to open up the media from within served as a way of co-opting journalists by providing them with fantasies of internal political renewal. By creating a narrative in which state-run journalism and criticism from within were compatible, the system deterred journalists from alternative political mobilization.

Fantasies of internal renewal within the system have managed to entice several generations of young journalism students who had to work for the state in order to obtain and validate their degree. However, official discourses of journalistic renewal contrast with journalists' reflections upon the difficulties they faced when trying to change the system from within. As a former employee of an official newspaper puts it:

> [Social work] was extremely frustrating. I do not mind investing time in my job, but as long as I can work. I would propose news stories [to

the editors], but they would only publish two paragraphs, and so biased! I was very bothered by that logic, or nonsense, because it lacked any logic [at all]. I felt like I was wasting my time. I felt really bad. I asked for a transfer and I said that, if they did not grant it to me, I would quit social work altogether. (R16)[10]

Cuban journalists are well aware of the obstacles they face when trying to change the system from within the state-media structure. The main barrier, according to them, comes in a very basic form: not being able to publish their work. When draft articles do not comply with the editorial line of the Ideological Committee of the Party, they are simply not published, or are partially published after a process of heavy ideological editing. Censorship prior to publication also affects the use of simple words, humor, or word games; that is, it also touches upon style.

> I got tired of negotiating simple words, sentences, concepts that were obvious . . . Soon, I was viewed as someone very critical towards the president of the country. They told me that I did not have the moral right to work there. (R9)

One of the problems the institutional media encounters is the need to co-opt young talented journalists so they complete their social work and hopefully stay on for the duration of their careers. Of course, this is an opportunity to shape their journalistic identities in ways that privilege ideological over professional goals. While it is undeniable that there are talented journalists working in the state-run media (Garcia Santamaria 2018b), the interviewees emphasize the system's failure in retaining talent. For instance, R16 considers that "talent is not something that prevails in the state-run media" and that "the state-run media ended up filled by the least talented people, those who take less risks in their career." Whether talented or not, the problem is that those who stay are less likely to push for change within the system.

The interviews show that fantasies of internal renewal operated hand in hand with journalists' rejection of political positioning. Young Cuban journalists are embedded in a system that automatically positions them in political terms; that is, a system that politicizes journalism, as discourse, and journalists, as subjects. The interviewees reveal that during their studies and first journalistic jobs they did not see themselves as political agents, not to say enemies of the system; their political identity was still unfolding. Most of the interviewees consider that the ability to read their daily struggles from a political standpoint took some time, and they were only able to do so after getting some distance from the events. However, some journalists were able to identify the political nature of the conflicts that they were experiencing from an early stage. For instance, one of the interviewees remembers wondering in college about the source of his problems: "What the hell am I living here? All this is a trick, all this is a lie. This is terrible! It was a conflict that started at a professional level but then, of course, had a social reading and a political reading that became truly clear to me" (R20). Most of the interviewees recognize that being an independent journalist is a political stance in itself. As the editor of an independent digital newspaper puts it, "this is a government that keeps the people sunk in a crisis. We have never announced: 'We are against the government.' But we have a position towards that" (R1).

The interviews reveal that young journalists only reject "the political" when they see it through the lenses of political polarization. Therefore, rejecting their political self has been a fantasmatic logic that allowed them to conceal the mismatch between their still-developing ideas and those of the system, but also has helped them fantasize about the possibility of breaking the vicious circle that automatically positions journalists in binary terms: as either soldiers or enemies.

Rejecting the Emotional Self

Journalism is "an emotionally charged" profession and the digital era has brought about an emotional redistribution of power and influence within it (Beckett and Deuze 2016). This is even more true in the Cuban case since political polarization leads to binary constructions of affective stances. In fact, the interviewees consider that the official media system pushes journalists toward the poles of the affective spectrum. By inflicting fear and rage, the system seeks to provoke an overtly emotional state in young journalists that makes them vulnerable and can even blind their rationality.

One of the ways in which the interviewees construct the difference between professional journalists and dissidents is precisely through an emotional lens. While professional journalists would be able to manage anger, despair, and outrage, dissident journalists are seen as emotionally taken by extreme feelings, thus creating polarizing accounts of reality that foster rage rather than debate. By positioning themselves beyond primary emotions, the interviewees construct their identity as opposed to the state, but also to others who presumably share their criticisms: activists and dissidents. For instance, one of the editors rejects the exercise of journalism under extreme emotional pressure and explains that he had to stop writing for a while until he was able to take hold of his emotions. This quote connects two important fantasies: the beatific fantasy of professionalism beyond emotionality and the horrific fantasy of emotions taking over identity:

> It was a moment of such anger and rage! Never again have I felt that kind of rage and asphyxiation with absolutely everything. You can perfectly understand how totalitarianism works, how it starts reducing your intellectual complexity, limiting you to feelings and sensations that can be very primary. Which is very understandable, because they also reduce your visual and emotional field. I felt a stage of rage, of resentment, of hate . . . that was not healthy. If I did not leave Cuba, I felt that something catastrophic was going to happen. That I was going to be buried in that mud. (R20)

At that moment, the editor was working for *OnCuba*, a private digital magazine that is legally accredited as a foreign media outlet but has its main newsroom in Havana. Preceding the recent wave of independent digital media projects, the magazine became a place where generations of young Cuban journalists experimented with doing journalism *outside* the official system, developing new identities while testing the boundaries of what could be said and tolerated in a relatively safe space.

The quote reveals a widely shared image of dissidents as being emotionally taken over by extreme feelings, as being "buried in the mud." Emotionality is seen as a personal failure that has negative professional outputs, since it weakens journalists' ability to think with a cold mind, leading to bias. The interviewees seem to understand the frustration that dissidents go through because they have experienced the repressive capacity of the system in their own skin. In fact, the interviewees recognize that the system tries to emotionally destabilize journalists and, by doing so, to mobilize their rage in a way that pushes them toward the extremes of the soldier versus enemy line. According to this emotional logic, the system would be more comfortable reproducing extreme positions than allowing visceral paradoxical identifications with it. Overall, the shared view that emerges from the interviews is that good journalism cannot be emotionally contaminated because it would lose balance, and this applies both to those who thrive within the state-run media and to those who despise it.

Investing in the Cynical Self

This chapter aims at overcoming simplistic accounts of journalists being co-opted by the system and thus lacking all agency. In fact, it argues that investing in cynical fantasies of well-being has an agentistic power because it allows them to fantasize about circumventing the system—even if to a modest extent. Cynicism here is not seen in pejorative terms but as a resource that employees often use when they are "cynically enlightened" about exploitative practices, but "act as if they are not" with the aim of tricking the system (Fleming and Spicer 2003, 164). There have been some studies of employees' use of cynical fantasies in a way that ends up reinforcing the system (Clarke 2012; Glynos 2008; Contu and Willmott 2006). However, even if cynicism can cover up the need for a political breakthrough by providing a fantasy of internal freedom, it can also enable creative forms of resistance.

The use of creative cynicism has long been a tool of journalists operating in restrictive contexts. For instance, Cuban journalists working for the state often joke about cynically engaging in "poetic sorcery" (*brujería poética*) or "playing the lyrical violin" (*tocar el violín lírico*) as ways of embellishing dull and bureaucratic texts (Garcia Santamaria 2018b). While the "lyrical violin" is commonly played when covering agricultural news in a way intended to boost the public's optimism about crop yields and food availability, "poetic sorcery" refers to the embellishment of national symbols, such as the flag, the anthem, or historical milestones (Garcia Santamaria 2018b).

Cynical fantasies appear in the interviews, for instance, in quotes from journalists who consider themselves "lucky" because being bad students allows them to be placed in less prominent media outlets that are less ideologically demanding. In a way, identifying themselves as "bad students" or "bad workers" has provided journalists with a scapegoat (R09), a justification for showing no interest at all, even refusing to work altogether. Cynical fantasies have given journalists the impression that their subjectivity cannot be reduced to the system but exceeds it by far. The fantasy of being able to fool the system through cynicism can be seen in the following excerpt:

> I entered journalism school with a lot of naïveté. I didn't have a critical view of the profession or what it was to be a journalist. My critical view developed throughout my career. In my case, restrictions were minor because I was a bad student and they sent me to smaller media outlets for my internships. (R9)

In a way, cynicism can be seen as a tool that allows journalists to mediate between an externally imposed "official" identity and a still incipient identity that they have yet to see as political: a desire to free their voice. In other words, cynical fantasies enable a dialogue between an (apparently) fixed identity and its failure to saturate the meaning of who they are, personally and professionally speaking. In this sense, the development of young journalists' identities means that agency is constantly tested against the backdrop of inherited discourses and practices, exploring extreme positions by navigating the places in between, even if cynically.

Investing in the Professional Self

As we have seen, the interviewees consider that politics have been appropriated by the two extremes of the political spectrum: the state and dissidents, both claiming to speak in the name of the people. Therefore, they invest in fantasies of independence and professionalism as a way of distancing themselves from politics, concealing their often incipient political positions. This is key for understanding how the interviewees prefer to construct their identity in a way that is professional, rather than political. That is the main difference, for them, between journalism and activism.[11] Given the choice, the interviewees clearly position themselves on the side of professional journalism both as something that they possess (a journalistic training) and something they aim for (the professionalization of journalism in Cuba). This distinction can be seen in the following observation: "*Diario de Cuba, Cubanet* . . . those are Cuban media outlets as well. They suffer a stigma because they were some of the first ones and, since they are led by activists, they are very polarized" (R3).

While none of the interviewees dismisses the moral grounds of the dissident digital mediasphere, they construct boundaries of belonging (and exclusion) that are grounded in professional and intellectual values. Dissident journalists are seen not just as emotionally charged but also conditioned by political goals. The combination of these two elements is what would make them less "professional," leading them to promote an oversimplification of social reality that lacks intellectual complexity. And the interviewees believe that Cuban reality is nothing if not complex.

The interviewees' fantasies of professionalism offer important clues about what is valued in independent journalism and which fantasies have nourished the ethos of independent practice. What we find in the interviews is journalists' fantasy of being able to escape "the political," understood as political polarization. What emerges from journalists' discourse is a rejection of an overtly politicized and polarized conceptualization of journalism. There is the perception that the first independent media projects, such as those led by activists (like *14ymedio*, among others) or exiles (*Cubanet* or *Cibercuba*) contributed to binary narratives (R19). By clearly positioning themselves against the regime, dissidents would inadvertently feed the regime's friend versus foe narrative.

One of the consequences of rejecting both official and dissident practices as legitimate professional ways of exercising journalism is the creation of a narrow definition of journalism. By defining good journalists as those who have professional training and goals, the interviewees are drawing new frontiers of belonging that exclude those working for the state-run media, who might be "good journalists" but cannot express their talent within the system, as well as those who are activists and, therefore, lack journalistic training and professional goals—seen as damaging to the practice of journalism. In contrast, journalistic professionalism emerges as a fantasy that seems able to overcome political polarization and emotionalization and, therefore, open new positions: the grays, the in-betweens. However, this fantasy cannot escape having an exclusionary character as well: new identities are welcome, while others are rejected.

"The political" is an abstract concept that is not always easily recognizable in practice. What the interviews reveal is that young Cuban journalists did not consciously seek political goals in the workplace and, consequently, suffered censorship and harassment. In fact, it was by seeking professional fulfillment that they came to face political consequences. Far from experiencing a primacy of "the political," what journalists evoke in the interviews is an attack on their professional rights and their personal freedom, and it was only in retrospect that they attached a political meaning to their experience.

Fear of Rupture: The Paranoid Self

In her analysis of late socialist Cuban cinema, Humphreys (2019) sees paranoia and ambivalence as common positions toward the Revolution. The term "paranoid readings," which she borrows from Sedgwick and Frank (2003), denotes a way of examining social reality that unearths what remains suspicious yet hidden. In this section, paranoia is understood as a two-way suspicion between the state, which suspects that journalists are trying to threaten the system, and journalists, who suspect that the system will punish them harshly if they are judged as being "too critical." Suspicion seems to travel from the top to the bottom of the system and, as fear circulates, it feeds a sense of collective paranoia about "counterrevolution" and repression.

The shared opinion is that the Cuban government has used journalists' fear and vulnerability as a way of silencing them, but also deterring critical ones from "moonlighting" in nonofficial publications. The interviews show that repression has gone hand in hand with the expansion of independent media outlets. While journalists' early collaboration with the nonofficial publication *OnCuba* was seen as problematic, they only suffered moderate repression at their state-media jobs. However, as journalists started pushing the undefined limits of what was acceptable to say and do in the nonofficial press, experiences of repression grew in both intensity and frequency. This is exemplified in the following quote from a journalist who was completing social work at an official newspaper when he and his peers began collaborating with the independent digital press. This excerpt sheds light on the way failed attempts at co-opting journalists evolved into daily pressures and direct threats. Within months, all those who were completing their social work obligations at that newspaper left—sanctioned, expelled, or gone.

> I had published an article in *OnCuba* that was very bothersome. Then, one day, I was sitting in the [official paper's] newsroom and I saw a man I did not know standing behind me. He introduced himself as a state security official. This man took me to an office and interrogated me for an hour and a half about my work. He asked me to collaborate with state security and also insinuated that, if I did not, they could declare me a counterrevolutionary and my life could become hell. This is the kind of threats and harassment that we started receiving from the state security forces. That was at the workplace, but we also realized that several state security officials were looking for information about each of us in our neighborhoods. (R7)

As another journalist puts it, fear is instinctive and, when you are under its effect, it blurs the range of possibilities you perceive, making rupture with the system seem impossible: "For a long time, I felt that I was not scared, that I could do whatever I wanted and I was happy [...]. But then the moment of fear arrived and, when you are scared, you lose your reason" (R17). The way in which threats turn journalists' fear into paranoid fantasies is increased through peer-to-peer interaction. It is not necessary that all journalists suffer threats, harassment, or punishment; they become aware of what could happen to them because it has in fact happened to their colleagues. Once again, state repression pushes journalists to the edges of their emotional selves, creating horrific fantasies that block their ability to think properly and to use their agency in order to perform an ontological rupture with the system.

Conclusion: Fantasy and the Deterrents of Ontological Rupture

This chapter has taken a postfoundational logics approach to the role of fantasmatic logics in shaping Cuban journalists' practices in the state-run media. Young journalists' investment in fantasies means that they allow themselves to be partially invested in the system while also fantasizing about going beyond it. The interviews reveal that journalists' fantasies are a way of positioning themselves beyond politics and emotions, rejecting an excessive politicization and emotionalization of their profession. Instead, the interviewees invest in professional fantasies, sometimes in a cynical manner, in order to navigate daily pressures. However, fantasies are not always pleasant, and horrific fantasies of paranoia serve as a reminder of the power of fear in deterring journalists' ontological rupture with the system.

Drawing on sensitizing concepts from discourse theoretical analysis, this chapter has examined the apparent paradox of journalists who are "viscerally" invested in the Revolution yet fantasize about a rupture with it. This paradox takes place because Cuban journalists' professional and ideological identification with the Revolution can never fully saturate their identity. The internal instability of the official discourse and its interaction with competing articulations of Cuban reality leads young journalists to experience a "failed structural identity" that activates the search for new identity choices (Laclau 1990, 44).

The identity of Cuban journalists has always been complex, characterized as it is by continuous attempts to negotiate their personal freedom and their professional conditions with the system (Garcia Santamaria 2018a). However, older generations of journalists have lived in a context in which the state media system was hegemonic, leaving them with two clear ways of rupture: leave journalism and/or leave the country. However, younger generations are immersed in a digital revolution that is progressively disrupting the state media's hegemony with competing digital media projects. While digital technologies have contributed to a dislocation of official discourses about journalism, this does not mean that they have agentistic power but that they are able to mediate people's agency. Therefore, the dislocation of official journalism has come with a dislocation of Cuban journalists' professional identities, creating new opportunities for personal, ideological, and professional identification. It is in their ability to contest the system and to choose between competing identifications that journalists' political agency emerges.

The interviews have proved useful for understanding why young journalists can be gripped by revolutionary discourses and practices yet feel unable to work within the power relationships that were created in the name of the Revolution. That is why all the interviewees decided, at some point, to break away from the system and to invest themselves in independent media projects. The final decision, as complex as it was, seemed shaped by a series of confluences that rendered their fantasies unable to comfort them any longer. First, journalists came to realize the failed promise of an internal renewal of official Cuban journalism embedded in the official "updating" of economic and social structures. Almost simultaneously, hopes of depolarization were dashed when the reestablishment of diplomatic relations with the United States began to falter in 2016, especially following Barack Obama's state visit to Cuba and Donald Trump's election. In this context, Cuba received an outpouring of global media attention and many young journalists found a public beyond the island that was eager to hear "in-between" voices. They also found international organizations willing to offer them professional training and financial support for their projects. The fantasy of being able to reach a public "out there" helped journalists to progressively abandon fantasies of internal renewal and to position themselves as pioneers in the independent mediasphere.

It is common to assume that the Cuban independent mediasphere is unavoidably oppositional and inherently democratizing. However, this chapter has demonstrated the analytical failure of simplifying narratives that equate journalistic alterity with political opposition, overlooking the complex processes of identification, co-optation, negotiation, and resistance in which Cuban journalists operate, at both a personal and a professional level. Independent journalists have created new boundaries of journalistic belonging that go beyond the polarized media system of the early 2000s. But by establishing boundaries of belonging, they inevitably exclude those who are politically or emotionally saturated, at either pole of the official-dissident spectrum.

Faced with pressures to subjugate journalism to politics, journalists have used the fantasmatic logics of professionalization as a way of liberating their own goals from an over-politicized structure that threatens with annihilating their dreams. However, whether the avoidance of an open "political" positioning is a useful professional strategy in the long term or simply a way of delaying direct confrontation with the system remains an open question.

Notes

1. An ontological approach focuses on social relations rather than on content, which has an ontic nature (Laclau 2005, 153). The focus on ontology comes with the realization of an excessive obsession with the "ideological content" of (anti)revolutionary discourses (Holbraad 2014).

2. The goal is to assess journalists' self-interpretations while not reducing explanations to subjectivity alone, since their decisions intertwine with other social, political, and material orders that establish boundaries of (im)possibility (Glynos and Howarth 2007, 6).

3. Fantasy is not used here in its usual meaning. While common definitions highlight the idea of exiting the real world and immersing oneself in pleasant imagined realities, in postfoundational discourse analysis fantasies are defined as a way of concealing the

constructed nature of discourses about the social world. This means that fantasies are inherent to the way in which we relate to the social world and make sense of it.

4. It is important to highlight that, from a postfoundational discourse analysis perspective, all discourses and discursive positions are constructed and unstable. Therefore, it is always possible to find fissures and to contest them.

5. This quote is from a letter José Martí sent to the editor of the Argentine newspaper *La Nación* on June 10, 1887, where he claimed that Cuban journalists like himself were not afraid of dying in battle because they had the soul of a soldier in them.

6. See Henken 2011 for an early study of Cuba's "blogosphere" that highlights this dilemma.

7. I arrived in Cuba in 2013 as part of a research stay at the Faculty of Communication, University of Havana. It was a time in which there was a lot of debate about a possible aperture of journalistic practice in Cuba. For my doctorate, I interviewed many academics and journalists who were working for the state-run media, of all ages, and who fought relentlessly for a journalistic-led change. Having met them, I have no doubt of their honesty and professionalism. However, as hopes did not materialize, many young journalists started collaborating with independent media outlets, or created their own. I had the chance to observe this transition firsthand during my doctoral research stays, between 2013 and 2017. It is only thanks to my ethnographic work in Cuba that I have been able to develop a network of trusted academics and journalists who were key for accessing the interviewees, and convincing them to share very intimate experiences, both of hope and of fear, with me.

8. Cuban journalism students have the chance, and the duty, to do internships at the end of each semester. This is different from social work, which is conducted upon graduation. More information about these internships, or *prácticas laborales*, can be found here: http://www.fcom.uh.cu/practicas-laborales.

9. The term "logic" does not refer to logical or causal mechanisms, since social logics are always limited by the context in which they develop and by other competing logics (Laclau and Mouffe 1985: 142).

10. All interviewees are anonymized, only identified by the letter R (for respondent) and a randomly assigned number. They have all worked for the state-run media to then disengage themselves from it and become independent journalists.

11. For instance, Abraham Jiménez Enoa, editor in chief of the independent magazine *El Estornudo* was recently quoted to the effect that, in Cuba, independent journalism should not be confused with political activism (García 2019).

REFERENCES

Barker, Chris. 2004. *The Sage Dictionary of Cultural Studies*. London: Sage.
Beckett, Charlie and Mark Deuze. 2016. "On the Role of Emotion in the Future of Journalism." *Social Media + Society* 2(3): 1–6.
Buckingham, David. 2008. "Introducing Identity." In *Youth, Identity, and Digital Media*, edited by David Buckingham. Cambridge: The MIT Press.
Butler, Judith. 1997. *Excitable Speech: A Politics of the Performative*. New York: Routledge.

Carpentier, Nico. 2017. *The Discursive-Material Knot: Cyprus in Conflict and Community Media Participation*. Bern: Peter Lang Publishing Group.

Clarke, Matthew. 2012. "Talkin' 'Bout a Revolution: The Social, Political, and Fantasmatic Logics of Education Policy." *Journal of Education Policy* 27(2): 173–191.

Contu, Alessia and Hugh Willmott. 2006. "Studying Practice." *Organization Studies* 27(12): 1769–1782.

Cubadebate. 2019. "¿Qué política se plantean el estado y el gobierno para la comunicación social?" July 17, 2019.

Fleming, Peter and Andre Spicer. 2003. "Working at a Cynical Distance: Implications for Power, Subjectivity and Resistance." *Organization* 10(1): 157–79.

García, Iván. 2019. "Abraham Jiménez: 'Los medios independientes en Cuba no confunden activismo político con periodismo.'" *Diario Las Américas*, October 21, 2019.

Garcia Santamaria, Sara. 2018a. "Digital Media and the Promotion of Deliberative Debate in Cuba." Internet Policy Observatory, University of Pennsylvania.

Garcia Santamaria, Sara. 2018b. "The Historical Articulation of 'The People' in Revolutionary Cuba. Media Discourses of Unity in Times of National Debate (1990–2012)." Ph.D. thesis, Department of Journalism Studies, University of Sheffield.

Garcia Santamaria, Sara. 2019. "La Construcción Histórica del Pueblo Cubano en Momentos de Debate Nacional." In *En Cuba, Periodismo es Más (+): Transposición, Redundancia y Dinamismo Profesional*, edited by Martín Oller Alonso. Havana: Cuadernos Artesanos de Comunicación.

Gardner, Andrew. 2004. *Agency Uncovered: Archaeological Perspectives on Social Agency, Power and Being Human*. London: Routledge.

Geoffray, Marie Laure and Armando Chaguaceda. 2015. "Medios de Comunicación y cambios en la política de información en Cuba desde 1959." *Temas de Comunicación* (29)1: 171–196.

Glynos, Jason. 2008. "Ideological Fantasy at Work." *Journal of Political Ideologies* 13(3): 275–296.

Glynos, Jason and David Howarth. 2007. *Logics of Critical Explanation in Social and Political Theory*. New York: Routledge.

Glynos, Jason and David Howarth. 2008. "Structure, Agency and Power in Political Analysis: Beyond Contextualised Self-Interpretations." *Political Studies Review* 6(2): 155–169.

Henken, Ted A. 2011. "Una cartografía de la blogósfera cubana: Entre 'oficialistas' y 'mercenarios.'" *Nueva Sociedad* 235 (September-October).

Henken, Ted A. 2017. "Cuba's Digital Millennials: Independent Digital Media and Civil Society on the Island of the Disconnected." *Social Research: An International Quarterly* 84(2): 429–456.

Holbraad, Martin. 2014. "*Revolución o Muerte*: Self-sacrifice and the Ontology of Cuban Revolution." *Ethnos* 79(3): 365–387.

Humphreys, Laura-Zoë. 2019. *Fidel Between the Lines: Paranoia and Ambivalence in Late Socialist Cuban Cinema*. Durham and London: Duke University Press.

Lacan, Jacques. 1999. *The Seminar of Jacques Lacan. Book XX, On Feminine Sexuality: The Limits of Love and Knowledge*. New York: W. W. Norton & Company.

Laclau, Ernesto. 1990. *New Reflections on the Revolution of Our Time*. New York: Verso.

Laclau, Ernesto. 2005. *On Populist Reason*. London: Verso.

Laclau, Ernesto and Chantal Mouffe. 1985. *Hegemony and Socialist Strategy: Towards a Radical Democratic Politics*. London: Verso.
Mouffe, Chantal. 2000. *The Democratic Paradox*. London: Verso.
Repnikova, Maria. 2017. *Media Politics in China: Improvising Power Under Authoritarianism*. Cambridge: Cambridge University Press.
Roudakova, Natalia. 2017. *Losing Pravda: Ethics and the Press in Post-Truth Russia*. Cambridge: Cambridge University Press.
Sedgwick, Eve Kosofsky and Adam Frank. 2003. *Touching Feeling: Affect, Pedagogy, Performativity*. Durham: Duke University Press.
Stavrakakis, Yannis. 2005. "Religion and Populism in Contemporary Greece." In *Populism and the Mirror of Democracy*, edited by F. Panizza. London: Verso.
Yurchak, Alexei. 2003. "The Soviet Hegemony of Form: Everything was Forever, Until It was No More." *Comparative Studies in History* 45(3): 480–510.
Yurchak, Alexei. 2006. *Everything was Forever, Until It was No More: The Last Soviet Generation*. Princeton: Princeton University Press.
Zicman de Barros, Thomas. 2020. "Desire and Collective Identities: Decomposing Ernesto Laclau's Notion of Demand." *Constellations*: 1–11.
Žižek, Slavoj. 2014. *Event: A Philosophical Journey Through a Concept*. New York: Melville House.

9

Perceptions of and Strategies for Autonomy among Journalists Working for Cuban State Media

ANNE NATVIG

According to the Cuban academic Julio García Luis (2013, 127), friends or colleagues visiting Cuba have often asked him the following question: "Why, with your passionate Revolution, do you nevertheless have such a boring press?" One possible answer may be found by revisiting the well-known words of Fidel Castro: "Within the Revolution, everything; against the Revolution, nothing" (Castro 1961). Working for the state media in Cuba is difficult for journalists wanting to pursue "Western" professional ideals such as criticism and debate. This chapter addresses how some of these journalists navigate within the strict frame of what the Cuban Communist Party (Partido Comunista de Cuba, or PCC) defines as appropriate information for the public. The chapter seeks to answer the following research questions: What perceptions of autonomy do journalists working for Cuban state media have? What strategies do these journalists apply to broaden their journalistic autonomy?

Most journalists who work for Cuban state media are products of an extensive five-year university education in which the professional ideals they are taught are much closer to standard "Western" principles and paradigms of critique and debate than the reality they encounter once employed as members of the state media apparatus. This makes for difficult initial adjustments, constant professional compromises, and general discontent with the dearth of information offered to the people. The frustration of these journalists has increased through the recent expansion of Internet access on the island and by the veritable explosion of independent digital media outlets, which extend its reporters a far greater tolerance of journalistic autonomy. Indeed, these start-ups have been built around a clear expectation of such autonomy combined with the classic journalistic ideals of impartiality, investigation, critique, and the generation of debate (Henken 2017).

The Competing Roles of the Cuban State Media and the "Blogosphere"

The function of the state media is to support the policies of the PCC. Moreover, all state media outlets are subject to the regulation and control of the PCC's Ideological Department (ID). As explained to me by the participants in this study, the lines of communication and control between the ID and the newsrooms can take various forms,[1] such as phone calls or personal visits where editors are informed by representatives of the ID about the Party's current media agenda. As *Granma* is the country's leading newspaper and the PCC's "official organ," what is written here is interpreted as a guide to other newspapers, which often reprint or digitally republish its articles verbatim. As a general rule, if *Granma* avoids a sensitive issue, no other newspaper will touch it.

A new policy on Information and Communication Technologies (referred to as TICs in Spanish) was approved as a decree law by Cuban President Miguel Díaz-Canel on July 4, 2019 (Díaz-Canel 2019).[2] Another TICs policy document, which supposedly has been approved by the Political Bureau of the Communist Party, has been in informal circulation for more than a year. Some journalists have considered it a slight loosening of control on state media. Others see little or no change in the new policy, except that it does not prohibit non-state actors specifically (*Periodismo de Barrio* 2018; Rodríguez 2018). In sum, there is a lot of confusion about what kinds of independent digital media are allowed and what are not in the wake of this new legal framework. Moreover, what if any real impact these new policies will have on state media is also so far unclear.

While the decree law does not state the rights and obligations of media outlets, the policy document does. It says: "The director of every media outlet is responsible, in a personal and nontransferable way, for the execution of the informative, editorial, and cultural policy in his or her organ" (PCC 2018, 12). At the same time, this policy document states that the PCC is "the director of social communication in the country, draws up the general policy for its development and controls it" (PCC 2018, 10). This means that there is a certain degree of autonomy within each newsroom. The various editors in chief decide what is printed or broadcast but the PCC plays an oversight role. According to the higher-ranking journalists included in this study, it is important to avoid crossing the invisible line that would provoke the ID of the PCC to become directly involved in evaluating specific content. Thus, editors are responsible for anticipating and preemptively censoring topics the ID may object to. The risks of being punished or dismissed, for stepping out of line or across this invisible line is therefore a strong motivator for self-censorship. Furthermore, editors are often given this role by the PCC because they have proven over many years to be supporters of the system, and this makes the autonomy of journalists further down in the journalistic hierarchy extremely dependent on their particular editor. As noted by Garcés (2013), only fifty percent of leaders in the Cuban state media have journalistic training and in many cases this influences editorial decisions away from professional considerations and toward the interests of the PCC.

With the recent expansion of the Internet in Cuba, however, various kinds of non-state digital media have also appeared on the national scene, undermining the hegemony of the top-down Cuban state media system. Most non-state media—international newspapers and wire services such as *El País*, *New York Times*, *Reuters*, *EFE*, and the Associated Press—are accredited by the state-run Foreign Press Center (*Centro de Prensa Internacional*, or CPI) and risk losing authorization and legal residency status if they are too critical of the government.[3] On the other hand, the wide variety of emergent, independent media outlets (both those whom Henken (2017) calls "digital millennials" as well as the more bold "digital dissidents") tend to be more outspoken in their criticism of the Cuban government and its policies than the foreign press. As a result, these island-based independent digital media startups receive a constant stream of harassment and are periodically blocked from access via the state-controlled national servers whether via the island's growing web of public Wi-Fi networks or over the mobile 3G connections made available in December 2018.

Foreshadowing the appearance of these digital indie media outlets, a number of independent blogs were launched from Cuba starting around 2007–2008. The state's response to this was twofold. On the one hand, it portrayed the most prominent and overtly critical unauthorized bloggers as U.S. government mercenaries (or "lackeys of imperialism"); on the other, it actively and publicly embraced a handful of other blogs and bloggers, attempting to use them as a tool to counter what it considered "anti-Cuban" content online (Henken 2011; Vicari 2015). Following this, state media journalists were given Internet access from their homes under the condition that they open a blog (ostensibly a personal, unmediated space) representing an official point of view. Currently, the Cuban Union of Journalists (Unión de Periodistas Cubanos, or UPEC) lists over 160 blogs written by journalists from all over the country (UPEC 2018). However, when one attempts to access these blogs, most either stopped publishing after 2012 or have been discontinued or deleted altogether (which is when the Cuban blogosphere started to wane). This trend is almost the reverse for the thirty blogs listed by *Granma*, where the majority are still active.

This is important because to some degree the blogging format could potentially still constitute an opportunity for freer expression for journalists working for Cuban state media. Now, most of the previously active independent bloggers have merged into journalistic collectives, creating their own island-based news outlets (such as *14ymedio*, *Periodismo de Barrio*, *El Toque*, *El Estornudo*, and *Tremenda Nota*), something that Marreiro (2014, 30) had presciently foreseen. And for their part, Cuban youth are not taking to blogging but, rather, creating their own YouTube channels (Associated Press 2018) or signing up for Twitter (*OnCuba* 2019; Pentón 2019), or, more commonly, Instagram or Snapchat (or Tinder!) accounts, like other young people all over the world.

Journalistic Autonomy in Authoritarian Contexts

In order to understand journalistic autonomy in Cuba, it is relevant to briefly review differing understandings of autonomy around the world. According to Jane B. Singer, U.S. journalists consider autonomy to be fulfilling "their public service obligations of informing the citizenry, free from the influences of government or of obligations to any other force" (2007, 81). This is coherent within the professional milieu of the "detached watchdog" that Thomas Hanitzsch describes as "prototypical of the Western journalist" (2011, 485). Monitoring political and economic elites in this way ("keeping them honest" or "holding them accountable") is a function of journalism globally, and support for this role is found in countries worldwide (2011, 487).

Katrin Voltmer and Herman Wasserman (2014, 189) find that there are two parallel, and often conflicting, processes taking place when journalists in emerging democracies interpret press freedom. One understanding leans toward the premises common in what they call "Western discourses," such as claiming membership in a global professional community where holding those in power to account is a primary journalistic value. Another way of interpreting press freedom, however, is through historical and cultural aspects that may be in contradiction to this "Western notion." For instance, the way journalists perceive their role in society may guide how they define their responsibilities connected to freedom of the press. For example, in authoritarian countries like China, Indonesia, Russia, and Uganda the "opportunist facilitator role" dominates (although it is also found in all types of political regimes, and in the West). Journalists in these countries see themselves largely as supportive of the government and cooperative with its official policies, a role which has come about through diverse political and historical factors in the respective countries (Hanitzsch et al. 2011, 282).

The presence of the state in news organizations is experienced by journalists as a limiting force in their perceived professional autonomy. Democratic forms of government are therefore a major condition for journalistic autonomy (Reich and Hanitzsch 2013, 149). Thus, analyzing autonomy in authoritarian countries calls for a somewhat different approach than studies focusing on journalistic autonomy in democracies. Journalists in authoritarian societies may negotiate between various goals, in addition to the fulfillment of their ideal role as professional journalists.

After the 1952 revolution, the Egyptian press was put under political control. In order to maintain some of the professional progress they had enjoyed before the revolution, journalists found closeness to those in power, through a role as experts or advisers a way to expand their autonomy. Also, by redefining their role in society toward that of "eyewitness or historian," journalists could develop counternarratives to official contemporary or historical accounts. In addition, new digital media outlets have exposed Arab journalists to Western journalistic practices. This has served as a bridge between cultures, which young Arab journalists have used to reform their societies (and their practice of journalism) from within (Mellor 2009, 318).

During the Soviet era, Estonian journalists practiced various forms of "silent resistance" against restrictions on their autonomy. Their strategies included emphasizing apolitical subjects to diminish the official ideological discourse and using linguistic means of circumventing the demands of the ruling party (Lauk and Kreegipuu 2010). Jingrong Tong (2009) holds that, in more liberal Chinese media organizations, external pressure from the government on the newsrooms makes self-censorship an important strategy for exposing social ills. For instance, by carefully calibrating reports by including official discourse, a sensitive issue can be addressed. Tong argues that this selective way of writing indeed increases autonomy as it helps newsrooms bypass political minefields and increase the possibility of publication on politically sensitive topics. However, as Reich and Hanitzsch (2013, 152) suggest, there is a need for more qualitative data on how autonomy is experienced and negotiated by journalists in authoritarian and transitional societies. This chapter hopes to contribute to this body of literature by focusing on Cuban perceptions of and strategies for autonomy within the structure of Cuban state media.

Professional Autonomy

According to Silvio Waisbord (2013, 45–71), the liberal ideal of journalism as a marketplace of ideas is not sufficient to guarantee true autonomy. For journalism to be able to report on publicly relevant matters, it needs to distance itself from both state and corporate interests. In particular, Waisbord distinguishes between "press autonomy" and "professional journalism" (2013, 53). The first refers to the importance in democracies of guaranteeing the independence of the press from the state, while the latter is linked to a central element of professionalism: "the need to control boundaries vis-à-vis external actors (the state, the market, and organized politics) in order to serve the public interest" (2013, 54).

However, in liberal capitalist contexts, erecting a principled and impenetrable firewall between journalistic practice and corporate interests is an almost impossible ideal to achieve. But professional journalists do not necessarily succumb to external actors' attempts of control; autonomy is also contingent on journalists' own willingness to preserve boundaries of the profession. Strategies for maintaining autonomy consist of trying to maintain or regain sovereignty over their professional jurisdiction or attempting to make livable arrangements that strike a principled balance between professional journalistic ideals and outside forces such as the market, the government, or bureaucracy. The result is a constant negotiation between professional considerations and nonprofessional anticipations (Waisbord 2013, 150).

The Cuban scholar Julio García Luis (2013, 87) considers that the media has "the transcendent role as producer and reproductive agent of the political system, of the values, and of the culture of society." The press can be viewed as an open system that interacts with other systems such as the political, juridical, economic, cultural, or individual. These systems relate to each other in different ways. If it is an *obligatory* relation, the system is *rigid*. If it is possible to substitute one element with another and keep functioning, the relation is *optional* and thus more *flexible* (2013, 88). These elements constitute what "regulates" the press (as opposed to the outright control of it as state propaganda). At the same time, the press is a system in itself, with its own internal structures that are able to "self-regulate" its activity. However, "self-regulation" is only functional if a good "regulation" exists; otherwise it is merely a euphemism for "self-censorship."

García Luis also argues that the constant external threats to Cuba from the U.S. in the years following the triumph of the 1959 Revolution (often understood as a "state of siege" that gave birth to a "siege mentality" among

Cuban officials) caused Cuban leaders to see the role of journalism as one directly related to the interests of the Communist Party and the defense of national sovereignty embodied by the Revolution and state socialism (2013, 90–101). This has fatally undermined the Cuban press's ability to "self-regulate." Therefore, it has lost the authority to make decisions and choose the best solutions to professionally fulfill its role in society—becoming a mere propagandistic instrument of the political-ideological system. This is not a judgment about the journalists working in the media themselves as good or bad professionals. Instead, it is about the system itself, a system which—in García Luis's consideration—Cuba should have been able to change in the years since the early 1960s. For example, in a questionnaire to which Cuban journalists responded, García Luis found that only 11 percent considered media leaders to have power over editorial decisions while over 50 percent considered the leaders of the PCC to exercise most influence over the media. According to García Luis, such regulation may in turn cause the people working in state media to be "like little birds in their nest, waiting for you to feed them everything [already] chewed up" (2013, 158).

Methodology

The data analyzed here consists of in-depth interviews with twelve journalists who work in Cuban state media. These interviews were conducted during a fieldwork trip to Cuba in 2016. Due to the challenges of access for foreign researchers and the sparse diffusion of research originating in Cuba (and a general lack of research itself) little research on state media journalists has been done. The exclusive selection of state media journalists was not the original intention. I had initially hoped to draw on a more diverse sample of practicing journalists so that I could compare the experiences and struggles for journalistic autonomy across different kinds of outlets, including those who work for non-state outlets. However, the process of applying for and being granted a research visa by the Cuban government made a more inclusive approach impossible.

To secure participants' anonymity, journalists were given pseudonyms and placed within three age categories: young (20–34), middle-aged (35–49), and senior (50+). Participants ranged from newly graduated reporters to long-established editors, but titles and affiliations have been omitted. The responses from the journalists interviewed are not applicable to all journalists throughout Cuba. However, they are indicative of key journalistic trends and strategies and offer some illustrative points of view on autonomy for state media journalists in a changing society.

The interview guide used in the research was inspired by the framework of the *Worlds of Journalism Study* (WJS 2012). It covered daily routines, autonomy, and changes in the Cuban media landscape, while also leaving room for participants to elaborate on subjects particularly important to them (Bryman 2016). Important questions for this study were: What does journalistic autonomy mean to you? Who decides which stories should be prioritized? How much do you decide over your journalistic production? Have any of your articles been withheld or rewritten? I have translated transcriptions of these interviews from Spanish to English and verified them with a native Spanish-speaking proofreader. Additionally, for this project, five group interviews with journalism students were conducted. I will refer to data from these interviews to supplement my quotations from the working journalists themselves.

Perceptions of Autonomy

When asked to define autonomy at a general level, most of my interviewees defined it as a responsibility residing between obligations to the collective and to the individual. A young reporter, Carlos, believes that the media should uphold values such as "anti-imperialism, defending ideas and struggles of the third world, supporting the weak and not the strong [. . .], and it should defend Cuban independence and sovereignty." Autonomy for him is then both protection of Cuba as a nation-state and personal agency in the journalistic profession: "Autonomy is the capacity of every individual, every journalist, to guide their actions, their written works towards these values. [At the same time,] nobody needs to come and tell me what I should write, how I should write it, or in which form." However, when describing what autonomy means in practice, the journalists answer in diverse ways. Many start by claiming that journalists work with substantial self-determination. For instance, the middle-aged reporter, Luis, says:

> I do not believe that censorship exists here. Censorship is when there is a dictatorship and there is a censor that comes with a red pen and a magnifying glass and draws a line and harasses you. [. . .] I mean, nobody writes because they are commanded, mandated, forced. That is impossible.

Many journalists who work in the state media emphasize the importance of freedom from corporate interests. A middle-aged reporter, Juan, exemplifies this by claiming: "I believe the Cuban journalist sometimes works with a little more freedom than in many places of the world. I mean the journalist edits his story, he does not have to negotiate with the owners or his superior." Nevertheless, the Cuban state media depends on the degree of liberty the PCC grants it at any given moment. Juan continues his argument by saying that his journalistic autonomy depends on the topic not being "very important," which implicitly means an issue that does not question the political leadership.

This leads to the second part of what autonomy means for journalists: something situated "within the limits." Journalists often explain these limits by referring to the "editorial guidelines" of each media outlet. As senior reporter María explains, the problem with these guidelines is that neither do they grant much autonomy nor are they always followed. Juan claims that if one agrees with the editorial line there is substantial space for movement. If one does not agree, however, one should leave and "look for another place to work, that could be in a foreign media outlet or you could make your own blog."

Strategies of Autonomy

Leaving the state media and entering another type of outlet is more easily said than done. The content, writing style, and remuneration in non-state media are key elements that attract young journalists to this emerging option, but there is not room for everyone. Many young journalists therefore attempt to keep one foot in the more stable but less autonomous state sector and another in the more unreliable but freer and better-paid independent realm (García 2016). Another way for state media journalists in Cuba to gain autonomy is to avoid the coverage of sensitive or particularly "delicate" topics. For example, the young reporter Tania considers that "this is an exercise of balance and battle. National issues, relating to the domestic reality, are the most difficult themes to breach [in one's journalism]."

Several journalists say that they have never experienced censorship, but then they also emphasize that they work with issues on the margins of what may be considered political by the PCC, such as culture, information technology, or international subjects. The young reporter Jorge says: "I used to write about sports, which is no big deal. So, it was not politics or national issues." Among journalism students the avoidance of politics is also reflected when they discuss in which state media outlet they would like to spend their two to three-year obligatory internship after graduation. None of the students wanted to work on domestic issues, although several commented that they know there is censorship in sports and cultural reporting as well.

The structural conditions of the state media are not favorable for journalists who want to denounce social problems or institutional failures through their work. According to the journalists interviewed, the Cuban News Agency (Agencia Cubana de Noticias, or ACN) functions as a "headquarters" for determining which events and stories the state media should cover. Journalists may also propose subjects for coverage, but the events of "maximum interest for the state" often leave few resources for other stories. One of the journalists interviewed had several strategies for overcoming the limitations when covering the news. Working in a state broadcasting company, the journalist volunteered to host an early morning program:

> That gave me many opportunities because I got to have a space there of ten minutes, to talk about whatever politics I wanted. At that time [in the morning], there were not many decisions made, so there aren't many bosses who bother you too much because of the contents that you are covering, and I had a lot of freedom. And there were things that I said in that time slot that were never repeated later during the day, but I said them in the morning.

Another way of creating a space for strong opinions is to get a prominent person, tolerated by the PCC, to state it. Intellectuals in Cuba enjoy a wider space of autonomy than journalists, and can therefore make more challenging public claims, even if these too always must remain "within the limits" (Garcia Santamaria 2017, 33). In a broadcast series interviewing the aforementioned group, the journalist promoted stories of hard work and sacrifice—but it was also:

> ... an excuse to expose some of the problems of the press. And some very strong things were said, things that I could never have stated in the news [myself], but if [the Cuban intellectual] Raúl Garcés is telling me, then Raúl Garcés is telling me. And this content is heating up the debate on the problems that the media in Cuba have with the authorities.

This means that the relative freedom of prominent intellectuals and academics can promote a trickle-down effect to expand the autonomy for journalists working for state media outlets.

Using Blogs

Among the many contradictions in the Cuban state media system, one that is particularly restraining on journalistic ideals is that everything printed in state newspapers may be interpreted as official policy. This means that journalists cannot make critical comments about foreign regimes in the state media, as this may be interpreted as a message from the Party, which in turn can cause difficulties in bilateral relations. For instance, as indicated by the young reporter Carlos, if a Middle Eastern country were to lend Cuba money, state newspapers would then be unable to write about human rights violations in that country. Responding to the push and pull between state obligations and professional ideals, some journalists feel they have no choice but to leave the profession. Others still remain within the official media but resolve to avoid sensitive topics or become resigned from doing much serious work at all, which according to Carlos can be understood as a strategy of protest (but can also arguably be taken as a form of consent, obedience, acquiescence, and self-censorship).

However, in addition to collaboration with non-state outlets, another strategy for autonomy among state media journalists is to turn to their personal blogs. Indeed, three of the participants in this study used blogs for this specific purpose. The middle-aged reporter Roberto explained that it would be impossible for him in his official journalistic work to directly question a minister or directly criticize someone in the government, Party, or bureaucracy: "I wouldn't do that, because I know that it won't be published. You don't write to not get published. I'd put that in my blog." He said that there have been reactions to his using his blog in this manner but refrained from specifying how these episodes played out or what they were in relation to. Instead, he simply (if a bit cryptically) claimed: "I am still here, but one also [has to] know the rules of the game."

The young reporter Carlos considers his blogging strategy to be "a way of applying pressure so that people understand that what was published on the Internet, on the blog, could easily have appeared in the [official] paper without being considered a catastrophe." In fact, he claims that several times editors, even "leaders," have called him to say that his blog posts could have been published in the news outlet, which also is the case with one of his stories. Carlos says he has not had any problems with the content of the blog, which he considers to be true to the values mentioned earlier (anti-imperialism, support for the weak, etc.). If one day he encountered problems, he said, "I would refer to those values, and if they do not agree with those values, I would quit my job."

It seems that keeping a certain degree of transparency toward the political elite is key in order to be able to continue blogging as a way to let off steam. Roberto says he started working with a government institution, informing them about important issues in his blog, and this raised awareness in other governmental bodies such as the Ideological Department. Importantly, he managed to make a relevant ministry see that there were subjects lacking proper reporting in the state media: "I do not think that any government institution has been surprised with the things I have done, because they knew that I was involved in this."

Another journalist, a middle-aged reporter named Ernesto, has experienced how difficult it is to know where the limit is for acceptable utterances in blogs. Once, he wrote a blog post on a public march by self-employed workers and was afterward fired from his news outlet. However, the UPEC got involved, and he was allowed to return after a month-long layoff. A while later, he published a speech made by a government official at an internal meeting on his blog. This caused him to be fired permanently, and he was also suspended from the UPEC. Ernesto says: "What was said [at the meeting] was such an elemental thing. Everybody knew it. It is not like I revealed a state secret. [...] I didn't think it would create such a big thing. If I had known, I wouldn't have published it, because I lost my job." Ernesto contends that the autonomy he thought he had had on his blog turned out to be a fiction since he could not publish anything there that went against the agenda of the state media outlet where he worked: "I mean, if you go outside the line of what they want you to say, or what is supposedly correct for a journalist to publish, the same thing that happened to me will happen to you." The self-censoring effect such layoffs can have on other journalists working for state media should not be underestimated.

Navigating Autonomy

Managing boundaries with external actors is an important feature of what Waisbord (2013) defines as "professional journalism." Ideally, neither states nor corporations should exercise influence over journalistic decisions. While such a normative ideal is difficult to obtain in any political system, the role of the state media as promoters of the PCC "party line" in Cuba makes this impossible to achieve for journalists who practice their profession in these official outlets. Still, it does not mean that such journalists have completely given up maintaining, negotiating, navigating, or eventually regaining autonomy within official structures.

The extensive university education where criticism and debate are encouraged rather than avoided is a big advantage for Cuban journalists. They are well aware of the possibilities of criticism, accountability, and debate in their practice of journalism if the structure would allow them develop these journalistic traits.[4] Indeed, this may be the case for many journalists in countries with limited media freedom. Examining twelve countries with limited or no media freedom, Josephi (2010) concludes that "journalism education cannot be used as a sign of how free or not free the country's media system is."

Although Cuban state media journalists fall firmly within the "loyal facilitator role" (Mellado et al. 2017; Olivera and Torres 2017), Cuban journalism students show a much greater interest in political issues than their counterparts in Ecuador and Venezuela. About half of the Cuban student respondents (N=383) claim to be very or extremely interested in politics (Alonso et al. 2017, 254). The stark contrast between a strong journalistic preparation coupled with interest in politics, and the disconcerting reality in state media outlets, make the dissonance between ideals and practice difficult to swallow for journalism graduates (Natvig 2018).

As for how state media journalists define autonomy, they find themselves torn between a dual responsibility: they should consider the needs of the nation, but at the same time work without interference from the PCC. The Cuban system (often referred to as a "regime" by its critics) is a heavily politicized subject, not only internally, but also—perhaps especially—internationally. Cuban journalists are acutely aware of the possible resonance a media story can have far beyond the shores of the island. They are thus bound, both formally and informally, to certain obligations to protect the state, especially since the siege-like atmosphere on the island allows the government to conflate itself with the Party and the nation. Anyone who has wandered the streets of Havana, or any other Cuban town, knows that political discussions are abundant among vendors, friends, and families. It is revealing that, despite the high level of interest in politics displayed by journalism students, established journalists seek to avoid this subject in their work because of the implicit limitations on autonomy. Although some journalists argue that it is a collective responsibility to work from within in creating structures to broaden autonomy, most consider the system to be too rigid to change without political will from above.

Even the emerging crop of independent, non-state media startups on the island often carefully engage in strategic avoidance of politics as an important survival strategy. For example, many use *el paquete* (a digital compilation of a wide variety of media circulated via flash drives) as a method of distribution. However, the distributors of this service assiduously follow the "no porn and no politics" rule. Lacking a legal basis, this practice of self-censorship is one of the costs of staying in the game (Henken 2021).

If stories are seen to be questioning the political regime (state socialism or the Revolution), censorship, withdrawal of tolerance, or outright repression awaits. This outcome was the fate of the influential independent magazine

El Estornudo (Álvarez 2018; Álvarez 2019). Upon its being blocked, its editors published a letter saying that its editorial decisions would not "move an inch" toward the expectations of the political powers. An easier path for journalists, whether official or independent, is to simply avoid these "areas of contradiction," as some journalists put it. Writing about sports, culture, or technology makes the dissonance between journalistic ideals and reality easier to bridge, and contradictions appear more seldom. However, even in these safer thematic areas, one can never be fully confident of when or how a new "area of contradiction" might suddenly appear in what would otherwise be an innocuous topic or story. In other words, the line between what is considered "within the [digital] Revolution" and outside or even against it is perhaps purposely nebulous, leading to the common practice of self-censorship by journalists working in both the state and independent media.

As noted by both Waisbord (2013) and García Luis (2013), autonomy is a precondition for journalistic practice, and a legal framework is an essential element to secure journalistic autonomy. While Cuban journalists and intellectuals have called for less dependence on the PCC (Elizalde 2013; Garcés 2016; García Luis 2013), these demands remain theoretical and avoid direct criticism of the political elite. As mentioned earlier, the newly established Cuban communication policy and decree law (a process which has taken five years, and of which journalists in this study have had great expectations) has not defined a framework securing journalistic autonomy, but rather created further confusion about the invisible parameters drawn by the PCC.

For those journalists who choose to write on the difficult topic of politics, one way to carve out space for opinions that differ from the Party line is to find programs and publications that are less scrutinized or to use intellectuals accepted by the PCC as a foil or a voice of complaint. However, this way of moving around requires a certain status within the journalistic hierarchy and thus is not easily accomplished by the average or rookie reporter. More accessible platforms for expanding autonomy are blogs, collaboration with non-state outlets, or leaving the state media altogether.

The fluidity of what can and what cannot be written without consequences is perhaps the most striking aspect of the analysis of the three bloggers interviewed for this chapter. Roberto and Ernesto are largely at opposite ends of the spectrum in how they approach the invisible "glass ceiling" of tolerated expression. Roberto accepts a certain limitation on autonomy by striving toward keeping different bureaucratic units of the PCC informed about his planned blogging activities at any given time. Such openness runs the risk of backfiring since their knowledge of his intentions could lead to his being prohibited from posting stories he deems important. On the other hand, he has thus far been able to stay in the "game" for a long time and has managed to expand his autonomy and to gain a modicum of political acceptance for his agenda. This approach directly relates to strategies described by Waisbord (2013) in journalists making livable arrangements with outside forces to protect shares of autonomy.

In contrast, Roberto adheres to ideals closer to standard "Western," liberal democratic paradigms of autonomy such as denouncing social problems and exposing malfunctions. He considers that information relevant to people's lives should be published and he should be able to do this on his own blog. However, in an authoritarian state where even the role of critically minded "state-friendly journalistic blogs" committed to the revolutionary project are potentially suspect, such ideals are likely to provoke negative consequences. In losing his job and the following chain of events leading to difficulties in getting a new job, he completely lost his space to maneuver. The third blogger, Carlos, has given up his job in the state media and started working for a non-state media outlet. Editors and leaders in the non-state media are mostly professionally trained journalists themselves. Despite having to avoid politics, they often prioritize stories that simply are unavailable in state media. Although Carlos pragmatically (and idealistically or perhaps a bit naively) sought to use his blog as a way of improving the state media from within, it seems that the "system" did not appreciate his efforts.

Conclusions

Fidel's "Words to the Intellectuals" may in fact sum up some journalistic strategies for autonomy in the Cuban state media. If journalists move within boundaries ("within the Revolution") and are always aware where the often arbitrary line of the acceptable is drawn at any given moment, they are likely to expand their degree of autonomy and keep their jobs. My interviews have shown that if journalists move too far "outside," much less turn "against the Revolution," all bets are off and all doors to autonomy "within the Revolution's" media system are shut, making it impossible for them to maintain a career as a journalist in the state media.[5] While there is general agreement that the state media is too far removed from the public agenda and too concerned with the political agenda (Elizalde 2013), a common way of seeking journalistic autonomy is merely by avoiding national issues and politics. Therefore, the state media remains "fossilized" (Marreiro 2014: 7), stuck within a Cold War paradigm recently exacerbated by the return to an antagonistic policy by the U.S. Trump administration.

The recent ascension to the Cuban presidency of Miguel Díaz-Canel has so far not shown any promising signs of more autonomy for state or non-state media actors. Indeed, in his speech to the UPEC in 2018 Díaz-Canel criticized non-state media outlets in general, and those he claimed to have financing from the U.S. government in particular, stating that: "they have been escalating the attack on what unites us–the Party–and what defends us–our press–continually disqualifying both and trying to fracture and separate what comes from the same root and grows in the same trunk." This quite visually shows what the leadership of the Party consider to be the role of journalists working for the state media: They are to defend the political leadership and the Revolution from outside forces. In fact, Díaz-Canel considers Cuban journalists and the Party to be two branches of the same tree. According to the president, this task is so important that the interests of the individual are unimportant (*Granma* 2018).

Thus, while the Revolution may still wield considerable power, it has also created a media system incompatible with journalistic autonomy from the political leadership, forcing many journalists to take creative risks to achieve a modicum of autonomy. It seems that the state media will remain "boring" as described by García Luis (2013: 123). However, as this chapter has shown, journalists apply various strategies to gain autonomy from this "too close for comfort" relationship. For instance, issues that might not pass otherwise can be addressed in publications that receive little editorial scrutiny. Others channel stories through their personal blogs, while making sure that stories are not very confrontational. Also, having Cuban intellectuals comment on issues that may be controversial, is a way of getting something published, because of the freer leeway some prominent intellectuals enjoy in Cuba. Finally, many journalists maintain jobs in both state media and the non-state media, as this allows them a broader range of autonomy.

Notes

1. Journalism students interviewed for this study explain that during periods of practical training they often encounter sensitive issues when writing articles, and many have had their work rewritten or been told to change content themselves. It seems that newly educated journalists or journalism students learn to navigate sensitive issues through "socialization" (Breed 1955, 328). Journalism students also appear more willing to oppose established norms than do journalists working in the state media (see Natvig 2018).

2. Briefly outlined, the objectives of the decree law are as follows: continue the "computerization" of the country, develop TICs as an instrument in the defense of the Revolution, promote access and "responsible use" of TICs by the population, and promote the

use of TICs among state and government bodies, as well as securing the "technological sovereignty" of TICs in the development of the computerization of the country (Díaz-Canel 2019, 764).

3. Mauricio Vicent of *El País* lost his accreditation because the CPI considered his coverage offered a "partial and negative" image of Cuba (*El País* 2011). The same reason was given for not renewing the visas of Gary Marx of the *Chicago Tribune* and César Gonzáles-Calero of the Mexican newspaper *El Universal* (Reporters Without Borders 2007). For the same reason, Fernando Ravsberg, formerly of the BBC, closed his blog *Cartas Desde Cuba* after reporting from the island for almost thirty years (Pentón 2018).

4. The fallout over the recent July 2019 case of the official Cuban media's total silence in the face of rolling blackouts that the government had previously publicly promised would not occur is a good example of this dilemma. In a pair of tweets sent out on July 18, Elaine Díaz, a former professor of digital journalism at the University of Havana and now director of the independent news site *Periodismo de Barrio*, called Cuba's state journalists to task for their journalistic failure with a direct reference to the role critical pedagogy played in their university educations. "During these days of silence about the blackouts, I have been asking myself how so many journalists could remain mute. How could they reconcile what they had learned in the academy with their news blackout?" (https://twitter.com/elainediaz2003/status/1152015188456955905) "How could they read and debate *In Cold Blood*, the Watergate case, the reportage of Tom Wolfe, *La noche de Tlatelolco*, [. . .] and still remain silent today. Remain silent everyday. Or report only part of reality?" (https://twitter.com/elainediaz2003/status/1152015195050348544).

5. For instance, the former state media journalist Reinaldo Escobar, who is now running the independent digital startup *14ymedio* with Yoani Sánchez, "went too far" when working at *Juventud Rebelde*. In 1988 he wrote an article about a principal who did not let pupils with long hair enter school buses, although it was not in the school rules. It created a scandal, and since he did not try to make good afterward, he was expelled from the Young Communist League (UJC) and lost his position as a reporter with the newspaper (Rodríguez 2013).

References

Alonso, Martín Oller, Dasniel Olivera Pérez, Carlos Arcila Calderón et al. 2017. "La cultura periodística pre-profesional en el triángulo de las Bermudas del periodismo latinoamericano: Cuba, Ecuador y Venezuela." In *Cultura(s) Periodística(s) Iberoamericana(s). La diversidad de un periodismo propio*, edited by Martín Oller Alonso, 223–274. La Laguna (Tenerife): Sociedad Latina de Comunicación Social.

Álvarez, Carlos Manuel. 2019. "Tres años sin paracaídas." *El Estornudo*, March 14, 2019.

Álvarez, María Eugenia. 2018. "Director de El Estornudo quiere que la revista crezca por su periodismo y no por la censura." *IJNET*, March 12, 2018.

Associated Press. 2018. "Flying high: Cuban YouTubers dream big despite poor internet access." March 14, 2018.

Breed, Warren. 1955. "Social Control in the Newsroom: A Functional Analysis." *Social Forces* 33(4): 326–335.

Bryman, Alan. 2016. *Social Research Methods* (5th ed.). Oxford: Oxford University Press.
Castro, Fidel. 1961. "Words to the Intellectuals." http://www.cuba.cu/gobierno/discursos/1961/esp/f300661e.html.
Díaz-Canel, Miguel. 2019. Decreto Ley No. 370, "Sobre la informatización de la sociedad en Cuba." July 4, 2019. https://www.gacetaoficial.gob.cu/pdf/GOC-2019-O45.pdf
Elizalde, Rosa Miriam. 2013. "El consenso de lo posible." Ph.D. Thesis, University of Havana, Havana.
El País. 2011. "El régimen cubano retira la acreditación al corresponsal de *El País* en La Habana." September 4, 2011.
Garcés, Raúl. 2013. "Siete tesis de la prensa cubana." *Cubadebate*, July 14, 2013.
Garcés, Raúl. 2016. *El desafío de la construcción de nuevos consensos. Controversias y concurrencias latinoamericanas.* Asociación Latinoamericana de Sociología.
García, Alejandra Elizalde. 2016. "¿Dónde están los jóvenes periodistas?" Diploma Thesis, University of Havana, Havana.
García Luis, Julio. 2013. *Revolución, Socialismo, Periodismo. La prensa y los periodistas cubanos ante el siglo XXI*. Havana: Pablo de la Torriente.
Garcia Santamaria, Sara. 2017. "The Historical Articulation of 'the People' in Revolutionary Cuba. Media Discourses of Unity in Times of National Debate (1990–2012)." Ph.D. thesis, University of Sheffield, Sheffield.
Granma. 2018. "Discurso de Díaz-Canel en la clausura del X Congreso de la UPEC." July 15, 2018.
Hanitzsch, Thomas. 2011. "Populist disseminators, detached watchdogs, critical change agents and opportunist facilitators: Professional milieus, the journalistic field and autonomy in 18 countries." *The International Communication Gazette* 73(6): 477–494.
Hanitzsch, Thomas, Folker Hanusch, Claudia Mellado, et al. 2011. "Mapping Journalism Cultures Across Nations." *Journalism Studies* 12(3): 273–293.
Henken, Ted A. 2021. "The Opium of the *Paquete*: State Censorship, Private Self-Censorship, and the Content Distribution Strategies of Cuba's Emergent, Independent Digital Media Startups." *Cuban Studies* 50.
Henken, Ted A. 2011. "A Bloggers Polemic: Debating Independent Cuban Blogger Projects in a Polarized Political Context." *Cuba in Transition* 21: 171–185.
Henken, Ted A. 2017. "Cuba's Digital Millennials: Independent Digital Media and Civil Society on the Island of the Disconnected." *Social Research* 84(2): 429–456.
Josephi, Beate. 2010. "Conclusions." In *Journalism Education in Countries with Limited Media Freedom 1*, edited by Beate Josephi: 253–259. New York: Peter Lang.
Lauk, Epp and Tiiu Kreegipuu. 2010. "Was it all pure propaganda? Journalistic practices of 'silent resistance' in Soviet Estonian journalism." *Acta Historica Tallinnensia* 15.
Marreiro, Flávia. 2014. "Continuity and Change in the Cuban media under Raúl Castro." University of Oxford: Reuters Institute Fellowship paper.
Mellado, Claudia, Mireya Márquez-Ramírez, Jacques Mick, Martín Oller Alonso, and Dasniel Olivera. 2017. "Journalistic performance in Latin America: A comparative study of professional roles in news content." *Journalism* 18(9): 1087–1106.
Mellor, Noah. 2009. "Strategies for Autonomy." *Journalism Studies* 10(3): 307–321.
Natvig, Anne. 2018. "Cuban Journalism Students: Between Ideals and State Ideology." *Journalism Education* 7(1).

Olivera, Dasniel and Leydi Torres. 2017. "Análisis del periodismo en Cuba: el predominio del rol profesional leal-facilitador de los periodistas en el contenido de las noticias de prensa." In *Cultura(s) Periodística(s) Iberoamericana(s). La diversidad de un periodismo propio,* edited by Martín Oller. La Laguna (Tenerife): Sociedad Latina de Comunicación Social.

OnCuba. 2019. "'Bajen los precios de Internet,' exigen los cubanos en Twitter." June 2, 2019.

PCC. 2018. "Política de Comunicación Social del Estado y el Gobierno cubanos." https://www.periodismodebarrio.org/2018/12/que-dice-la-nueva-politica-de-comunicacion-cubana/

Pentón, Mario J. 2018. "Ravsberg: 'Tengo que callarme porque soy extranjero, pero eso no va a pasar con los jóvenes cubanos.'" *El Nuevo Herald,* July 13, 2018.

Pentón, Mario J. 2019. "Cuban officials invite dialogue on Twitter—but only with citizens who don't criticize." *Miami Herald,* March 8, 2019.

Periodismo de Barrio. 2018. "¿Qué dice la nueva política de comunicación cubana?" December 2, 2018.

Reich, Zvi and Thomas Hanitzsch. 2013. "Determinants of journalists' professional autonomy: Individual and national level factors matter more than organizational ones." *Mass Communication and Society* 16(1): 133–156.

Reporters Without Borders. 2007. "Two Havana-based foreign correspondents ordered to leave." February 23, 2007.

Rodríguez, Andrea. 2018. "Cuba slightly loosens controls on state media." Associated Press, June 21, 2018.

Rodríguez, Yusimi. 2013. "Cuba: Interview with Reinaldo Escobar, An Independent Citizen." *Havana Times,* February 27, 2013.

Singer, Jane. B. 2007. "Contested Autonomy." *Journalism Studies* 8(1): 79–95.

Tong, Jingrong. 2009. "Press self-censorship in China: A case study in the transformation of discourse." *Discourse & Society* 20(5): 593–612.

UPEC. 2018. "Directorio de Blogs de periodistas cubanos." http://www.cubaperiodistas.cu/index.php/directorio/directorio-de-blogs-de-periodistas-cubanos/

Vicari, Stefania. 2015. "Exploring the Cuban blogosphere: Discourse networks and informal politics." *New Media & Society* 17(9): 1492–1512.

Voltmer, Katrin and Herman Wasserman. 2014. "Journalistic norms between universality and domestication: Journalists' interpretations of press freedom in six new democracies." *Global Media and Communication* 10(2): 177–192.

Waisbord, Silvio. 2013. *Reinventing Professionalism: Journalism and News in Global Perspective.* Hoboken, NJ: Wiley.

WJS. 2012. "Worlds of Journalism Study. Master questionnaire 2012–14." http://www.worldsofjournalism.org/research/2012-2016-study/methodological-framework/

10

Independent Media on the Margins

Two Cases of Journalistic Professionalization in Cuba's Digital Media Ecosystem

ABEL SOMOHANO FERNÁNDEZ
AND MIREYA MÁRQUEZ-RAMÍREZ

When *El Estornudo,* an independent digital magazine founded in Cuba in 2016, covered the wave of Cuban emigrants stranded in Central America, the outlet was exercising a particularly innovative conception of journalism on the island. The same can be said when *Periodismo de Barrio*, another independent digital outlet founded in 2015, covered the rampant water pollution produced by Ronera Santa Cruz—the country's largest rum distillery. By giving visibility to such topics—normally absent from the Cuban Communist Party (PCC)-controlled official press—this fresh brand of Cuban journalism performed a watchdog function and displayed a civic mission through a commitment to public service.

These outlets aim to fill the void left by the state-ruled official media by embracing the watchdog and civic models of journalism. Both distance themselves from the official media but also from the realm of political activism, and instead follow the professional frameworks, norms, and values of journalism that they consider appropriate to navigate the restrictions that they face. In this chapter, we argue that a process of journalistic professionalization is taking place at these two independent media outlets. Their journalists subscribe to norms that guide their work, possess specialized knowledge and skills, have developed autonomy by maintaining control over their work, and are unequivocally guided by the ideal of public service (Aldridge and Evetts 2003; Deuze 2005; Waisbord 2013).

The focal aspects of this chapter are the interplay between the changing Cuban social and political context and the normative roles to which journalists adhere. In the emergent digital ecosystem on the island, both *El Estornudo* and *Periodismo de Barrio* stand out for their relevance in the national landscape and their international prestige, as well as for their distinctive topical focus, alternative news agendas, and the professional profile and educational background of their staffs. Both organizations were founded and are run by young innovators, most of whom are university graduates in journalism. *Periodismo de Barrio* was launched to conduct investigative journalism, especially about environmental issues. For its part, *El Estornudo* emerged with a focus on narrative and literary journalism (creative nonfiction) aimed at capturing the deterritorialized and diasporic condition of contemporary Cuba. Likewise, through their work, they want to surpass the lack of coverage about Cuban social, economic, and political reality in the official press. They also defend the idea that journalistic logics are different from political activism and thus strive to separate both realms. Both outlets advocate for the professionalization of independent Cuban journalism.

In exploring these issues, this chapter contributes to the debate over journalistic professionalization of news outlets that both springs "from the inside-out" (Hughes 2003) and at the same time, exists on the margins of the dominant Cuban media system. We explore the professional and normative milieus of these journalists, in order to understand the emerging models of journalism to which these digital outlets adhere, the norms and missions that their members pursue, and the relevance of these views in the broader discussion of journalistic roles.[1]

We argue that these developments bear the signs of a vibrant journalistic profession in growth. In *Periodismo de Barrio* the perceptions about journalists' professional models reveal a culture discursively entrenched in both liberal but also traditional socialist norms, but only in its ideal variation. *El Estornudo*, for its part, is open in assuming a more adversarial and critical position toward established powers, but from the perspective of professional journalistic standards and a public service mission that strives to be critical, not from the perspective of political activism per se. The analysis of these two cases yields rich experiences that reveal similar perceptions of journalists about their roles in society and the professional models that guide their work, although with certain differences in their referential frameworks.

The first section of the chapter briefly reviews the larger theoretical discussion about journalistic professionalization and media transition. We then survey the way in which journalistic models have been historically conceived and materialized under socialism, highlighting the particular values associated with those models. Next, we describe the main characteristics of different strands of Cuban journalism. Finally, we focus on the particular journalistic models guiding *Periodismo de Barrio* and *El Estornudo*, and conclude with a reflection on the significance of the findings for debates on journalistic professionalization and innovation.

JOURNALISTIC PROFESSIONALISM AND MEDIA DEMOCRATIZATION: THEORETICAL DISCUSSION

Our discussion is inserted within debates about the professionalization of journalism in authoritarian political contexts. Given that neither *Periodismo de Barrio* nor *El Estornudo* are circumscribed by state control or driven by a corporate, for-profit bottom line, the professionalization processes they are undergoing are not (yet) being propelled by typical factors such as media privatization, political democratization, or economic liberalization. These factors tend to underpin the processes of media democratization and journalistic professionalization in many cases covered in the existing "transitology" literature (Sparks 2008; Voltmer 2013). In fact, scholars of media transitions in postcommunist societies have debated and relativized the impact and adoption of Western-inspired legal frameworks, policies, patterns of ownership, and journalistic roles on the actual practices and conditions of autonomy in these countries (De Smaele 1999; Lauk 2009). This literature analyzes whether visible "changes" exist in journalistic norms, roles, and practices in postcommunist societies or are still embedded in old-school "continuity" (Sparks 2008; Gross and Jakubowicz 2013; Voltmer 2013).

Most of this literature agrees that the processes leading to full media democratization have been "tortured" (Gross and Jakubowicz 2013). On the one hand, regardless of changes implemented at the structural, systemic levels, there are still patterns of continuity that prevail at the agency level, that is, in the cultural fabric that connects the collusive relation between media proprietors and politicians, or the hierarchical, sometimes sycophantic relation between journalists and sources. On the other hand, even when agents do manage to change their mindsets, certain systemic factors and the structural logics of property and ownership tend to hinder change (Örnebring 2012).

To account for these processes in detail, Hughes (2003) argues that a cue to understand them is to explore "the internalization of shared cognitive and normative frameworks across time and space" (2003, 90). Often, it is the unwritten, informal rules that guide organizational practices and missions, rather than formal norms. She argues that while some organizations can impede change and protect stability, others can build the conditions that enable innovation and change. "Changing environmental conditions, new role models, and contact with influential change agents promoting differing frameworks can stimulate the formation of new cultures and cognitive identities" (Powell 1991, 197–201, cited by Hughes 2003, 92).

Indeed, this is the case at both *Periodismo de Barrio* (*PdB*) and *El Estornudo* (*ElEs*), where change is inherent to the logic of the medium. Their young innovators reject the status quo and, as university graduates in journalism, have renounced their adherence to the official media and come together to launch their own independent media startups based on mutual support and shared values, roles, and social missions. According to Katrin Voltmer (2013, 26), functions and practices associated with the watchdog and civic roles of the press are crucial in democratic societies, hence the appearance and consolidation of these characteristics is taken in the literature as a good sign of either a transition to come or a transition already in progress with respect to journalistic professionalization.

However, the question remains as to what drives change of normative journalistic mindsets and patterns of professionalization in authoritarian and change-adverse settings. According to Hughes (2003, 99), either media owners can push change from above, or new cohorts of journalists can push from below, or ultimately, staff can desert publications that clash with their new values to launch their own. We also observe that some journalists avoid the pathway of "stability" altogether and start from scratch. The two digital Cuban media outlets profiled here are paradigmatic cases of independent professional journalism that followed this latest route. They are not state-run, not state-regulated, but also not clandestine in nature or dissident in orientation.

The recent emergence of both outlets has been made possible by the gradual "digital revolution" taking place on the island. With the affordances of new digital innovations in their respective geographical locations—some abroad—these Cuban journalists embracing new values have launched their own media startups and implemented their own missions and norms. Are these changes signaling, at some level, a gradual democratization of the media in the island? As Ruiz (2006) contends, the existence (or not) of a political transition process is closely related to a society's capacity to build independent communication. However, we lack the benefit of the hindsight gained by past transitions in what are now postcommunist countries, and Cuba has not yet experienced the seismic political or economic changes that took place elsewhere. We can only attest that a process of professionalization is taking place on the island based on its own context and logic, and with a potential to inspire a new generation of Cuban journalists.

While liberal values and outside norms are deeply ingrained in the fabric of professional norms and practices in both outlets, the only key difference is that *Periodismo de Barrio* also consciously draws its professional culture and norms from an "imagined should-be" vision of democratic socialism. As a result, we observe the development of context-driven, professional ideologies, and journalistic norms emerging on the island today based on the watchdog and civic functions long neglected by the official media. These two functions are not only cementing these outlets' journalistic missions, but also providing them with professional legitimacy (Waisbord 2013), societal respect, and prestige inside and outside the island. This prestige might sometimes safeguard them against certain types of aggressions.

We focus on journalistic roles because, as Donsbach (2012) claims, *role perception* has a strong influence on journalists' professional behavior, explaining differences between various news cultures. For this reason, here we explore two preestablished role dimensions: journalists' conceptions about the relationship between journalism and established powers—what their position toward power ought to be—and journalists' conceptions about the relationship between journalism and the audience—how they think about their public (Donsbach 2012; Hanitzsch et al. 2011). Based on these two approaches, our interviewees identify with a professional model close to the "liberal watchdog" function of journalism with respect to established powers, whereas they identify with a civic, public service model with respect to their audience. In the normative, liberal sense, a watchdog function of journalism aims to monitor and act as a check on established powers and public institutions in order to yield accountability, whereas a civic function provides citizens with the information they need to make political decisions, advocates for citizen causes, and makes visible their voices, needs, and rights (Kovach and Rosenstiel 2001).

Journalism Models in Socialism

Unlike the liberal model of the press, the socialist model has been scarcely researched and theorized as such. Instead, most literature has referred to the journalistic models existing in current or former socialist and Soviet countries (Voltmer 2013; Lauk 2009; Gross and Jakubowicz 2013). Research has highlighted the authoritarian traits, propagandist nature, and political instrumentalization of the press in socialist countries (Siebert, Peterson, and

Schramm 1963; Simons and Strovsky 2006). However, it is worth focusing on how the functions of the press have been conceived and devised generally under socialism in order to understand the normative discourse that is prevalent in Cuba.

Although the classic work by Siebert, Peterson, and Schramm (1963) refers to a "Soviet Communist" theory of the press, there is a need to make two fundamental precisions. First, their considerations about the role of the press in socialist societies fall short of "theory" as they suffer from considerable theoretical underdevelopment. Second, the figures referenced in the text—Marx, Lenin, and Stalin—although they are historically important, are also insufficient in accounting for the complex range of views about the role of media outside the liberal model of the press. While it is possible to find in Marx and Lenin a formulation of the media as an instrument for class struggle, it is Lenin who developed specific ideas about the role of the media in a socialist state (Romano 1987; Coca 1998; Siebert, Peterson, and Schramm 1963). For example, he conceived of the press as an instrument for the party and the state in the organization of the new socialist society. Before the October Revolution in Russia, he stressed the media's functions as organizers, propagandists, collective agitators, or forums to devise political tactics, among others. For his part, Stalin confirmed and implemented Lenin's mission of the media as state and party instruments, its propagandistic and agitative dimension, but saw their missions as strictly imposed and controlled by established powers.

More recent literature on dictatorships claims that autocrats use the mass media to sustain their opacity, fiction, isolation, massification, and monopoly (Ruiz 2006), making them instrumental to regime survival. For these purposes, a reporting style in these regimes and certain journalistic missions are important: journalists are viewed as public workers and publicists in Russia (De Smaele 1999) and their pieces tended to be analytical or didactic rather than informative or factual. In the case of China, a country still politically aligned with socialism, an extensive literature agrees that the Chinese Communist Party (CCP) has consistently used the media as an instrument to set the agenda, propagate official policies, monitor public opinion, and rally regime support (Tang and Iyengar 2011).

Despite all of this, there are also certain socialist ideals as democratizing processes within the Marxist tradition, from which not only the socialization of property—but also of power—can be fostered and achieved. Within these ideals of democratic socialism, the functions of the media can transcend their mere political instrumentalization and avoid the dictates of autocrats and political agents external to the press. In fact, this vein of the Marxist tradition sees the press as a potential trigger of active citizen participation in public affairs and as an engine of political transformation (Luxemburgo 2006; Gramsci 1997). However, within the actual logic of the political implementation of socialism, there are few actual journalistic referents that channel these democratic functions.

The lack of a serious discussion about the democratic potential of the media in a socialist framework is driven by three factors. First, the actual historical experience of authoritarianism in the self-branded "socialist" regimes undercuts claims of a press that truly represents the people. Second, there is little theoretical foundation or popular understanding of the multiple varieties and/or possibilities of different "socialisms." Finally, the expansion of the liberal model of the press as a core ideal underlying the structuration of media systems and journalistic practices across the world has made it difficult to imagine, much less theorize, alternative pathways of journalistic professionalization. Hence more studies are needed to explore how journalists have attempted to practice their profession with a modicum of autonomy within the rigid parameters of historically existing socialism (see Garcia Santamaria and Natvig, this volume, for two studies of this struggle within Cuban state media).

Journalism in Cuban Socialism: Between Ideals and Practices

For many years, the PCC, its principal political figures, and the Union of Cuban Journalists (UPEC) have historically emphasized—likely paying lip service to—the various functions that the press must follow: critically analyzing the sociopolitical environment, promoting the mobilization and organization of citizens, and generating platforms for citizen debate and dialogue. However, these functions of the official press—the only one with legal recognition domestically—stem from an essentially "reproductive" view of the reigning political system. That is, these roles have not translated into a daily critical practice as the press—no matter how self-critical it may aspire to be—has been conceived of as a tool to sustain and defend the existing political order.

Indeed, a comparative news content study of news stories from Mexico, Chile, Ecuador, Brazil, and Cuba (Mellado, Márquez-Ramírez, et al. 2017) yielded the following results with respect to the performance of the loyal-facilitator, watchdog, and civic roles in Cuba's official press. The Cuban press presents an overwhelming predominance of a "loyal-facilitator" role, an almost null presence of the watchdog role (along with Chile), and a middling position in the performance of the civic role, just above Brazil and Chile. These results suggest that while the press is generally complacent toward elites, there are certain spaces that do address citizens' voices and needs in the official press.

It has been statistically corroborated that lower levels of press freedom and democratic development significantly decrease the presence of criticism or questioning in the news (Márquez Ramírez et al. 2020). Thus, the type of political regime in Cuba does pose a continuing threat to the monitoring function of the press to a much greater extent than other organizational or individual factors. However, the civic role does have better chances to materialize in this socialist regime, as findings show that Cuban newspapers often exhibit more background information, local impact, and citizen perspectives in their news articles than newspapers in other countries (Mellado et al. 2017).

This helps to understand the context in which independent digital media face both opportunities and challenges. On the one hand, it is now possible to speak of a new stage in the exercise of journalism in Cuba that can be defined by several common traits: the type of stories being told, the storytelling styles and formats used, the young people behind such projects (nearly always journalists educated at Cuban universities), and the innovative hybrid online/offline digital channels of distribution and consumption of their stories (see Díaz in Fernández, Álvarez, Díaz, and Colunga 2017). At the same time, these digital outlets have faced myriad obstacles, including their unregulated, *alegal* character, the severe limitations to Internet access on the island, and the challenges to their economic stability and long-term sustainability. Even more worrisome, staff at these media are routinely subjected to pressures, attacks, and detentions, in addition to online harassment.

Even journalists who work for official media who dare collaborate with these independent digital outlets can expect reprisals (Díaz 2018; CPJ 2016). This situation of continuing risk and vulnerability places these media outlets "on the margins" of Cuba's official media system. Building international prestige and professional legitimacy has helped to safeguard some of them from the most extreme attacks. This recognition can be linked, in part, to the active journalistic models—watchdog and civic—that underlie their coverage. The following section analyzes the way in which journalists at *PdB* and *ElEs* endorse specific models of journalism within the specific context of the Cuban media system.

Conceptions of Journalistic Models in *Periodismo de Barrio* and *El Estornudo*

Periodismo de Barrio: Civic and Vigilance Values within the Socialist Frame

In 2015, *Periodismo de Barrio* published a code of ethics that expresses its advocacy of plurality in the public sphere, commitment to human emancipation, and the democratization of communication. The code also expresses an intention to practice a form of journalism that channels the processes of human liberation: "any social emancipating project that is based on people's ability to think freely demands responsible, rigorous, and honest journalism" (*Periodismo de Barrio* 2015, our translation). This manifesto highlights the freedoms of expression, the press, and information as necessary conditions for social participation and to maintain national sovereignty, democracy, solidarity, human dignity, and the environment. There are also clear references to the Cuban Constitution's language on freedom of expression and the press within the purposes of a socialist society. In this respect, an important aspect of this code is related to a defense of democratic socialism, protected by the principles of socialization of the different spheres of social life. Moreover, there is a rupture with the liberal ideal of objectivity, a defense of the independence of journalistic practice, the respect for Cuban sovereignty and national identity, and a commitment to transparency about the outlet's funding sources. They endorse self-regulation and take full individual responsibility for their work.

The very publication of a code of ethics and declaration of principles links *PdB* to a civic model of journalism that inscribes itself in a very peculiar frame. This entails what might be called a "double fracture." On the one hand, this approach breaks with the authoritarian nature of the historical experiences of socialism, specifically with the authoritarian traits deployed in the Cuban political system's relationship with the media. On the other hand, there is a rupture, at least discursively, with other political alternatives *outside* socialism. All statements are mutually inclusive and inserted within the broader principles of socialism, rather than devised in opposition to it. This journalistic stance implies that there is *a good and ideal* milieu of socialism to which the medium aspires, and which can ideally be achieved through different journalistic principles and practices, different from Cuba's existing official media. For its part, the liberal models of journalism translated into the watchdog and civic roles are entrenched in their professional mindsets.

PdB's staff has assimilated and naturalized the view of socialism as a normative framework. For example, a journalist we interviewed claimed to identify with the socialist model because "a predating" capitalism has proven to be no solution for the world's problems. He stresses that the socialism with which *PdB* aligns "is not the one currently existing in Cuba. It is with another model that perhaps has not yet been put into practice, but that we want to think possible or at least try" (R1, our translation).[2] In his view, this socialism must be oriented "towards the emancipation of the people, not the preservation of power" (R1).[3] While another respondent acknowledged that the medium's code of ethics supporting socialism garnered a great deal of debate, she supports the view that "a journalism like the one that *PdB* conducts, within the socialism as proposed by *PdB*, is very harmonic" (R2).[4]

The type of journalistic mission attributed to this imagined brand of socialism becomes clearer in other interviews with *PdB* staff members. Some respondents recognize that their approach to the profession clashes directly with what they deem as "erroneous" ideas about journalism in Cuba. "What mainly restricts the practice of journalism generally in Cuba, be at the state or non-state media, is the vision of the government and of those getting to decide what is journalism," said R3.[5] She sees a deformation in society's conceptions about the role of journalism, a deformation found both among the people and in official circles. Respondents also pointed out that deformed ideas about journalism's role in society impact the performance of the official press. In that sense, the defense of certain journalistic models on the part of interviewees is framed in reaction to a negative vision about the official media in Cuba. From their point of view, the professional models endorsed by their outlet—despite their being defined as "socialist"—have found no resonance or reception among the official press.

PdB's staff identifies with the watchdog role of the press, viewed as a critical position with respect to the locus of power in society (R3)[6] and to the exercise of journalistic scrutiny (R1).[7] Staffers also associated this watchdog approach with a balanced examination of both the problems and achievements of the country. One staff member argued that the vigilant model should be centered around examining and "narrating" Cuba "with all of its nuances: the lights and the shadows" (R4).[8] For another interviewee, this scrutinizing intention is associated with a commitment to the community. This has to do with the nature and priorities of *PdB* as a journalistic organization, as in the following example:

> We attend the meetings and assemblies, the discussions of municipal assemblies. Why do we go? Because we want to know what it is that the

local government is proposing, and we want to evaluate that the decisions approved at the municipal assemblies are actually carried out or at least in the municipalities that we are interested in, those we have been working with. (R5)[9]

This vigilant, watchdog model is also linked to the proactive, advocacy character of their news pieces. Their idea of advocacy involves transcending mere denunciations and advancing toward concrete actions and proposals. From her perspective, this task consists of proposing pathways and "valid tools" for problem-solving (R5).[10] Envisioning a journalism of solutions is therefore part of journalists' perceived mission at *PdB*.

They also endorse the watchdog function of holding the powerful to account on behalf of citizens (R2).[11] This practice is directly connected to the civic model in the journalistic culture of these professionals, which is understood as doing journalism in the service of society (as opposed to serving a particular party, ideology, boss, owner, or shareholder). Interviewees noted that a central criterion that determined the stories and topics they covered was their relevance for society (R3).[12] Also as part of this model, *PdB* prioritizes stories about neighborhoods, local communities, and community members. They claim to respect the individual "voices" of their interviewees and the value of the particular views they share about their communities (R5).[13] "In the few pieces that we managed to do in the [hurricane-ridden municipality of] Baracoa,"[14] recounted one respondent, "the biggest weight of the story relied on the people telling us their experiences" (R4).[15]

In the view of the staff, *PdB*'s goal is focusing on facts and on people because the "true protagonists" of the stories should be the ones getting to speak. This does not imply an endorsement of an aseptic position on the part of the journalist, but an opportunity for the protagonists of their stories to speak for themselves. At the same time, *PdB* is committed to telling stories that contain verifiable information, but without necessarily endorsing the objectivity value as such. Our five respondents at *PdB* are convinced that the news production process, in itself, opens the door for professional subjectivity. Giving voice to the leading characters of the stories and presenting verifiable data in their work provide the type of journalism they conduct with rigor and responsibility (see Henken, this volume, for a similar discussion as related to *14ymedio*).

Their normative expectations to conduct civic and watchdog roles coexist—in a creative tension—with limitations to performing them in actual practice. The obstacles of limited access to official spaces and information together with the almost total absence of transparency on the part of governmental agencies and officials are among the most chronic challenges in their effort to verify the information they publish. Still, *PdB*'s reporters try to do their best in transcending mere speculation and refraining from publishing uncorroborated or unverified information (R4).[16] Another limitation respondents face is a lack of training in carrying out in-depth, investigative journalism and the mastery of investigative tools and methods. Aware of this restriction, they openly admit being in a constant learning process (R3).[17]

The emphasis that *PdB* places on the values and practices of the watchdog model—such as scrutiny, balance, and commitment to local communities, among others—as well as the values and principles related to the civic model—such as journalism as a public service or giving voice to ordinary citizens—translate into an effort to professionalize journalistic practice in Cuba, operating independently from the official media system but doing so, discursively, within a socialist frame. The meanings associated with these values and the multiple hardships faced in the founding and development of *PdB* reveal an enduring, unresolved tension between an ideal brand of socialism that these journalists advocate and the reality of the authoritarian socialism historically practiced in Cuba.

El Estornudo: The Activation of Antagonistic Values

The tagline at *El Estornudo*, an outlet launched in 2016, describes the site straightforwardly—if a bit facetiously—as: [an] "independent magazine of narrative journalism, made from inside Cuba, outside Cuba, and while we're at it, about Cuba." The site contains sections offering chronicles, columns, profiles, interviews, opinion pieces, and photo galleries. Its "Brief Letter of Introduction" begins as follows: "The journalist is an athlete and journalism a long-distance race. Convinced that the office and the commandments result in arthritis, we decided to place ourselves at the starting line and independently establish an online magazine of chronicles about Cuba" (*El Estornudo* 2016).[18] In this statement, the transnational character of the journalists associated with the site stands out. Moreover, these journalists have conferred upon themselves—without visiting any "offices" or following anyone else's "commandments"—the right and responsibility of chronicling Cuba. The text also presents an intention to narrate Cuba from the position of its deterritorialized character together with overt criticism of the official press. At the same time, it declares a commitment to a narrative journalism that is both questioning and vigilant of Cuban power brokers as well as honest, balanced, and fair. This "who are we?" document also emphasizes the project's economic and political independence.

Interviews conducted with staff members at *El Estornudo* show evidence of a particular conception of the watchdog and civic models of journalism hinted at in the "Brief Letter" quoted above. One interviewee conceives of vigilance not only as the scrutiny of established powers, but as a process of visibilization of the affairs hidden behind official discourse. In their view, the watchdog model of the press connects with a critical function conceived not from the perspective of oppositional political activism per se but from the demands of the profession itself. Associated with this idea are the practical requirements of the profession, such as contextualization, provision of analysis, or nuanced examination of reality in their reporting; hence, *ElEs* staff advocates for the professionalization of journalism.

This does not mean, however, that they distance themselves from political demands. Indeed, professionals at *ElEs* defend the possibility of claiming a political agenda but from the perspective of the inherent "dramatic logic" of journalistic storytelling (R6); that is, from a position that "respects the standards, formats, and narratives of in-depth, questioning journalism."[19] Likewise, our respondents from *ElEs* understand the watchdog model as a panoramic and nuanced analysis of Cuban reality that addresses the multiple dimensions of existing social problems (R7)[20] and confronts established powers with a critical attitude (R8).[21]

When asked to illustrate content that employed the functions associated with the watchdog role, they mentioned examples such as election coverage, their (non-advocate) treatment of former president Raúl Castro and current president Miguel Díaz-Canel in their reporting, as well as commentary by columnist and UK-based Cuban academic Juan Orlando Pérez (R9).[22] Moreover, their conceptions about the civic model of journalism relate not only to reporting on social demands, but in setting the agenda so these demands gain visibility in the public debate. They observe a disconnection between different segments of society and social groups and aim to assume the responsibilities that state agencies or institutions—even or especially Cuba's official media institutions—have systematically failed to conduct.

One respondent put it this way:

When we have published [. . .] stories about the life conditions in unhealthy, illegal neighborhoods [. . .], the neighborhoods that proliferate on the peripheries of large cities [. . .], we see a strong demand within those communities for a legal recognition of their status, but there is not a connection with the rest (of the population). Those who don't live there have no interest in the matter, they haven't even heard about it, they don't care either, so the press [has the responsibility of] putting this matter on the table. (R6)[23]

The civic model also relates to the possibility to debate the effects that certain processes and political decisions have for Cuban society (R10).[24] One interviewee (R9)[25] gave two examples. One, the special coverage of Cuban migration to various European countries following the end of the policy that used to grant legal status to Cubans by default once they set (a dry) foot on U.S. soil. The second case involved the coverage of a self-described "artivista" (activist/artist) who organized an alternative art festival in defiance of state cultural policies and organizations. The visibilization of these cases contrasted with the deafening silence in the official media.

As with *PdB*, the support of the normative expectations of these roles and models that inspire *ElEs* go hand in hand with a realization of the severe limitations of always practicing them. Interviewees acknowledge their insufficient training to activate these models in their daily journalistic practice due to the absence of watchdog traditions in Cuba's journalistic culture (R6).[26] At the same time, they identify severe restrictions on access to information: the monitoring function of journalists becomes all but impossible when access to official and other key sources is denied (R7).[27] Crucially, it is possible to identify in *ElEs* an intention to conduct an interrogatory, vigilant journalism that is not necessarily grounded in the principle of objectivity, but in fairness and honesty.

Finally, unlike *PdB*, *ElEs* has not explicitly asserted their inclusion within the democratic socialist ideal or leftist ideological tradition. Nevertheless, their adversarial stance toward the established system and their commitment to citizens are central in the professional role conceptions of the outlet. Despite not officially declaring any particular adscription to a model, there is a recurring support for values and norms associated with the liberal model of journalism, but adapted and resignified within the specific conditions of Cuban reality. Both outlets defend the practice of journalism under the logic and norms of the profession, and identify neither with the propagandist function of the official press nor with any practice of journalism that is driven by the logic of political activism per se.

Discussion: The Emerging Agents of Change in the Profession

The birth and development of *El Estornudo* and *Periodismo de Barrio* illustrate the growing diversification of Cuba's media landscape, one that manifests itself in the components of their professional and organizational cultures, such as roles and values, missions, and practices. Triggered by a context of authoritarian rule, governmental opacity, lack of transparency, limited press freedom, and economic hardships, journalists at these outlets are devoting their work to the potential transformation of their immediate reality by challenging these conditions and becoming potential agents of change. Many of these factors could have prompted the configuration of alternative mindsets for journalists at both outlets, whose portfolio of collaborators attests not only to a great diversity of professional and educational profiles—including graduates from Cuba's most prestigious universities—but also to a variety of geographic locations.

These two media organizations share common traits in their trajectories, a similar vision about journalism as a profession, and the aspirational models that guide their practice: context-driven approaches toward the civic and watchdog roles. Within the ad hoc framework of a Cuban brand of civic journalism, both outlets share an ambition to transcend the mere disclosure of unreported affairs or the showcasing of voiceless characters, although these matters are among their top priorities. The professional identities and expectations at *Periodismo de Barrio* and *El Estornudo* appear to be motivated by a commitment to public service, a vocation for in-depth reporting and quality journalism, and by an aspiration to conduct their practice at the highest possible standards of verification, fairness, and balance.

In *PdB*, alternative socialist ideals and their democratic potential for transformative action appear to stimulate the outlet's mission, expectations, practices, and informative agendas, at least discursively. Of course, to avoid repression and gain a certain degree of safety and legitimacy in the eyes of the government, it could be convenient for the outlet to give lip service to an idealized version of the socialist discourse. One cannot blame the outlet for seeking shelter in socialist ideals considering that their working context is plagued with institutional fragility and legal jeopardy. However, the news agendas and staff motivations as found in our interviews with staff attest to the genuineness of their democratic socialist convictions.

Likewise, the vigilant function epitomized by the watchdog model of journalism (a core mission of the liberal model of journalism) also finds widespread support and endorsement at both outlets. In established democracies, the mission of watchdog journalism is that of making power accountable to the public (Voltmer 2013). However, our findings suggest that this view falls somewhat short of what journalists at both *Periodismo de Barrio and El Estornudo* intend. Such an ideal of public accountability might not only be implausible or premature in a context of authoritarian, opaque, and hierarchical rule, but also the denunciation of wrongdoing *per se* appears insufficient to solve Cuba's most pressing social problems and concerns. Instead, they envision a watchdog brand of journalism that transcends the mere unveiling of wrongdoing and provides in-depth analysis and prospective focus, bringing possible solutions to the table. In doing so, they strive to affirmatively build the communities they want and, in the process, the very fiber of citizenship.

Similarly, journalists at both outlets see it as their duty to fill that void by ensuring that the propagandist function of official media does not infect their work. The alternative nature of these two digital outlets is that, just as with digital media startups in established democracies (Wagemans, Witschge, and Deuze 2016; Carlson and Usher 2015), small, independent media not only tend to depart from established, mainstream media but explicitly situate themselves in opposition to the media status quo. They wouldn't be alternative otherwise. However, in Cuba, such an orientation toward "independence" is not only connected to new technological affordances and a tech-savvy generation of young entrepreneurs. It also involves a rupture with established politics of polarization, as these outlets claim to distance themselves from both the regime and the political opposition. In their view, both have negatively affected the professionalization of journalism.

Instead, *PdeB* and *ElEs* defend their work under the logic of professional practice. This does not mean their work is "apolitical" or abstains from advocating for political change at some level. Their work certainly carries political consequences and channels many political causes as voiced by citizens, but such "political" actions are grounded in—and emanate from—the normative functions and logics of professional, independent journalism (such as scrutiny, accountability, and citizen empowerment), not from a priori political causes or partisan agendas. Whether both outlets are considered part of the "opposition" by official or external actors, or by actors who aim to use their work to advance certain political causes, is another matter. Instead, these journalists prefer to build a professional journalism brand based on credibility and trustworthiness, fairness, balance, and factual evidence on the grounds of quality.

In that sense, we find that both outlets rely on a "meta-journalistic" discourse of self-presentation toward their publics (Carlson and Usher 2015) from which their projections and discourses of professional legitimacy are established. They appeal to traditionally liberal conceptions of journalism, such as the watchdog and civic functions—greatly undermined in the Cuban context—while also advocating for specific standards and narrative storytelling not widely practiced on the island. In that sense, we are witnessing a "situated form of innovation" at these outlets, also manifested in their sui generis processes of media management and news production. We can also note an interplay with traditionally normative functions widely shared by journalists around the world. Both outlets have undoubtedly become key innovators in their trade.

CONCLUSION

As Hughes (2003, 112) asserts, holding alternative ideas about journalism and power within the dominant existing institutional setting is key for the creation of successful change agents. Undoubtedly, both *PdB* and *ElEs* are agents of professional change in that respect. Their guiding norms and practices challenge the official media status quo. They defend their autonomy and maintain control over their work. Considering that these organizational milieus have not yet expanded far enough to trigger the democratization of the Cuban media at large, it remains to be seen the extent to which these professional models of civic and watchdog journalism can spread to other newsrooms and become naturalized not only as normative roles but also as reporting practices.

For now, the watchdog and civic models of journalism are the conduits that channel these transformative intentions, at least at the normative level: future research needs to evaluate the extent to which they have actually materialized in practice. Certainly, Cuban political and economic realities, as well as the island's recurring social problems, triggered this transformative agenda at these outlets, but one cannot deny that the influence of liberal conceptions of journalism has likely reached Cuban ears through many channels, such as journalism education, training and professional development, manuals and handbooks, peer socialization, other digital outlets across Latin America, and growing technological development such as social media use and Internet access in the island.

Moreover, many other alternative digital startups have sprouted on the island. However, alternative media holding oppositional values in Cuba is not a new phenomenon (as richly illustrated in the contribution to this volume by Lima Sarmeinto). Indeed, during periods of upheaval, challengers of the status quo have always relied on the latest technological developments of their day to better convey their ideals. As digital outlets require fewer material, technological, economic, and human resources to operate, and as young professionals take full advantage of digital affordances to build credible media brands, we conclude that there is a case to make for the positive impact of digital technologies in facilitating substantial media change at the organizational and individual levels of news production. In that sense, the digital revolution is indeed fostering the professionalization of journalism in Cuba.

By pursuing new visions of journalism, these digital outlets are undergoing professionalization processes that we hope can inspire in other newsrooms. As never before, a Goliath-sized press traditionally characterized by its publicist-propagandist role is facing competition from young independent news professionals. Through innovative digital narratives and storytelling, but above all, armed with the professional tenets of journalism, *Periodismo de Barrio* and *El Estornudo* refuse to play along with the traditional loyal-facilitator role of the Cuban press. They have taken matters into their own hands, with clearer principles and more horizontal working relations that aim to expand the civic values of Cuban society. The invaluable merit is that in doing so, they have not only built a profession with ethical principles and values, a body of knowledge and skills unique to these journalists, but also become directly accountable and responsive to their audience. Both are a small sample—significant nevertheless—of the vibrant and complex emergent ecology of independent digital media in Cuba.

Acknowledgments

The authors wish to thank both Mexico's National Council of Science and Technology (Conacyt) and the Postgraduate Research Assistance Program at Universidad Iberoamericana, Mexico City, for providing funding for this research. We are also grateful to all of the Cuban journalists who agreed to be interviewed for this study, and to the editors and reviewers for their insightful feedback.

Notes

1. This study is based on qualitative, phenomenological research. We conducted ten in-depth interviews with actors who played a significant role in launching and developing both indie media startups. Interviews were conducted from December 2017 to March 2018 and from mid-February to September 2019. We drew our research participants from the editorial boards and stable of reporters and collaborators working for both outlets and asked about their missions and roles, as well as their narrative practices.

2. Journalist 1, *Periodismo de Barrio*, personal interview, February 27, 2019.
3. Ibid.
4. Journalist 2, *Periodismo de Barrio*, personal interview, March 24, 2019.
5. Journalist 3, *Periodismo de Barrio*, personal interview, January 7, 2018.
6. Ibid.
7. Journalist 1, *Periodismo de Barrio*, personal interview, February 27, 2019.
8. Journalist 4, *Periodismo de Barrio*, personal interview, December 22, 2017.
9. Journalist 5, *Periodismo de Barrio*, personal interview, December 8, 2017.
10. Ibid.
11. Journalist 2, *Periodismo de Barrio*, personal interview, March 24, 2019.

12. Journalist 3, *Periodismo de Barrio*, personal interview, January 7, 2018.
13. Journalist 5, *Periodismo de Barrio*, personal interview, December 8, 2017.
14. On October 11, 2016, a number of reporters from *Periodismo de Barrio* were detained while trying to cover the aftermath of hurricane Matthew in the eastern part of the country. They were freed a day later without charges, but the events prompted an editorial a few days later: *Periodismo de Barrio*, October 16, 2016, https://www.periodismodebarrio.org/2016/10/quienes-tienen-derecho-a-contar-un-pais/.
15. Journalist 4, *Periodismo de Barrio*, personal interview, December 22, 2017.
16. Ibid.
17. Journalist 1, *Periodismo de Barrio*, personal interview, January 7, 2018.
18. Note that the phrase, "a long-distance race" ("una carrera de fondo") has a (perhaps intended) double meaning: "Long-distance race" and "serious or major career."
19. Journalist 6, *El Estornudo*, personal interview, March 27, 2018.
20. Journalist 7, *El Estornudo*, personal interview, January 5, 2018.
21. Journalist 8, *El Estornudo*, personal interview, February 18, 2019.
22. Journalist 9, *El Estornudo*, personal interview, February 8, 2018.
23. Journalist 6, *El Estornudo*, personal interview, March 27, 2018.
24. Journalist 10, *El Estornudo*, personal interview, April 15, 2019.
25. Journalist 9, *El Estornudo*, personal interview, February 8, 2018.
26. Journalist 6, *El Estornudo*, personal interview, March 27, 2018.
27. Journalist 7, *El Estornudo*, personal interview, January 5, 2018.

References

Aldridge, Meryl, and Julia Evetts. 2003. "Rethinking the Concept of Professionalism: The Case of Journalism." *The British Journal of Sociology* 54 (4): 547–564.
Carlson, Matt and Nikki Usher. 2015. "News Startups as Agents of Innovation." *Digital Journalism* 4 (5): 563–581.
Coca, César. 1998. *Lenin y la prensa*. Bilbao: Universidad del País Vasco.
CPJ (Committee to Protect Journalists). 2016. "Conectar a Cuba: Más espacio para la crítica, pero restricciones frenan avance de libertad de prensa." September 28, 2016.
De Smaele, Hedwig. 1999. "The Applicability of Western Media Models on the Russian Media System." *European Journal of Communication* 14 (2): 173–189.
Deuze, Mark. 2005. "What is Journalism? Professional Identity and Ideology of Journalists Reconsidered." *Journalism* 6 (4): 442–464.
Díaz, Elaine. 2018. "Medios emergentes en Cuba. Desafíos, amenazas y oportunidades." SembraMedia, January 11, 2018.
Donsbach, Wolfgang. 2012. "Journalists' Role Perception." In W. Donsbach, ed., *The International Encyclopedia of Communication*: 106. London: Blackwell.
El Estornudo. 2016. "Breve carta de presentación." March 14, 2016.
Fernández, Patricio, Carlos Manuel Álvarez, Elaine Díaz, and María Antonieta Colunga. 2017. "Existe nuevo periodismo en Cuba." Facultad de Comunicación y Letras, Universidad Diego Portales, Santiago, Chile, August 10, 2017. https://www.youtube.com/watch?v=737YNIUW1io&feature=share.
Gramsci, Antonio. 1997. *Gramsci y la filosofía de la praxis*. Havana: Ciencias Sociales.

Gross, Peter and Karol Jakubowicz, eds. 2013. *Media Transformations in the Post-Communist World: Eastern Europe's Tortured Path to Change*. New York: Lexington.
Hanitzsch, Thomas, Folker Hanusch, Claudia Mellado, et al. 2011. "Mapping Journalism Cultures Across Nations: A Comparative Study of 18 Countries." *Journalism Studies* 12 (3): 273–293.
Hughes, Sallie. 2003. "From the Inside Out: How Institutional Entrepreneurs Transformed Mexican Journalism." *International Journal of Press/Politics* 8 (3): 87–117.
Kovach, Bill and Tom Rosenstiel. 2001. *The Elements of Journalism*. New York: Crown Publishers.
Lauk, Epp. 2009. "Reflections on Changing Patterns of Journalism in the New EU Countries." *Journalism Studies* 10 (1): 69–84.
Li, Ke and Colin Sparks. 2018. "Chinese Newspapers and Investigative Reporting in the New Media Age." *Journalism Studies* 19 (3): 415–431.
Luxemburgo, Rosa. 2006. *Obras Escogidas*. Ediciones Digitales Izquierda Revolucionaria.
Márquez-Ramírez, Mireya, Claudia Mellado, María Luisa Humanes, et al. 2020. "Detached or Interventionist? Comparing the Performance of Watchdog Journalism in Transitional, Advanced, and Non-Democratic Countries." *International Journal of Press Politics* 25 (1): 53–75
Mellado, Claudia, Mireya Márquez-Ramírez, Jacques Mick, Martín Oller, and Dasniel Olivera. 2017. "Journalistic performance in Latin America: A Comparative Study of Professional Roles in News Content." *Journalism* 18 (9): 1087–116.
Örnebring, Henrik. 2012. "Clientelism, Elites, and the Media in Central and Eastern Europe." *International Journal of Press Politics* 17(4): 497–515.
Periodismo de Barrio. 2015. "Código de ética."
Powell, Walter W. 1991. "Expanding the Scope of Institutional Analysis." In *The New Institutionalism in Organizational Analysis*, edited by Walter W. Powell and Paul J. DiMaggio. Chicago: University of Chicago Press.
Romano, Vicente. 1987. "Introducción." In Carlos Marx and Federico Engels, *Sobre prensa, periodismo y comunicación*, 9–38. Madrid: Taurus ediciones.
Ruiz, Fernando. 2006. "Medios de comunicación alternativa y dictaduras en transición." In Rafael Rojas, ed., *Cuba hoy y mañana. Actores e instituciones de una política en transición*, 207–224. Mexico City: Planeta/CIDE.
Siebert, Fred S., Theodore Peterson, and Wilbur Schramm. 1963. *Four Theories of The Press*. Urbana and Chicago: University of Illinois Press.
Simons, Greg and Dmitry Strovsky. 2006. "Censorship in Contemporary Russia Journalism in the Age of the War Against Terrorism: A Historical Perspective." *European Journal of Communication* 21 (2): 189–211.
Sparks, Colin. 2008. "Media Systems in Transition: Poland, Russia, China." *Chinese Journal of Communication* 1 (1): 7–24.
Tang, Wenfang and Shanto Iyengar. 2011. "The Emerging Media System in China: Implications for Regime Change." *Political Communication* 28 (3): 263–267.
Voltmer, Katrin. 2013. *The Media in Transitional Democracies*. Cambridge: Polity Press.
Wagemans, Andrea, Tamara Witschge and Mark Deuze. 2016. "Ideology as Resource in Entrepreneurial Journalism." *Journalism Practice* 10 (2): 160–177.
Waisbord, Silvio. 2013. *Reinventing Professionalism: Journalism and News in Global Perspective*. Cambridge: Polity Press.

IV
BUSINESS AND ECONOMY

11

Online Marketing of Touristic Cuba

Branding a "Tech-Free" Destination

REBECCA OGDEN

Beginning amid local conditions of severe austerity, as Cuban tourism has increased steadily since the early 1990s, the island's status as an anomaly in tourism's general trend toward homogenizing "McDonaldization" (Ritzer 1998) has been reconfigured as one of its main attractions. Given Cubans' widely held desire to get online—especially pronounced among the island's frustrated millennials—it is perhaps ironic that Cuba continues to be voted among the best "tech-free destinations" by journalists and tourists on travel websites such as Lonely Planet. Indeed, the travel magazine *Wanderlust* includes Cuba in a top ten list of "digital detox" destinations, selected on the basis of the "always on" tourist's quest to embrace "powering down and tuning in to the world right before your eyes" (Higgins 2017). Far from being a nuisance for visitors, Cuba's absence of Internet and social media "can be a very liberating experience," according to tourist advice posts (Oag 2018). Travel to Cuba has often meant liberation from the "agitation" and "assault" of marketing and online hyperconnectivity (Cohen 2008). For those who normally enjoy low cost and unrestricted access to the World Wide Web, the digital is frequently framed as a burden to "escape" from in favor of more "authentic" experiences while on vacation.

Nevertheless, the Internet has also been crucial to oxygenating Cuba's current global trendiness and the various markets that have sprung up to take advantage of it. As this chapter will explore, tourism branding by both state and foreign tour operators relies heavily on digital media. In particular, short videos posted online with the intention of going "viral" (being widely shared, often through social media platforms) are a key mechanism in what we might refer to as the digital dimension of the "tourist gaze" (Urry and Larsen 2011), which can be defined as the highly visual way of categorizing, essentializing, and knowing places through tourism. In the Cuban context, the dissemination of short videos set to music has been crucial to the successful tourism campaign, "Auténtica Cuba," launched by Cuba's Ministerio de Turismo (MINTUR) in 2010 and still in use today. During this same period, the volume of images of Cuba circulated online by tourists, journalists, and other observers, has symbolized an intensely visual focus trained on the island, and on Havana in particular (Dopico 2002; Quiroga 2005; Kent 2019).

This chapter considers the key role played by video content produced and circulated by MINTUR and by two foreign tour operators, combining interviews with their creators with content analysis of the videos themselves. The chapter argues that these videos highlight authenticity, disconnectivity, human-to-human contact, and a return to sensual pleasures as Cuba's principal comparative advantage, implicitly linking this status with the uneven and deferred development of digital technologies on the island. Despite the tendency toward this image and narrative, the chapter proposes that MINTUR has adopted an increasingly strategic approach to disseminating the Cuban "nation brand" through digital platforms from the mid-2000s to the present, and that viral videos, social media, and Web content are central to manipulating positive images of the nation in the context of tourism marketing.

Tourism and the (Digital) Nation Brand

Tourism has been perhaps the dominant lens through which attention on Cuba has been directed in recent years, a lightning rod for much of the (often lamenting) discourse of Cuba's sudden aperture to global flows since the 1990s. While the sociocultural, economic, and ideological challenges associated with the accelerated expansion of the industry during the Special Period, including the devaluation of state jobs, the emergence of *jineterismo* (the broadly conceptualized "hustling" of tourists, often synonymized with informal and sexualized encounters), and the demarcation of tourist-only spaces (or so-called tourist apartheid) have received significant scholarly attention, the symbolic currency of the island's image as it is articulated through tourism has not attracted the same interrogation. Nevertheless, it is clear that tourism plays a significant role in articulating the established understanding of places and shaping expectations of visitors (Silver 1993); that is, tourism's enunciative or "world-making" authority (Hollinshead 1999; Hollinshead 2007).

The 1990s in particular saw an increase in the number of social scientists examining the function of tourism to "make, remake, and/or de-make specific peoples, places, or pasts" (Hollinshead 2004, 25), to authoritatively articulate who a population is and what ought to be celebrated (or hidden) about particular peoples or places (Hollinshead 2004, 31; Horne 1992). This, in turn, may determine how "emergent populations" legitimize and define themselves, to use Keith Hollinshead's phrasing (2004, 36). Thus, tourism's worldmaking enactments, write Hollinshead, Ateljevic, and Ali (2009, 428), have "a constitutive role over what we know about populations and destinations . . . [that] can become contextually sovereign in its normalizing and naturalizing effect." Hollinshead (1999) is especially convincing in describing the ways in which actors and institutions at many levels use tourism (often unsuspectingly) to mediate and normalize myths, stereotypes, narratives, and interpretations through their inclusion in tourism texts and tourism promotional materials, and in the suppression or the denial of other traditions/storylines. Through these discursive and lived processes, the tourist experience of place is socially constructed, projected, and neatly contained, normalizing essentialized ways of life in the host country and signposting that which is important or valuable (Kirshenblatt-Gimblett 1998).

According to John Urry's much-cited conceptualization, the enunciative authority of tourism lies in its highly visual modes (Urry 1990): the tourist gaze. Urry uses this term to refer to the way places are consumed through tourism by the experience of gazing upon or viewing a set of different scenes, landscapes, or townscapes and the industries that help to construct and develop that gaze by drawing our attention to particular objects of apparent value (1990, 1). In a general sense, then, the tourist gaze refers to the largely unconscious force by which peoples, places, and pasts are labeled, classified, and performatively represented in and through tourism (Urry 1990). For Urry, the visual also refers to the mind's eye, in the sense that "tourism paradigmatically involves the collection of signs . . . when a small village is seen, what is captured through the gaze is a sight of the 'real olde England'" (1992, 172). In this sense, the notion of a place is built up long before travel takes place, then, as an anticipation or fantasy that is reinforced through multiple non-tourist cultural forms, such as film, TV, music, literature, journalism, and videos (Urry 1990, 3). This daydreaming process does not appear autonomously but instead involves a constant "working over [of] advertising and other media-generated sets of signs" (Urry 1990, 13).

The emergence and consolidation of an industry of nation-branding "experts"—engaged by governments to crystallize and articulate their national identities more cohesively, persuasively, and competitively—implicates a new series of actors, aims, and results involved in tourism's worldmaking and the tourist gaze (Aronczyk 2013; Fehimović and Ogden 2018; Morgan et al. 2007). Employing the techniques and rationale of corporate public relations (PR) and advertising, nation branding offers nation-state elites the opportunity to capitalize on national resources—assets of a nation's landscape and culture, for example—and market them to global others through the use of vehicles such as logos, slogans, hashtags, and social media campaigns. Rather than flattening the world out into a homogenous sameness, globalization has, according to Dinnie, revitalized the importance of national identity (2015, 8), heightening the need to be visible and original, unique, or even exotic in the competitive marketplace.

Converting national identity into a competitive brand does more, then, than capture flows of capital in competitive marketplaces such as tourism in the Caribbean but also reconfigures the state's legitimacy as custodian of national and cultural resources. Rather than simply considering Cuba's branding efforts as an acquiescence to global forces, it is instead possible to consider how Cuba, a country that has been subject to intensely divisive speculation, scrutiny, and critique from abroad, may engage tourism branding as a vehicle of positive, autochthonous articulations of the nation, as well as an essential source of income. Indeed, attempts to exercise soft power and strategically circulate modern images of the nation and Revolution have been an established feature of revolutionary international relations, including through international sports programs (Huish 2011), medical missions (Kirk and Huish 2007), and via broadcast media (Rivero 2015). While directed first and foremost toward economic competitiveness, tourism branding may also echo broader political aspirations, including how the nation hopes to be seen by others.

Despite the promise of control seemingly offered by the nation-branding industry, critics warn that aspirations to create new national storylines and images must be tempered by a recognition of those that are already familiar to the target market: nation branding often recycles common myths, stereotypes, and clichés, based on its directive to resonate with its global audience, or rather, market. Moreover, the question is not whether to brand, but how to do so and how to control the branding process and message. The image of the nation, warns Keith Dinnie (2015, 166), already exists in the imaginations of others: branding appears to offer the opportunity to use the expertise of PR and marketing professionals to mold it and harness it toward various economic and political ends; to generate and consolidate soft power in diplomatic contexts, to corral citizens toward a common national goal, and to attract capital through promoting foreign investment or tourism. Clearly, visibility and control over image are not synonymous in these contexts. Digital technologies and online media in a globalized world appear to convey access to a global audience, and have been eagerly embraced by some governments for the purposes of nation branding and diplomacy

(Christensen 2013). Conversely, exposure to global media and technologies and the multiplicity of voices, images, narratives, and interests that they host, challenges the control over the nation brand that nation-states now seek.

Cuba's hypervisibility in the media, particularly online, has fueled tourists' interest to see the island "before it changes," as the pervasive refrain has it. At the same time, the Internet has allowed a global audience to see the explosion of emerging markets and the myriad social, moral, and economic contradictions associated with the sector, often through the postings of high-profile bloggers (Sánchez 2015),[1] even while domestic exposure to those same discourses has been severely limited. A deluge of images of the island (and especially Havana) for foreign consumption (Dopico 2002), symptomatic of a renewed fascination with Cuba and the Revolution, has found a captive viewership of "armchair tourists." The extraordinary commercial success of the Buena Vista Social Club's albums, tours, and eponymous documentary (Wenders 1998) was indicative of this sudden nostalgic interest (Finn 2009).[2] Images circulated online by photographers, journalists, tour operators, and tourists have extended through new media the "distinct aesthetic quality" of architectural decay and candid portraiture of "photogenic poverty" (Duong 2014, 164) that has characterized visual representations of post-Soviet Cuba (Hernandez-Reguant 2009, 13).

Tourists themselves have contributed to this visual proliferation, sharing photos on social media and thus participating in Cuba's digital tourist gaze. However, due to the delayed and incomplete access to the Internet on the island, the increasing volume of images of Cuba online has tended to come from outside.[3] Moreover, images of Cuba circulated online tend to privilege a fetishized nostalgic aesthetic, in which a vision of a crumbling Havana functions as a visual shorthand for the "fallen" Revolution and resilient population (or alternately as an indirect criticism of the U.S. embargo), and represents nostalgia for the world "as some hoped it might be" (Whitfield 2008, 22). Photographs of Cubans using Wi-Fi hot spots in city centers, their faces lit up by smartphone screens, now also frequently appear in journalists' and tourists' photos on social media platforms, speaking again to the vague ideological anxiety surrounding Cuba's increased connectivity. In short, Cuba's valued status as untouched and unspoiled, and thus somehow more authentic, is closely related with the staggered and uneven development of digital technologies on the island.

This status is somewhat misleading given what Cristina Venegas (2010) describes as the simultaneous and mutually reliant development of tourism and technology in Cuba. The use of digital technology in the sector, particularly within the visible lobby areas of upscale hotels in Havana, Venegas notes, became a marker of Cuba's distinction and competitive, modern edge (2010, 101). In fact, tourism's expansion would not have been possible without the foundation of telecommunications (Venegas 2010, 101). Strategic online visibility showcased Cuba as an independent socialist nation-state and provided the means to further capitalize on global fascination with the country (Venegas 2010, 126). Venegas contends therefore that concerted efforts to develop tourism have turned the sector into a "site of advanced information technology" (2010, 19). Simultaneously, a "spillover" effect of "upgrading, modernization, and increased efficiency of domestic productive capacity" has been generated as a result of tourism expansion (Carty 2009, 172). Moreover, information technology has been utilized as a strategic tool to enhance the sector's competitiveness: in the last decade MINTUR and the National Institute for Economic Research have launched coordinated efforts of tourism data collection and analysis (Miller et al. 2008, 274).

Despite these insights and the recent significant changes in access and use of mobile technology analyzed in this volume and elsewhere (Grandinetti and Eszenyi 2018),[4] some popular and academic discussions tend to still emphasize Cuba's deferred and incomplete access to the Internet and implementation of digital technologies through a "language of lack" (Laguna 2017, 169) and citing censorship and repression (Geoffray and Chaguaceda 2015). The intersection of technology, tourism branding, and sector infrastructure is therefore worthy of further analysis and updating. How are digital media used to articulate the national image in the competitive marketplace of tourism both by MINTUR and foreign tour operators? How do these efforts encounter or oppose the persisting marketability of Cuba as a pre-globalized, pre-digitized time warp?

"Auténtica Cuba"

Within the crowded marketplace of international tourism, a brand plays to a country's strengths by identifying and emphasizing singularity and value in its cultural and geographic resources. Any nation's brand design is centered on the notion of comparative advantage of identifying a source of distinction that carves out a niche in the marketplace. Given that the homogenized Western imaginary of the Caribbean has tended to "flatten" the region out (Sheller 2003; Sheller 2004), making the vision of an idyllic beach (sun, sea, and sand—and sex) equally attractive in any island setting, tourism branding has increasingly sought to distinguish countries from their competitors by highlighting other unique offerings, cultural assets, and characteristics. For example, Jamaica's 2012 "Get All Right" strategy emphasized the prestige of its music industry and history, the campaign video cutting between shots of white sands and studio mixing desks, set to Bob Marley's "One Love" (Visit Jamaica 2014). Likewise, through its tagline, "The Place You Thought You Knew," Mexico's recent promotional strategy appeared to nod to both the reputation for drugs-related violence earned from global news coverage and television series like *Breaking Bad*, and the broad range of tourist experiences it offers. Beyond beaches, the Dominican Republic has sought to market its diversity with its slogan: "The Dominican Republic Has It All" (Dominican-Days 2010).

Similarly, Cuba's current USP, or "unique selling point" is predicated on the idea that the island is distinct from its regional competitors: Mexico's "Riviera Maya," the Dominican Republic, and Jamaica. Indeed, Cuba aims to attract visitors based on the notion that it is unlike any other destination in the world. The recent campaign aiming to communicate this message, "Auténtica Cuba," was designed by Brandworks, a Canadian advertising agency commissioned by MINTUR in 2010. This was the first time that MINTUR had deviated from their own media planning and buying strategy to appoint an external agency. As Michael Clancy, Brandworks' director described in an e-mail, MINTUR sought an "objective vision" to overcome a slump in the European market and build on the steady flow of Canadian tourism, Cuba's single biggest sending country. Brandworks designed, developed, and produced a campaign that would work across traditional (TV, print, OOH or out-of-home advertising—billboards, tram, and taxi "wraps"), digital (a geo-targeted website in seven languages, YouTube videos), and social platforms (Facebook and search engine marketing). While the production was directed wholly by Brandworks, the agency used Cuban "fixers" on the ground, and were generally accompanied by MINTUR representatives "eager to learn about how [Brandworks] produced film, video, and still photography" (Clancy, personal communication, December 10, 2018).

First, the Brandworks team's objective was to identify Cuba's distinguishing selling point, "the 'heart and soul' of the country . . . what made Cuba special" (Clancy, personal communication, December 10, 2008). Drawing on their own online qualitative study across twenty-nine countries and based on two investigative trips to Cuba, their key findings indicated that Cuba was "more than a beach" encompassing "many rich and positive associations . . . with incredible depth and dimension." In particular, it became evident that "Cuba was a place stuck in time." Michael Clancy recalls that the study responses overwhelmingly focused on the fact that there were "no signs of globalization" and thus, "an urgency to see it before it changes." The campaign thus centered fully on a single word—*auténtica* (authentic)—which would symbolize Cuba's uniqueness, "zest," and preservation from globalization. Rather than being a disadvantage, the absence of digital technologies and "American influences" and sense of isolation from the wider world were identified as its comparative advantages. However, as Clancy described, there were serious concerns among MINTUR representatives that this approach would create unwelcome associations that Cuba was "backward" and "poor." Addressing these concerns, he recalled "we had to aggressively argue that their unadulterated culture was a real tonic for the rest of the world."

In tourism scholarship, authenticity is a contested concept (Wang 1999). While authenticity may refer to objects that are certifiable or may be accurately attributed to local and "traditional" ways of life, the notion of *experiential* authenticity hallmarked by Brandworks refers instead to transcendence of the mundane everyday and the (temporary) fulfillment of the "real" self (Wang 1999, 360). Authenticity of experience is rooted in nostalgia and romanticism, as Nina Wang describes, "because it idealizes the ways of life in which people are supposed as freer, more innocent, more spontaneous, purer, and truer to themselves than usual (such ways of life are usually supposed to exist in the past or in childhood)" (1999, 360). As Dean MacCannell has also outlined, the sense of authenticity in cultural experiences of tourism is corroborated by access to intimate "back spaces" and the "real lives" of visited populations (MacCannell 1973; MacCannell 1999). Intimacy and interiority are central to the perception of authentic experience (Cohen 2010, 162).

Moreover, disconnection from digital technologies is an essential new facet of the discourse of touristic authenticity (Molz 2012, 122). The apparent burden of constant connectivity is seen by many to be offset by "authentic" experiences and intimate connections with locals (Cohen 2010) and fellow tourists—even if, paradoxically, tourism is largely organized through technology and tourists in fact desire to stay in contact with those at home. The very notion of what it means to "escape" when travelling is cast into new light by the spread and use of modern technologies (Molz 2012, 142). In the context of Cuba, many have conflated advances in Internet availability and use with more generalized exposure to global flows in highlighting the attractiveness and urgency of the island's dwindling "authentic essence [and] unaltered state" (Chase 2017). For instance, travelers posting to the Tripadvisor forum frequently make comments that valorize forced disconnection in Cuba. One comments, "You have no choice but to disconnect in Cuba, which is what makes it a vacation."[5] Another contributor echoes this sentiment, joking that "travel agents should offer Cuba as a detox destination for those addicted to social media."[6] The positive associations of being offline while

Figure 11.1. Stills from the "Auténtica Cuba" promotional video. AutenticaCuba YouTube channel, June 23, 2010. https://www.youtube.com/watch?v=99IBtics0wQ&t=218s.

visiting Cuba endure in journalistic and touristic discourses, even if, as Molz argues (2012, 139) the idea of escaping modernity is somewhat illusory.

Brandworks communicated the overarching idea of authenticity which defined the "Auténtica Cuba" campaign through a number of creative approaches. In the campaign videos, original music written and performed in Spanish by Cuban artists highlighted Cuba's cultural wealth. Videos avoided the voice-over format, a common but heavy-handed approach typical of other campaigns (such as the child voice-over who pleads for the viewer to see that Colombia is full of "good people" in "Colombia is Passion").[7] In contrast, photography and video footage used in Brandworks' Cuba campaign fulfilled an imperative to engage "powerful visuals . . . intimately capturing sights, sounds, and faces of Cuba" (Clancy, personal communication, December 10, 2018). The spectacular staging of "normal" Cuban life was integral to the campaign. To this end, Brandworks traveled across the country, filming and photographing real people in authentic (non-staged) contexts (both Cubans and tourists), rather than actors. Such an approach marked a clear departure from previous campaigns, which foregrounded conventional tourist spaces and activities rather than "ordinary" locals in typical surroundings (Ogden 2017). It also belied the somewhat stringent state regulations to control contact between tourists and locals and to limit the spread of tourism beyond demarcated enclaves (Espino 2000; Sánchez and Adams 2008, 32). Instead, the "powerful visuals" of the campaign offered tourists a candid portrait of Cubans engaged in everyday activities in the street, at weddings, at sports events, and in school and work uniforms (see figure 11.1).

Videos shared online allow a global audience to connect with this spontaneous, affectively charged and sensory experience of Cuba—to recognize and consider positively the intimate "sights, sounds, and faces of Cuba," as Brandworks had envisioned. In addition to traditional print and OOH marketing techniques, the campaign also relied on a brand-new, unified digital component. Brandworks reported that they had to counteract extreme reluctance on the part of MINTUR decision makers to direct marketing spending on search engine marketing (SEM), YouTube, and the website, given that no such marketing strategy already existed. The rationalization was to exploit a moment in the "unique purchase funnel" of tourism (Pan and Crotts 2012, 86), that is, the first two of the three stages of tourism advertising: dreaming, planning, and booking. Compelling visuals of authentic ways of life and experiences in the campaign images and videos—interventions in the tourist gaze—would address the "dreaming stage." Before the "Auténtica Cuba" campaign, Cuba had not taken advantage of the highly personal and engaging potentialities of the Internet in fueling this "dreaming stage." In addition, since MINTUR had not, at this point, relinquished control of online booking to a Web-based foreign operator such as Expedia or Travelocity, the planning and booking stages were stymied by a lack of information online. A great deal of work and planning went into the official website, in order to engage and encourage tourists to seek out information to turn piqued interest into bookings (and sales).

The website would also, as Brandworks saw it, inspire trust among travel providers to sell Cuba to potential tourists rather than recommending competitors. Visible advertising builds confidence: the nation's brand presents a spectacular, cohesive, and modern image to others. The campaign also spoke to players in the tourism trade, whose cooperation in sales is essential, and to investors, for whom the assurance that Cuba was a solid, self-aware option warranted their spending. Without a singular, cohesive identity articulated in the brand through accessible, modern media, building this confidence would be a challenge, due to the contemporary imperative for online visibility. If the competitiveness of the nation's image can be squandered through a lack of concerted branding strategy, as some advocates have warned (Dinnie 2015, 166), then failure to make the brand visible online also risks the ignorance and indifference of investors, stakeholders, and customers. There is also the risk that alternative visions of the nation will crowd out the tourist gaze and obscure the nation-state's desired brand messaging.

The Digital Tourist Gaze: Other Interventions

Other interventions in the digital tourist gaze of Cuba have paid similarly high attention to the notion of spontaneity and authenticity in the everyday. Viral videos in particular have been exploited by other agencies in order to pique tourist interest in Cuba. The first to be analyzed here, "Mi Cuba Querida" ("My Beloved Cuba"), by bespoke travel operator The Wind Collective, engages slick production values and emotive voice-overs, more in the style of a movie trailer. The Wind Collective describe themselves as "a community expressing freedom through travel and creativity [who] engage in local experiences, build our community, and live our best lives." This brand identity is expressed in both its digital marketing and the itineraries advertised on the website, which include "boutique Cuban styled accommodation," professional photo shoots, creative workshops, and "giving back" sessions, through which participants "dedicate some time to local communities" and "shine a light" (The Wind Collective n.d.). The spontaneity and creativity that this description associates with the brand is evident in the choice of camera shots and editing techniques in the "Mi Cuba Querida" video, which has been viewed just under 5,700 times at the time of writing (February 2020). Drone shots that take in streets of urban architecture are followed by intimate close-ups of Cuban faces and hands, repairing old pans, holding candles in church, and handling fruit. The camera follows an emaciated stray cat as it jumps over a dirty puddle in the street (figure 11.2). There is an accelerated montage of portraits of Cuban faces staring directly into the lens. This is a highly sensory, gritty vision of Havana (no other Cuban locations are featured), where the intimacy and immediacy of the everyday lived experience, of *resolviendo* ("making do" or "making ends meet"), become key subjects.

Figure 11.2. Still from "Mi Cuba querida" video. Wind Collective YouTube channel, July 25, 2018. https://www.youtube.com/watch?v=PEeBCildXTc&t=28s.

The video's voice-over, narrating over sounds of children playing and dogs barking, extends this sensory mode, frequently rising and breaking with emotion:

> Imagine. Imagine a morning. A morning unlike any other morning... ever since, and just like every other morning up until then. Then imagine all those mornings of the world, my world—gone, almost in an instant. And everywhere, I see Cuba. I taste Cuba. I feel Cuba. Because Cuba is there. I will lay my head on her shoulders. Once more [voice breaks] in her arms. Her arms around me. *Mi Cuba querida.* (Hunnigan et al. 2018)

This narration vaguely invokes the passage of time that expedites Cuba's aperture to the world and seemingly inevitable change from authenticity to overexposure. Simultaneous manipulation of footage reinforces this perspective. Footage is speed-ramped—alternately and suddenly sped up and slowed down—with clouds flying across the cityscape in a time-lapse. Hyperlapse footage (using time-lapse with moving rather than static shots) of city-center buildings and crash zoom transitions made in the edit also enhance the sense of movement, and elicit the discourse of transience and precariousness that has become synonymous with Cuba "in transition." The narration is otherwise not straightforward to interpret. The personification of Cuba as a receptive, sensual woman is anything but novel, since the figure of the sexualized *mulata* is central to the Cuban cultural imaginary (Mendieta 2000; Kutzinski 1993) and for whom the relevance of race, gender, and class in Cuban discourses are also implicated in contemporary understandings of the *jinetera* (sex worker, hustler) (Daigle 2015, 27). In short, the video presents travel to Cuba as a return to the familiar intimacy of a lover's embrace.

This vision of Cuba is familiar, precisely because of the proliferation of images in the tourist gaze that build a sense of anticipation and recognition long before travel takes place (Urry 1990). The experience of tourism thus becomes a vision of witnessing first-hand the Cuba that has been represented in similar ways, in literature, photography, branding, and cinema. Indeed, the dramatic voice-over, sense of narrative, and sometimes "moody" tone of the images furnish the "movie trailer" sense of the video; the caption also invites the viewer to "watch this video and delve into a cinematic world." While not informative or indicative of tourist activities on offer, this type of content contributes to the "dreaming" stage of the tourism purchase "funnel." The tourist gaze refers thus to the mind's eye or the daydreaming imaginary of place (Urry 1990), the broader ocularcentrism of tourism which compels the

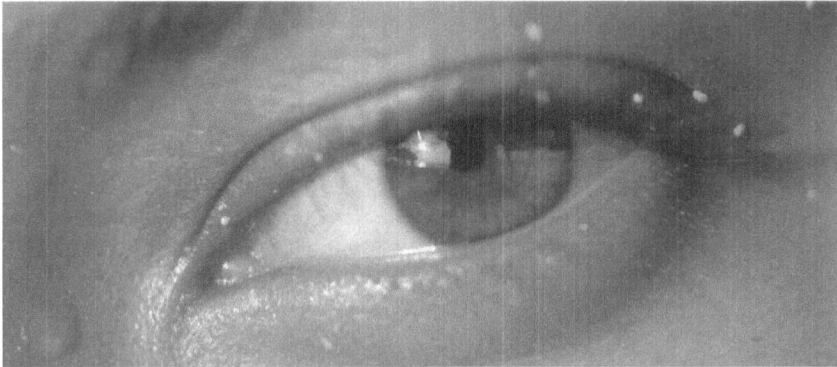

Figure 11.3. Still from "Mi Cuba querida" video. WindCollective YouTube channel, July 25, 2018. https://www.youtube.com/watch?v=PEeBCildXTc&t=28s.

tourist to gaze on intimate "back-spaces." Small wonder, then, that a close-up of an eye is a recurring motif in this video (figure 11.3).

The majority of the video's footage appears to have been filmed using a DSLR (digital single-lens reflex) camera, a small, portable camera which enables filmmakers to produce high-quality images using less invasive equipment than a larger film camera. The intimate feel of the video, which relies on spontaneous and uninhibited movements in its subjects and between photographer and subject, is therefore ensured by the device.

Another recent viral video, circulated by tour operator Responsible Travel, similarly engages sensual and sensory representation of the city and its inhabitants. Eschewing modern tourism infrastructure and only infrequently featuring iconic tourist sites, the camera is instead trained on lines of drying laundry, couples embracing, and people carrying out quotidian, domestic tasks. The caption confirms this choice of urban subjects and scenes:

> Cuba's beaches and bays are a must, however stepping into Havana . . . presents a nostalgic world of classic cars, crackling transistor radios, and clacking dominoes whilst children play with handmade toys in the street. Meander into the countryside to find farmers riding horses through forests, oxen ploughing fields, wheelbarrows spilling over with homegrown veg, and rocking chair–bound residents sipping rum on the porch. (Responsible Travel 2017)

This nostalgic vision highlights a sensory immersion in sounds (clacking dominoes, crackling radios) and smells and tastes (homegrown produce, rum) that belong to a traditional, pre-digitized world, highlighting the significance of the sensory body to touristic experiences which break the

254 · Rebecca Ogden

Figure 11.4. Still from "Mi Cuba querida" video. WindCollective YouTube channel, July 25, 2018. https://www.youtube.com/watch?v=PEeBCildXTc&t=28s.

mundaneness of home (Edensor 2006). Authenticity here idealizes simpler ways of life as they may be associated with the past, in the ways that Wang describes (1999, 360)—involving rudimentary transport and socializing without screens. Moreover, the aestheticization of underdevelopment, evinced in many shots of laundry drying in the street, are common to both Wind Collective and Responsible Travel videos (figure 11.4). In both rural and urban settings, the Responsible Travel video cites evidence of traditional ways of life as points of interest within the tourist gaze, elevated not only as sites worth visiting and gazing upon but as a marketable distinction of the destination.

In both these examples, the brighter colors and upbeat music of the "Auténtica Cuba" campaign are replaced with more dramatic music and grittier, yellow and sepia tones—most likely the result of postproduction "grading." The videos are addressing slightly different markets: the "Auténtica Cuba" video is directed toward North American and European tourists in general, its concept derived from market research in those same regions. The videos produced by Wind Collective and Responsible Travel clearly target a more self-identified creative, independent tourist. Tourists who pursue a backpacking style and identity of tourism may be especially driven to explore profound experiences of intimate contact with "locals" (Cohen 2003; Conran 2011; Uriely, Yonay, and Simchai 2002).

Nevertheless, the central concept that combines each promotional strategy is authenticity—an essentialized and idealized nostalgia of the everyday, satisfied in one of the last places still "protected" from hyperconnectivity and globalization, which are often framed as a burden of life in the global North. Videos like these function in a different way from still billboard images or slogans because they elicit the visual, auditory, and olfactory dimensions, in intimate details of place, evoking "being there." In offering the possibility of sharing and watching these evocations at home, viral videos are a compelling marketing tool. Beyond the production costs, video's global reach is not dependent on budgets. If they are interesting and engaging, and thus worth sharing, they can be highly cost-effective.

Furthermore, in registering views, shares, and comments, viral videos offer the possibility to track impact in terms of numbers, global reach, and positive and negative responses. Creating content such as videos that can be shared by the same consumers they target also suggests the potential for brand "co-creation," a tactic that has evolved in nation branding which engages the active participation of individuals (Volcic and Andrejevic 2011) to either "crowdsource" ideas and material, gauge feedback, or collaborate in the spread and longevity of the brand through, for instance, likes and shares of a given campaign on social media (Gómez Carrillo 2018). Such a "loop" or social feedback cycle may be compared to a form of digital word-of-mouth, which some have argued may have greater impact than typical mass media marketing on consumer decision-making (Pan and Crotts 2012, 81). The success of such campaigns in influencing consumers increasingly relies on creators' ability to capture these online audiences and engage them to participate. One of their "achievements," as Brandworks saw it, was convincing MINTUR of the necessity of spending on digital marketing.

However, it is also clear that controlling the images and narratives of the touristic brand is not a straightforward exercise, precisely because other operators, stakeholders, and consumers make interventions in the tourist gaze. Tensions between the valorization of Cuba's pre-globalized, pre-digitized authentic "essence" and unwelcome suggestions of backwardness (a reported concern of MINTUR's during the brand creation process) are pushed to their extreme in some of these external interventions. Branding the nation as a destination means that first, the brand must speak primarily to the desires of the target market, and second, that it competes for attention among other online articulations. Indeed, these articulations include blog and social media posts, shared photographs, virtual "check-ins," and Tripadvisor reviews circulated by tourists themselves. This dilemma was highlighted by a senior manager at the state-owned company Havanatur, who made the following remark in an interview: "[as a tourist] you might take a couple of photos and you put them online with the caption 'this is Cuba.' But you have the power to caption a spectacular image of the Bellas Artes museum 'this is Cuba,' or, you have the power to say 'this is Cuba' with a photo of somewhere else ... From outside Cuba, you can post what you want."[8]

Conclusion

In December 2018, Cuba's then tourism minister Manuel Marrero Cruz posted the following message on his official Twitter account:

> Today we approve the communications plan of the Ministry of Tourism for 2019. The majority of its actions will be on the Internet and its networks. You can't move forward in tourism without using the highways of new technology. #CubaSafeDestination #TourismWithQuality.[9]

Clearly, there has been a transformation in the last decade from reluctance to invest in and develop digital marketing strategies to an embrace of technology in tourism practice and infrastructure. As a discussion with a senior sales manager at Havanatur confirmed, each Cuban state tourism agency (Havanatur, Cubanacán, Gaviota, etc.) has its own digital marketing representative or team. Marrero Cruz's use of hashtags—#CubaDestinoSeguro and #TurismoConCalidad—which have recently begun to appear in the short videos, images, and posts circulated by the social media accounts of state agencies, suggest a strong sense of cohesion in brand messaging, and indeed, a new message. While rival destinations have been linked with organized crime, kidnappings, and violence, Cuba's low crime rate (#CubaSafeDestination) appears as another distinguishing selling point.

However, although marketing touristic Cuba relies on digital channels and networks to circulate and communicate these narratives and images to global audiences, this chapter has shown that branding strategies have reinforced, implicitly or explicitly, nostalgic and romanticized value in the island's isolation from global capitalist and digital flows. In tending to frame children playing in the street, lines of drying laundry, and sensory pleasures, this nostalgic aesthetic also fetishizes a pre-globalized and pre-digitized world, a preserved time warp where tourists have a chance to put down device screens and experience authenticity, that is, to fulfill their true selfhood and have "unmediated contact with the Other" (Cohen 2010, 154). Although tourism in the Caribbean may satisfy a quest to travel to a premodern time "unburdened" by constant connectivity, the competitiveness of the industry itself relies on spectacular visibility online.

Online nation branding in Cuba demonstrates one of the ways that the Internet is not "postnational" or globalized, but instead expresses localization and embeddedness (Pitman and Taylor 2013, 4). The Internet allows nations to articulate their assets in new ways and to chart the impact and spread of such articulations. In the contemporary age of hypervisibility, to neglect online iterations of a brand campaign is to risk irrelevance, indifference, and invisibility to a largely "connected" target market. The opportunities of viral videos in particular to draw consumers and citizens into corroborating the summative outcome of these efforts lies in their networkedness and their online shareability. Yet, amid this hypervisibility and in the context of twenty-four-hour media coverage and the "always on" lifestyle (Thompson 2005), the heterogeneity of images and narratives accessible via the Internet prevent creators from maintaining total control and cohesiveness of brand messaging. Thus, the anxieties that representations of traditional ways of life can be seen as a "tonic" in a hypermediated world, or as evidence of backwardness and poverty, reveal the impossibility of fully controlling such tropes. This chapter has also demonstrated that alternative visions of the immediacy and intimacy of the urban everyday, which more explicitly evoke the nostalgia of technological underdevelopment, can also vie for attention and inform the tourist gaze.

Notes

1. See Henken's contribution to this volume for an analysis of the transformations in the fifteen-year public career of blogger turned digital newspaper director Yoani Sánchez.

2. To paraphrase Esther Whitfield's keen analysis, *Buena Vista Social Club* is a hugely successful film (and series of albums) built on Western nostalgia about a band that never existed and a club that no longer exists (2008).

3. See Duong's contribution to this volume, appropriately titled "Images of Ourselves," for a trenchant study of "mediascapes" created by Cubans themselves.

4. These include the development of tourism-related cell phone apps (such as the restaurant guide AlaMesa, the private homestay directory Cuba Junky, the private-sector business directories Isladentro and ConoceCuba, and the travel planner HabanaTrans), the now commonplace Wi-Fi hot spots, and the introduction of 3G and 4G cell phone coverage during 2018 and 2019.

5. See Tripadvisor comment here: https://www.tripadvisor.co.uk/ShowTopic-g580450-i10244-k5759271-Wifi_at_the_tryp-Cayo_Coco_Jardines_del_Rey_Archipelago_Ciego_de_Avila_Province_Cuba.html.

6. See Trip Advisor comment here: https://www.tripadvisor.co.uk/ShowTopic-g285732-i398-k4840330-Wifi_spt-Holguin_Holguin_Province_Cuba.html#36134921.

7. Rafael Suarez Buelvas, 2008. Colombia Is Passion-(Inglés), YouTube. Accessed January 29, 2019. https://www.youtube.com/watch?v=Hn4hMEOpF8o.

8. The original quote in Spanish reads: " . . . a lo mejor tiraste dos fotos y pusiste 'eso es Cuba.' Pero tienes el poder de poner 'esto es Cuba' en una foto espectacular del Museo de Bellas Artes, o tienes el poder de poner 'eso es Cuba' en una foto de otro sitio . . . desde afuera, puedes poner lo que tú quieras."

9. The original tweet in Spanish reads: "Hoy aprobamos el plan de Comunicaciones del Ministerio de Turismo para el 2019. La mayor cantidad de acciones serán en Internet y sus redes. No se puede transitar bien en el turismo; sino es por las autopistas de las nuevas tecnologías. #CubaDestinoSeguro #TurismoConCalidad."

References

Anonymous. N.d. Wind Collective: Cuba. The Wind Collective Trips. Last accessed, December 13, 2018. https://www.thewindcollectivetrips.com/cuba.

Aronczyk, Melissa. 2013. *Branding the Nation: The Global Business of National Identity.* Oxford: Oxford University Press.

Carty, Victoria. 2009. "Capitalist Measures within a Socialist Model: A Commodity Chains Analysis of the Emerging Cuban Tourism Industry." *Canadian Journal of Latin American and Caribbean Studies* 34 (67): 163–195.

Chase, Simons. 2017. "Cuba Is Headed for a Tech Revolution." *TechCo*, January 13, 2017.

Christensen, Christian. 2013. "@Sweden: Curating a Nation on Twitter." *Popular Communication* 11 (1): 30–46.

Clancy, Michael. 2018. E-mail to Rebecca Ogden. 18 December.

Cohen, Colleen Ballerino. 2010. *Take Me to My Paradise: Tourism and Nationalism in the British Virgin Islands.* Piscataway, NJ: Rutgers University Press.

Cohen, Eric. 2003. "Backpacking: Diversity and change." *Journal of Tourism and Cultural Change*, 1(2): 95–110.

Cohen, Roger. 2008. "Paris-Cuba." *The New York Times*, December 7, 2008.

Conran, Mary. 2011. "'They Really Love Me!' Intimacy in Volunteer Tourism." *Annals of Tourism Research*, 38(4): 1454–1473.

Daigle, Megan. 2015. *From Cuba with Love: Sex and Money in the Twenty-First Century.* Berkeley: University of California Press.

Dinnie, Keith. 2015. *Nation Branding: Concepts, Issues, Practice.* London: Routledge.

DominicanDays. 2010. "Dominican Republic Has It All." YouTube. https://www.youtube.com/watch?v=tORVMM7y3Wk.

Dopico, Ana Maria. 2002. "Picturing Havana: History, Vision, and the Scramble for Cuba." *Nepantla: Views from South* 3 (3): 451–493.

Duong, Paloma. 2014. "Amateur Citizens: Culture and Democracy in Contemporary Cuba." Ph.D. thesis, Columbia University.

Edensor, Timothy. 2006. "Sensing Tourist Spaces." In *Travels in Paradox: Remapping Tourism*, edited by Claudio Minca and Tim Oakes, 23–45. Lanham, MD: Rowman and Littlefield.

Espino, Mayra D. 2000. "Cuban Tourism during the Special Period." *Cuba in Transition* 10: 360–373.

Fehimović, Dunja and Rebecca Ogden, eds. 2018. *Branding Latin America: Strategies, Aims, Resistance.* Lanham, MD: Lexington Books.

Finn, John. 2009. "Contesting culture: a case study of commodification in Cuban music." *GeoJournal*, 74(3): 191–200.

Geoffray, Marie Laure and Armando Chaguaceda. 2015. "Medios de comunicación y cambios en la política de información en Cuba desde el 1959." *Temas de Comunicación* 0 (29): 171–196.

Gómez Carrillo, Paula. 2018. "Covert Nation Branding and the Neoliberal Subject: The Case of 'It's Colombia, NOT Columbia.'" In *Branding Latin America: Strategies, Aims, Resistance*, edited by Dunja Fehimović and Rebecca Ogden, 95–111. Lanham, MD: Lexington.

Grandinetti, Justin and Marie Elizabeth Eszenyi. 2018. "La Revolución Digital: Mobile Media Use in Contemporary Cuba." *Information, Communication and Society* 21 (6): 866–881.
Hernández-Reguant, Ariana. 2009. *Cuba in the Special Period: Culture and Ideology in the 1990s*. New York: Palgrave Macmillan.
Higgins, Emma. 2017. "10 Breathtakingly Beautiful Places that are Perfect for a Digital Detox." *Wanderlust*, January 9, 2017.
Hollinshead, Keith. 1999. "Surveillance of the Worlds of Tourism: Foucault and the Eye-of-power." *Tourism Management* 20 (1): 7–23.
Hollinshead, Keith. 2004. "Tourism and the New Sense." In *Tourism and Postcolonialism: Contested Discourses, Identities and Representations*, edited by M. Hall and H. Tucker, 25–42. London: Routledge.
Hollinshead, Keith. 2007. "'Worldmaking' and the Transformation of Place and Culture: The Enlargement of Meethan's Analysis of Place and Change." In *The Critical Turn in Tourism Studies: Innovative Research Methods*, edited by I. Ateljevic, A. Pritchard, and N. Morgan, 165–196. Oxford: Elsevier.
Hollinshead, Keith, Irena Ateljevic, and Nazia Ali. 2009. "Worldmaking Agency–Worldmaking Authority: The Sovereign Constitutive Role of Tourism." *Tourism Geographies: An International Journal of Tourism Place, Space and the Environment* 11 (4): 427–443.
Horne, Donald. 1992. *The Great Museum: The Re-presentation of History*. London: Pluto.
Huish, Robert. 2011. "Punching above its Weight: Cuba's Use of Sport for South–South Co-operation." *Third World Quarterly* 32 (3): 417–433.
Huish, Robert and John M. Kirk. 2007. "Cuban Medical Internationalism and the Development of the Latin American School of Medicine." *Latin American Perspectives* 34 (6): 77–92.
Hunnigan, Clemar, Mark Szekelyhidi, and Barbabas Kelemen. 2018. "Authentic Travels Ep01 Cuba: Mi Cuba Querida." Wind Collective. Accessed February 25, 2020. https://www.youtube.com/watch?v=PEeBCildXTc&t=5s&index=4&list=WL.
Kent, James. 2019. *Aesthetics and the Revolutionary City: Real and Imagined Havana*. Basingstoke: Palgrave Macmillan.
Kirshenblatt-Gimblett, Barbara. 1998. *Destination Culture: Tourism, Museums, and Heritage*. Berkeley: University of California Press.
Kutzinski, Vera M. 1993. *Sugar's Secrets: Race and the Erotics of Cuban Nationalism*. Charlottesville and London: University Press of Virginia.
Laguna, Albert Sergio. 2017. *Diversión: Play and Popular Culture in Cuban America*. New York: NYU Press.
MacCannell, Dean. 1973. "Staged Authenticity: Arrangements of Social Space in Tourist Settings." *American Journal of Sociology* 79 (3): 589–603.
MacCannell, Dean. 1999. *The Tourist: A New Theory of the Leisure Class*. Berkeley and Los Angeles: University of California Press.
Mendieta, Raquel. 2000. "Exotic Exports: The Myth of the Mulatta." In *Corpus Delecti: Performance Art of the Americas*, edited by Coco Fusco, 43–54. London, New York: Routledge.
Miller, Mark M., Tony L. Henthorne, and Babu P. George. 2008. "The Competitiveness of

the Cuban Tourism Industry in the Twenty-First Century: A Strategic Re-Evaluation." *Journal of Travel Research* 46 (3): 268–278.

Molz, Jennie Germann. 2012. *Travel Connections: Tourism, Technology and Togetherness in a Mobile World*. London: Routledge.

Morgan, Nigel, Annette Pritchard, and Roger Pride. 2007. *Destination Branding*. London: Routledge.

Oag, Caron. 2018. "5 Essential Travel Apps to Download for a Trip to Cuba." *Caledonia Worldwide*, April 19, 2018.

Ogden, Rebecca. 2017. "Living the Brand: Authenticity and Affective Capital in Contemporary Cuban Tourism." In *Branding Latin America: Strategies, Aims, Resistance*, edited by Dunja Fehimović and Rebecca Ogden. Lanham: Lexington Books.

Pan, Bing and John C. Crotts. 2012. "Theoretical Models of Social Media, Marketing Implications, and Future Research Directions." In *Social Media in Travel, Tourism and Hospitality: Theory, Practice and Cases*, edited by Marianna Sigala, Evangelous Christou, and Ulrike Gretzel, 73–85. Farnham, UK: Ashgate.

Pitman, Thea and Claire Taylor. 2013. *Latin American Identity in Online Cultural Production*. London: Routledge.

Quiroga, José. 2005. *Cuban Palimpsests*. Minneapolis: University of Minnesota Press.

Responsible Travel. 2017. "Responsible Travel Presents: Cuba." YouTube. https://www.youtube.com/watch?v=nfdJKU-iinU&t=24s&index=6&list=WL.

Ritzer, George. 1998. *The McDonaldization Thesis: Explorations and Extensions*. London: SAGE.

Rivero, Yeidy M. 2015. *Broadcasting Modernity: Cuban Commercial Television, 1950–1960*. Durham: Duke University Press.

Sánchez, Peter M. and Kathleen M. Adams. 2008. "The Janus-faced Character of Tourism in Cuba." *Annals of Tourism Research* 35 (1): 27–46.

Sánchez, Yoani. 2015. "En la patria de la solidaridad no hay extranjeros." *14ymedio*, October 12, 2015.

Sheller, Mimi. 2003. *Consuming the Caribbean: From Arawaks to Zombies*. New York: Routledge.

Sheller, Mimi. 2004. "Demobilizing and Remobilizing Caribbean Paradise." In *Tourism Mobilities: Places to Play, Places in Play*, edited by Mimi Sheller and John Urry, 13–21. New York: Routledge.

Silver, Ira. 1993. "Marketing Authenticity in Third World Countries." *Annals of Tourism Research* 20 (2): 302–318.

Thompson, John B. 2005. "The New Visibility." *Theory, Culture & Society* 22 (6): 31–51.

Uriely, N., Yonay, Y. and Simchai, D., 2002. "Backpacking experiences: A type and form analysis." *Annals of Tourism Research* 29(2): 520–538.

Urry, John. 1990. *The Tourist Gaze: Leisure and Travel in Contemporaries Societies*. London: SAGE.

Urry, John. 1992. "The tourist gaze 'revisited.'" *American Behavioral Scientist* 36(2): 172–186.

Urry, John and Jonas Larsen. 2011. *The Tourist Gaze 3.0*. London: SAGE.

Venegas, Cristina. 2010. *Digital Dilemmas: The State, the Individual, and Digital Media in Cuba*. Piscataway, NJ: Rutgers University Press.

Visit Jamaica, 2014. "Jamaica: The Home of All Right." YouTube. https://www.youtube.com/watch?v=59s9DRB9BuQ.

Volcic, Zala and Mark Andrejevic. 2011. "Nation Branding in the Era of Commercial Nationalism." *International Journal of Communication Systems* 5 (0): 21.

Wang, Nina. 1999. "Rethinking authenticity in tourism experience." *Annals of Tourism Research* 26 (2): 349–370.

Wenders, Wim. 1998. *The Buena Vista Social Club*. United States: Artisan Entertainment.

Whitfield, Esther. 2008. *Cuban Currency: The Dollar and "Special Period" Fiction*. Minneapolis: University of Minnesota Press.

12

"A Una Cuba Alternativa"?

Digital Millennials, Social Influencing, and *Cuentapropismo* in Havana

JENNIFER CEARNS

"Vengan a conocer nuestra plataforma, formen parte, ¡tomen acción en esta batalla por documentar y mostrar al mundo una Cuba ALTERNATIVA!"[1] read the invitation, which pinged up through yet another WhatsApp group to which I'd been added by Frank, my digital entrepreneur friend in Havana. He was one of several friends I had who, having completed university degrees that were unlikely to lead to satisfying or well-remunerated work for the state, had set up their own businesses, using emerging digital technologies and networks to celebrate the various unsung countercultural trends that saturate Havana's exclusive events lineup. Frank and others like him are riding the crest of a growing wave in Cuba, the result of a potent combination of increasing Internet and social media access (at least in central Havana), and further concessions to Cuba's euphemistically dubbed *cuentapropistas* (i.e. "those who count on themselves" or self-employed people). Implicit within this euphemism, however, is an inherent binary forming at the heart of Cuban society: an all-pervasive sense of "them" (the state) versus "us" (those active in the so-called non-state sector). Moreover, for some *cuentapropistas* who operate in the even more liminal digital space of Cuba's emerging hybrid economy, this can bring with it a heightened vulnerability in a country where Fidel Castro's famous declaration, "Within the Revolution, everything; against the Revolution, nothing" (1961) still strongly resonates as the country's official "cultural policy."

This chapter considers how an emerging generation of Cuban "millennials"[2] are becoming digital entrepreneurs, launching businesses that operate within a relatively new world of social media and Internet access in Havana. I follow Jean and John Comaroff in considering three essential aspects of this so-called millennial moment: "the shifting provenance of the nation-state and its fetishes, the rise of new forms of enchantment, and the explosion of neoliberal discourses of civil society" (2001, 3). The digital age has only increased the fetishization of Cuba in the visual imaginary of a world tourism industry seeking out the "authentic" at every turn. This project has coincided with Cubans' own increasing access to digital media, resulting in a growing desire to have a voice in the representation of their homeland in a public digital space, while engaging in dialogues about what Cuban society can and will be in a digital, globalized age.

The chapter draws upon ethnographic research conducted in Havana between March 2017 and September 2018 to consider how a relatively small but culturally influential set of young Cubans has been negotiating these shifts in an altogether complex sociopolitical and technological context. Their businesses often operate in a liminal space within Cuban ideological norms.[3] Although technically legal and within the remits of *cuentapropista* licenses, many of these young Cubans are coming under increased scrutiny and pressure from both the state and regular members of society for their celebration of a cultural "alterity," parallel perhaps to "hipster" youth movements seen around the world, but which in Cuba might be interpreted as countercultural, counter-Cuban, or indeed counter-Revolutionary.[4] Ironically however, for some this stems not so much from a particular stance against the Revolution or from resistance to the Cuban state, but rather from a social or cultural positioning against hegemonic and stereotyping visions from the outside of a fetishized or "exotic" Cuba they reject. Paradoxically, this is a position which, arguably, puts them back in line with Cuba's Revolutionary ideals of resistance to colonialism, U.S. imperialism, and global capitalism.

This chapter follows several such entrepreneurs as they navigate the emerging systems of regulation and normativity that surround both digital media and *cuentapropismo* in Cuba, as well as when interfacing with other liminal digital spaces such as *el paquete* and the SNETs (akin to intranets) of Havana.[5] It examines some of the pitfalls of this world, as several of the entrepreneurs encounter tensions with the police, family, or neighbors due to their activity, before considering to what extent young digital entrepreneurs are redefining what it means to be Cuban, as digital media facilitate increased interaction with modes of expression from outside of Cuba. For several of these digital entrepreneurs, their celebration of cultural "alterity," even if through tangential association with the aesthetics of fashion and music movements from abroad, can be inherently, if unwittingly, political statements, which can in turn create tensions for them both at home and at work. And yet our own notions of what constitute "revolution" and "resistance" are also called into question when considered within the Cuban context, as lived practices belie a subtler interplay between various coexisting notions of "resistance," "rebellion," and "revolution" within an evolving Cuban identity politics.

The Rise of Digital Entrepreneurs in Havana

> How could a one-party socialist state that still monitors e-mails, curtails freedom of the press, and limits private enterprise create a digital society, which is premised on the open exchange of information and trade? (Ashby 2001, 18)

It is all too easy to presume that, because Cuba's digital and technological panorama does not mirror that of, say, the United States, it would be an odd place to set up a "digital" business. It is well known that the island has limited Internet connectivity. High costs, slow speeds, censorship, and a frustrating lack of privacy when online due to the very public nature of the most common access points,[6] all continue to characterize getting online (Freedom on the Net 2018). Indeed, Ashby captures this conundrum explicitly when he juxtaposes some of the characteristics of Cuba's well-known "surveillance state" with its seemingly contradictory efforts to create a "digital society," as quoted in the epigraph above (2001). Yet in practice this situation has proved galvanizing for some of Cuba's millennial generation, with deficiencies in access to infrastructure, capital, and information spurring remarkable creativity when it comes to digital platforms. At the time of my departure from Cuba after my latest round of field research, one of my contacts was in the process of constructing a new business, which he hoped to launch internationally within a few years, and which would offer digital storage and archiving services (similar to what we might think of as "the cloud") without reliance on Internet access. As a teenager, without online access, he had learned to take apart and rebuild computers, cell phones, and eventually whole digital systems and networks. This knowledge, patience, and aptitude for *invento* (an all-important Cuban popular term for creativity and inventiveness of ambiguous legality) all stood him in good stead in what is a notoriously challenging marketplace even with dependable Internet access. Despite its frequent fetishization as the "off-line island" (Helft 2015) or "the island of the disconnected" (Henken 2017), therefore, Cuba is arguably a fertile land for digital entrepreneurship, and Cubans' "make do and mend" attitude has fomented a particularly widespread saturation of digital content.

The most renowned of these means undoubtedly remains *el paquete* ("the package"), a highly efficient and profitable island-wide data distribution system that has been called Cuba's "largest private employer" (Press 2015), and summarized as "the Internet distilled down to its purest, most consumable, and least interactive form: its content" (García Martínez 2017). This weekly (nowadays daily) distribution of digital content including music videos, international soap operas (ranging from South Korean to Turkish), antivirus updates and apps, digital magazines, classified advertisements, and more crosses the island by boat, plane, car, bus, bike, and even on foot (thus the term "sneaker net") to reach a substantial proportion of the population. Layers upon layers of *paqueteros*, or distributors, participate in this marketplace, which can cost as little as a few Cuban pesos (approximately $0.20 U.S. cents), and which delivers a curated selection of digital content on USB sticks and hard drives door-to-door (Cearns 2021).

The content which circulates through *el paquete* also circulates daily, within Havana at least, through the city's SNETs (García Martínez 2017). These started out as ad hoc local area networks (LANs) or *intra*-net systems wired up by teenagers in the outskirt suburb of Villa Panamericana in Eastern Havana for the purposes of gaming (Press 2017), but have now expanded to include at least forty-four thousand people spread all across Havana, according to my contacts who worked across several of the locally deployed and managed networks. Access costs around US $1 a month and depends upon living in the right neighborhood to be able to run a cable from a preexisting connection. Once "online," members can browse a veritable treasure trove of games, videos, music, and chat rooms from the comfort of their own homes, and can share data and chat in real time with friends across their neighborhood. Moreover, the entire contents of *el paquete*, including its dozens of pdf-format magazines made by various digital entrepreneurs across Havana, are also liberally shared throughout these networks.

For the majority of young millennials in Havana for whom Internet access is a considerable challenge, these "alternative" sources of digital connectivity are a vital means of staying up to date with the latest music, fashion, gossip, and events. For a smaller elite however, Internet access itself is also an everyday aspect of normal consumption. "El Internet es de respirar, está en el aire" ("you breathe the Internet, it's in the air") explained Frank, as he fiddled with the Nanobox he had screwed onto a bracket from the ceiling of his office. For those with access to money (typically those with relatives in Miami, which in turn most likely means the white middle classes), such devices can be bought through the black market for a few hundred U.S. dollars and installed to extend or amplify state Internet signals from Wi-Fi hot spots to private dwellings a block or two away. Internet access can then be enjoyed in the privacy of one's home or office, albeit still typically at the high cost of $1 per hour charged by the state telecom monopoly, ETECSA. For people like Frank, who runs a social influencing business in El Vedado (a middle-class neighborhood of Havana),[7] or my various other contacts who work in digital marketing or produce digital magazines, regular Internet access is an essential tool of the trade. For them, reliable Internet access is a tool which also implicitly belies a degree of social capital, not infrequently bought with money from contacts overseas, and possible in part due to the maintenance of close social relations with neighbors on higher floors who can host the antenna for them, or at the very least not snitch ("*chivatear*") on them to the authorities.

Cultural Alterity and National Identity

One thing most of my contacts within this emerging digital entrepreneur "social set" in Havana had in common was a mutual self-identification as *alternativo* (alternative), and a desire to distinguish themselves from "los cubaneos, los cubiches, and los cubanazos" while still resolutely declaring inclusion within *la cubanidad*.[8] These *habaneros* might be considered the local equivalent of "hipsters," and were not to be found grinding to Cuban *son* tracks wearing tight neon clothing, as one so often sees in Cuban music videos. Nor were they sipping *mojitos* and dancing *salsa*, as a hegemonizing and exoticizing foreign gaze so often projects onto Cuba. No, these young twenty- and thirty-somethings were educated, artistic, creative, middle-class, and seeking modes of expression that encapsulated all of this alongside a keen awareness of international trends, combined with a proud sense of their Cuban identity.

As a small but culturally influential elite group, these millennials occupy a hazy space within Havana's cultural and political landscape, however. On the one hand, they explicitly seek "the alternative"; a statement which is inherently problematic in a one-party state which often interprets any expression of "alterity" as a threat to a hard-won "Revolutionary" status quo. Moreover, such "alt" movements clearly map onto issues of social class, which in Cuba is irrevocably bound up with transnationalism and access to Cuba's large, relatively wealthy, and multifaceted diaspora. To recognize these countercultural movements would be to acknowledge the existence of a middle class or an emerging bourgeoisie, which is fundamentally at odds with Cuba's Revolutionary project.

On the other hand, these millennials assert strong claims to a Cuban identity. Moreover, they proudly incorporate strands of their *cubanidad* into their adoption and adaptation of trends started overseas. For example, one emerging music producer in Havana's countercultural scene has spearheaded a new genre—*afrofuturismo tropical*—which he envisions as connecting Cuban sounds with those of the larger African diaspora and other Caribbean aesthetics (Du Graf and Cromwell n.d.). The name of his recording label—*guampara*—is a colloquial word for machete, a symbol for the Cuban fight for liberty, and importantly a symbol which can be deployed (and interpreted) in multiple, seemingly contradictory ways: as nationalistic in its representation of the insurgent struggle of Cuba's *Mambises* (independence rebel fighters) against colonial oppression, as a statement of the (ongoing) Afro-Cuban struggle for equality, and as a call for freedom of expression in an authoritarian state.

The issue of whether or not Havana's countercultural advocates see themselves as political actors is a fraught one, however, for Havana is a place where all action is potentially political, yet such politics can be mobilized in several concurrent directions at once. Indeed, Havana is a place where seeming paradoxes take some unpacking. It is not uncommon for people to criticize the state and wholeheartedly defend the Revolution in practically the same breath (Holbraad 2014). The fluidity of lived experience requires a certain flexibility in approach, a skill acquired and honed from birth, and rarely set aside. It is therefore not paradoxical, but in fact entirely logical, that young counter-cultural *habaneros* might at once recognize themselves within potentially countercultural/"alternative" aesthetics while at the same time fiercely self-identifying as proudly Cuban, and staunchly defend their choice to stay put rather than leave for Miami.

Indeed, in so doing they arguably follow the Revolutionary ideals they have been taught since infancy. One can be a product of the Revolution, live within it, abide by it, perpetuate and promulgate it, resist it and actively condemn it all at once. Revolutionary Cuba has long defined itself as constituting a powerful "alternative" to capitalist global hegemony, and the Revolution has overseen the continuation of "a long Cuban history of elaborating an alternative version of modernity" (N. Miller 2008, 694). One might even argue that the championing of cultural alterity has not been peripheral to Cuba's self-image, but central to it, and has perhaps been its lasting achievement.

Getting Online at the CDR

I first met William at the famed Fábrica de Arte Cubano[9] while he was shooting images of a local rap artist for his upcoming music video. He was in his early thirties, mixed race, and would have looked at home in any hip-hop video, fusing dreads and a Caribbean beanie hat with a baggy American football T-shirt and sneakers. Like many of his age and cultural cachet in

Havana, he had got into the Fábrica that night for free through his wide array of social contacts, and saw the venue as an important place both for networking and for getting footage of people dressed "the right way." The Fábrica becomes a fashion parade on Fridays, as young *habaneros* take their newest outfit for a night out. William's job was to capture the action and recycle it in music videos to harness an image of Havana as young, hip, and alternative, or in his words, "un Brooklyn a lo cubano" ("a Brooklyn, Cuban-style").

William was from El Cerro, a working-class neighborhood which has also become the heart of Havana's digital boom. Of all of Havana's SNET intranets, El Cerro's is one of the largest and most influential.[10] As a freelance photographer, William's work in the music video business invariably came through contacts, and the SNET proved an invaluable way for him to stay in the loop. When he noticed an upcoming pool party was being advertised on the Súmate network (the SNET's version of Facebook, literally meaning "add yourself" or "join up," which explicitly mirrors the aesthetic of the international social network), he dashed off a quick message in the chat box to find out if they wanted any of it to be filmed for further promotion; within five minutes it was all confirmed and he'd sorted out a weekend of paid work for himself.

For young freelancers like William, uninhibited social connection such as that offered by digital networks is a primary and powerful currency in a media landscape where for the majority, even phone calls and text messages remain prohibitively expensive. As the SNET connection is a set payment per month, rather than per use or per minute as regular Internet access is in Cuba, William can browse as long as he likes, from the privacy of his front room, and make himself available more consistently for upcoming work. Moreover, he can also source the tools of his trade online. In fact, his Zeiss camera lenses were ordered through the network from a neighbor who put up an ad stating his cousin in Miami could (for a price) order things on Amazon and ship them to Cuba.

A few weeks later, to his dismay, William was cut off from El Cerro Cerrao. The guy who administered the network in the immediate streets of William's house had gone abroad, bequeathing his "patch" to a friend, who in turn had decided to up the prices considerably. A few blocks away, we knocked on a door bearing a plaque saying "Presidente del CDR" (President of the Committee for the Defense of the Revolution), only to be invited by Jessica, the local CDR president,[11] into a small apartment with pictures of Che Guevara and Fidel Castro smiling down from the walls onto a central table with a computer and various gaming consoles. Jessica sat on a rocking chair in the corner, re-stitching a dress, while her twenty-eight-year-old son Guillerme and my friend William sat at the computer surveying who else was then connected to the network. Slightly surprised that someone so outwardly in favor of the Revolution would partake of the delights of El Cerro Cerrao, I asked Jessica if she took issue with her son being online all day long. "Oh, not really!" she smiled back at me, "only when he hogs the computer all the time. He has to get off when my girlfriends and I want to watch our soap opera! Anyway, where do you think I got the frames for all those pictures from? Besides, the network is real life [la red es la realidad], it's where you'll find the real Cubans, making ends meet [la red es donde hay los cubanos de verdad, inventando]."

Jessica and her family were further evidence of a truth borne out constantly in the chaotic refrain of daily life in Havana; seeming juxtapositions can be in one instance reified and upheld, only to collapse the following instant in the maelstrom of day-to-day survival. Jessica and her family engaged in ostensibly "counter-Revolutionary" activity on a daily, indeed, hourly basis, yet they also personified much of what the Revolution arguably represented. Moreover, their entire lives were framed by it; the family's apartment (on the top floor) was in a central location so that they could administer the Revolution from their front door to their neighbors; they were in fact its very physical manifestation in the community. For Jessica, real life simply wasn't as black and white as "within the Revolution, everything; against the Revolution, nothing." The hard realities of life demanded a more nuanced negotiation of parallel worlds. Their status as local representatives of the Revolution undoubtedly afforded them certain opportunities, but their comfort was driven almost entirely by their digital entrepreneurship, which provided additional income as and when needed. William and his friends, like most Cubans in their early thirties I knew who had grown up under a more rigid notion of "Revolution," had learned to balance the older social rules of life under socialism with some of the opportunities offered with increasing entrepreneurial opportunity and digital connectivity.

Social Influencing in Havana

When Frank left college, he got himself a *cuentapropista* license and set up a small shop in El Vedado fixing phones. After a few years, and having saved up some money, in 2018 he decided to open up a second business in "social influencing," an emerging commercial space within Havana's expanding digital market. Tall, pale-skinned, and impossibly cool, Frank is a well-known presence in Havana's hipster scene, and is well connected with music producers, models, photographers, bloggers, and the like. Indeed, it was upon realizing that he himself represented and embodied much of what in Havana is deemed "alternative" or "countercultural" that Frank saw a business opportunity: to use digital networks combined with his own social networks and presence to promote alternative events across Havana, and charge in the process. In his own words, his business is:

> An audiovisual platform with the purpose of giving visibility, socializing, and connecting the Cuban alternative world. Our vocation is to create a multidisciplinary space supported by artists, projects, and influencers that exist beyond the conventional framework. We support and defend the essence of the artist, spaces with good taste, good ideas, and the attitude of the dreamer.

Havana has long had an influential "alternative" scene, and indeed, the role of what loosely might be termed "the arts" has always been important in Havana's cultural sphere. For political scientist Sujatha Fernandes, the arts in Cuba are of pivotal importance as a means of "evaluating competing political alternatives" (2006, 3) in a historical moment of growing contradictions, greater repression of formal political activities by the state, and the emergence of new social (and economic) bases for action. Yet crucially, those artists "who work in transnational spaces of production and exhibition address global concerns and issues rather than confront the socialist state directly" (184). The new element in this mix, however, is the immediacy of digital technology, even in a landscape like Havana where Internet access can be so challenging. One still has to move in the right circles to be invited to these events, and in that regard social networking has barely changed in Havana, the only difference being that this activity is now modulating onto networks like Facebook, Instagram, WhatsApp, *el paquete*, and the SNETs, which bring with them further (profitable) opportunities for promotion.

Through his sizable networks, Frank is now able to promote several events per night to targeted audiences across Havana. One Friday evening we went to the launch of a new "clandestine" nightclub in the heart of Chinatown: on the rooftop of what otherwise appeared to be an entirely residential street was perched a new bar designed to resemble an opium den, with portraits of old Chinese-Cuban neighborhood denizens, and various craft beers on the menu. Havana's most exclusive DJ duo—a lesbian couple who mix electronica with Caribbean influences—was at the deck while Havana's young and cool swayed. There was no sign or name on the door; to get in one showed the bouncer a WhatsApp invitation, which was distributed through a closed group. The next night we attended a similar event, this time on a rooftop of an apartment looking down onto the American Embassy. Strobe lighting flecked the pool as models, artists, and musicians garbed in floral T-shirts swigged beer and exchanged Instagram details.

Such events happen every night in London, Paris, New York, and many other cities across the world. Havana is no exception. But what is exceptional is the cultural capital on parade at these nights out in the Cuban capital; every aspect of the proceedings, from the clothing, to the haircuts, to the music, to the slang, demonstrates a close acquaintance with aesthetics and fashion trends outside of Cuba. That is not to say they are wholeheartedly adopted—to be sure, trends are blended with notably "Cuban" styles—but such trends belie both a degree of access to the "outside world" and a degree of interest in alternative symbols of trendiness and cool. This particular party, which involved a fashion parade of the work of Cuba's top designer and a famous local band, put the organizers back about US $10,000, I later learned, which is a significant sum of money anywhere in the world. This was a celebration of social capital and economic affluence, which in contemporary Havana usually involves some degree of foreign contact, as much as of cultural alterity.

For some, increased contact with international cultural counterparts both on and off the island through digital media provides a new facility at finding like-minded people. Sujatha Fernandes has demonstrated how for Cuban rappers their styles are also a way of exhibiting their cross-national identifications, of "asserting a collective sense of black identity in contrast to the racially integrative program of the Cuban state" (2006, 128). Yet at the same time, they continue to promote (some of) the ideals of the Revolution, for they are critical of the emergence of consumerist values and practices among the more commercial rappers, and identify with the official characterization of Cuba as a "rebel nation." Similarly, Havana's LGBTQ community, which for a long time has lived in the shadows of the state, is also using these emerging digital networks to consolidate their position on Havana's cultural events scene. One such conversation took place on a WhatsApp group Frank had set up to promote the Chinatown nightclub opening (figure 12.1). A girl asked if there were any lesbian-friendly events going on that night. A whole new thread started up as suggestions were added to the forum from ordinarily silent observers: in fact there was an invitation-only event happening that very night that would combine Havana's LGBTQ scene with local fusion genres such as "tropical afro-futurism," that blend international influences with local "flavor."

This is a shifting world for millennials in Havana; a world which recognizes taboo class structures, economic prosperity, the profitability of new digital enterprises, and "bling" (broadly defined), but which still pays lip

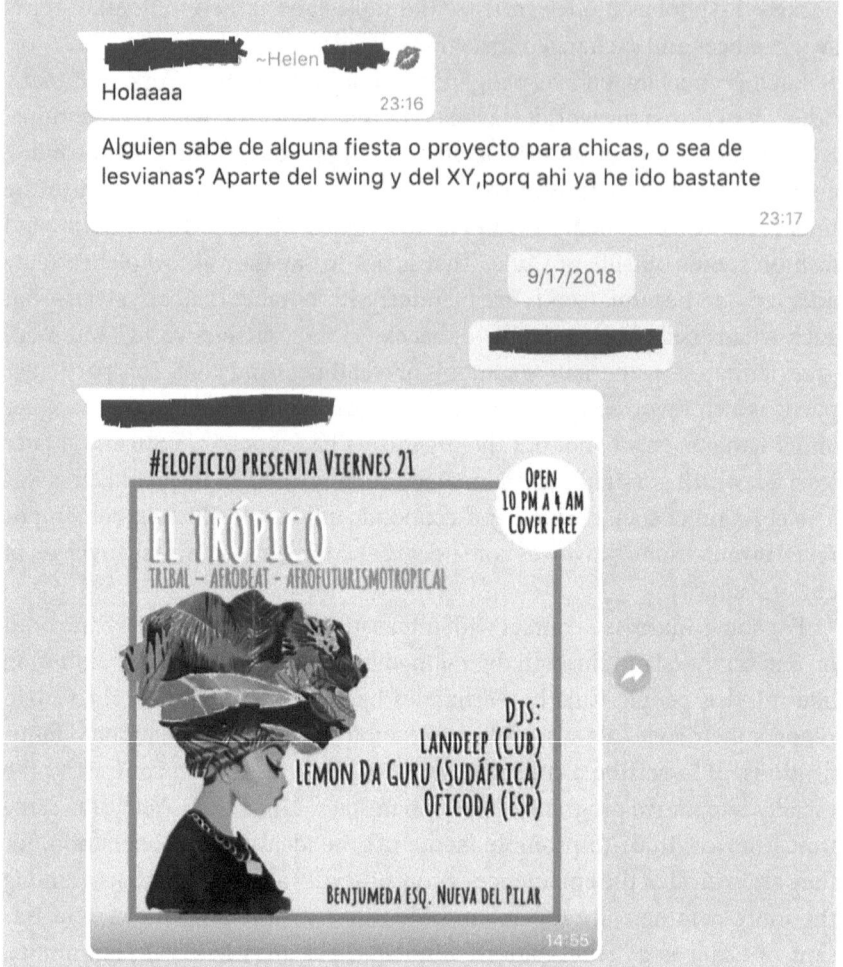

Figure 12.1. WhatsApp thread seeking "alternative" lesbian cultural events. Author's photo, September 2018.

service to rules from the old egalitarian order. The word "alternative" is a problematic one, and to be successful, digital entrepreneurs like Frank have to code switch between social worlds as they navigate a new path. Frank has learned this the hard way, and as he sits idly in his office connected to his Nanobox station Wi-Fi booster, he inspects each customer as they walk in the door to evaluate how they should be dealt with. Several of the older customers who frequent his original business (the one that fixes cell phones) bristle as they notice that the term *compañero* (comrade) is slowly and quietly being displaced by *señor* (the more bourgeois "sir" or "Mr.").

One evening after office hours, as we sat browsing YouTube videos, one such older gentleman passed by. He was high up in the neighborhood's CDR, and wanted help upgrading his phone's software. The news that the shop had closed, but that he was welcome to return in the morning, was not met with the same politeness with which it was supplied. "Profiteering lowlifes [*delincuentes aprovechadores*] like you aren't going to tell me what I can and can't do!" Frank shrugged at me, "Some people don't like change I guess!"

As Frank's new business has boomed, he has also come under increasing scrutiny from the state. In the week running up to the expensive rooftop party he was organizing, he was pulled over on his electric scooter by the police as many as three times a day and asked for his "papers." To Frank's mind, the increase in such generalized "harassment" was directly linked with his quick success in growing his business. A false denunciation by a neighbor the following week led him to be thrown in an overcrowded jail cell for three days while his business partner came up with the money to pay a fine. Frank emerged with a black eye and a determination to make his business even more successful. But this pressure has not gone unheeded either, he is now making inquiries into obtaining a passport, with the hope of expanding his business to Mexico or Panama and so be able to continue to grow unimpeded. In Havana's digital entrepreneurial landscape, an invisible "line" patrolled by the state still limits the degree to which one can expand or prosper unchecked.[12] In its effort to "update" socialism and pump some market-driven efficiency and productivity into the moribund Cuban economy, the government has explicitly outlawed the private concentration of wealth or property.

Liminal Public Spheres, "Revolution," and "Resistance"

For William, Jessica, and Frank, the emerging digital public forums of social media in Havana are providing new spaces for locating and connecting with like-minded people, and making a living. Emerging digital technologies have the power to divert social encounters into a somehow altogether more ephemeral "space," and therein lies their latent potency. Social media have long been associated with locating new publics and what Juris refers to as "emerging logics of aggregation," that is, their supposedly inherent ability to harness otherwise disparate energies and unite "underground" resistances into movements (Juris 2012).

Some individuals in Havana do utilize digital technologies for political (counter-Revolutionary) purposes. *El paquetico* is an excellent example. Much like *el paquete*, *el paquetico* or "the little package" circulates hand to hand through flash drives, typically once a week, and mostly in Havana. It contains items downloaded from the Internet that are censored by the Cuban state and studiously avoided or filtered out by the compilers of the more tame and commercial—if still independent and widely sought after—*paquete*. *El paquetico* normally includes news reels from Miami Spanish-language television broadcasts, humor (often at the expense of the Castro brothers), and articles that express critical opinions of the Cuban State in one form or another. The founder of *el paquetico*[13] consciously imitated the methods of distribution that have been so successful in *el paquete* to provide what he terms an "alternative voice," albeit one which he only dares circulate to a small circle of trusted friends, who in turn circulate it further. Even here then, amidst a conscious network of resistance within Havana, digital social media are not typically implemented as widespread "calls to arms"; instead, WhatsApp, Facebook, and Havana's indigenous digital networks of distribution are utilized to share content with known and trusted friends, and thus celebrate the privacy of these digital spaces, in contrast to the public spaces of Wi-Fi access across Cuba.

Daniel Miller and his colleagues have defined the emerging uses of social media as "the colonization of the space between traditional broadcast and private dyadic communication, providing people with a scale of group size and degrees of privacy" that they term "scalable sociality" (D. Miller et al. 2016, 9). I would add that in the context of contemporary Cuba as both an authoritarian state and one with limited digital access, these emerging public/private digital "spaces" are of critical importance in capturing the dynamics of Cuban sociality, which in turn is in a constant state of negotiation between the supposedly hard binaries of state/public, power/freedom, etc. For Paloma Duong, the public domain in Cuba reveals

> an autonomous subjectivity increasingly invested, and exercised, in this sense of "news about ourselves." The search for, and dissemination of, a certain kind of individual data links the subject as an individual to a larger political body, offering a challenge both to prevailing accounts of social autonomy and to information blackouts mediated by the state. (2013, 11)[14]

Certainly in terms of *effect*, public domains have this capacity in Cuba. Change, albeit gradual and piecemeal, can occur as digital technologies facilitate greater discussion around political or politicized topics. In this way, traditional patterns of cultural and media hegemony are slowly being reworked (and perhaps undermined). It would be impossible to rule out the potential role of digital technologies and social media in these changes.

Yet while there are clear exceptions, mostly among bloggers and journalists, who might use such technologies for explicitly political ends, the vast majority of my contacts who regularly used these networks for countercultural or "alternative" motives were not doing so in a consciously political (and much less a counter-Revolutionary) way. For them, these networks are a way of connecting with friends, sharing pictures, and organizing a night out (but not a protest); a chance to dance, not to revolt. As I have described above, some take an additional step and utilize digital social networks in entrepreneurial ways. An ethnographically informed analysis of the rising use of digital technologies and social media in Havana must consider the majority, for whom such networks are merely an extension of their everyday lives, which they do not necessarily view in political terms, but in the far more nuanced and negotiated terms of *invento* and *sobrevivencia* (survival). This is not to dispute the potential for political action simply as a consequence of the increasing use of the Internet among millennials, but an important distinction should be drawn here between the majority—who seek individual expression, social connectedness, and an amorphous sense of "alterity" in their use of digital media—and a tiny minority, for whom political action is the primary, conscious, and intentional aim.[15]

I agree with Sujatha Fernandes therefore that these "artistic public spheres" are not bound, but rather overlap with market forces, state institutions, and the countercultural as "sites of interaction and discussion among ordinary citizens generated through the medium of art and popular culture" (Fernandes 2006, 2–3).[16] To recognize the possibilities for transformative politics within digital networks in Cuba is not to say that these networks are themselves associated with resistance or dissent by Cubans. While some political actors undoubtedly do use digital media to facilitate their political agenda, my own research shows that they often use Havana's digital networks as alternative means of contacting preexisting acquaintances to discuss mutual topics of interest, not to recruit members to new systematic movements of resistance. Mona Rosendahl (1997) has suggested that the widespread experience of participation in the Revolution has been one of the main reasons for its survival, and indeed, people's experiences of participation have not been limited to attending military parades or watching state news broadcasts. Participation has been cultural as well as economic, social, and political, and thus the Cuban Revolution cannot easily be separated out from any one aspect of everyday lived experience.

This logic plays out in the case of all the stories I have shared here. William spent an increasing number of hours connected to the SNET as the network provided him with distraction from his troubles, entertainment, an "edge" over competitors to gain more work, and ultimately, a way of realizing his social capital into more tangible assets, a strategy common to most *cuentapropistas*. His interests in working in the "alternative" sphere of rap and hip-hop music video production arose not so much because of any messages of political resistance that those movements might embody, but more because of a sense of solidarity with other Afro-Cubans, many of whom he had grown up with in El Cerro. His introduction to the world of hip-hop music videos had in fact come through the cousin of his *Santero* priest, who knew he was looking for work. William did have a strong desire to leave Cuba, and discussed this in the SNET's chatrooms with friends, but this desire was related more to his desire to be reunited with his children (who had moved to Italy with their mother) and to work on the production of the more extensive international music videos he consumed through *el paquete*, than it was to a political motive to leave Cuba.

Then there's Frank, whose "call to arms" with which I opened this paper seemed so political. His focus upon branding himself a "social influencer" has certainly got him noticed, and of late has attracted increasing levels of attention from state actors. On the third occasion he was pulled over by police and had his electric scooter impounded, he furiously muttered, "¡Esto se llama RE-PRE-SIÓN!" ("This is called REPRESSION!"), and vowed to expedite his attempts to get a foreign passport. Yet the following day, I heard him criticize "how hard things are" ("la cosa está dura") and, in practically the same breath, defend socialism from the slander of some Americans in a bar who had wrongly assumed such things were black and white in Cuba.

His primary motivation in curating and promoting "la alternatividad cubana" (Cuban alterity) was a deep-seated sense of pride in an *habanero* identity that fused various multicultural elements and which he saw as defying both foreign appropriating attempts to pigeonhole his city as increasing flows of tourism advance hegemonic depictions of *cubanidad,* and the popular (or "*bajo*") cultural forms of *cubaneo* that dominate Havana's more public spaces. His objective was more a cultural project of what he would deem "progression" (*progreso),* and he lauded digital social media more for its ability to exclude than to include. Ironically, for a kind of media that is often uncritically assumed to democratize the communicational sphere for everyone, the "public" spheres of Havana's emerging digital spaces were optimal for their relative privacy and exclusivity when compared with word-of-mouth (*radio bemba* or the rumor mill) on the street, which included not only "lower" forms of culture but also increased risk of potential condemnation from or conflict with others.

Finally, we have Jessica and her son Guillerme, who perhaps most neatly encapsulate the paradox of interactions in everyday life in Havana. Jessica saw no contradiction in both working for the state—indeed physically representing the state within her community as president of the local CDR—and systematically disobeying or undermining it. In her mind, the two elements were both fundamentally true and necessary. She had been born into the Revolution. Her parents had fought for it and had been respected members of the Party. So as she and her mother polished the CDR plaque on the door, her son perched at the computer table, selling cushions the pair had stitched with various aphorisms using threads bought online via a neighbor's relative abroad on one screen, and launching various memes at friends through the chat forum open on another. Spotting my own incredulous look as I surveyed the scene from the opposite corner, she chuckled and said, rather appropriately using a sewing metaphor, "la vida es un labor de retazos fascinante, no?!" ("Life's a fascinating patchwork isn't it?!").

Conclusion

The supposed democratizing potential of digital media has captured the attention of an international neoliberal set and there has clearly been an expectation that such movements would impact Cuba.[17] Such debates, when combined with an oftentimes fetishizing view of Cuba as a fading bastion of an "offline" world, have centered on the phrase "digital revolution," which, when applied to Cuba, is doubly intoxicating. In Havana, which enjoys greater digital connectivity than the rest of Cuba, this has certainly been true for political activists, bloggers, and independent journalists, many of whom have received extensive attention from foreign journalists and researchers alike (including numerous chapters of this volume). As Cristina Venegas describes,

> [d]igital media seeps into the everyday life of Cubans just as currents of political transition breathe greater dimension to individual expression and visions for the future. The generation of Cubans joining the digital era are grandchildren of the Revolution, without firsthand memories of its victories and accomplishments. Their lot has been defined by the hardship of extreme times. This generation and its aspirations, complaints, and desires is changing and intensifying the nature of opposition to the government through fresh forms of expression. (2010, 184)

Yet I have argued here that, while digital media have undoubtedly realized new opportunities for those in Havana who wish to express counter-Revolutionary views, these voices are a distinct minority among Havana's emerging digital millennials. The majority of the capital's millennials are drawn more to these networks to share selfies and memes than political opinions, much less galvanize collective resistance to the state. This is true even of a smaller subset that identifies with growing countercultural or "alternative" movements in Havana, despite the fact that this very "alterity" is a problematic ideology to proclaim or identity to embody in Cuba. Emerging digital millennial entrepreneurs are utilizing Havana's digital media networks to forge and further their own career paths, but this principally involves realizing social connections with people they already know, not using digital media to reach into "the beyond." Moreover, in some cases it is the very exclusivity of certain digital networks, as opposed to their potential for inclusion, that is so appetizing to many of my "hipster *habanero*" contacts.

Finally, a close reading of ethnographic data points to how conceptions of "revolution" and "resistance," or of state and civil society as diametrically opposed terms, is restrictive in its analytical scope when applied to the Cuban case. Not only are these terms ideologically loaded and frequently co-opted in a Cuban context, they also ignore much of the social, economic, and moral complexity navigated by Cubans on a daily basis. A nuanced analysis of how countercultural movements are emerging and utilizing digital networks in Havana reveals a seemingly paradoxical truth: these "movements," if we can even call them that, can both express tension with the Revolutionary project and the state, and at the same time embody and even celebrate part of its message. Most importantly, many of these countercultural or "alternative" actors do not see themselves as political actors, and indeed, frequently and quite explicitly avoid participating in what they consider to be "politics."

Perhaps then, emerging digital networks in Havana highlight the death of the binary in Cuba, where moves toward a world where self-employed "social influencers" can even exist are perhaps a tacit admission that old realities were unsustainable. Digital technologies merely reveal in a new way the complex reality of Cuban sociality that has in fact long existed: within the Revolution everything; against it, around it, through it, with it, across it, in spite of it . . . everything.

Notes

1. Title translation: "Toward an alternative Cuba"? Translation of message: "Come and find out about our platform, take part, take action in this battle to document and show the world an ALTERNATIVE Cuba!"

2. Broadly understood as the generation born from the mid-1980s to the mid-1990s, who thus lived through the "special period" of economic hardship in Cuba (following the

demise of the Soviet Union) as children, and have set up their own businesses as Cuba has "transitioned" into a new economic period.

3. I understand "liminality" here in the sense used by anthropologists Arnold Van Gennep and Victor Turner in their studies of religion and ritual, whereby they describe an ambiguity that occurs in the middle stage of rites of passage, when participants no longer hold their pre-ritual status but have not yet begun the transition to the status they will hold when the rite is complete (Gennep 1977; Turner 1969). In this case, I allude to the ambiguity experienced by those entrepreneurs poised between what might (very crudely) be characterized as "socialist" and "postsocialist" Cuba.

4. The word "revolution" has a particular ideological resonance in the Cuban context. In this chapter, I use "revolution" with a small *r* to refer to the concept more broadly, and "Revolution" with a capital *R* to refer to the Cuban Revolution of 1959 and the ideologies attached to it. The same is true for the adjectives "revolutionary" and "Revolutionary."

5. These terms are discussed fully later in the chapter, but in brief, *el paquete* refers to a network for the distribution of digital content spanning the island of Cuba, while SNETs or "Street Networks" (in Spanish: *la red*) are akin to intranets and operate as digital networks for sharing content within neighborhoods in Havana, as well as in some other towns across Cuba.

6. This meant using Wi-Fi hot spots in public parks, at least up until a limited 3G mobile service was launched in December 2018.

7. The notion of socioeconomic class is a problematic one in relation to Cuba, given the Revolution's intention to dismantle class disparities. Nonetheless, Cuban society remains stratified according to various socioeconomic principles (for example, access to relatives abroad who can provide remittances), and as such, I follow others in maintaining Cuban society is driven by notions of class (Eckstein 2010; Weinreb 2009), and, indeed, this is a crucial element influencing access to digital technologies on the island.

8. Fernando Ortiz (1881–1969), Cuba's premier anthropologist, defined *la cubanidad* as "the generic condition of [being] Cuban" (1940, 166). *Cubanía, cubiche*, and *cubaneo*, however, refer to what is considered a dominant Cuban temperament (Pérez-Firmat 1997, 4), which in contemporary Havana typically suggests an overt liking of *reggaetón* music, tight clothing, and lots of "bling," and overall brings to mind an aesthetic associated with the lower classes.

9. The "Cuban Art Factory" or F.A.C. is an old peanut oil factory in the far western section of Havana's once upscale Vedado neighborhood, which has recently been converted into a one-of-a-kind venue that celebrates cultural alterity among Havana's hipster elite and foreign tourists alike, but which is also managed indirectly by the state. It includes multiple bars, music and performance spaces, an art gallery, and a private "*paladar*" restaurant.

10. In local argot, this local area network is proudly referred to as "El Cerro Cerrao," or "El Cerro closed off."

11. Committees for the Defense of the Revolution (Spanish: Comités de Defensa de la Revolución), or the CDR, are a network of neighborhood committees across Cuba. The organizations, described as the "eyes and ears of the Revolution," exist to promote social welfare and report on counterrevolutionary activity. As of 2010, 8.4 million Cubans of the national population of 11.2 million were registered as CDR members (Sánchez 2010).

12. See also Henken's discussion of "la linea roja" (Henken 2016).

13. I conducted ethnographic interviews from July to August 2018 with the founder of *el paquetico*, but for the sake of anonymity do not reveal his name here. For more about *el paquetico*, see Henken's article, "The Opium of the *Paquete*" (2021).

14. Also see Duong's contribution to this volume, chapter 14, titled "Images of Ourselves."

15. This point echoes the central argument of Geoffray's contribution to this volume, chapter 6, "Digital Critique in Cuba."

16. See also Gray and Kapcia 2008; Fernández 2000.

17. Such as the new U.S. Cuba Internet Task Force (Marsh 2018) and prior U.S. State Department attempts to spur regime change via "liberation technology" (The Guardian 2014).

References

Ashby, Timothy. 2001. "Silicon Island: Cuba's Digital Revolution." *Harvard International Review* 23 (3): 14–18.

Castro, Fidel. 1961. *Palabras a Los Intelectuales*. Havana: Ediciones del Consejo Nacional de Cultura.

Cearns, Jennifer. 2021. "Packaging Cuban Media: Communities of Digital Sharing in Cuba and Its Diaspora." *Cuban Studies* 50.

Comaroff, Jean, and John L. Comaroff. 2001. "Millennial Capitalism: First Thoughts on a Second Coming." In *Millennial Capitalism and the Culture of Neoliberalism*, edited by Jean Comaroff and John L. Comaroff, 1–56. Durham, N.C: Duke University Press.

Du Graf, Lauren, and Rose Marie Cromwell. n.d. "Cuban Revolutions." Topic. Accessed October 12, 2018. https://www.topic.com/cuban-revolutions.

Duong, Paloma. 2013. "Bloggers Unplugged: Amateur Citizens, Cultural Discourse, and Public Sphere in Cuba." *Journal of Latin American Cultural Studies* 22 (4): 1–23.

Eckstein, Susan. 2010. "Remittances and Their Unintended Consequences in Cuba." *World Development* 38 (7): 1047–1055.

Fernandes, Sujatha. 2006. *Cuba Represent! Cuban Arts, State Power, and the Making of New Revolutionary Cultures*. Duke University Press.

Fernández, Damián J. 2000. *Cuba and the Politics of Passion*. Austin: University of Texas Press.

Freedom on the Net. 2018. "Cuba Country Report." https://freedomhouse.org/report/freedom-net/2018/cuba.

García Martínez, Antonio. 2017. "Inside Cuba's DIY Internet Revolution." *Wired*, July 26, 2017.

Gennep, Arnold van. 1977. *The Rites of Passage*. Edited by Gabrielle L. Caffee and Monika Vizedom. London: Routledge.

Gray, Alexander I., and Antoni Kapcia. 2008. *The Changing Dynamic of Cuban Civil Society*. Gainesville: University of Florida Press.

Helft, Miguel. 2015. "No Internet? No Problem. Inside Cuba's Tech Revolution." *Forbes*, July 1, 2015.

Henken, Ted A. 2014. "Is Cuba 'Open for Business'?" *Cuba Counterpoints*.

Henken, Ted A. 2017. "Cuba's Digital Millennials: Independent Digital Media and Civil Society on the Island of the Disconnected." *Social Research* 84 (2): 429–456.

Henken, Ted A. 2021. "The Opium of the *Paquete*: State Censorship, Private Self-Censorship, and the Content Distribution Strategies of Cuba's Emergent, Independent Digital Media Startups." *Cuban Studies* 50.

Holbraad, Martin. 2014. "Revolución o Muerte: Self-Sacrifice and the Ontology of Cuban Revolution." *Ethnos* 79 (3): 365–87.

Juris, Jeffrey S. 2012. "Reflections on #Occupy Everywhere: Social Media, Public Space, and Emerging Logics of Aggregation." *American Ethnologist* 39 (2): 259–79.

Marsh, Sarah. 2018. "U.S. State Department Creates Cuba Internet Task Force." *Reuters*, January 23, 2018.

Miller, Daniel, Elisabetta Costa, Nell Haynes, et al. 2016. *How the World Changed Social Media*. Edited by Daniel Miller. London: UCL Press.

Miller, Nicola. 2008. "A Revolutionary Modernity: The Cultural Policy of the Cuban Revolution." *Journal of Latin American Studies* 40: 675–96.

Ortiz, Fernando. 1940. "Los Factores Humanos de La Cubanidad." *Revista Bimestre Cubana* 21.

Pérez-Firmat, Gustavo. 1997. "'A Willingness of the Heart: Cubanidad, Cubaneo, Cubanía.'" *Cuban Studies Association Occasional Papers* 8.

Press, Larry. 2015. "El Paquete Update—Cuba's Largest Private Employer?" *The Internet in Cuba* blog, September 14, 2015.

Press, Larry. 2017. "Data on SNET and a Few Suggestions for ETECSA." *The Internet in Cuba* blog, November 10, 2017.

Rosendahl, Mona. 1997. *Inside the Revolution: Everyday Life in Socialist Cuba*. Ithaca and London: Cornell University Press.

Sanchez, Isabel. 2010. "Cuba's Neighborhood Watches: 50 Years of Eyes, Ears." Agence France-Presse (AFP), September 27, 2010.

The Guardian. 2014. "US Secretly Created 'Cuban Twitter' to Stir Unrest and Undermine Government." April 3, 2014.

Turner, Victor. 1969. *The Forest of Symbols: Aspects of Ndembu Ritual*. Ithaca, NY: Cornell University Press.

Venegas, Cristina. 2010. *Digital Dilemmas: The State, the Individual, and Digital Media in Cuba*. New Brunswick, NJ: Rutgers University Press.

Weinreb, Amelia. 2009. *Cuba in the Shadow of Change: Daily Life in the Twilight of the Revolution*. Gainesville: University Press of Florida.

V

CULTURE AND SOCIETY

13

Without Initiation Ceremonies
Cuban Literary and Cultural E-zines, 2000–2010

WALFRIDO DORTA

In the early 2000s, a group of young Cuban writers and artists published a series of literary e-zines, some of which were active until the end of that decade.[1] *Cacharro(s)* (2003–2005), *33 y 1/tercio* (2005–2010), and *The Revolution Evening Post* (2006–2008) are three such e-zines that will be discussed here. Despite their importance, they have not received the critical attention they deserve. That importance lies, among other things, in the fact that they pluralized the artistic and critical discourses on the Cuban cultural landscape through different strategies which included the dissemination of texts not published by official state institutions. Furthermore, these e-zines displaced the sociability dynamics from the institutional context (controlled by the state and traversed by filters of ideology and politics) to the "fields" of e-mails and portable data storage devices, intermediate spaces without full virtuality (due to the lack of Internet connection at the time), but much less controlled by state supervision.

Thus, these e-zines challenged the digital disconnect in Cuba through their distribution via e-mail, e-mail newsletters, and thumb drives. They were never affiliated with any official institution (or opposition political group, for that matter). Most of them were created before the explosion of blogs and digital media that took place on the island during the second decade of the twenty-first century. Some of them are currently archived on blogs and websites, but can be hard to find due to their digital dispersion.[2] I propose that these projects are a direct precedent of the Cuban "independent digital mediasphere" and constitute the prequel to the coalescence of "Cuba's independent media ecosystem" (Henken 2017, 430, 453), specifically regarding the specialized media on Cuban literature and culture. I also hold that these cultural e-zines served as key precedents for the future appearance, pluralization, and "diasporization" of the Cuban blogosphere.

Specifically, this chapter focuses on three e-zines and describes their distinctive characteristics and editorial profiles through their content and design. I begin by introducing ideas developed by the scholars Cristina Venegas, Paloma Duong, and Ted Henken about the Cuban digital media-sphere and the alternative blogosphere. I also introduce the points of contact between these projects and *Diáspora(s)*, a prior analog media venture. Each of the following sections focuses on one specific e-zine. First, I comment on the transgressions of *Cacharro(s)* in terms of its editorial policy and its covers, as well as its perhaps deliberately ambiguous political orientation. Second, I review *33 y 1/tercio*'s intermedial dialogue with music and the record as objects, as well as the multiplication of referential universes that this e-zine brings forth centered around not only literature, but also television and punk culture. Finally, I comment on the *The Revolution Evening Post* from the ideas of seriality and spectacle, as well as the referential shift from the written word to multimedia that it promotes; a change that is innate to the young Cuban writers who began to publish in the early 2000s, and who are mostly the protagonists behind the e-zines analyzed here (sometimes referred to as la Generación Cero [the Zero Generation]).

New Citizen Avatars: Cultural E-zines and Autonomous Subjectivities

Scholars like Cristina Venegas (2010), Paloma Duong (2013) and Ted Henken (2017), among others, have studied the development of digital media and the alternative blogosphere in Cuba. The e-zines that this essay focuses on do not fit within the profile of the examples they study,[3] among other reasons, because these e-zines were created mostly offline although using digital technology. They were distributed via e-mail or on thumb drives and did not originally "live on" the Web, in part because very few Cubans (including their creators) had Internet access at the time. Nevertheless, I argue that projects like *Cacharro(s)*, *33 y 1/tercio*, and *The Revolution Evening Post* are examples of "personal platforms and intellectual communities" that "test the boundaries of censorship and expression" as stated by Venegas in her pioneering book *Digital Dilemmas*. Furthermore, the creators of these cultural and literary e-zines were motivated by the desire to create "alternative social identities," "[n]ew avatars of citizens, (. . .) [and] [a] new social imagination" (Venegas 2010, 184).

For her part, Duong (2013, 386) studies Cuban independent blogs, as "a vehicle for the repositioning of autonomous subjectivities" through the use of digital media. This description can also apply to the literary and culture e-zines of the first decade of the 2000s, for they too wanted to create new spaces of expression outside the official institutions, and in that manner challenge not only the technological inadequacy, but also the regulatory framework for discourse inside the island. Despite their inadequate offline production and distribution conditions (and thus their slim possibilities of "success" and of reaching a wide audience), the e-zines were "emergent democratic discourses" (384) as Duong points out regarding the later independent blogs.

Like those later blogs, the e-zines were published between 2000 and 2010 by young creators who did not wait to be authorized by the official channels of legitimization, but instead decided to build their own distribution channels and audiences through the meager technology resources available in the early 2000s. Duong goes on to suggest that the practices of the alternative Cuban blogosphere gave visibility to a new political entity: the "amateur citizen," a public figure that combines cultural amateurism and amateur citizenship, while also embodying an emergent democratic ethos. The figure of the "amateur citizen" is also a way to understand the culture and literary e-zines and their promoters, more so when they were dealing, in the early 2000s, with technologies and tools that would become more widespread in the second half of the decade; during which the alternative blogosphere and the Cuban independent digital mediasphere had access to more tech resources, even if Cuba continues to have one of the lowest rates of Internet connectivity in the region.

It is worth noting the remarkable youth, at the time, of the collaborators in the e-zines (and later in many of the blogs) who included Orlando Luis Pardo Lazo (thirty-two, born in 1971), Elena Molina (seventeen, born in 1988), Lizabel Mónica (twenty-two, born in 1981), and Jorge E. Lage (twenty-six, born in 1979). It adds an important distinction to the figure of the "amateur citizen" because to the very few experiences of autonomy that they may have had is added their scarce formal training in handling technological resources. Despite the e-zines' restrictions in circulation (which was limited to e-mails, newsletters, and thumb drives) and the lack of larger or more complete digital interaction (that was possible later on platforms like blogs, websites, and eventually social networks like Facebook and Twitter), these projects were, for their creators, exercises of individual autonomy that "call into question the normative patterns of participation inherent to an understanding of civil society where popular mobilization stands in for participatory citizenship" (Duong 2013, 384).

There is also a continuity of intention between these three e-zines and a prior project promoted by the writers Carlos A. Aguilera, Rolando Sánchez

Mejías, and Pedro Marqués, among others: *Diáspora(s)* magazine (1997–2002). The dangers of the analog distribution of *Diáspora(s)*, which was illegally disseminated in Cuba through physical photocopies, contrast with the relative ease and legality of the e-zines, which were distributed by e-mail. Yet, the e-zines are a continuation of the disruptive intention of *Diáspora(s)* when it comes to positioning themselves outside official channels, given that both its content and distribution strategy short-circuited Cuba's institutional framework and filter. The young creators of these e-zines saw the distribution of cultural—especially literary—texts as woefully inadequate, so they responded with their own distribution strategies that broke the state's restrictive logic in a gesture similar to that of *Diáspora(s)*. Herein lies a continuity of political gestures in the sense in which Jacques Rancière (2006) conceptualizes politics: as the reconfiguration of the distribution of the sensible; an introduction of "dissensus" (as opposed to consensus) and acts of subjectivization starting from the logic of the disagreement.[4]

According to the writer, blogger, and activist Orlando Luis Pardo Lazo (2014) (who was involved in both *Cacharro(s)* and *The Revolution Evening Post*), in the early 2000s young artists and writers lacked cultural projects with the dynamic energy of previous projects like "Paideia," "La Azotea de Reina," or *Diáspora(s)* magazine.[5] The e-zines created by the young artists and writers fit, according to Pardo Lazo, right in the emptiness left by the disappearance of those projects of intellectual autonomy. The advent of the new century brought silence, but also a new regenerative opportunity: "[it] didn't bring the 2000s, but the '0s. We had to start from zero," stated the artist sarcastically (2014, 9).

Despite the lack of Internet connection, those years were, paradoxically, a "golden decade of digital magazines" (Pardo Lazo 2014, 10). This phenomenon is seen by Pardo Lazo as "eminently urban, Havanan [*habanero*], and amateur, but with the airs of inhabiting a First World megalopolis" (11). Without previous ceremonies that would allow these young ones to publish their texts (lacking both the official mechanisms that would give them a certain legality and the official recognition as published authors), the early 2000s e-zines recognized and promoted atomicity and multiplicity as signs of identity. In common they have the delocalization of the digital virtuality: their distribution through that same virtuality, and their aspiration to disseminate texts and images beyond physical contexts and state institutions. Their different editorial poetics and naming policies are witnesses to the multiplicity of their interests and aesthetics. *Cacharro(s)*'s dossiers represent an ironic game with state surveillance that does not exclude an acute awareness about the transgressions to said state surveillance. *33 y 1/tercio*'s music tracks suggest an intentional levity associated with pop music and youth culture. *The Revolution Evening Post*'s "episodes" evoke seriality and spectacle.

Cacharro(s): Transgressive "Dossiers"

The e-zine *Cacharro(s)* was published between 2003 and 2005, releasing a total of seven issues. Its main coordinator was Jorge A. Aguiar Díaz.[6] For the first three issues, the team consisted of Rebeca Duarte (the pseudonym of Lizabel Mónica),[7] Pedro Marqués de Armas,[8] Juan Carlos Flores,[9] and another team member who wrote under the pseudonym Pia McHabana (Orlando Luis Pardo Lazo).[10] In the other four issues, only Aguiar Díaz and Duarte appear. The e-zine was distributed mostly by e-mail, but also by thumb drive. It was sent to approximately five hundred e-mail addresses, in groups of one hundred at a time due to Gmail's restrictions. It was one of the first Cuban e-zines distributed via e-mail to recipients both inside and outside the island. However, its coordinators received confirmation of delivery mostly from people abroad.[11]

Cacharro(s) can be seen as a continuation of *Diáspora(s)* magazine to which it "pays homage" through its own title (the final *s* placed between parentheses), although the general tone of the e-zine is more direct, crude, and playful than that of *Diáspora(s)* (Timmer 2013). The staff at *Cacharro(s)* and the roster of what appears under the name Proyecto Cacharro(s) combined both members of *Diáspora(s)* like Pedro Marqués and Ismael González Castañer, as well as younger writers like Lizabel Mónica and Pardo Lazo. Conscious transgression is central to *Cacharro(s)*, thus the presentation of each issue as a "dossier" that contains files, texts, and images not preapproved by Cuba's cultural commissars, and therefore discarded as not belonging within state ideology and to the "insular tradition" (Aguiar Díaz 2003, 5) echoing the careers of the Cuban writers mentioned by Aguiar Díaz (2003, 5) in the "Preliminar" from "dossier 1": Jorge Mañach (1898–1961), Lino Novás Calvo (1903–1983), Calvert Casey (1924–1969), and Guillermo Cabrera Infante (1929–2005).

Cacharro(s) is built from these "detritus" rescued and given new meaning in a narrative that highlights their transgressive potential. The e-zine is also built on a simultaneously meager and rich collection of texts which is common to all the e-zines analyzed here. Given the precarious access to cultural products from abroad, these texts are the product of a labor that is at the same time patient and nonsystematic. The editors accumulated them from different sources and then assembled them into these e-zines. Obviously, from this reassemblage an editorial policy is born, but we should not ignore the fact that said policy is a mix of equal parts contingency and deliberate intention.

These "dossiers" are designed, ironically, for readers-censors who would ban their content if they could exert their control given that each issue includes censored authors (like Cabrera Infante and Lorenzo García Vega) and because the covers contain a series of transgressions (illustrated below). Thus, each issue of *Cacharro(s)* is the victorious result of an escape from control of the censors. In *"Preliminar,"* a text that functions as the e-zine's manifesto or editorial poetics, Aguilar Díaz refers to the impossibility (legal and material) of the existence of independent magazines (2003, 5). Against such impossibility, *Cacharro(s)* was produced.

Cacharro(s)'s presentation shares many characteristics with the discourse of *Diáspora(s)*. In both there is a criticism of "literary nationalism"; of the Cuban literary field "so pacified and conforming that is no longer a field but a Garden of Eden for certain state fictions"; and of the "provincialism of Cuban literature" (Aguilar Díaz 2013, 5). There is also a consciousness of "literary guerrilla" (7) that aspires to undermine those political constraints in the Cuban cultural field that dictate what can and cannot be published. Hence, *Cacharro(s)*, like *Diáspora(s)* before it, pushes for a rereading of the island's cultural and literary archives through authors like Reinaldo Arenas and Guillermo Rosales (to whom they dedicated the e-zine's first issue and who—having died by suicide in exile—were ignored or actively censored in Cuba); or filmmakers like Nicolás Guillén Landrián, excluded from the national culture scene for many years. Texts and authors in *Cacharro(s)* overlap to a great extent with those of *Diáspora(s)*. This overlap may be seen as a desire by Aguiar Díaz and the rest of the e-zine's team to extend the disruptive effects of *Diáspora(s)* and to create a confluence of interests around the publication of censored authors and the criticism of literary nationalism.[12]

A brief text that opens issue 6/7 (2004) addresses the discomfort of trying to locate the e-zine within existing political categories. Such classifications are plagued by clichés and misunderstandings that failed to account for the transgressive nature of *Cacharro(s)*. The important thing is that the e-zine was produced in Cuba under adverse circumstances, without institutional backing of any kind (governmental or private, inside or outside of Cuba). That "orphanhood," however, is not enough to classify the e-zine as "independent" or "dissident," categories loaded with implications in the Cuban political landscape from which *Cacharro(s)* wanted to distance itself, or at least question. In this way, we can understand *Cacharro(s)*'s political gesture according to Duong's ideas about the Cuban alternative blogosphere (2013, 386) which "displaces the language of traditional ideological opposition used by dissident discourse with the demands of an informed citizen." That positionality inserts a political subject that does not understand civic participation in accordance with teleological narratives, but which looks at the public sphere as a set of plural interests subject to negotiation.

Each issue of *Cacharro(s)* opens with a transgressive cover. This ironic and subversive exercise "rescues" texts from (mostly official) publications whose placement within *Cacharro(s)* allows them to be read as samples of an absurd compilation. For example, issue 6/7 creates a temporal deception by picturing the chief of the secret police on its cover without clarifying the date or origin of the document. The picture thus becomes an archetypical example of a member of the secret police who surveils and enforces the existing order, and who is celebrated for it in a pompous fashion regardless of the reigning political regime. Other images are even more ironic. The cover for issue 2 (2003), for example, reproduces the cover of the pedagogical pamphlet *Course on Scientific Communism* published by the Ministry of Public Health in 1980 (figure 13.1). Further disruption and absurdity occurs when the reader realizes that the course was offered by Havana Psychiatric Hospital.

Further deepening this sense of irony is the fact that the issue is dedicated to the poet Luis Marimón (1952–1995) and the filmmaker Nicolás Guillén Landrián (1938–2003) both of whom were marginalized by the official Cuban cultural apparatus, eventually falling victim to insanity. Luis Marimón left Cuba for the United States in 1994 and died there a year later from alcoholism. By 2003, when issue 2 of *Cacharro(s)* appeared, his work was largely unknown among the Cuban literary world.[13] Similarly, Nicolás Guillén Landrián was a filmmaker who suffered censorship, persecution, incarceration, and psychiatric internment in Cuba (including electroshock therapy). Due to his irreverent and experimental documentaries that violated the aesthetics promoted in the 1960s and 70s, he was expelled from the Cuban Film Institute (ICAIC) in 1972. By 2003, when *Cacharro(s)* dedicated its second issue to him, his work was largely forgotten in Cuba.[14]

These ironic and transgressive games mark *Cacharro(s)*. The e-zine's pages, distributed by e-mail in Word or pdf formats, are deliberately filled with dead hyperlinks, revealing an unfulfilled yearning for connectivity due to Cuba's precarious technological situation at the time. In spite of that lack of connectivity, the texts in *Cacharro(s)* cross ideological barriers and create a crisis for the state's exclusionary logic by distributing the works of authors discarded by that very logic. In a way, just as *Cacharro(s)* wishes to continue the aesthetic disruptions of *Diáspora(s)*, the e-zines I analyze in the next sections, *33 y 1/tercio* and *The Revolution Evening Post*, seek to make

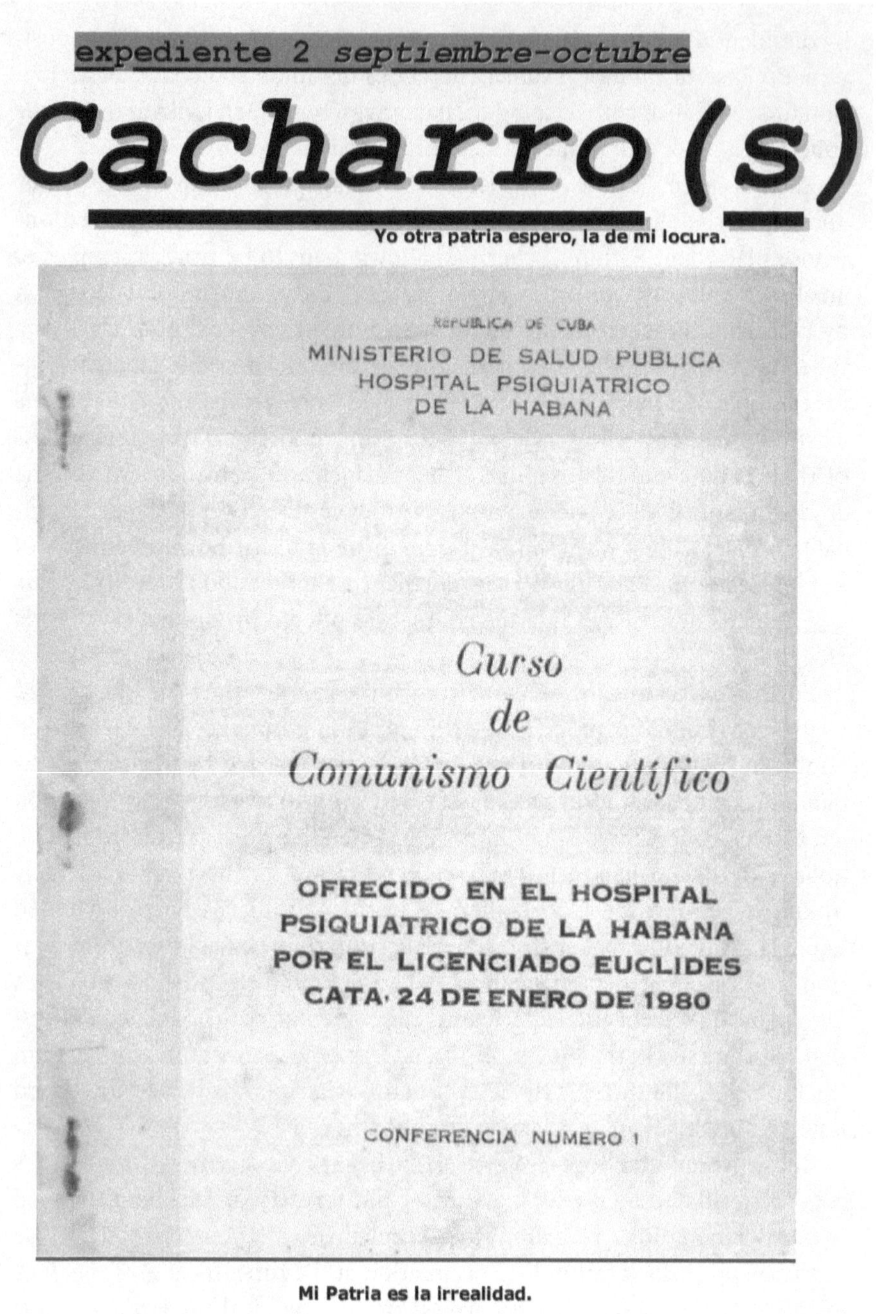

Figure 13.1. Cover image of *Cacharro(s)*—Issue 2, September–October 2003. Credit/Source: Blog *Revista Cacharro(s)*, http://revista-cacharros.blogdiario.net/img/expediente_2_septiembre-octubre_2003.zip. Used with permission.

Cacharro(s)'s disruptions longer-lasting, while also adapting them to their creators' evolving interests.

33 Y 1/TERCIO: INTERMEDIALITY AND PLANNED JUVENILE LEVITY

The e-zine *33 y 1/tercio* (2005–2010, with a total of sixteen issues) was created primarily by the writers Raúl Flores,[15] Jorge E. Lage,[16] and Elena Molina.[17] In most issues only an "editorial team" appears in charge of the e-zine, except in issue 6 (2007) where the individual names of the above-mentioned authors appear as members of the team. *33 y 1/tercio* was created on the basis of precarious access to online information. It is also crafted with an evident logic of chance. That is, its pages reveal a carefully reasoned project based on particular references and sensibilities, lending it a certain identity and making it distinct from former such projects.

Each installment of *33 y 1/tercio* carries a distinguishing title. For example, "33 y 1/tercio" (issue 1), "el laberinto" (issue 2); "toma 3" (issue 3); "toma 14" (issue 3, repeated); "aquí en 3" (issue 4); "bitch" (issue 14), and "isla que se hunde" (issue 14). As can be seen, the consecutiveness is sometimes interrupted (there are two third issues and two fourteenth issues) because the publication deliberately plays with the idea that these repeated issues are EPs (records that contain more tracks than a "single" but fewer than an LP). Indeed, part of the identity of *33 y 1/tercio* is built on the intermedial dialogue that has music and the record as its subject. This e-zine is therefore a very clear example of what Irina O. Rajewsky calls an "intermedial reference," a specific case of intermediality in which "the media product uses its own media-specific means, either to refer to a specific, individual work produced in another medium (. . .) or to refer to a specific medial subsystem (. . .) or to another medium *qua* system" (2005, 53–54).

The name, *33 y 1/tercio* (33 and a third), refers to the speed used to play back music on vinyl. Another, less explicit reference is to the performance "33 1/3" (1969) by the composer John Cage: a participative sound installation in which twenty-four phonographs with speakers and more than three hundred LPs were placed in a room without chairs. The audience that entered the performance was not given any instructions, although in the end people began to play the records on the turntables and that way generated a collective sound mix. "33 1/3" was a piece typical of Cage's indeterminate style, which aimed to break down the barriers between the audience and the performer, and between sound and music. Some of these participative and interactive qualities can be found in *33 y 1/tercio* where the texts being published (essays, stories, poetry) are presented as "tracks" of the different "albums" which are the issues of the e-zine.

The opening texts of some of the issues of *33 y 1/tercio* contain multiple musical references. For example, in the piece "play" from issue 1 (2005) that serves as the introduction for the entire e-zine, music, and specifically the LP, appear as routes to both knowledge and escape: "to see the ghost of an LP turning on the plate of the phonograph: the/ answer to all our inquiries./ that acetate plate turning at 33/ and one third revolutions/ took/ us/ to/ another/ dimension" (*33 y 1/tercio* 2005, 5). At the same time, Rajewsky's moments of "intermedial reference" multiply. In text, there are references to the transformation of words into different digital file formats ("jpgs," "tiffs," or "mp3s"), to the proximity of the language to videoclip aesthetics, and "to the 3-minute duration of a song/ on/ the/ radio" (5–6). Literature is thus evoked in some of its non-canonical and peripheric forms, far from the prestige of the authorized ones: "literature/ pop lit, thrash writing, paperback writers,/ splatterlight fiction" (6; in English in the original); a reference that becomes relevant in the Cuban context for these "degenerate" variants are not the ones that appear in cultural magazines or books.

The structure of this editorial text, "play," resembles a poem in prose with verses of different lengths, and in which appear fragments of other texts placed in simulated randomness, like a quote from American writer Ronald Sukenick, or a headline from CNN. In light of the "intermedial reference," the intertextual resource (and consequently the entire text) can be seen as an example of sampling in which portions from other recordings are repurposed. These mechanisms contribute to what in the editorial is referred to as "the atomized perception of an atomized cultural multiverse" that helps "to expand boundaries that were once imposed/ to erase them." On this action plan, and on that desire is where the media paradigm shift that occurs among the young Cuban writers that begin to publish in the 2000s vis-à-vis previous authors, is concentrated.

Some of the younger authors, like those who created the e-zine *33 y 1/tercio*, are more interested in the universe of American TV series, low-budget movies, or MTV loops. In fact, *33 y 1/tercio* published an abundant number of essays on the relationship between literature and television, punk, and TV series, from authors like Eloy Fernández Porta and Vicente Luis Mora. This paradigm shift brings a multiplication of referential universes (not only those related to literature), an atomization with a different identity from the homogenous cultural projects sponsored by the state and the pleasure of being part of said atomization and plurality (and of producing it as well).

33 y 1/tercio's covers are also part of the e-zine's "intermedial references" for they are similar to pop and rock album covers in which the young faces are the main characters, or where there appear images of a well-rehearsed banality. Its visual appearance evokes a teenage and young adult aesthetic, but its contents go well beyond gestures of self-complacent, age-specific rebelliousness. There is a well-planned lightness to seduce readers. For example, some issues feature a group of idle youth sitting on a park bench looking defiantly at the camera and whose attitude contrasts with others of "revolutionary" youth engaged in fulfilling "tasks" handed down to them by the state and its institutions.[18]

Together with that apparent lightness, *33 y 1/tercio* shows a clear awareness of the possibilities of participation offered by digital media as opportunities for the construction of autonomous subjectivities, which are not structured on vertical power relationships. Instead, they take advantage of the disruptive potential of atomization and disintegration in a context where hierarchies impose the main modalities of political participation:

> The blog, like the Internet itself, points to a politics of the personal, and those who dare make statements like "the minimal effectiveness of disintegration" and similar others must take into account a more current view of history [and read] the social corpus from fractality and complexity rather than from the pyramid. And no gesture should be underestimated. (*33 y 1/tercio* 2007, 5)

Some of the texts also directly question relations with the national cultural archives that are ruled by the state's diktats. *33 y 1/tercio* advocates for the elimination of the "historical determinism transplanted to the literary landscape" (*33 y 1/tercio* 2008, 4). In other words, a literary canon is formed originating with the state with which young writers must have had a relationship motivated by a debt to or the cult of certain legitimized figures with the subsequent exclusion of other uncomfortable ones (who are named in the text of the e-zine, like the writers Virgilio Piñera, Reinaldo Arenas, and Carlos Victoria). Therefore, it is imperative to "attempt re-readings of the precedents without political or institutional meddling" (*33 y 1/tercio* 2008, 4).[19]

A series of thematic nuclei traverse the sixteen issues of *33 y 1/tercio*. For example, the e-zine published many essays on American authors usually unmentioned in state cultural magazines, including David Foster Wallace, Chuck Palahniuk, Jonathan Franzen, Bret Easton Ellis, and Jonathan Lethem, as well as texts by these same authors. There are also sci-fi and speculative fiction authors like Rudy Rucker, Philip K. Dick, J. G. Ballard, and

Stephen King.[20] The Latin American literature that appears on *33 y 1/tercio* steps away from the veneration of the now-canonical authors of Latin American Boom. Instead, the e-zine included authors like Álvaro Bisama (better aligned with pop and trash aesthetics), Heriberto Yépez, and Rafa Saavedra. There is also the important presence of Juan Villoro and Ricardo Piglia (not so much through fiction, but through essays on writing); of other authors like Roberto Bolaño, Rodrigo Fresán, and Alberto Fuguet, and by more "rupturist" writings from Pedro Lemebel, César Aira, and Néstor Perlongher. In contrast, the e-zine published very little Cuban literature. Texts by Cabrera Infante and Calvert Casey appear in some issues. Some members of the so-called Generación Cero[21] to which some of those in charge of creating *33 y1/tercio* belong, like Jorge E. Lage, Raúl Flores, Legna Rodríguez,[22] Agnieska Hernández,[23] and Jamila Medina,[24] are published as well.

Significantly, the e-zine republished works by Rolando Sánchez Mejías and Lorenzo García Vega that had already appeared on *Diáspora(s)*, together with new ones by the same authors, as well as pieces by Carlos A. Aguilera, Rogelio Saunders, Ricardo A. Pérez, and Antonio José Ponte. Other continuities exist between *33 y 1/tercio* and *Diáspora(s)* since works by Thomas Bernhard, Gilles Deleuze, Ror Wolf, and Russian avant-garde artist Daniil Kharms appear in both. Additionally, there is one set of essays from *33 y 1/tercio* that could have been published by *Diáspora(s)* given its similar interest in criticizing the state: "State Terrorism" by Albert Camus (issue 11, 2008); "State 'Horrorism'" by Carlos Rehermann, and "Meyerhold's Letter" by Sergio Pitol (issue 14, "isla que se hunde," 2010).

In sum, *33 y 1/tercio* shares with *Cacharro(s)* the mordant tone of its editorials and the questioning of the institutionally dictated relations with the Cuban cultural archives (especially the literary one). As an e-zine, *33 y 1/tercio* stands out for its youthful light appearance, its covers with defiant young people, idle and glamorous, and for the intermedial relationships that it establishes with music and the record as objects. With this coverage, the e-zine's editorial policy multiplies the referential universes of the island's cultural publications and takes advantage of the disruptive potential of digital atomization. The last e-zine I analyze here, *The Revolution Evening Post*, adds other ironic and playful nuances to the spectacularity exhibited by *33 y 1/tercio*.

The Revolution Evening Post: Seriality and Spectacle

The writers Pardo Lazo, Jorge E. Lage, and Ahmel Echevarría created the e-zine *The Revolution Evening Post* (*TREP*), which published eight issues between 2006 and 2008. Its issues or "episodes" did not follow a chronological order. They were numbered as follows: 5, 6, 7, 2, 3, 4, 1, 8 in order to break away from the classic linear structure of literary magazines. *TREP* was distributed through e-mail to approximately four hundred subscribers.[25] According to its creators, this e-zine featured "irregular writing," an idea that refers to the type of texts they wanted to promote. That is, they wanted to publish texts written for nonspecialized media like book reviews and chronicles, as opposed to fiction as is customary in most literary magazines. The e-zine's name, *The Revolution Evening Post*, aims to put the Cuban "Revolution" (an event heavy with historical and political connotations) in a less exceptional, lighter, and more serialized context, with reference to the American magazine *The Saturday Evening Post* (1897–1969). The "revolution" would not, then, be a unique event, but a repetition of minor, almost local events, archived in a digital publication that evokes an analog era. In any case, *The Revolution Evening Post* is an ambiguous name that combines references to the analog with its digital distribution by e-mail. Echevarría points out this ambiguity:

> What comes to your e-mail inbox? The ideal texts to read in the "dusk" of the Revolution? Readings for this moment in which the Revolution slows down its rpm. and lets you take a breather? Or simply texts that force you to decrease the revolutions of the narratives the institutions are telling you [. . .]? (Mesa 2010, 13)[26]

All issues of *TREP* are called "episodes," thereby imagining them as installments of a TV series. When one contrasts the classification of these "episodes" with that of the "documents" assigned to the issues of *Diáspora(s)*, one can see the shift from the written word to the broadcast as the referential universe of these young writers. The first page in each issue of *TREP* is an image from an American entertainment magazine (*Rolling Stone, Playboy, Esquire, Maxim*) replaced by the words *The Revolution Evening Post* in a font and color similar to the original (figure 13.2). This "interventionist" sensibility is central to *TREP*'s editorial policy, because what the e-zine sets out to do is insert works by Cuban authors, mostly young ones, into a context not circumscribed by the Cuban context, and place those texts at the same level of those circulating outside Cuba. The creators of the e-zine take on this enterprise with all their limitations seeing it as a ludic fantasy, but nevertheless encouraged by its imaginary nature.

Every *TREP* cover carries the words: "We have been cordially invited to be part of Chilean literature in Cuba. Of course, we have accepted. There was no initiation ceremony. Better that way" (*The Revolution Evening Post*

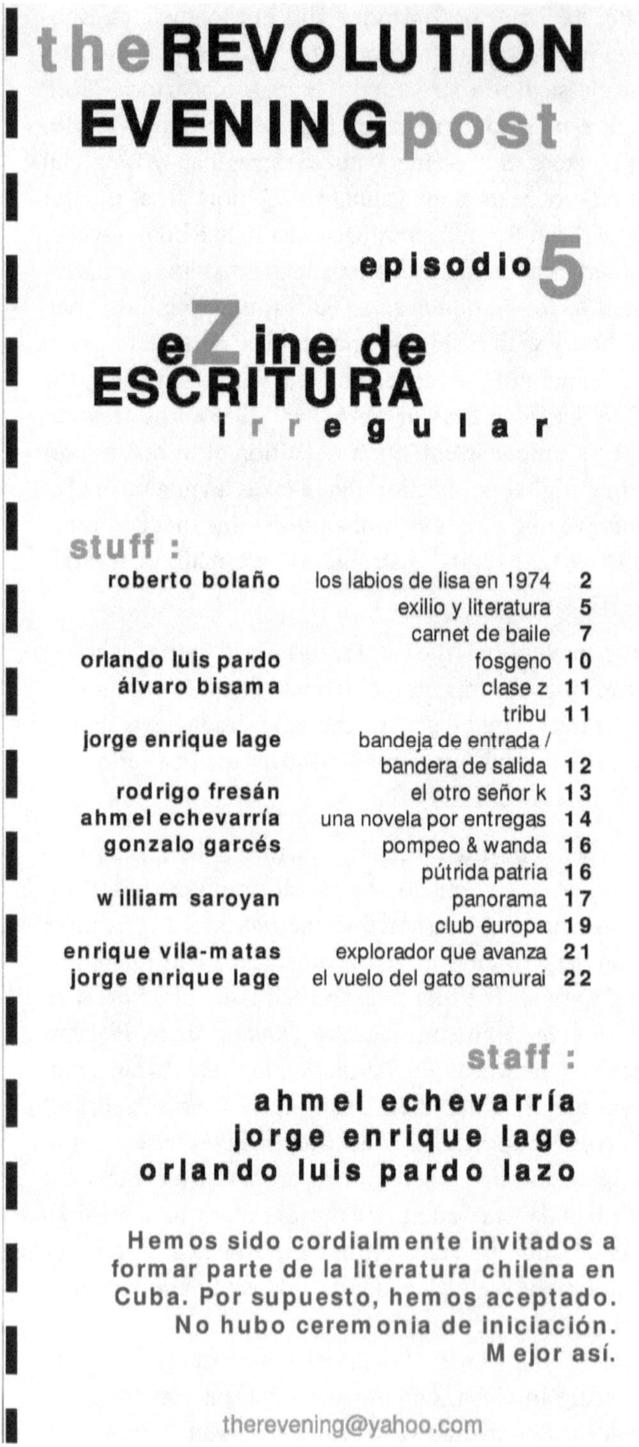

the REVOLUTION EVENING post

episodio 5

eZine de ESCRITURA
irregular

stuff :

roberto bolaño	los labios de lisa en 1974	2
	exilio y literatura	5
	carnet de baile	7
orlando luis pardo	fosgeno	10
álvaro bisama	clase z	11
	tribu	11
jorge enrique lage	bandeja de entrada / bandera de salida	12
rodrigo fresán	el otro señor k	13
ahmel echevarría	una novela por entregas	14
gonzalo garcés	pompeo & wanda	16
	pútrida patria	16
william saroyan	panorama	17
	club europa	19
enrique vila-matas	explorador que avanza	21
jorge enrique lage	el vuelo del gato samurai	22

staff :

ahmel echevarría
jorge enrique lage
orlando luis pardo lazo

Hemos sido cordialmente invitados a formar parte de la literatura chilena en Cuba. Por supuesto, hemos aceptado. No hubo ceremonia de iniciación.
Mejor así.

therevening@yahoo.com

Figure 13.2. Partial cover image of *The Revolution Evening Post*—Episode 5, 2006. Credit/Source: Blog *Fogonero Emergente*, http://static.scribd.com/docs/jlipmwwlfikv2.swf. Used with permission. Note: The original cover image used by the editors of *The Revolution Evening Post* has been cropped here to eliminate their willfully unauthorized reproduction of the cover of *Rolling Stone* (Issue 1007, August 24, 2006), featuring a scantily clad Christina Aguilera. The cultural and technological appropriation and resignification that e-zines like *TREP* engaged in at the time in Cuba is not something we can imitate here for fear of violating copyright.

2006, 1). This is a nod to the beginning of *The Savage Detectives* (1998) by Roberto Bolaño: "I have been cordially invited to be part of visceral realism. Of course, I have accepted. There was no initiation ceremony. Better that way." An homage, a parody, and a positioning in regard to Bolaño inspires the creators of *TREP*, as Lage states, "for what he can represent in the future of Hispanic American literature" (Mesa 2010, 21). The absence of these "ceremonies" refers to the fact that the creators of *TREP* (and the other e-zines discussed here) did not wait for authorization from Cuba's literary community to distribute their material. Nor did they ask permission before creating their own communities of interest, their own channels of content distribution.

The promise of delocalization and the yearning for a fluidity that is not tied to the framework of a national literature (objectives to which the three promoters of *TREP* allude several times in an interview [Mesa 2010]), are embodied by the author of *The Savage Detectives*. "To be part of Chilean literature in Cuba" is to introduce estrangement and distance within a space controlled by institutional editorial policies that determine the circulation rules of cultural texts and the dynamics of state magazines; it is "to contaminate and disseminate ways of writing: hence the politicity of our gesture," says Pardo Lazo (Mesa 2010, 22). The phrase that is repeated on each cover of *TREP*, explains Lage (Mesa 2010, 21), speaks of "an outward look [. . .] To look at those things we were reading outside a Cuban context is to create within Cuban literature, a literature that is not so as much, that is not part of the domestic tradition." One of the guiding ideas of the e-zine is to emulate the spirit of magazines outside of Cuba that not only publish texts about literature, but about cinema, fashion, and television, with bylines by authors who have frequent, personal columns. Lage, Pardo Lazo, and Echevarría want to write as if they were one of these authors; as if there was "nobody looking to play the censor or the curator following an editorial policy," Pardo Lazo argues (Mesa 2010, 22).

The Revolution Evening Post shares with *Cacharro(s)* and *33 and 1/tercio* (and, in turn, all these e-zines with *Diáspora(s)*) this policy of dissemination of texts and authors. The creators of these e-zines wanted to reduce the distance between Cuban readers and literary and cultural texts that were published outside Cuba through the circulation of e-zines by e-mail. In other words, they wanted to connect disconnected readers and create a simulation of a current and present when, in reality, the temporality of cultural consumption was a deferred one. The creators of *The Revolution Evening Post* are especially aware of these contradictions. Lage points out that the e-zine was distributed by e-mail but its recipient is a reader who did not have access in real time to the materials the e-zine reproduced (Mesa 2010, 22).

Visually, the intention of the creators of *TREP* was to play with "bad design," breaking the traditional association between literary text and an image of an artist or designer on the same page, which is usually the case in literary magazines; to build a more kinetic design, one that is more linked to pop and lighter fare (Echevarría, in Mesa 2010, 23). In all of *TREP*'s "episodes" appear texts by Lage, Pardo Lazo, and Echevarría which reveal their desire to make their own authorial presence stronger, in contrast to the previous e-zines *Cacharro(s)* and *33 y 1/tercio* where they acted more as editors. Another notable difference is that *TREP* did not publish "op-eds" because neither Pardo Lazo nor Lage wanted to reproduce this practice which they saw as echoing "literary" magazines.

Diáspora(s) and *The Revolution Evening Post* are set apart from each other by the repertoire of texts each published. Dominant in *TREP* are Latin American authors, almost completely absent from *Diáspora(s)*. The creators of both projects also chose, generally speaking, different literary models to articulate them. One possible explanation is that the creators of *TREP* read, as part of their literary education,[27] some of the writers published by *Diáspora(s)*, like the Central Europeans (Thomas Bernhard, Ror Wolf, and Milan Kundera, among others) and thus prioritize other literary traditions. Hence, we find in *TREP* a first group of writers closer in age to the members of Generación Cero (born in the 1970s), some of whom had already been published in *33 y 1/tercio* like Álvaro Bisama and the Mexican Heriberto Yépez.[28] They also published a second batch of Latin American authors like Bolaño and Mario Bellatin. Furthermore, other writers from Cuba's Generación Cero also appeared in *TREP* like Anisley Negrín and Raúl Flores.

Like *33 y 1/tercio*, the amount of Cuban literature published in *TREP* is minimal. Contemporary authors include Antonio José Ponte and Pedro Juan Gutiérrez. Authors from the Cuban Republican Period (who built their careers before 1959) like Miguel de Marcos (1894–1954) and Carlos Montenegro (1900–1981) link through shared interests and their readings of the Cuban literary archive, the writers from Generación Cero with those of the *Diáspora(s)* group. Thus, *The Revolution Evening Post* is an interventionist e-zine: The insertion of its name on the covers of well-known American entertainment magazines denotes a yearning for connectivity and of an opening beyond the boundaries of the Cuban publishing space controlled by official institutions. *TREP*'s creators wished to disseminate writings and manners of reading that were "alien" in the Cuban cultural landscape, and to that end did not wait for authorization. Instead, they built their e-zine as if there were no censorious gaze.

Conclusion: The Expansion of the Cuban Digital Landscape

The e-zines *Cacharro(s)*, *33 y 1/tercio*, and *The Revolution Evening Post* were projects of creative autonomy without institutional affiliation that tested not only the limits of expression within the Cuban cultural landscape, but also the limits of the analog dissemination permitted by the state. Despite precarious access to technology, and in a context of virtual disconnection, the e-zines' creators distributed them by e-mail, thumb drives, and newsletters, trying to reach the largest possible number of readers in Cuba who were in turn also disconnected from the information immediacy of the Internet. These digital magazines served as precursors to the expansion of the independent blogosphere (2007–2014) and later to the proliferation of independent digital newspapers and magazines (2014–present) in Cuba, while also being artifacts that exist halfway between analog and digital culture.

Without waiting for authorization or legitimization from upper echelons, these authors/editors created new spaces for expression, and thought of themselves as part of a multifaceted digital landscape. They contributed to the expansion and development of that digital landscape from their respective editorial policies and imaginaries: the awareness of state surveillance and transgression as engines of the "dossiers" of *Cacharro(s)*; the challenge of the intermedial "music albums" of *33 and 1/tercio*, with their pop and light appearance; and the interventionism of the "episodes" of *The Revolution Evening Post*, which sought to be a "strange" and "unauthorized" object in the insular discursive landscape of Cuba. All these e-zines gathered texts and images with a mix of randomness and conscious planning. They had a sustained—and at the same time ephemeral (for they lasted for relatively short times)—will for disagreement and critical intervention.

The disruptive energy of these e-zines together with their desire to break down the barriers of the dissemination of edgy authors and texts are the bases for the subsequent expansion of the island's independent blogosphere. A later, transitional project like *Voices* (2010–2014)[29] gathered part of that energy, publishing literary texts next to others of a markedly political orientation by authors both inside and outside Cuba. Pardo Lazo was its main editor and blogger Yoani Sánchez also collaborated. Some of the creators discussed here continued on to their own projects, now with the benefit of the interactive framework of blogs and websites. Jorge A. Aguiar Díaz managed the blog *Fogonero Emergente* (2007–2010) with news about alternative cultural and political projects in Cuba. Pardo Lazo continues to maintain his blog *Lunes de Post-Revolución* (2008–present) where he publishes texts and videos. Lizabel Mónica has created several blogs and websites including *Proyecto Desliz* (2007–present). And Jorge E. Lage is the director of *Hypermedia Magazine* (2016–present), a transnational, digital publication of Cuban-themed opinion articles and essays on arts and literature.

In the last few years, the Cuban digital landscape has grown considerably. In it coexist projects like the aforementioned blogs with others of a more journalistic character, such as *El Toque* (2013–present), a multimedia platform that publishes news, chronicles, and interviews focused on Cuban youth; *14ymedio* (2014–present), a digital newspaper that publishes daily reportage and opinion pieces on everything from Cuban politics and human rights to food shortages and transportation bottlenecks; and *El Estornudo* (2016–present), an independent magazine of narrative journalism with hard-hitting and very diverse stories about Cuba.[30] The pluralization of the cultural discourses in Cuba, and the democratization of its public sphere cannot be imagined without the active role of these projects and of the e-zines that appeared and were distributed by e-mail and thumb drives in the early 2000s. None of them waited for a legal status in accordance with the restrictive norms of the Cuban state, nor did they wait to be authorized to begin their digital journey. In those rebellions lie the greater part of their disruptive potential.

Notes

1. E-zine is an industry term for magazines distributed by any electronic means, like e-mail, and that boomed in the late 1980s and early 1990s. Its predecessor is the zine, a type of independent, underground publication from which the e-zine inherits some of its characteristics like the use of more cost-effective technologies, their opposition to the sociocultural mainstream, a noncommercial ethos, and the emphasis on personal communication, as Frederick Wright points out in his history of zines and their transition into e-zines.

2. *Cacharro(s)* can be found on the blog *Revista Cacharro(s)* (http://revistacacharros.blogspot.com/). All issues of *33 y 1/tercio* are on the blog *Revista 33 y 1/tercio* (http://revista33y1tercio.blogspot.com/). Some issues of *The Revolution Evening Post* are dispersed through various blogs, such as *Fogonero Emergente* (http://jorgealbertoaguiar.blogspot.com/) and *Lunes de Post-Revolución*. (http://orlandoluispardolazo.blogspot.com/).

3. Venegas (2010) focuses on various "electronic genres" (157) used by Cubans that she labels: "official stories" (161), "personal stories" (164), "emotional geographies" (168), "blogostroika" (172), and "videostroika" (178). Duong (2013, 375) studies "the encounters and dialogues between the alternative blogosphere and key intellectual and cultural actors in contemporary Cuba," while Henken (2017, 453) analyzes independent projects he calls

"digital dissidents," "digital millennials," "critical digital revolutionaries," and "the digital diaspora."

4. See Dorta (2015b, 2016) for an analysis of the means of production, reproduction, and circulation of *Diáspora(s)* magazine, as well as its materiality and editorial profile.

5. Paideia (1989–1990) was a cultural policy project promoted by intellectuals, writers, and artists like Rolando Prats, Jorge Ferrer, Ernesto Hernández Busto, among others, that questioned the official system of culture and tried to restore a critical agency to obtain more autonomy. It did not come to fruition due to its prohibition by Cuba's official institutions. Young artists frequently met on the roof of the poet Reina María Rodríguez's building to read and discuss their works in the midst of the scarcity of the 1990s and later.

6. Jorge A. Aguiar Díaz (born 1966) is a writer and literary promoter. He founded the Narrative Workshop "Salvador Redonet" and the Creative Writing Lab "Enrique Labrador Ruiz" in Havana and published the book, *Adiós a las almas* in 2002. He also oversaw the blogs *Fogonero Emergente* and *Cacharro(s)* in which the homonymous e-zine would end up dwelling.

7. Lizabel Mónica (born 1981) is a writer and editor. She coordinates the alternative cultural distribution project Desliz, the magazine of the same name, and also blogs like *Cuba Fake News* among others. According to her own account (personal communication, June 20, 2019), she adopted the pseudonym at the suggestion of Jorge A. Aguiar Díaz, who feared repercussions not only for being part of the magazine's team but also due to her relative youth (twenty-two at the time).

8. Pedro Marqués de Armas (born 1965) is a poet and essayist. Founder of *Diáspora(s)*, among his books are Óbitos (2015) and *Prosas de la nación: Ensayos de literatura cubana* (2017). He's a codirector of the digital literature publication *Potemkin Ediciones* and maintains the blog *Hotel Telégrafo*.

9. Juan Carlos Flores (1962–2016) was a poet and experimental performance artist. Among his books are *El contragolpe (y otros poemas horizontales)* (2009). He committed suicide at the age of 54.

10. Orlando Luis Pardo Lazo (1971) is a writer, photographer, and blogger. Editor of digital magazines like *Voces* and anthologies of recent Cuban literature like *Generation Zero: An Anthology of New Cuban Fiction* (2014). He maintains the blog *Lunes de Post-Revolución*.

11. Lizabel Mónica and Pardo Lazo, personal communication, June 20, 2019.

12. Notable authors who appear in both *Cacharro(s)* and *Diáspora(s)* include Pedro Marqués de Armas, Rolando Sánchez Mejías, Rogelio Saunders, José Kozer, Juan C. Flores, Emilio Ichikawa, and Guillermo Cabrera Infante as well as the philosophers Jacques Derrida, Peter Sloterdijk, and Hans Magnus Enzensberger.

13. His works have been recognized little by little, mostly through the actions of his daughter, Yanira Marimón.

14. Young filmmakers have since created various documentaries dedicated to him, including *Café con Leche* (2003) by Manuel Zayas and *Retornar a La Habana con Guillén Landrián* (2013) by Raydel Araoz and Julio Ramos. Julio Ramos and Dylon Robbins also recently edited a book on his life and work, *Guillén Landrián o el desconcierto fílmico* (2019, Leiden: Almenara).

15. Raúl Flores' (born 1977) publications include *La carne luminosa de los gigantes*

(2008) and *Paperback Writer* (2010). Between 2004 and 2008 he ran Espacio Polaroid, a space that featured audiovisual materials, underground music, readings, and performance art.

16. Jorge E. Lage (born 1979) is a writer and editor who has published *Archivo* (2015) and *Carbono 14: Una novela de culto*. He collaborates with digital outlets like *Diario de Cuba* and *Hypermedia Magazine,* of which he is also a cofounder.

17. Elena Molina (born 1988) is a writer and cultural activist.

18. Sara Garcia Santamaria (2017, 134–135) studies, for example, how the daily newspaper *Granma* (the official newspaper of the Cuban Communist Party) builds the identity of every generation of young people through elements like emotional involvement with national symbols, respect for the country's heroes, and acts of revolutionary affirmation.

19. Rafael Rojas (2006, 2009) has studied the politics of memory of the Cuban state regarding intellectuals and artists, as well as the state's exclusionary practices that guarantee its control of the literary space.

20. Sci-fi and cyberpunk are important elements in the work of some young Cuban authors such as Erick Mota, Michel Encinosa Fú, Jorge E. Lage, and Elaine Vilar Madruga.

21. See Dorta (2015b) for the characteristics of the literature of Generación Cero.

22. Legna Rodríguez (born 1984) has published books of various genres like *Mi novia preferida fue un bulldog francés* (short stories, 2017) and *Miami Century Fox* (poetry, 2017).

23. Agnieska Hernández (born 1977) has written plays as well as stories. Among her books are *Panóptico en dos estaciones* (2009) and *Sol negro* (2011).

24. Jamila Medina (born 1981) is an editor, essayist, storyteller, and poet. Among her works are *Del corazón de la col y otras mentiras* (2013) and the seminal essay *Diseminaciones de Calvert Casey* (2012).

25. Pardo Lazo through personal communication, June 30, 2019. Pardo Lazo also points out that on occasion, Gmail would block the mass e-mails that he tried to send because of the high number of recipients.

26. Leopold Mesa is the pseudonym of Reinier Pérez-Hernández.

27. In a recent interview, Lage and Pardo Lazo explain how they read *Diáspora(s)* thanks to the suggestion of Jorge A. Aguiar Díaz, one of the creators of *Cacharro(s)*.

28. Other Latin American authors published in *TREP* are the Chileans Rafael Gumucio and Alejandro Zambra; the Argentine Gonzalo Garcés; the Peruvians Santiago Roncagliolo and Daniel Alarcón, and the Mexican Rafael Lemus.

29. All back issues of *Voices* are archived at: http://www.100yaldabo.com/voces.htm.

30. See Henken (2017, 2021, and this volume) for a more in-depth analysis of these and other projects.

References

33 y 1/tercio. 2005. "play." *33 y 1/tercio* 1: 5–6.
33 y 1/tercio. 2007. "download 33." *33 y 1/tercio* 8: 5.
33 y 1/tercio. 2008. "push." *33 y 1/tercio* 11: 4–5.
Aguiar Díaz, Jorge A. 2003. "Preliminar." *Cacharro(s)* 1: 5–7.
Bolaño, Roberto. 2006. *Los detectives salvajes*. Barcelona: Anagrama.

Cacharro(s). 2003. [Portada]. *Cacharro(s)* 1: 1.
Cacharro(s). 2004a. "Guillén es el Poeta Nacional." *Cacharro(s)* 4: 1.
Cacharro(s). 2004b. [Portada]. *Cacharro(s)* 6/7: 1.
Cacharro(s). 2004c. "Como saben nuestros amigos y suscriptores. . . ." 6/7: 4.
Dorta, Walfrido. 2015a. "Conversa en Benefit Street (sobre literatura cubana reciente)." *Diario de Cuba,* March 14, 2015.
Dorta, Walfrido. 2015b. "Políticas de la distancia y del agrupamiento. Narrativa cubana de las dos últimas dos décadas." *Istor. Revista de Historia Internacional* 63: 115–135.
Dorta, Walfrido. 2016. "Materia pobre para la intensidad: Diáspora(s) en el Periodo Especial." *La Noria* 11: 46–50.
Duong, Paloma. 2013. "Bloggers Unplugged: Amateur Citizens, Cultural Discourse, and Public Sphere in Cuba." *Journal of Latin American Cultural Studies* 22 (4): 375–97.
Ecured. *Revista Juventud Técnica.* N.d. https://www.ecured.cu/Revista_Juventud_T%C3%A9cnica. Accessed June 18, 2019.
Garcia Santamaria, Sara. 2017. "The Historical Articulation of 'the People' in Revolutionary Cuba: Media Discourses of Unity in Times of National Debate (1990–2012)." Ph.D. thesis, University of Sheffield.
Henken, Ted A. 2017. "Cuba's Digital Millennials: Independent Digital Media and Civil Society on the Island of the Disconnected." *Social Research* 84 (2): 429–56.
Henken, Ted A. 2021. "The Opium of the *Paquete*: State Censorship, Private Self-Censorship, and the Content Distribution Strategies of Cuba's Emergent, Independent Digital Media Startups." *Cuban Studies* 50.
Mesa, Leopoldo. 2010. "Postrevolution suave, cordial, amable, divertido." *Upsalón* 8: 20–26.
Pardo Lazo, Orlando Luis. 2014. "Preface." *Cuba in Splinters. Eleven Stories from the New Cuba,* 7–13. Edited by Orlando L. Pardo Lazo. Translated by Hillary Gulley. New York, London: OR Books.
Rajewsky, Irina O. 2005. "Intermediality, Intertextuality, and Remediation: A Literary Perspective on Intermediality." *Intermédialités* 6: 43–64.
Rancière, Jacques. 2006. *The Politics of Aesthetics.* Translated by Gabriel Rockhill. New York, London: Continuum.
Rojas, Rafael. 2006. *Tumbas sin sosiego Revolución, disidencia y exilio del intelectual cubano.* Barcelona: Anagrama.
Rojas, Rafael. 2009. *El estante vacío, Literatura y política en Cuba.* Barcelona: Anagrama.
The Revolution Evening Post. 2006. "Hemos sido cordialmente invitados. . . ." *The Revolution Evening Post* 1: 1.
Timmer, Nanne. 2013. "La Habana virtual: Internet y la transformación espacial de la ciudad letrada." *CiberLetras: revista de crítica literaria y de cultura* 30.
Venegas, Cristina. 2010. *Digital Dilemmas: The State, the Individual, and Digital Media in Cuba.* New Brunswick, NJ: Rutgers University Press.
Wright, Frederick A. 2001. "From Zines to E-zines: Electronic Publishing and the Literary Underground." Ph.D. thesis, Kent State University.

14

Images of Ourselves

Cuban Mediascapes and the Postsocialist "Woman of Fashion"

PALOMA DUONG

Citizens of former communist regimes "have been deprived of media images of themselves for thirty years," remarks Sylvie, the main character of Chris Kraus's novel *Torpor* ([2006] 2015, 185). A middle-aged, American intellectual on her way to Romania, Sylvie muses about the recognizably outdated fashion of the "Easties" while passing through East Berlin in 1991. Beyond Kraus's astute dramatizations of the Western intellectual's engagement with the postsocialist milieu in the novel, here I am interested in how the relationship between media and its publics in "actually existing socialism" has been portrayed and conceptualized, and how it is *remediated* in the postsocialist context. In other words, the issue is not whether citizens in historical communisms were deprived of media images of themselves, but rather, what kind of media images of themselves they were offered, and by whom. Furthermore, like most of us, twenty-first century Cubans—or at least an increasing number of them—can generate, access, and share images of themselves beyond those created by official state media or by an exoticizing foreign gaze. How new media agents engage a contested visual archive in the process of representing themselves and the nation is particularly relevant, then, given the symbolic weight attached to revolutionary Cuba by the multiple constituencies that claim its historical legacy within and beyond its national borders. Specifically, this chapter examines images of the postsocialist Cuban "woman of fashion," as a key to understand the social and media contexts in which Cuban postsocialism is produced, and experienced, as a mediascape.

Mediascapes, a term coined by Arjun Appadurai, are the cultural landscapes where the everyday social experience of meaning, values, and worldviews is created and disseminated in a multimedia, multiagent context (1990, 298). The Cuban postsocialist mediascape accommodates competing visions of a present where nation-state and transnational markets, the Communist Party and global finance, meet informal and hybrid economies mediated by local digital cultures. This mediascape is "postsocialist" in several ways: despite the country remaining nominally socialist and governed by a self-styled Communist Party, Cuba's economy, culture, and society engage a wide range of mixed models caught between the old bureaucratic command economy and the new domestic and international market investments, between the former horizons of egalitarian social justice and the new differentiated demands for recognition, though socioeconomic inequality continues to grow. Access to the public sphere remains heavily contested, but the state monopoly on traditional mass media technologies has to contend with the persistent challenges of digital connectivity, and with new patterns of travel and migration. The expansion of transnational capitalist markets, the proliferation of digital media, and the reorganization of state and non-state economic sectors shape this postsocialist mediascape, where mass consumerism is a novelty, but where socialism, as a political imaginary and as a collective memory, "passes, but it does not pass away" (Krasznahorkai [1989] 2000).

Reflecting on an iconic subject of this mediascape, as I argue is the postsocialist "woman of fashion," invites a critical reflection on how Cubans see themselves, how they want to be seen, and how they imagine and construct the world(s) they inhabit. Dominant discourses about Cuba focus on established narratives about the isolated provincialisms of the socialist mediascape, the exuberance and exceptionalism of its tropical and political conditions, or the beleaguered fortitude of its allegorical battle against historical time. They traffic in different versions of the (dis)enchantment with the Cuban Revolution. "Frozen in time" has become synonymous with Cuba's identity as a new global destination, despite the major social, cultural, and economic changes that have taken place over the last thirty years. Yet Cuba continues to be presented as being on the brink of an imminent transformation forever postponed: from exile salsa star Willy Chirino's 1991 classic "Nuestro día (ya viene llegando)" ("Our day (it's coming)") to the latest reports in the *New York Times*, "No one can predict what will happen to Cuba in the coming years, which is why you must rush there now. As in, right now" (Larsen 2018). This expectation of imminent change must by definition be indefinitely suspended and constantly fed: "I want to go before it changes" is a recurrent motif in narratives from afar in which the island or its 1959 Revolution function as an international object of desire.[1]

Meanwhile, the global market emerges as a national object of desire instead, a localized desire that is codified and managed differently within and beyond Cuban borders by different constituencies and stakeholders. The online version of *Granma*, the main newspaper of the Cuban Communist Party (PCC), hosts a permanent link to a comprehensive guide for international investment in Cuba. It also explains the legal frameworks of the free-trade zone inaugurated in the port of Mariel in the languages of Cuba's main commercial partners in the twenty-first century: Italian, Vietnamese, Portuguese, Russian, and Chinese. However, while the government aggressively courts international investments, its domestic policies scramble to update the Cuban economic model while maintaining the political status quo and extolling the virtues of socialist morality.[2] The new president, Miguel Díaz-Canel, who joined Twitter on October 10, 2018, has constructed his digital footprint around these two main themes: the insistence on a unified national identity and culture with the hashtag #SomosCuba (#WeAreCuba), and the continuum of the Cuban revolutionary socialist project into the twenty-first century with #SomosContinuidad (#WeAreContinuity), a hashtag heavily promoted by the PCC and other institutional media outlets as well.[3]

Both of these dominant narratives stress, and desire, different versions of a change without changes. If the Cuban postsocialist context, as I argue here, is better understood by the explosion of images that chronicle both continuities and transformations in everyday life at the meeting point of digital cultures and informal economies, what are these new media images, how and by whom are they generated, and how do they differ from top-down images of postsocialist Cuba? The aesthetics of what I call "portable postsocialisms" and the media agents that produce them challenge persistent visions of a Cuban reality they no longer recognize as their own: the sordid, eroticized apocalypticisms of the post-Soviet years of the "Special Period" (1990–1999), the siren song from a historically exotic location ripe for emotional and commercial investments as promoted by the foreign gaze, and the identity of abiding underdog of principled humanist socialism projected by official state discourse.

Looking more closely at narratives of transformation across a range of these media practices can give a measure of changed social concerns and cultural meanings that avoid simplified dichotomies. The focus of these stories has shifted from migration to upward mobility, from marketability of tropical sexuality to the desire for recognition of racial and gendered subjectivities, from epic futures (never) to be built to imminent presents (always already) under construction. Specifically, the postsocialist Cuban woman of fashion, and the discourses around her practices of consumption and beautification, synthetize but also update these anxieties around the end of the national socialist project and its trials with altered economic and media landscapes. These are the images I turn to below.

The Aesthetics of Portable Postsocialisms and the Cuban Woman of Fashion

These transformations are particularly evident in the aesthetics of the emergent advertising and entertainment offers that circulate primarily through offline mobile apps, DIY Wi-Fi networks, and "sneakernets," and which make domestic and international audiovisual content available to the general public outside of official media channels. This new media ecology is characterized by the portability, digitalization, and massification of the former analogue, underground sharing networks of bootleg content. Now partly monetized and home to the first comprehensive, country-wide system of commercial advertising for local consumers since the elimination of commercial publicity and private enterprise, the most well known of these sneakernets is *el paquete semanal* (the weekly package).

No discussion about digital media in Cuba can avoid *el paquete* (as many of the essays in this collection illustrate), a weekly release of about 1 terabyte of multimedia data. And there is much to say about it: it is the first, and as of 2019, the only, nationwide non-state mass media distribution platform in Cuba since 1959. It is the largest repository of the advertising system for local businesses and for the informal circulation of national and international news, entertainment, digital tools, and textual and audiovisual materials. The *paquete* remediated, centralized, and monetized its predecessors in the underground cultural economy: private video and game rental banks, illegal satellite antennas, and organized communities for bootleg copying and sharing. It is the unofficial platform for the consumption of the official global culture industry, but it is also the vehicle for the expansion and legitimation of the informal and emergent local economies, which exist in permanent tension with state enterprises and official discourse as much as with transnational capital and its images of Cuba.

What *el paquete* is not, however, is an offline "Internet in a hard-drive," the next phase in the struggle against communist Big Brother, or the harbinger of corrupting McDonaldizations of national media consumption, as some of the most extreme coverage portrays it to be. In fact, the kind of international attention *el paquete* has generated says as much about the assumptions that outsiders project onto Cuba and the supposedly liberating role of media technologies, as it does about *el paquete*'s rise to prominence as a local phenomenon and socioeconomic tool.[4]

The postsocialist "woman of fashion" is featured regularly in these window-pages where hybrid economies and digital cultures meet. Her presence in this mediascape underscores the political stakes and technological challenges of new media agents producing images of themselves, and the degree to which an emerging consumer culture caters to a changing image of the Cuban woman. One of the most representative examples of this phenomenon consists of intervening international publicity with local advertising and promotion. For example, the category of "Revistas Internacionales" (International Magazines) in *el paquete* holds modified pdfs of fashion and gossip magazines like *Cosmopolitan* and *¡Hola!*. Along with their original ads—largely irrelevant for most Cuban consumers—these digital copies include publicity for relevant local businesses and services. (A similar procedure applies to copied TV shows, which may feature lower-third ads of local businesses and services.) Full-page ads for three local photography studios, one hair salon, and a party organizing service stand between the cover of a pdf version of the Spain *Cosmopolitan* issue of May 2015 and the original publicity included in the magazine, a Chloé perfume and a Clinique lotion.[5] When the pdf opens, the subtly made-up, inviting bashful smiles of actress Paula Echevarría, the cover model, and Clémence Poésy, the perfume model, framed by floating tresses in deliberately impromptu poses, share the spotlight with provocatively dressed anonymous Cuban teens looking directly at the camera, with half-open mouths and tilted heads, brightly colored makeup, extravagantly dyed and curled hair, gem-studded acrylic nails, and hips and pelvises angled prominently forward and sideways (figure 14.1).

These hair salons and photography studios offer long-lasting, bedecked evidence of *quinces* (short for *quinceañera*, the celebration of girls, and sometimes boys, turning fifteen), weddings, and other special events. Their forms of representation and their kindred media practices index the irruption of what George Yúdice (2016) has called "el pueblo feo" ("the ugly people") in the generation of aesthetic content. Authorship and ownership of one's own image, individual and collective, determine when such vernacular media literacies are in play, defined not just by active spectatorship but by active participation in the production of culture at large. The sheer number of photography studios and hair salons advertised on these platforms may strike the casual observer as disproportionate. And the prominence of ads for photography studios would seem to contradict the thesis that digital producibility puts the authorship of their own images in people's hands. But

Figure 14.1. "Yindra" is featured in *Primavera*, March 2, 2015, and in the ad for the studio Essence in *el paquete*'s version of *Cosmopolitan*, May 2015. Credit/Source: *El paquete semanal*, Issue of Monday, June 1, 2015.

this would be a simplistic way to understand these forms of authorship, the enduring inequalities in access to technology and know-how, and the way these factors and knowledges are organized within a specific social context and local economy.

With smartphones and tablets, with preset filters and image-editing software, with online and offline sharing networks and platforms, Cubans too have become adroit producers of images of themselves. The fast-growing numbers of cell phone lines in use reported by the state telecommunications company ETECSA since the service began in 2008 (5.4 million lines registered in 2019 and counting) indicate that Cuba has followed the leapfrogging logic of most Latin American countries and developing regions, adding first-time mobile before PC users who access social media and the Internet primarily, and even exclusively, via portable devices. Internet access is slow, expensive, with highly regulated traffic and mostly available in fixed hot spots throughout the country, but pilots to expand home and mobile Web access were rolled out in 2017 and 2018, respectively.

However, equipment and know-how are unevenly distributed and inconsistently regulated: modems are only available on the black market, the legally sold Huawei phones remain prohibitively expensive, and GPS devices remain technically illegal to import even if nearly every arriving passenger has one embedded in their smartphone. The business of unblocked or used phones and prepaid credit supports the growth of mobile telephony, a sizable, transnational informal sector dependent upon the established Cuban diasporas and the new forms of travel available to Cubans. *El paquete*'s business model relies on the specificity of this mediascape: on the inequality of individual literacies, on uneven access to Web content and media infrastructure, and on the state monopoly of mass media. (ETECSA's public Internet offer servers, for example, block port 80 and other data transfer Internet protocols, which in the standard HyperText Transfer Protocol or HTTP of the World Wide Web normally allow the transmission of linked content and files between a client computer and the Web host.) As such, sneakernets are lucrative at various levels: at the level of copying and distribution of existing content, but also, much as other established private digital media conglomerates elsewhere, at the level of production of original material and from direct advertising revenues from local businesses.

This emerging advertising network and its effective use of pdf manipulation is another example of what Lisa Gitelman argues are the ways in which born-digital texts question the "intrinsic reliability" and fixedness of print media, and establish new standards of publishing by redefining what counts as publishing (2014, 117–118, 131). These practices highlight discrepancies between the uses for which a technology is designed and the purposes for which it is deployed by actual, everyday users. In doing so, emergent producers and consumers also realize the collective desire to participate in a global economic logic, creating a virtual leveling space where, in turn, the local businesses and emerging advertising industry seek legitimation among well-established brands and their consumer imaginaries while expanding their national presence. They also shift the importance from cover to content: while the political importance of both the magazine/journal format and the poster charged covers with great symbolic weight in Cuban literary culture (as Walfrido Dorta's contribution to this volume attests), the digital file, with its search function and easy scrolling, equalizes the value of the pages for readers more interested in useful, quickly accessible information than on the politics of the front page.

These practices also highlight other ways in which Cuban postsocialism has become portable: renewed Miami and Latin American exchange flows have left their own mark on the transformation of *quinceañeras* in Cuba in the last few decades, as in every other aspect of popular culture and fashion. The increasingly fashionable lavish celebration of *quinceañeras* in Cuba again is a prime example of the remixes of national customs, international fashion, personal aspirations, and media cultures that prop up a growing sector of the private economy and mark the rites of adult womanhood as initiations in an emergent consumer culture. A "born again" tradition deeply marked by immigration as Julia Álvarez documents in *Once Upon a Quinceañera* (2007), and as the classic sitcom *¿Qué pasa USA?* humorously addressed in its first episode (1977).

Expensive and elaborate photo and video sessions, property rental and band hires for parties, and costuming and hairdressing reinforce the well-established trope of representing social success via the enactment of consumption. These updated rituals of womanhood have been the subject of analysis of several photographic series (Niurka Barroso's 1999 *Vestidos de ilusión*, Frank Thiel's 2014 series *15*, and Diana Markosian's *Quince* from 2018) and, in the national press, of at least two highly critical articles in the long-running Cuban magazine *Bohemia*, "Vals de las apariencias" (2005) and "Historias detrás de un abanico" (2015). The latter reports that some of the latest fashions involve *quinceañeras* exchanging traditional hairdos for those seen on the TV series *Vikings* and *Game of Thrones*, and posing in commercial establishments with shopping bags from international brands without local stores such as Victoria's Secret. A new local magazine, *Primavera* (Spring), circulating in *el paquete* and fashioned after international outlets whose target audience is the teen, promises in turn to equip the Cuban *quinceañeras* with the latest tools to navigate adult femininity and the logistics of its celebration.

Cuban Women, Economic Crisis, and Consumer Imaginaries

As a key constituency of its transformative politics, if not always on their own terms, and as one of the most affected demographics by the economic crisis of the 1990s, it is not surprising that (the representation of) woman has been one of the privileged sites of a collective reckoning with an uncharted national destiny.[6] Esther Whitfield in literature (2008), Nora Gámez Torres in popular music (2012), and Velia Cecilia Bobes from the vantage point of sociology (2001), have each analyzed how the special period stoked gender stereotypes, especially that of the prostitute or *jinetera*, that were predicated on allegorical representations of a Cuban socialism in crisis, and on anxieties of male inadequacy confronting an economic and sexual competition with a foreign, usually European and well-to-do male other. Cubans were challenged by forms of female empowerment, recognition, and sexual agency in the pursuit of material independence that went beyond the double burden of the socialist woman, whom the Cuban Revolution—through the Federación de Mujeres Cubanas (Federation of Cuban Women) in particular—had recruited in large numbers into the workforce, but whose primary role in household and child-rearing responsibilities remained rooted in traditional social norms and reinforced by cultural stereotypes.

When the Cuban government pursued tourism and dollarization as a way out of economic collapse, the *jinetera* became an immediate target of social criticism, the most recognizable dramatic character in allegorical representations of the national crisis, and a testament to the declining morality—or long-term ineffectiveness—of the socialist project. The semantic effect of this tendency has been that updated sexist assumptions have resurfaced as part of a system of signification in which consumption, Cuban women, and sexual (im)morality became frequent common bedfellows in the social text. It is my contention that the postsocialist woman of fashion participates in these imaginaries where consuming images of women stand for the dangers of the broader consumerism paradigmatic of the transformations of economic, cultural, and media practices underway.

In popular music, for instance, the core tropes around the Cuban woman of fashion have not changed much from the 1990s, but key details of the plot have: Los Van Van's musical hit "La moda" ("Fashion") and its video clip stage a compelling combination of these updated elements. The song lyrics of "La moda" tell the story of two professional women—"'La China' has a Ph.D. in science and 'Dolores' in economics"—who want to get keratin treatment and hair extensions. The song sounds two alarms: that hair treatments are dangerous if applied by the wrong hands, and that the price of beauty treatments and the popularity of new fashions are astronomically inflated, and breaking the men's banks. The song points to a subtle change in the discourses around the postsocialist woman of fashion and to her role in the representation of consumer anxieties in Cuban popular culture, where a weak will and material interest drove Cuban women into the arms of a dollar-wielding foreigner before, the dangerous element now is consumer culture proper:

> "It's just that today's prices
> Are not those of the past
> How expensive is keratin!
> And extensions, even more . . .
> . . .
> Men want to get a divorce."

Wielding a vast repertoire of tricks and products deployed in the pursuit of (mass-produced) ideals of female beauty, youth, and grace, her spending habits, frivolous or enfranchising, alternatively fuel the economy or deplete pockets of men in the process of becoming worthy of their possession/gaze.

Filmed in the privately owned Darocha hair salon, which advertises in *el paquete*, the video-clip tells a parallel story: that of the hairdresser who, seen taking cash from her clients—and the men in their lives who pay for their treatments—extracts a surplus by selling hair products and extensions of questionable provenance, and goes from having a studio in her living room to an upscale locale, while the global stock prices of keratin are shown to surpass those of oil. Besides the jabs at the stock market's and sole trader's winning bets on Cuba's hybrid economy, the social and regulatory costs of the self-employment model is a common trope in many approaches to the critique of Cuba's new consumer culture, which highlights the restoration of classes and the growing economic inequality but skirts the structural and historical roots of these problems.

Looking at these examples it would seem, too, that Cubans are overwhelmingly concerned with hair. Like cleanliness, hair has a long history as a social marker of race, class, and gender in the national imaginary and remains an important cultural signifier. (Cuban cleanliness as national virtue, and the inescapable gendered images it mobilizes, becomes a subject of parody, for example, in the third vignette of Arturo Infante's 2007 short *Gozar, Comer y Partir* [Enjoy, Eat, and Leave] and in the Cuban-American lifestyle blog "My Big Fat Cuban Family.") The images of socialist apocalypse and (self-)eroticized sordid survival that predominate in the dirty realism aesthetics of 1990s cultural production had their everyday counterparts in a collective preoccupation second only to food scarcity: lack of water, shampoo, soap, deodorant, menstrual pads, and cleaning supplies. Or as Frank Delgado captures in his 1996 song "*La Habana está de bala*" (Havana is a bullet): "Havana is very dirty, Havana has lice, Havana has parasites . . ." Consequently, the cult around hair products and treatments and the popularity of hairdressing are as much historical sociocultural phenomena as they are the result of concrete economic decisions: the licenses for hairdressers were among the first authorized forms of self-employment, and they partly redressed a collective preoccupation with grooming and cleanliness that was a signature of the 1990s economic crisis. As the manager of the household, moreover, cleanliness, and beauty and cleaning products, remained overwhelmingly the concern of the (post-)socialist woman.

Woman, historically, has been the object-subject of consumption par excellence. Whether satisfying the traditional constructs of the male gaze, as resignified practices of sexually assertive self-empowerment, or articulating a notion of common and narrowly defined experience of womanhood, the "Woman of Fashion" endlessly reproduced in the advertising system specifically, and in culture more broadly, "is simultaneously what the reader is and what she dreams of being..." (Barthes 1990, 261; McRobbie [1978] 2000, 69). Embodying the new forms of consumer culture in particular, the woman of fashion has been an emblematic subject of what Jelača, Kolanović, and Lugarić-Vukas call "the restructuring of feeling" in postsocialism: caught between allegorizations of the national economy, the exercise of unsanctioned social agencies, and the pressure of performance under pervasive conservative, contradictory, and patriarchal expectations of womanhood (2017, 4). From very different angles, the trap-reggaeton artist Señorita Dayana, the artwork and performances of multidisciplinary artist Susana Pilar Delahante Matienzo, the poetry of Reina María Rodríguez, and the fashion label Clandestina, respond to these challenges of navigating the postsocialist Cuban mediascape from the intersection of nation, markets, and gender by creating their own images of the Cuban woman of fashion.

IMAGES OF THEMSELVES

During the 2015 Havana Biennial, Delahante Matienzo organized a beauty contest called "Lo llevamos rizo" (We Wear It Curly) that brought attention to the links between the disciplinary modes of racialized sociability and expectations of beauty on the one hand, and the hair treatments and procedures, like keratin, aimed at subduing the natural, curly growth of Afro hair into straightened locks on the other. Delahante Matienzo's installation *Dominadora inmaterial* (Immaterial Domatrix, 2012–2013), in turn, documented her online activity as Flor Elena Resident in Second Life during an artist residency in Germany. As Flor Elena, Delahante Matienzo became the financial dominatrix of as many as twenty virtual slaves who paid real life money that was then cashed in through the platform. The avatar is a dark-skinned, curvy, big-haired woman; Flor engages with a long line of archetypical—and allegorical—representations of the Cuban woman as objects of desire of both national and international imaginaries, from Cirilo Villaverde's foundational novel *Cecilia Valdés* (1839) to Iberia airline's controversial 2007 advertising video of its flights to Cuba. As a study of an extreme—and virtual, and temporary—inversion of the more familiar dynamic of Cuban sexual tourism, it functioned as an art fundraising project as much as an ethnographic document of Internet and capitalism. It also called attention to aesthetic expectations of the national in the art market, and to those who find pleasure in financial punishment via the digital sociabilities where capital can be resignified and redistributed otherwise. At the same time, Delahante demonstrates the capacity of the situated work of art to complicate our assumptions about media, capital, and image, and to make visible the libidinal, gendered economies underwriting commodity exchange.

For her part, Señorita Dayana is arguably the most successful female Cuban singer of urban genres to date. Also known as "la que no tiene ni perro ni gato" (she who has neither dog nor cat), with this signature and the popularity of songs like "Soltera" ("Single"), "La mentira" ("The Lie"), "Te Choca" ("It Shocks You"), and "Tenemos el control" ("We Have Control"), Señorita Dayana has managed to gain visibility in one of the most male-dominated areas of Cuban culture: popular dance music. With "La mentira" for example, a song about the necessity of lying to men—and, incidentally apropos, a 2017 commercial for a cosmetic surgery clinic in Miami—she recasts the stereotypical female subject presented as manipulative and a spendthrift ["No me digas que soy mala ni calculadora" ("Don't tell me that I'm bad or calculating")] as a strategy for survival in a world structured by the expectations of male desire: "Las mentiras que te digo son las que a ti te enamoran" ("The lies I tell you are those that make you fall in love"). In a context of unequal power dynamics where the burden of emotional labor takes the form of de-escalation and pacification, she offers:

> A lot of lies, so that you don't get stressed
> So that you are happy, and not upset
> So that you are an addition, and not a subtraction
> You want to subdue me and I don't think so.

In "Te Choca," her take on the song about success against all odds—an obligatory genre in the repertoire of any urban singer—is somewhat different in tone from those of her most popular peers. Praising one's natural talents, boasting of audience popularity and street credibility, and claims of being number one or pioneers in one thing or another, are staples of the genre, as hits like Gente de Zona's "El animal" ("The Animal"), El Micha's "Único en mi peso" ("The only one in my weight"), Los 4 with La Charanga Habanera's "Lo que tengo yo" ("What I have"), and Yomil y Dany's "Me imagino" ("I imagine") showcase. While also framed as a story of hard work and of having finally made it, "Te Choca" highlights the role of supporters and collaborators, a subject enjoying the spoils of her triumph that is always plural, and the inordinate hostility and verbal violence she has faced in a cutthroat music industry and in a predominantly male genre. "It shocks you," Señorita Dayana ripostes to the figure of a former detractor addressed throughout the song "that now you have to copy even my clothing style."

A very different proposal, the fashion label Clandestina began in 2014 as a design initiative by women under the direction of artist Idania del Río, and gained press coverage during a Q&A with Obama during his March 2016 visit. Since 2018, the company advertises as the first "Made in Cuba" design and clothing company to sell its products online. Their 2018 collection, "Made in Cuba: País en Construcción" ("A Country in Construction"), was developed in collaboration with Google and unveiled in a fashion show at the Museo Nacional de Bellas Artes in Havana, Cuba's leading art museum. Clandestina illustrates the complexities of representation and creativity in the postsocialist context, where the combination of cultural projects and commercial ventures has a fighting chance at success. The project shows that being independent and alternative no longer automatically translates as anti-official and underground (thereby provoking the concomitant state repression), denoting a changing relationship between Cuban local producers (artisans, entrepreneurs, and *cuentapropistas*), global markets, and the heretofore all-controlling state.

Clandestina designs feature cheeky slogans like "99 percent Cuban design," "Actually, I'm in Havana," and "vintrashe" (trashy vintage) that ironize but also incorporate global fashion trends, local referents, and recycled materials, playfully trafficking in ambiguously deployed political symbols. Their hard currency prices put them at the same level of other global brands, which means that their work is, and should be, valued on par with those of any other international designer, that it must provide a living wage to their creators, but that also makes them unaffordable for most working Cubans. Their brand name capitalizes on the synthesis of several historical and political traditions of the nation without distinction, remixing symbols of prerevolutionary republican modernism, socialist iconography, and eco-friendly tropicalism. It presents itself as a social and ecologically conscious project for the promotion of world-class design by Cuban women, and as a trendy fashion label and clothing company startup both. Clandestina illustrates the porous frontier between the sole traders, artistic projects, and non-state economic and social actors, and the necessary rhetorical (and political) strategies for successfully representing themselves, and the idea of a rebranded Cuba, in a global mediascape.

More importantly, Clandestina is an exceptional project that eclipses a dark trove of other "clandestine" popular fashions: the massive informal market for cheap clothes, cleaning, and beauty products with which they coexist, and where most Cubans satisfy these necessities. Because state stores, which also sell secondhand clothes bought abroad in bulk, cannot fully satisfy the demand for basic consumer goods, a parallel market of clothing resellers and traveling bulk buyers is thriving. They import mostly Chinese-made products and counterfeit goods brought from Mexico, Ecuador, Brazil, Miami, Russia, and other common shopping destinations of Cuban "mules." This submerged economy sustains the aspirations of everyday Cubans to be, and remain, worldly fashionable. Indeed, in Reina María Rodríguez's *The Book of Clients* (2005), secondhand clothes, confiscated and inherited clothes, containers of cheap clothes, become opportunities to reflect on how fashion, like poetry, compensates for the horrors of the everyday. Poem by poem, the indulgence of the woman of fashion is remade as a tactic in which the pursuit of beauty can be a form of self-knowledge, survival, (in)sanity. These are themes explored, for example, in the poem "The dress": "¿Quién puede traspasar la pasión de un vestido?" ("Who can pierce the passion of a dress?); and in the text "La pacotillera" ("The materialist"): "Déjenla mentir. Que crea en la negación del tiempo . . ." ("Allow her to lie. Let her believe in the negation of time . . .") (71, 115).[7]

In the poem "¿Una cara de reina?-dices" ("The face of a queen?-you say") the corporeal estrangement of wearing secondhand clothes captures the reluctant resignation of a woman in a consignment store: "Hoy ha sido frívola y se ha comprado una blusa/ para la premiación de lo que no le han dado/ ni le darán" (She was frivolous today and bought herself a blouse/for the award ceremony [of the prize] they didn't give her, and never will) (83). Rodríguez, reading Barthes, renders the dress as artisanal commodity, as status symbol, as shroud of gendered obligations, and as metaphor for the aesthetic effect of the poem upon the body politic. Rodríguez's investigations into the zones where images of a public Cuba intersect with the intimate and with the representation of (its) women are explicitly developed further in *Variedades de Galiano* (2008), where Rodríguez's own photographs and poems close with a commentary on recent work by Cuban women photographers: "This is how we pee subject to the undertow . . . The nation is also woman and gives births, disguises herself, camouflages with the colors of dusk, with the clouds passing through the sun and the blood" (201).

Delahante Matienzo, Señorita Dayana, Clandestina, and Rodríguez each provide singular and contrasting counterarguments about the roles that the Cuban woman has been called to play in these postsocialist consumer imaginaries and portable mediascapes. Their aesthetic proposals do not rely on the business of (revolutionary) disenchantment, nor do they easily fold into the usual demonization of the woman as paradigmatic subject-objects of consumer culture and foreign fashion. Their chosen names and the titles of their works—*señorita, clandestina, dominadora, pacotillera*—already point to the rejoinders that reshape their public images in their own terms, while at the same time embodying the structural, mediatic, and social contradictions in which they operate. They address the gendered readings of the Cuban present at the sociological and the metacritical levels both. This cursory survey across diverse cultural forms—a teen magazine, a performance artist, a reggaeton singer, a fashion brand, a poet—subscribes several of the proposals to read the postsocialist Cuban mediascape we have suggested so far. Embedded in the digital, symbolic, and hybrid economies of the postsocialist context, the images we have discussed here reject the dichotomies in which Cuba is flattened and instrumentalized as political fodder.

Immanent Mediascapes

Before hard currency stores and "the minoritarian markets" were established in Cuba (state-organized import and stores for small-scale, unrationed commerce of consumer goods steeply priced in dollars or their equivalent in Cuban convertible currency), consumer markets were nonexistent outside of the informal economy. In fact, within the socialist bloc, Cuba occupied an extreme position in debates about the role of material incentives in the period of transition to full communism (Mesa-Lago 1972, 50–51). For the majority of the population basic goods were subsidized, rationed, and distributed to the family unit, and the possibility of acquiring higher-end commodities (refrigerators, bicycles, cars, TVs) was an incentive tied to state employment and ideological performance as a *trabajador de vanguardia* (vanguard worker). Consequently, consumption remains a problematic site for the articulation of postsocialist identities, disproportionately burdening women as a subject-object of consumption. At the same time, all consumers are also increasingly involved in the creation of media images of themselves as producers and as participatory spectators. Like other new social types, the postsocialist woman of fashion makes a spectacle of defying and reflecting upon the expectations made of revolutionary men and women: the modesty, sacrifice, constancy, industriousness, self-effacement that characterized representations of the worker-hero and the worker-mother as ideal-types.[8] (The protagonists of the films *Retrato de Teresa* from 1979, and *Una novia para David* from 1985, are classic representations of those revolutionary female values.)

As the site of historical experiments in media, cultural, and political democratization—whatever their heterogeneous legacies are today—the production of images of Cuba, and of images by Cubans, always takes place under a hypervigilant gaze through which its media subjects are routinely reduced to testaments of foreign-inflected consumerisms or state-sanctioned cultural policy. This was recently and devastatingly illustrated by legal language enforcing Decree Law 349 (2018) that seeks to expand official jurisdiction over the cultural politics of the private sector. The portable, self-produced images of an emergent consumer culture often serve as easy ammunition in arguments across the political spectrum, be it denouncing the corrupting cultural and economic influences arriving from abroad and in detriment of hard-won socialist and nationalist values, or showing the failures of the Cuban revolutionary project to transform the (vulgar, hedonistic) working masses in the long term. These are attempts to convert such images into mere scapegoats of political arguments, or that reduce them to sensationalized and flattened objects of curiosity.

For cultural studies of postsocialism, this is both a political and a conceptual challenge, as Enzensberger argued in his theorization of socialist media already in 1970 after his visit to Cuba:

> The attractive power of mass consumption is based not on the dictates of false needs, but on the falsification and exploitation of quite real and legitimate ones without which the parasitic process of advertising would be redundant . . . Socialists and socialist regimes which multiply the frustration of the masses by declaring their needs to be false, become the accomplices of the system they have undertaken to fight. (Enzensberger [1970] 1982, 24, 26)

Three decades later, Colin Sparks's analysis of postcommunist media transitions impugns any critical project that cannot let go of the image of the state as "a kindly, if regrettably bureaucratic, agency of social regulation," and does not investigate seriously alternative forms of "self-activity and self-emancipation" (1998: 191). Differentiated demands for cultural, social, and political agency characterize the mobile network society and are always geopolitically situated practices (Castells et al 2007: 51). The postsocialist woman of fashion illustrates how we can no longer discuss the society of the spectacle without considering these demands expressed in new forms of cultural and media-making agency; whereby "we are all turned into actors," as Enzensberger highlights in his "Constituents of a Theory of the Media" ([1970] 1982). These media practices, however, are no longer recognizable as building blocks toward a radical emancipation mediated by a state organized around a homogenizing party ideology. These are some of the key questions posed to any postsocialist theory of media by the contemporary demands of its new constituents.

The rhetoric and the policies that have shaped Cuban postsocialism and the concrete role the Cuban state and its socialist legacy have had in Latin American's so-called pink tide, moreover, are in dialogue with what Verónica

Gago has called "the return of the state" in Latin America: an alliance between state developmentalist interventionism and the restructured interests of transnational capital, a pact that presents itself under the guise of a progressive force while its political representatives declare themselves the enemies of the very neoliberal logic they are successfully deploying (Gago 2017, 3). Cuba tends to be singled out as a regional exception with respect to the rest of Latin America, but the path from crisis to selective abundance, from ideological collapse to the language of state-led recovery has followed a parallel and in no small measure interdependent course with respect to the patterns Gago observes (2017, 5). The Cuban mediascape therefore registers its postsocialist context, but also offers a double critique to the prevalent mystification of the state by the Latin American left—which monopolized definitions of socialism and critiques of capitalism—and to the capitulation to neoliberal myths of capitalist success through corporate governance. Suggesting the concept of "cultural capitalism" for (post)socialist contexts along similar lines, Jelača, Kolanović, and Lugarić-Vukas note that only the critical analysis of cultural hybridity as the logic of postsocialist economies can speak to the precarization of life under, and the disappointments with, both the socialist past and the capitalist present (2017).

The postsocialist woman of fashion invites us to think beyond binary critiques where Cuban images of change and continuity, consumerism and socialism, are reduced to the neoliberal and national(ist) hegemonic strategies that channel legitimate desires and needs onto the narrow spheres of privatization and statecraft. I want to avoid reducing citizenship to consumerism, but any serious critique of the culture industry and the expansion of consumer culture in Cuba cannot forget that the state has had a very successful run with its own commodification of Cuban culture. Those who look to the Cuban state, in its current form, as a possible ally against consumer culture and capitalist exploitation rely on binary oppositions such as socialism vs. capitalism, or local vs. global, that no longer obtain. In Cuba, like everywhere else, there are strategies and agencies at work that are never one-dimensional, and that are at once responses to a shared geopolitical and technological present, and locally tailored interventions.

Cuba does not need to be fetishized as a privileged epistemic place or ideal laboratory, as a passive subject-object always on the verge of awakening, as it has been before innumerable times. The larger question, then, is whether the continuities, more than the differences, between actually existing socialisms and actually existing capitalisms ought to be rethought. Extractivist exploits, state repression, corporate intrigue, organized media piracy, participatory cultural agents, and the emergence of new tech elites complicit in the external and internal digital segregation of users are not unique to Cuba nor alien to Latin America's recent history. The challenge remains how to recognize systemic global dynamics in their particular expressions, and how to scale critiques accordingly. The degree to which we can read and deploy media images of ourselves conditions our capacity to critically engage the multiple mediascapes we inhabit, and the social values and political economies that simultaneously shape and are (re)produced by them.

NOTES

1. As Cuban-American artist and essayist Coco Fusco has argued, there is an enduring line of reasoning that does not distinguish between criticism of U.S. foreign policy and blanket defense of the Cuban government, nor, I would add, between the different stages of the 1959 Cuban Revolution. Remaining within the binary logic of the Cold War and conflating official state discourse with the variety of political opinions and attitudes in the country, these arguments, still widespread among American progressives, "deny Cubans agency as thinking subjects" (2013). After the reactivation of U.S. tourism to Cuba in December 2014 (later curtailed in 2019), news outlets began to report in 2015 the increased volume of Canadian and European visitors rushing "to see it before it changes," wary of the transformations that an American rapprochement would bring to the island (Wetherall 2015; Zabludovsky 2015; Hamre 2016).

2. See the special editions of the "Documents of the Seventh Congress of the Communist Party" (Tabloids I and II, 2017) and "Foreign Investment Opportunities Portfolio," accessed June 28, 2019, at http://www.granma.cu/especiales/cartera-de-oportunidades-de-inversion-extranjera. While the country continues to aggressively pursue foreign capital investment, the new 2018 guidelines for self-employment were widely perceived not only as a political move to reaffirm strong centralized control over the growing non-state economic sector, but also as measures that largely missed the larger structural issues afflicting overall economic growth and diversification, and above all, national food sovereignty. See *Gaceta Oficial* 35 Extraordinaria, July 10, 2018, and, for example, Henken 2018.

3. Most of Díaz-Canel's tweets since October 2018 feature one or both of these hashtags. See, for example, Díaz-Canel, Miguel. Twitter Post. July 1, 2019, 4:04 AM. https://twitter.com/DiazCanelB/status/1145649310266249216.

4. See the *"paquete"* dossier edited by Jennifer Cearns in *Cuban Studies* 50, 2021, for more on this.

5. *El paquete semanal*, June 1, 2015.

6. The tendency toward a feminized representation of the Cuban nation has a long tradition in literary and visual culture. Its origins date to the history of the representation of the new world and to Cuba as the key port to the Hispanic Americas, and has been reinforced as a "foundational fiction" of the modern nation ever since (Sommer 1991). It has also existed in symbolic tension with its counterpart, the patriarchal chauvinism and militant masculinities that underwrite Cuba's modern and revolutionary nation-building discourses.

7. *Pacotilla* refers to merchandise of inferior quality, and *pacotillero/a* is one who either

peddles it or likes to buy a lot of it indiscriminately. This connotation in Cuban Spanish refers to a ubiquitous female consumer of cheaply made goods. The *pacotillera*, who consumes at the expense of her man's money, is the subject of popular timba songs Los Van Van's "La shopimaníaca" (1997) and Maykel Blanco y su Salsa Mayor's "La pacotillera" (2010).

8. For a material history of revolutionary fashion in Cuba, see María A. Cabrera Arús, "Beauty and Quality for All: A Vision of Fashion under Cuban Socialism," *The Oxford Handbook of Communist Visual Culture,* edited by Aga Skrodzka, Xiaoning Lu, and Katarzyna Marciniak (2019).

References

Arjun Appadurai. 1990. "Disjuncture and Difference in the Global Cultural Economy." *Theory, Culture & Society* 7:2 (1990): 295–310.

Barthes, Roland. 1990. *The Fashion System.* Berkeley: University of California Press.

Bobes, Velia Cecilia. 2001. "Las mujeres cubanas ante el periodo especial: ajustes y cambios." *Debate Feminista* 23: 67–96.

Buck-Morss, Susan. 2000. *Dreamworld and Catastrophe: The Passing of Mass Utopia in East and West.* Cambridge, MA: MIT Press.

Buck-Morss, Susan. 2008. "Theorizing Today: The Post-Soviet Condition." *Log*, No. 11: 23–31.

Castells, Manuel, Mireia Fernández-Ardèvol, Jack Linchuan Qiu, and Araba Sey. 2007. *Mobile Communication and Society A Global Perspective.* Cambridge, MA: MIT Press.

De Ferrari, Guillermina. 2007. "Cuba: A Curated Culture." *Journal of Latin American Cultural Studies* 16 (2): 219–40.

Delgado, Frank. 1996. "La Habana está de bala." *Trova-Tur.* Mutis. CD.

Enzensberger, Hans Magnus. [1970] 1982. "Constituents of a Theory of the Media." In *Critical Essays.* New York: Continuum.

Fusco, Coco. 2013. "Who's Afraid of Yoani Sánchez?" *Huffington Post*, March 27, 2013.

Gago, Verónica. 2017. *Neoliberalism from Below: Popular Pragmatics and Baroque Economies.* Durham: Duke University Press.

Gámez Torres, Nora. 2012. "Hearing the Change: Reggaetón and Emergent Values in Contemporary Cuba." *Latin American Music Review* 33 (2): 227–260.

Gitelman, Lisa. 2014. *Paper Knowledge: Toward a Media History of Documents.* Durham: Duke University Press.

Hamre, Jaime. 2016. "Surge of Americans Tests Limits of Cuba's Tourism Industry." Reuters, January 26, 2016.

Henken, Ted A. 2018. "'The Revenge of the Jealous Bureaucrat': A Critical Analysis of Cuba's New Rules for Cuentapropistas." *Cuba in Transition* 28: 231–238.

Kraus, Chris. 2015. *Torpor.* Cambridge, MA: MIT Press. Semiotext(e).

Krasznahorkai, László. 2000. *The Melancholy of Resistance.* Translated by George Szirtes. New York: New Directions.

Jelača, Dijana, Maša Kolanović, and Danijela Lugarić-Vukas. 2017. *The Cultural Life of Capitalism in Yugoslavia: (Post)Socialism and Its Other.* London: Palgrave.

Larsen, Reif. 2018. "Havana's Symphony of Sound." *The New York Times*, March 12, 2018.
McRobbie, Angela. 2000. *Feminism and Youth Culture*. New York: Routledge.
Mesa-Lago, Carmelo. 1972. "Ideological, Political, and Economic Factors in the Cuban Controversy on Material Versus Moral Incentives." *Journal of Interamerican Studies and World Affairs* 14 (1): 49–111.
Mitcherall, W.J.T. 2005. *What Do Pictures Want?: The Lives and Loves of Images*. Chicago: University of Chicago Press.
Rodríguez, Reina María. 2005. *El libro de las clientas*. La Habana, Cuba: Editorial Letras Cubanas.
Rodríguez, Reina María. 2008. *Variedades de Galiano*. La Habana, Cuba: Editorial Letras Cubanas.
Sommer, Doris. 1991. *Foundational Fictions: The National Romances of Latin America*. Berkeley: University of California Press.
Sparks, Colin, and Anna Reading. 1998. *Communism, Capitalism, and the Mass Media*. London and Thousand Oaks: SAGE Publications.
The New York Times. 2016. "Cuba on the Edge of Change." March 19, 2016.
Triana, Alexis. 2018. "El 349, Un Decreto En Torno a La Circulación Del Arte." (Interview with Alina Estévez, the HR director of the Ministry of Culture). *Granma*, November 29, 2018.
Wetherall, Tyler. 2015. "Cuba sees record bookings as tourists rush to see it before it changes." *The Guardian*, October 30, 2015.
Whitfield, Esther Katheryn. 2008. *Cuban Currency: The Dollar and "Special Period" Fiction*. Minneapolis and London: University of Minnesota Press.
Yúdice, George. 2016. "Músicas plebeyas." In *Memorias, saberes y redes de las culturas populares en América Latina*, edited by Graciela Maglia and Leonor Arlen Hernández Fox. Pontificia Universidad Javeriana, Universidad Externado de Colombia, and Institut français d'études andines.
Zabludovsky, Karla. 2015. "Americans Are Heading to Cuba, but the Europeans Don't Like It." *BuzzFeed News*, July 13, 2015.

Contributors

Jennifer Cearns (University College, London) is an anthropologist whose research has focused upon material and digital flows connecting Cubans on the island with communities across the world. She has conducted sixteen months of ethnographic research in Miami, Havana, Guyana, Panama, and Mexico, in pawn shops, funeral parlors, airport lounges, bus stations, and street market stalls, as well as following *mulas* across the region to understand networks of material and digital exchange. Her research has also explored Cuba's digital landscape, including *el paquete* and Havana's intranet networks (SNETs). She is the author of a recent article ("The Mula Ring") in the *Journal of Latin American and Caribbean Anthropology*, and is editor of a dossier on *el paquete* in *Cuban Studies* 50.

Walfrido Dorta is assistant professor of Spanish at Susquehanna University. He has published several articles on Cuban literature and culture in academic and cultural journals. He focuses on twentieth and twenty-first century Latin American and Hispanic Caribbean literatures and cultures, visual and media studies, and critical theory. He is currently working on the book manuscript *Political Dynamics and Cultural Projects in Cuban Post-Revolution (1989–2015): Paideia, Diáspora(s), and Generación Cero*.

Paloma Duong is assistant professor of Latin American and Media Studies at MIT. She researches and teaches courses on culture, media, and political philosophy in twentieth and twenty-first century Latin America. She has published articles on the Cuban blogosphere, Havana's apartment art scene, and Cuban cultural politics. She is writing a book titled *Portable Postsocialisms: Cuban Mediascapes after the End of History* that focuses on digital, participatory, and informal media and cultures in twenty-first-century Cuba.

Sara Garcia Santamaria is associate professor of media and communication at Universitat Ramon Llull and Universitat Jaume I. She holds a doctorate in journalism studies from the University of Sheffield (U.K.) and is a former research fellow at the Annenberg School for Communication, University of Pennsylvania. Some of her recent publications include "The Sovietisation of Cuban Journalism: The Impact of Foreign Economic Dependency on Media Structures in a Post-Soviet Era," *Journal of Latin American Communication Research* 6 (1–2) and "Alternative Cuban Journalism: A Comparative Approach to Indirect Violence," *Persona & Sociedad* 23 (2). Garcia is also the coeditor of the volume *Media and Governance in Latin America: Toward a Plurality of Voices*. Her research interests include media in restrictive contexts, safety of journalists, the intimization of politics, and populist political communication. She is vice chair of the Political Communication, IAMCR, and part of the research groups Media Flows and the Varieties of Democracy Project.

Ted A. Henken is associate professor of sociology and Latin American studies at Baruch College, City University of New York (CUNY). A past president of the Association for the Study of the Cuban Economy (2012–2014), Henken is the coauthor, with Archibald Ritter, of the book *Entrepreneurial Cuba: The Changing Policy Landscape*, the updated Spanish edition of which was published as *Cuba Empresarial* by Ediciones Hypermedia. He also coedited the country study *Cuba in Focus* with Miriam Celaya and Dimas Castellanos (ABC-CLIO). A noted specialist on the Cuban Internet, Henken has authored the articles, "The Opium of the *Paquete*: State Censorship, Private Self-Censorship, and the Content Distribution Strategies of Cuba's Emergent, Independent Digital Media Startups," *Cuban Studies* 50; "Cuba's Digital Millennials: Independent Digital Media and Civil Society on the Island of the Disconnected," *Social Research*; and "From Cyberspace to Public Space? The Emergent Blogosphere and Cuban Civil Society," published in *The Revolution under Raúl Castro: A Contemporary Cuba Reader*. Henken is also the author of the annual Freedom House report on the state of the Internet in Cuba, "Freedom on the Net."

Olga Khrustaleva is a freelance journalist and researcher. She came to the U.S. to study at the University of Missouri on a Fulbright scholarship and then continued her studies at American University in Washington, D.C. Khrustaleva has worked as a journalist, producer, and videographer in the U.S., Latin America, and her native country, Russia. Her work has appeared at *Al Jazeera*, the BBC, *Great Big Story*, and other media. Khrustaleva's professional interests include digital human rights, freedom of expression, censorship, and the role of technology in political processes. She was a 2016

Google Policy Fellow and researched Internet censorship in Latin America at the Chilean NGO Derechos Digitales (Digital Rights).

Marie Laure Geoffray is associate professor of political science and junior member of the French Academic Institute. She has published widely on contentious politics in Cuba, including the book *Contester à Cuba* and the articles "Transnational dynamics of contention in contemporary Cuba," *Journal of Latin American Studies* 47, and "Channeling protest in illiberal regimes: The case of Cuba since the fall of the Berlin Wall," *Journal of Civil Society* 10. She has also published methodological articles about the study of authoritarian regimes such as "Mettre la peur à distance. Retour sur une expérience ethnographique en contexte autoritaire," *Critique Internationale* 86.

A native of Havana, Cuba, Edel Lima Sarmiento is currently a doctoral candidate in the Department of Communications, Universidad Iberoamericana, Mexico City, where he researches the media-government relations under Batista's dictatorship, especially his strategies of press control. He is currently being funded by Mexico's National Council for Science and Technology (Conacyt). His research interests expand to the overall history of censorship and press control in the Cuban and Spanish presses. He has a bachelor's degree in journalism and a master's in communication science from the University of Havana, where he was adjunct professor of journalism. He also holds a master's in communications research as a historical-social agent from the University of Valladolid, Spain. Edel also worked as a journalist and editor at *Tribuna de La Habana* and *Juventud Rebelde,* and twice earned the *26 de Julio* prize, Cuba's most important journalism award, for his interviews with personalities in the cultural field. He is the author of the book *La prensa cubana y el machadato*, now in its second edition, awarded with the prestigious Pinos Nuevos national prize in social sciences. He has also published various research articles in the Cuban journals *Perfiles de la Cultura Cubana*, *Espacio Laical, Bibliotecas: Anales de Investigación, Santiago,* and *Islas.*

Carlos Manuel Rodríguez Arechavaleta is a research professor in the Department of Communications at the Universidad Iberoamericana, Mexico City. He has worked as a visiting researcher at Georgetown University and the University of California, San Diego, as well as at the Universidad Autónoma de Madrid, the Universidade de Porto, and the Universidad de Granada. His recent publications include, *La Democracia Republicana en Cuba, 1940–1952: Actores, Reglas y Estrategias Electorales* and "Del Constitucionalismo Republicano al Autoritario en el Siglo XX cubano," in Rafael Rojas et al., *El Cambio*

Constitucional en Cuba. His main research focus is the institutional history of the Cuban Republic and political transition in Cuba; democratization, civic activism and social movements; political communication and the public sphere in times of transition.

Mireya Márquez-Ramírez is professor of journalism studies and media theory at the Department of Communications, Universidad Iberoamericana, in Mexico City. Her research interests include comparative media systems and journalism cultures; sociology or professions, digital news production; journalism and labor; anti-press violence and sports journalism. She has published several articles on these topics in leading journals such as *Journal of Communication, Journalism, Press Politics* and *Journalism Studies*, as well as numerous book chapters in publishing houses such as Columbia University Press, Palgrave, Routledge, Nordicom, and others. She coedited the volume *Media Systems and Communications Policies in Latin America* and is currently investigating the transnational, collaborative and newsroom-less journalistic projects in Latin America. In her country, Márquez leads or co-leads some of the most high-profile cross-national comparative studies of her field, such as the *Worlds of Journalism Study* in Bolivia and Mexico, as well as *Journalistic Role Performance* and *Journalism Students Global*. She is a member of the scientific or editorial boards of UK's *Journalism Studies* and Spain's *Estudios sobre el Mensaje Periodístico*, both leading journals in their respective languages.

Anne Natvig is a doctoral candidate in the Department of Journalism at Volda University College and the University of Oslo, where she researches journalism in Cuban state media. Her areas of academic interest are journalism in Latin America, sociology, and social anthropology. Her most recent publications are: "Cuban Journalism Students: Between Ideals and State Ideology," *Journalism Education*; "Diverging ideals of autonomy: Non-state media in Cuba challenging a broken media monopoly," *Journal of Alternative and Community Media*; and "A place under siege: Self-censorship strategies among Cuban state media journalists," *Brazilian Journalism Research*.

Rebecca Ogden is a lecturer in Latin American studies at the University of Kent, UK. She is coeditor of the volume *Branding Latin America: Strategies, Aims, Resistance*. Ogden's current research interests lie in questions relating to reproductive politics, especially in Cuba and Mexico.

Alexei Padilla Herrera is a doctoral candidate in the Department of Communications at the Federal University of Minas Gerais, Brazil, where he earned a master's in communications. He holds a bachelor's in social communication from the University of Havana and a diploma in digital journalism from the Instituto Internacional de Periodismo José Martí. In Cuba, Padilla worked as a professor and journalist. He was also a member of the Cuban think tank Cuba Posible. His research focus is media and public space in Cuba.

Larry Press is professor emeritus of computer information systems, California State University, Domínguez Hills. Press is the author of the widely read blog, *The Internet in Cuba* (http://laredcubana.blogspot.com/). His many other publications on Cuban IT include, "A framework for assessing the impact of U.S. restrictions on telecommunication exports to Cuba," *Cuba in Transition* 25 (https://ascecuba.org//c/wp-content/uploads/2016/03/v25-press.pdf), which is based on his testimony to the U.S. International Trade Commission, "The effect U.S. trade restrictions on IT exports to Cuba," Washington, D.C., June 2015.

Abel Somohano Fernández is a doctoral candidate at the Department of Communications, Universidad Iberoamericana, Mexico City, where he investigates the conditions of journalistic production and oppositional models of independent digital media in Cuba. His research is funded by the National Council for Science and Technology (Conacyt). He holds two MA degrees in communication science and in social and political studies from the University of Havana, Cuba, where he was assistant professor of media and communications at the Faculty of Communications. Abel was a short-term visiting fellow at Madrid's Universidad Rey Juan Carlos, and Cartagena de Indias' Universidad Tecnológica de Bolívar. He is senior research assistant for the *Journalistic Role Performance* cross-national study in Mexico, for the *Worlds of Journalism Study* in Mexico and Bolivia, and for other research projects at his current department. At University of Havana, he was a team member of the research project *Journalism Students' Pre-Professional Cultures in Ecuador, Cuba and Venezuela*. He helped launch and manage the Cuban communications journal *Alcance*. Somohano's many publications include the coedited book *En Cuba, periodismo es más (+): Transposición, redundancia y dinamismo profesional*, a chapter on journalism graduates' professional trajectories, and an article in *Global Media Journal Mexico*.

Eloy Viera Cañive is one of the founders of the Collective of Many Voices Foundation, dedicated to supporting independent communication initiatives in Cuba. He has worked for seven years as a lawyer for the ONBC (La Organización Nacional de Bufetes Colectivos), Cuba's only independent organization that offers legal services to citizens. He has dedicated himself to the study of the Cuban regulatory system. He also coordinates *El Toque Jurídico*, a virtual space dedicated to the legal education of Cuban citizens.

Index

ABC, 58–60
Alma Mater (magazine), 59, 63
Alterity, 196, 263, 266, 271, 275–78
Alternative media, 51–68, 105–10, 150, 235
Apklis, 82
Auténtica Cuba, 242–54
Authenticity, 19, 242, 248–56
Authoritarian regimes, 11, 79, 89, 103, 120, 123, 136
Autonomy, 15–19, 55, 89, 118–31, 200–215, 219–35, 274, 287, 301, 330
Ávila, Eliécer, 87

Batista, Fulgencio, 52, 60–67
BlackHat (collective), 141
Boullier, Dominique, 138–50
Branding, 241–57, 276

Cachivache Media, 127, 146, 148
Castro, Fidel (former Cuban president), 8, 17, 32, 61, 78, 90, 98, 129, 200, 268
Castro, Raúl (former Cuban president), 32, 73, 88, 96, 104–9, 117, 187, 231
CDR (Committee for the Defense of the Revolution), 267–77
CENIAI (Center for Automated Interchange of Information of the Cuban Academy of Sciences), 31
Censorship, 1, 12, 30, 53, 56–63, 77, 83, 102–7, 118, 127–31, 136, 148, 169, 188, 193, 202–12, 246, 264, 286, 291

Cibercuba (news website), 65, 84, 87, 97, 104, 127, 192
CIGB (Center for Genetic Engineering and Biotechnology), 31
Citizen journalism, 2, 142, 157–73
Civic Journalism, 116–33, 233
Civil society, 5, 9, 15–18, 32, 61, 73–91, 96, 102, 122, 127, 136 142, 147, 263, 278, 287, 328, 333
Clinton, Bill (former US president), 10, 32
Communist Party, 1, 10, 32, 58, 60, 63, 95–100, 105, 109, 119, 143, 200, 206, 219, 224, 307
Comprehensive Computerization Policy, 96
Computer Youth Clubs (JCCE), 84
Condis, Camilo (Twitter influencer), 9, 20
Copyleft, 140, 145
Counter-revolutionary, 263, 269, 273, 275, 277
Cuban blogosphere (*blogósfera cubana*), 20, 102, 142, 157, 203, 285, 287
Cuban Constitution (1976, 2019), 60, 96, 106
Cubanet (news website), 65, 87, 97, 127, 146, 148, 192
Cuba Posible (think tank), 97, 103, 104
Cuentapropismo (self-employment), 143, 262–78

Decree Law 209, 129
Decree Law 349, 105, 108, 321

Democratic communication, 96
Democratization, 8, 11, 60, 67, 77, 97, 99, 103, 110, 116, 150, 221, 227, 235, 302, 320, 330
Denuncia (ABC's newspaper), 59–68
Diario de Cuba (news website), 65, 87, 97, 104, 127, 146, 192
Díaz, Elaine, 103, 175
Díaz-Canel, Miguel (Cuban president), 2, 7, 88, 105, 125, 201, 215, 231, 308
Dictator's dilema, 5, 29, 82
Digital critique, 136–51
Digital democracy, 10, 90
Digital entrepreneurs, 19, 262–62, 272
Digitalization, 13, 67, 139, 309
Digital marketing, 251, 255, 266
Digital millennials, 126, 202, 262–78, 328
Digital revolution, 1–21, 51, 68, 82, 86, 89, 166, 195, 213, 222, 235, 277
Discourse theory, 183, 184

El Estornudo (magazine), 7, 19, 97, 103, 127, 146, 158, 203, 213, 219–22, 227, 230–36, 302
El paquete semanal (the weekly packet), 30, 37, 82, 311
Entrepreneurship, 5, 38, 150, 264, 269
ETECSA (Empresa de Telecomunicaciones de Cuba, S.A.), 6, 29, 33, 36–42, 78, 81–87, 104, 126, 145, 170, 265, 311
Exceptionalism, 307
E-zines, 302
    Cacharro(s), 285–301
    Consenso, 159, 166, 173
    The Revolution Evening Post, 285–301
    33 y 1/tercio, 285–301

F/OSS (free/open source software), 13, 15
14ymedio (newspaper), 19, 66, 78, 81, 87, 97, 103, 104, 109, 126, 132, 142, 146, 148, 157–60, 166–74, 192, 203, 229, 302
Fábrica de Arte Cubano (FAC), 267
Fantasmatic logics, 180, 185–87, 194, 196
Fantasy, 19, 180–96, 243, 297

Federation of University Students (FEU), 63
Freedom of the press, 10, 53, 98, 107, 203, 264

GAFAM (Google, Apple, Facebook, Amazon, and Microsoft), 138, 141, 144, 148, 150
    Apple, 140
    Amazon, 4, 40, 268
    Facebook, 6, 12, 17, 41, 82, 88, 102, 142, 148, 170, 247, 268, 270, 274, 287
    Google, 7, 12, 40, 43, 77–80, 140, 142, 145, 167, 171, 318, 329
    Google Global Cache, 78
    Microsoft, 14, 15, 77, 140
Garbos (magazine), 126
Generación Y (blog), 157–75
Granma (newspaper), 1, 36, 61, 85, 99, 125, 129, 201, 203, 215, 308
Guardian, The, (newspaper), 172

Havana Times (news website), 9, 127
Hegemony, 1, 7, 11, 99, 116–33, 195, 202, 267, 274
Helms-Burton Act, 32, 100
Hora de Cuba, La (newspaper), 104
Hoy (newspaper), 63, 99
Hybrid regimes, 116–18, 130, 262, 307, 310, 315, 320

Ideological legitimation, 121, 128, 131
Independent media, 18, 19, 52, 53, 86, 103, 108, 126, 127, 146, 158, 180, 185, 192, 193, 195, 202, 213, 219, 222, 234, 285
    Independent blogosphere, 2, 20, 102, 142, 173, 174, 201, 203, 285–90, 301
    Independent digital newspapers, 2, 19, 78, 87, 90, 95–110, 122, 125–31, 142, 146–48, 168, 173, 175, 189, 301
    Independent journalism, 3, 101, 157, 172, 180–96, 200, 234
    Independent online journalism, 18, 117, 122, 127

Infomed, 31, 33
Information and communication technologies (ICTs), 1, 8–10, 74, 88, 90, 98, 101, 106, 150
Informatización (computerization), 3, 6, 36, 74, 106
Intimacy, 248, 251, 257
Inventos (inventions), 2, 76, 80, 82, 85

Jiménez Enoa, Abraham (Cuban journalist), 6, 8, 87
Joven Cuba, La (blog), 127

Kcho (Alexis Leiva Machado) (Cuban artist), 78, 86

LANs (local area networks), 4, 6, 84, 265
Law 88, 100, 107
LEO/MEO (low- and middle-earth orbit) satellites, 40
Liberal norms, 126, 128, 131, 149, 205, 214, 220, 223–27, 232–35
Liberation technology, 10
Lineamientos (Guidelines), 97, 105–8, 120, 208
Logics approach, 185, 194

Machado, Gerardo (former Cuban president), 58–60, 64–67, 78
Marxism-Leninism, 18, 95–98, 100, 109, 120, 224
Mediascapes, 20, 306–23
Mi Mochila, 84
Minidisk, 164
MINTUR (*Ministerio de Turismo*), 242, 246–50, 255
Movimiento 26 de Julio (M-26-7), 329

Nation branding, 243, 255
Nauta, 4, 36, 73, 170
Negolution (magazine), 146
Networked authoritarianism, 10, 12, 75
Networked public sphere, 6, 10, 12, 75
Normalization, 73–76, 86, 125

Obama, Barack (former U.S. president), 35, 43, 73–78, 103, 125, 196, 318
Observatorio Crítico, 97, 127
Official media, 3, 8, 64, 87, 101, 110, 129–31, 139, 144, 150, 157, 159, 169, 180, 185, 189, 210, 219, 222–35, 309. *See also* State media
Ontological rupture, 180–96

Pardo Lazo, Orlando Luis (writer), 20, 138, 287–89, 296, 299–305
Periodismo de Barrio (magazine), 19, 97, 103, 106, 127, 146, 148, 158, 175, 201, 203, 216, 219–23, 227, 232, 236
Play-Off (magazine), 126, 146, 148, 152
Polémica intelectual, La, 17, 22, 160
Postdata (website), 146–49
Postsocialist, 20, 279, 306–23
Professionalization, 18, 105, 117, 121, 128, 130, 146, 150, 192, 196, 219–36
Public space, 11, 17, 88, 101, 109, 162, 164, 328, 331
Public sphere, 6, 10, 12, 17, 59, 75, 90, 96, 102, 118, 120, 122, 130, 227, 273–76, 291, 302, 307, 330

Radio Rebelde, 60–68
Red ciudadana, La (citizen network), 163
Resolviendo (making ends meet), 251, 269
Revolución (newspaper), 62, 66, 99

Saavedra, Lázaro (Cuban artist), 14, 16, 20, 162, 174
Sánchez, Yoani, 1, 2, 19–23, 78, 86, 126, 138, 142, 157–74, 245, 249, 301
Santana, Omar (Cuban cartoonist), 3, 20
Self-censorship, 2, 30, 83, 103, 118, 202–10, 328–30
SNET (street net), 15, 19, 20, 38, 39, 84, 85, 268, 275
Social Communication Policy, 96, 105–9, 129
Social influencers, 278
Socialist norms, 220

Socialist press model, 18, 117, 120, 121
Social media, 3, 6, 8–13, 17, 19, 64, 67, 87–90, 103, 125, 148, 160, 167, 235, 241–48, 255, 262, 273–76, 311
    Twitter, 3, 6–9, 12, 17, 20, 41, 76, 84, 88, 102, 142, 165, 168, 203, 256, 287, 308
    WhatsApp, 6, 82, 170, 262, 270–74
    ZunZuneo, 76, 77
State media, 11, 20, 88, 95–110, 121, 126, 139, 158, 180, 188, 193, 195, 200–215, 225, 228, 306, 330
Surveillance, 8, 12, 18, 79, 87–90, 103, 109, 117, 129, 131, 148, 264, 288, 301

TCP/IP, 31, 32
Technological sovereignty, 14, 108, 145
Telecommunications, 18, 36, 40, 74, 89, 246, 311
Telepuntos (navigation rooms), 30, 36, 42
Temas (magazine), 165
3G (*datos mobiles*), 4, 6, 30, 37, 39–41, 73, 81, 170, 173, 202
TinoRed, 31–33
toDus, 81, 82

Transitional regimes, 116, 117, 130
Trump, Donald (former U.S. president), 74, 79, 117, 125, 131, 214

Updating (*actualización*), 116
U.S. Cuba Internet Task Force, 74, 75, 79, 80
U.S. Embargo, 14, 29, 31–35, 41, 42, 73, 74, 77, 80, 99, 100, 245
USAID (United States Agency for International Development), 76, 147
UUCP, 30, 31

Vanguardia (newspaper), 62, 103
Venegas, Cristina, 20, 245, 277, 286
Ventana 14 (podcast), 170, 171
Verde Olivo (magazine), 99
Vistar (magazine), 90, 126

Watchdog journalism, 233, 235
Wi-Fi, 4, 30, 36, 37, 42, 73, 78, 83, 170, 202, 245, 265, 272, 274, 309
Words to the intellectuals (speech), 98, 182, 214

X.25., 30, 31

REFRAMING MEDIA, TECHNOLOGY, AND CULTURE IN LATIN/O AMERICA

Edited by Héctor Fernández L'Hoeste and Juan Carlos Rodríguez

Reframing Media, Technology, and Culture in Latin/o America explores how Latin American and Latino audiovisual (film, television, digital), musical (radio, recordings, live performances, dancing), and graphic (comics, photography, advertising) cultural practices reframe and reconfigure social, economic, and political discourses at a local, national, and global level. In addition, it looks at how information networks reshape public and private policies, and the enactment of new identities in civil society. The series also covers how different technologies have allowed and continue to allow for the construction of new ethnic spaces. It not only contemplates the interaction between new and old technologies but also how the development of brand-new technologies redefines cultural production.

Telling Migrant Stories: Latin American Diaspora in Documentary Film, edited by Esteban E. Loustaunau and Lauren E. Shaw (2018; paperback edition, 2021)

Mestizo Modernity: Race, Technology, and the Body in Postrevolutionary Mexico, by David S. Dalton (2018; first paperback edition, 2021)

The Insubordination of Photography: Documentary Practices under Chile's Dictatorship, by Ángeles Donoso Macaya (2020)

Digital Humanities in Latin America, edited by Héctor Fernández L'Hoeste and Juan Carlos Rodríguez (2020)

Pablo Escobar and Colombian Narcoculture, by Aldona Bialowas Pobutsky (2020)

The New Brazilian Mediascape: Television Production in the Digital Streaming Age, by Eli Lee Carter (2020)

Univision, Telemundo, and the Rise of Spanish-Language Television in the United States, by Craig Allen (2020)

Cuba's Digital Revolution: Citizen Innovation and State Policy, edited by Ted A. Henken and Sara Garcia Santamaria (2021; first paperback edition, 2022)

Afro-Latinx Digital Connections, edited by Eduard Arriaga and Andrés Villar (2021)

The Lost Cinema of Mexico: From Lucha Libre to Cine Familiar and Other Churros, edited by Olivia Cosentino and Brian Price (2022)

Neo-Authoritarian Masculinity in Brazilian Crime Film, by Jeremy Lehnen (2022)

www.ingramcontent.com/pod-product-compliance
Lightning Source LLC
Chambersburg PA
CBHW031755220426
43662CB00007B/413